Media Law in New Zealand

Media Law in New Zealand

Ursula Cheer

This book was originally published as a monograph in the International Encyclopaedia of Laws/Media Law.

General Editors: Roger Blanpain, Frank Hendrickx
Volume Editor: Peggy Valcke
Associate Volume Editor: Eva Lievens

Wolters Kluwer

Published by:
Kluwer Law International B.V.
PO Box 316
2400 AH Alphen aan den Rijn
The Netherlands
Website: www.wklawbusiness.com

Sold and distributed in North, Central and South America by:
Wolters Kluwer Legal & Regulatory U.S.
7201 McKinney Circle
Frederick, MD 21704
United States of America
Email: customer.service@wolterskluwer.com

Sold and distributed in all other countries by:
Turpin Distribution Services Ltd.
Stratton Business Park
Pegasus Drive, Biggleswade
Bedfordshire SG18 8TQ
United Kingdom
Email: kluwerlaw@turpin-distribution.com

ISBN 978-90-411-6758-3

This title is available on www.kluwerlawonline.com

The Author

Ursula Cheer LLB(Hons)(Cant), LLM(Camb), PhD (Canterbury) is a Professor of Law specializing in media law at the University of Canterbury. She has published widely in the area of media law, and has a special interest in defamation and privacy law. Ursula completed her PhD in 2009, with the title: *Reality and Myth: The New Zealand media and the chilling effect of defamation law*. She is also author of *Burrows and Cheer: Media Law in New Zealand* (7th ed, LexisNexis, 2015), and a contributing author in the leading text, *The Law of Torts in New Zealand*, Thomson Reuters (2013, 6th ed, S Todd ed) where she writes on defamation and privacy. Ursula is a member of the editorial committee of the *Journal of Media Law* (Hart Publishers, UK) and a member of the editorial committee and international contributing editor of the *Media & Arts Law Review* (MALR) (LexisNexis Butterworths) CMCL, Melbourne Law School, Melbourne, Australia.

The Author

Table of Contents

Table of Contents

List of Abbreviations

AC	Appeal Cases
ACTR	Australian Capital Territory Reports
AJHR	Appendix to the Journals of the House of Representatives
All ER	All England Law Reports
All ER (D)	All England Direct Law Reports
ALJ	Australian Law Journal
ALR	Australian Law Reports
ASA	Advertising Standards Authority
ASCAB	Advertising Standards Complaints Appeal Board
ASCB	Advertising Standards Complaints Board
ATR	Australian Torts Reports
AULR	Auckland University Law Review
B	Baron
BCL	Butterworths Current Law
BSA	Broadcasting Standards Authority
CA	Court of Appeal
CJ	Chief Justice
CLR	Commonwealth Law Reports
CRNZ	Criminal Reports of New Zealand
DC	District Court
DCR	District Court Reports
DLR	Dominion Law Reports
ELRNZ	Environmental Law Reports of New Zealand
EMLR	Entertainment and Media Law Reports
ERNZ	Employment Reports of New Zealand
EWCA Civ	Court of Appeal (Civil Division)
EWHC	England & Wales High Court (Administrative Court)

List of Abbreviations

Fam	Law Reports, Family Division
FMCA	Federal Magistrates Court of Australia
GLR	Gazette Law Reports
HC	High Court
HCA	High Court of Australia
HKC	Hong Kong Cases
HRNZ	Human Rights Reports of New Zealand
IP	Issues Paper
IPR	Intellectual Property Reports
J	Justice
KB	Kings Bench
LJ	Lord Justice
LR	Law Reports First Series
LT	Law Times Reports
MCD	Magistrates' Court Decisions
M & W	Meeson and Welsby's Exchequer Reports
NSWLEC	New South Wales Land and Environment Court
NSWLR	New South Wales Law Reports
NSWSC	Supreme Court of New South Wales
NZAR	New Zealand Arbitration Reports
NZBORA	New Zealand Bill of Rights Act
NZFLR	New Zealand Family Law Reports
NZHRRT	Human Rights Review Tribunal of New Zealand
NZLC	New Zealand Law Commission
NZLJ	New Zealand Law Journal
NZLR	New Zealand Law Reports
NZLRev	New Zealand Law Review
NZOMSA	New Zealand Online Media Standards Authority
NZPD	New Zealand Parliamentary Debates
NZPrivCmr	New Zealand Privacy Commissioner
NZTC	New Zealand Tax Cases
ONCA	Ontario Court of Appeal
P	President
PC	Privy Council
PIB	Public Information Brochure
PIR	Post-Implementation Review

PRNZ	Procedure Reports of New Zealand
QB	Queens Bench
QWN	Queensland Weekly Notes
R	Report
SASR	South Australian State Reports
SC	Supreme Court
SCC	Supreme Court of Canada
SCR	Supreme Court Reports (Canada)
SO	Standing Orders
SP	Supplementary Paper
TLR	Times Law Reports
VCC	Victoria County Court
VR	Victorian Reports
VSC	Victoria Supreme Court
VSCA	Victoria Court of Appeal
WAR	Western Australian Reports
WLR	Weekly Law Reports

List of Abbreviations

Preface

Media law is a complex and growing subject worldwide, and New Zealand's media laws are merely part of this continued expansion. Within one of the most open economies in the world, the communications and broadcasting sector is continuing to expand and change. Government policy and practice is light-handed on broadcasting and more heavy-handed on telecommunications. In spite of this inconsistency, all forms of media continue to develop and change to make use of the new technological platforms available. All areas of media law are under pressure to cope with these changes. In this monograph, the author examines the New Zealand media market and its main players, the predominant infrastructure, and technological and economic developments affecting the sector. The sources of media law and the impact of freedom of speech are also outlined, as well as the role of journalists and the character of the profession, and the nature of journalistic liability in New Zealand. The main forms of general regulation of media are described, including the general laws such as defamation and privacy, and laws relating to access to public information and court reporting. The self-regulation of the print media in the form of the Press Council is detailed. This is followed by an in-depth analysis of the regulation of broadcasting in its current forms, including the differences relating to public and private broadcasting in New Zealand, the programme standards that apply, and how political broadcasting and advertising are regulated. The monograph is completed by a discussion of the issues of cross ownership and the desirability of an over-arching regulatory body.

General Introduction

§1. General Background of the Country

I. Political and Legal System of the Country

1. New Zealand was colonized by Britain in 1841. Its population ethnicity is now made up of nearly 74% European descendants of those mid-nineteenth century colonists, with the next largest group being nearly 15% indigenous Maori. The Asian population at close to 12% is the next largest and the fastest growing ethnic group in New Zealand.[1] The country has three languages: English, Maori and New Zealand Sign Language, the latter two being designated official languages by statute.[2]

Still a constitutional monarchy, politically, the country is a stable democracy utilizing a mixed member proportional (MMP) voting system every three years to vote in a unicameral parliament made up of the House of Representatives and the Governor-General. Queen Elizabeth II is the Queen of New Zealand, and the Governor-General is her representative and plays no part in the House of Representatives. However, the Queen's representative has an important constitutional role in the calling of elections, and in exceptional circumstances, in the forming a government and determining the life of Parliament.[3] New Zealand has an unwritten constitution, made up of such things as the Constitution Act 1986, decisions of the courts, the Treaty of Waitangi, the letters patent, Orders in Council, and unwritten constitutional conventions.[4]

2. When New Zealand was colonized in 1841, it adopted laws and courts based on those in Britain at the time. The court system that exists today is still hierarchical. The Supreme Court is New Zealand's highest court, and below, in descending order, are the Court of Appeal, the High Court and then District courts. These courts have general jurisdiction. Statute defines the jurisdiction of the Supreme Court, the Court of Appeal and the District court. However, the High Court has both statutory jurisdiction and inherent jurisdiction which arises at common law through the decisions of the judges.

1. *2013 Census*, New Zealand Government http://www.stats.govt.nz/Census/2013-census/profile-and-summary-reports/quickstats-about-national-highlights/cultural-diversity.aspx, accessed October 2013.
2. Maori Language Act 1987, and New Zealand Sign Language Act 2006.
3. http://www.elections.org.nz/voting-system/new-zealands-system-government and Electoral Act 1993.
4. See generally Joseph, *Constitutional and Administrative Law in New Zealand* (4th ed., Brookers Ltd, Wellington, 2014).

District courts deal with much of the day-to-day business in the court system, hearing most criminal cases and a large number of civil cases. However, if the amount in dispute is more than New Zealand Dollar (NZD) 200,000, or the alleged crime is more serious (such as murder), the case is heard by the High Court, which hears the more serious jury trials, the more complex civil cases, administrative law cases, and appeals from the lower courts and tribunals.

Cases that are appealed go to a higher court in the system, not necessarily that directly above. The appeal forum may depend on the nature of the decision, offence or dispute. District court decisions can be appealed to the High Court, or directly to the Court of Appeal if the law allows this. However, the Supreme Court is the final appellate court and appeals cannot go beyond it or into an overseas system. The Court of Appeal hears more appeals than the Supreme Court and is therefore the last appeal court for most cases in reality. To go to the Supreme Court requires leave to appeal. The Supreme Court Act 2003 requires that such appeals need to raise a significant legal point or a matter of general and public importance.[5]

The common law system of justice operating in New Zealand is based on an hierarchical system of precedent. This means where similar cases arise for resolution, the decisions of higher courts are binding on lower courts, and ultimately, the Supreme Court binds all other courts. Precedent is intended to give certainty and consistency to the law as it develops.

Specialist courts and tribunals exist outside the court system described above and are usually established by specialist statutes. In New Zealand, these include the Employment Court, the Environment Court, the Mäori Land Court, the Waitangi-Tribunal, Coroners Courts, the Broadcasting Standards Authority (BSA) and the Courts Martial Appeal Authority. The courts of general jurisdiction already described hear appeals from these courts and tribunals. Additionally, the High Court has special supervisory jurisdiction of them through a process of judicial review.[6]

II. Geography and Population

3. New Zealand is a remote archipelago in the South Pacific made up of two main islands, the North and the South, and the much smaller Stewart Island. Geographically it is 1.1 times the size of the United Kingdom, but has a tiny population of only 4.2 million people. The South Island is bifurcated by a set of magnificent mountains called the Southern Alps, also known as the Alpine Fault because they are the on-land manifestation of the intersection of the Pacific and Australian geological plates. Hence, New Zealand is prone to earthquakes. The country's weather is sub-tropical in the far-north, and sub-Antarctic in the far-south.[7]

5. Supreme Court Act 2003, s. 23.
6. Courts of New Zealand, The Structure of the Court System, http://www.courtsofnz.govt.nz/about/system/structure/overview, accessed 31 Jul. 2015.
7. Te Ara, the Enclopedia of New Zealand, http://www.teara.govt.nz/en/natural-environment/page-1.

III. Social and Cultural Values

4. New Zealand's founding document is the Treaty of Waitangi, signed between British Crown representatives and about 540 Māori rangatira (chiefs) representing the indigenous population in 1840. The document was intended to provide stability to the settlement process then taking place, and it was believed that annexing the country could protect Māori, regulate British subjects and secure commercial development. Three versions of the Treaty exist and debate about the intent and import of the process continues. For decades now, New Zealand governments have been engaged in a grievance and land loss settlement process with Māori, and attempts to develop and enhance a bi-cultural society based on the intention, spirit or principles of the Treaty are ongoing within society, culture and the law.[8] This process impacted on the major reorganization of broadcasting under the Broadcasting Act in 1989, which contains provisions intended to preserve and enhance the Māori language and culture. At the same time, government was also forced to take account of Māori interests in its sale of the radio spectrum under the Radiocommunications Act 1990.[9] The resulting regulation is described further below.[10]

§2. The Media Landscape

I. Overview of Media Markets and Main Actors

5. New Zealand media audiences are small – among the smallest in the world. There is not much of a market to fight over, but what market exists is governed only by basic competition legislation and mostly owned by offshore interests. In 2014, there were only six major commercial players, five of which are foreign-owned – these are Bauer Media, APN News & Media (Australian but with a large stake held by Irish company, INM), Fairfax Media (trans Tasman), MediaWorks (American private equity group Oaktree Capital is the largest shareholder in the company), and Sky TV (owned by offshore financial institutions). The only significant New Zealand-owned commercial media player is TVNZ – owned by the government.

Cross-mediaownership and promotion is common: APN News & Media and Fairfax Media dominate the print media in New Zealand, while MediaWorks Ltd and Sky TV dominate commercial television, and MediaWorks and APN dominate radio networks. Change in ownership by these offshore media proprietors is constant. For example, in 2013, the German Bauer Media Group bought APN's magazine stable.

8. 'The Treaty in brief', URL: http://www.nzhistory.net.nz/politics/treaty/the-treaty-in-brief, (Ministry for Culture and Heritage), updated 5 Aug. 2014, accessed 30 Jul. 2015.
9. Report of the Waitangi Tribunal on Claims Concerning the Allocation of Radio Frequencies, (Wai 26, 27 Nov. 1990): http://www.justice.govt.nz/tribunals/waitangi-tribunal/Reports/wai0026 and *Allocation of Radio Frequencies Report* (Wai 150). See also Report on Broadcasting Claim, (Wai 176, 22 Jul. 1994), http://www.justice.govt.nz/tribunals/waitangi-tribunal/Reports/wai0176 and Māori Language claim (Te Reo Māori claim Wai 11), http://www.justice.govt.nz/tribunals/waitangi-tribunal/Reports/wai0011, accessed 30 Jul. 2015. See.
10. See para. 227.

Additionally, financial institutions have been replacing media companies as media proprietors since 2010. By 2012, financial institutions such as equity funds owned over 50% of APN and Fairfax Media, and in 2013, Rupert Murdoch's News Corporation sold all 44% of its shares in SKY TV, now dispersed among various financial institutions.[11] However, there are smaller private broadcast companies too, such as Choice TV.

Alongside this ever-changing commercial market sits a small public broadcasting sector which is nonetheless constantly shrinking as government withdraws or freezes funding and increasingly applies commercial imperatives. This is made up of the state broadcasters TVNZ, (TV1, TV2, TV1 and TV2 Plus (which simply repeat programming from both channels an hour later)), Māori Television, (made up of the Māori TV and Te Reo channels, the latter broadcasting exclusively in Māori) and Radio New Zealand, made up of National Radio and the Concert Programme. Only the National Radio stations and the Te Reo television channel carry no advertising. TVNZ no longer has any public broadcasting imperative and is therefore essentially a commercial media corporation.

The newspaper sector is dominated by APN and its rival, Fairfax. The online presence for Fairfax, the *stuff* website, has greatest audience share in that platform.[12] No mainstream newspaper has paid digital subscriptions as yet. Allied Press is an independent, New Zealand-owned media company which publishes the *Otago Daily Times* and nine other publications, and also runs local Canterbury and Dunedin television stations. There is one major financial publication, *The National Business Review*, a privately owned weekly financial newspaper that funds its operations from advertising and print and digital subscriptions. In radio, APN owns the Radio Network operating seven brands, while rival, MediaWorks owns a similar share of the commercial radio audience.[13]

II. Broadcasting Infrastructure

6. Content is broadcast by diverse forms of transmission in New Zealand, including terrestrial, satellite, cable and digital. Technological change and uptake is high. Premium content, for example, live rugby, blockbuster movies and cult television shows were previously only available in New Zealand via pay television broadcaster, Sky TV. However, now such content, for example, English Premier League football, has become available via online streaming on many different platforms. Services such as Quickflix, Ezyflix, VideoEzy and Lightbox (a service

11. *New Zealand Media Ownership Report 2014* (AUT Centre for Journalism, JMAD, 5 Dec. 2014) http://www.aut.ac.nz/study-at-aut/study-areas/communications/media-networks/journalism,-media-and-democracy-research-centre/journalists-and-projects/new-zealand-media-ownership-report, accessed 30 Jul. 2015.
12. http://www.stuff.co.nz/, accessed 31 Jul. 2015.
13. *New Zealand Media Ownership Report 2014* (AUT Centre for Journalism, JMAD, 5 Dec. 2014), at 12–13, http://www.aut.ac.nz/study-at-aut/study-areas/communications/media-networks/journalism,-media-and-democracy-research-centre/journalists-and-projects/new-zealand-media-ownership-report, accessed 30 Jul. 2015.

run by Spark, previously the state telecommunications provider) have entered the online video streaming market. In response, Sky TV is soon to launch its own on-demand distribution service.[14]

Aspects of broadcast infrastructure are monitored and regulated by three Ministries – Broadcasting, Culture & Heritage,[15] and Business, Innovation & Employment.[16] However, the government intervenes in the market as little as possible. New Zealand's communications networks are predominantly owned and operated by private companies, with government regulating to ensure stability and attraction of investment.

Wireless technologies are recognized as critical for sectors such as broadcasting and government looks to manage radio spectrum to provide for new technologies and simultaneously protect the rights of incumbents, and prevent interference with legitimate use. The Telecommunications Act is being reviewed to ensure its regulatory scheme is compatible with a new fixed fibre network being rolled out over most of the country under two broadband initiatives – the Ultra-Fast Broadband initiative and the Rural Broadband Initiative.[17]

The government is concerned about cyber-security but wishes to maintain a free and open Internet. It therefore supports a multi-stakeholder model of internet governance.[18] Current priorities are connecting New Zealanders to high quality broadband and voice services, ensuring legislative frameworks keep pace with change, and enhancing the security and resilience of New Zealand's communications networks and services.[19]

III. Technological and Economic Developments on the Media Markets

7. Great change has occurred in the New Zealand broadcasting sector since 1989 when the sector was opened to competition as economic restrictions were relaxed to provide open entry to the industry broadcasting services. All special restrictions on overseas ownership of broadcasters were removed in 1991, allowing investment by overseas investors. Entry into the market is now provided for by the general law of competition under the Commerce Act 1986. Any technologies may be utilized to

14. See Briefing for the Incoming Minister of Broadcasting, October 2014, Ministry for Culture & Heritage, http://www.mch.govt.nz/sites/default/files/BIM%202014%20Broadcasting%20Oct%202014%20%28D-0564811%29.PDF, accessed 31 Jul. 2015.
15. http://www.mch.govt.nz/, accessed 31 Jul. 2015. Broadcasting is located within the Ministry Culture & Heritage.
16. http://www.mbie.govt.nz/, accessed 31 Jul. 2015.
17. Ministry of Business, Innovation & Employment, Communications: http://www.med.govt.nz/sectors-industries/technology-communication/communications, accessed 31 Jul. 2015.
18. National Cyber Policy Office, Department of Prime Minister and Cabinet, http://www.dpmc.govt.nz/ncpo, accessed 31 Jul. 2015.
19. See Briefing for the Incoming Minister of Broadcasting, October 2014, Ministry for Culture & Heritage, http://www.mch.govt.nz/sites/default/files/BIM%202014%20Broadcasting%20Oct%202014%20%28D-0564811%29.PDF, accessed 31 Jul. 2015.

supply broadcast services, and cable, microwave-distributed services, and satellites as well as traditional broadcasting techniques may be used. Pay television services are also permitted. SKY Television was New Zealand's first pay television network and began broadcasting in May 1990, and now delivers multiple subscription channels via digital satellite. SKY also owns free-to-air broadcast channel Prime.

These major broadcasting and telecommunications reforms resulted in increased demand for frequencies in the radio spectrum. The Radiocommunications Act 1989 provides the legislative framework for an administrative-based licensing regime and for a market-orientated regime for spectrum management based on tradable property rights. Broadcasters operating under warrants issued by the Broadcasting Tribunal on 1 July 1989 were entitled to a licence under the Radiocommunications Act. Auctions are regularly held for bandwidth, the latest being in 2013–2014, when the rights to the 700 MHz band were auctioned for 4G-LTE cellular use. This was described as a 'digital dividend' band and became available after New Zealand switched to digital television broadcasting, thus freeing up the former analogue broadcasting spectrum.[20]

New Zealand transitioned region by region from analogue to digital television in the four years from 2010 to 2013.[21] Television viewers migrated, and analogue transmission signals were switched off to enable radio spectrum space to be made available for sale by the government for telecommunication purposes, such as next generation mobile communication services. The transition to digital has been said to deliver improved reception quality of both picture and sound, a greater number of channels, and more onscreen features such as electronic programme guides and audio description to all viewers across the nation.[22]

The communications sector is now digitized in New Zealand, and the population has a rapid uptake of mobile devices and connectivity.[23] There is an increasing demand for online video content, and competition for online broadcast audiences has become significant with the entry into the market of telecommunication companies and internet service providers in a battle for on-demand video. New Zealand copyright laws are increasingly being placed under strain by these developments.[24] Television and radio still dominate audience share, but video on-demand services

20. See Radio Spectrum Management, Ministry of Business, Innovation & Employment, http://www.rsm.govt.nz/projects-auctions/spectrum-auctions, accessed 30 Jul. 2015.
21. See Ministry for Culture and Heritage website, http://www.mch.govt.nz/goingdigitalreview, accessed 30 Jul. 2015.
22. Cabinet Paper, Going Digital PIR, March 2014, Minister for Broadcasting, http://www.mch.govt.nz/sites/default/files/Going%20Digital%20PIR%20Cabinet%20paper%20March%202014%20%28D-0534168%29.PDF, accessed 30 Jul. 2015.
23. 2015 ICT Sector Report: http://www.mbie.govt.nz/what-we-do/business-growth-agenda/sectors-reports-series/information-and-communications-technology-report, accessed 30 Jul. 2015.
24. 'Sky, Spark, TVNZ, MediaWorks take action against CallPlus, other "global mode" ISPs', *National Business Review*, 2 Apr. 2015, http://www.nbr.co.nz/article/copyright-global-mode-ng-170966, accessed 28 Aug. 2015; 'Sky TV toughs out first year of true competition', *New Zealand Herald*, 21 Aug. 2015, http://www.nzherald.co.nz/business/news/article.cfm?c_id=3&objectid=11500827, accessed 28 Aug. 2015.

now have an increasing presence.[25] Established broadcasters are also making content available on web, mobile and tablet.[26]

§3. Sources of Media Law

8. Laws regulating media in New Zealand arise from numerous sources. The most common sources are statute and the decisions of the courts. Legal liability generally arises within the criminal and the civil law.

As to criminal liability, a number of statutory provisions impose duties on media for which breach constitutes an offence and penalties such as a fine or imprisonment may be imposed. For example, the offence of blasphemy remains on the statute books and carries a penalty of up to one year's imprisonment.[27] Fortunately, the leave of the Attorney-General is necessary before a prosecution may be brought.[28] Forms of incitement may apply to media,[29] as may a limited and rarely used hate speech provision in the Human Rights Act 1993 which makes it an offence to publish or broadcast threatening, abusive or insulting statements, these statements being intended and likely to excite hostility or ill will against, or bring into contempt or ridicule any group of persons in New Zealand on the ground of the colour, race or ethnic or national origins of that group of persons.[30] The country also has a comprehensive censorship classification system enforced and administered under the empowering legislative umbrella of the Films, Videos and Publications Classification Act 1993. This censorship regime centres on a finding that material is 'objectionable', and classification is supported by possession and publication offences.[31] Publications that promote or support, or tend to promote or support, certain types of behaviour listed in section 3(2) of the Act are automatically deemed likely to be injurious to the public good and can be banned or restricted.[32]

Non-statutory offences also exist, for instance, failure to comply with a court order suppressing an accused's name is a contempt offence. Contempt of court is

25. *New Zealand Media Ownership Report 2014* (AUT Centre for Journalism, JMAD, 5 Dec. 2014) at 28–29, http://www.aut.ac.nz/study-at-aut/study-areas/communications/media-networks/journalism,-media-and-democracy-research-centre/journalists-and-projects/new-zealand-media-ownership-report, accessed 30 Jul. 2015.
26. *New Zealand Media Ownership Report 2014* (AUT Centre for Journalism, JMAD, 5 Dec. 2014) at 30, http://www.aut.ac.nz/study-at-aut/study-areas/communications/media-networks/journalism,-media-and-democracy-research-centre/journalists-and-projects/new-zealand-media-ownership-report, accessed 30 Jul. 2015.
27. Crimes Act 1961, s. 123.
28. Crimes Act 1961, s. 123(4). New Zealand removed criminal libel from the statute book in 1992 and sedition in 2007: see Crimes (Repeal of Seditious Offences) Amendment Act 2007, and Defamation Act 1992, Third Schedule (Repealing the Defamation Act 1954, including ss 15 and 16).
29. For example: Sections 66 and 311 of the Crimes Act 1961.
30. See Human Rights Act 1993, s. 131, and *Brooker v. Police* [2007] 3 NZLR 91 (SC) at [61].
31. Films, Videos and Publications Classification Act 1993, ss 3, and Part VIII of the Act.
32. Numerous other statutes contain minor publication offences: see Ursula Cheer, *Burrows and Cheer on Media Law in New Zealand* (7th ed., 2015), Ch. 10.

not only defined by statute, but it is also punishable by fine or imprisonment in the same manner as a criminal offence.

Civil liability for media may arise from the decisions of the courts on the private disputes of New Zealand citizens and companies. Significant civil actions which exist in New Zealand include defamation,[33] privacy, breach of copyright and confidence, and trespass.[34] Statute can also establish civil liability, for example, section 61 of the Human Rights Act 1993 provides civil sanctions for published racist remarks. Complaints based on this racial disharmony provision may be made to the Race Relations Conciliator, whose office is part of the Human Rights Commission. The remedies are not punitive, but if the matter is not settled through conciliation, it can be referred to the Human Rights Review Tribunal. Among other remedies, the Tribunal may uphold the complaint, issue a declaration that the Human Rights Act has been breached, award damages or make a restraining order. Damages may be significant, covering pecuniary loss, loss of benefit, and humiliation, loss of dignity and injury to feelings. Media are exempt from liability under this provision for accurately reporting the remarks of others.[35]

Criminal and civil proceedings are quite different. However, there are times when the same conduct may render media liable to both types of proceedings. Thus, knowing breaches of copyright can sometimes give rise to criminal proceedings as well as civil proceedings for damages or injunction, and trespass is sometimes a criminal matter as well as a civil one. Breach of a statutory provision by media could also give rise to a civil action for damages by someone injured by the breach.[36] For example, in one case,[37] the High Court recognized an intrusion tort of privacy in a case where the defendant had already been prosecuted under the intimate covert filming provisions of the Crimes Act 1961.[38]

Media are also subject to the jurisdiction of a number of complaints bodies other than the courts. The Broadcasting Act 1989 lays down standards for broadcasting and provides for the formulation of broadcasting codes of practice, and sets up a BSA to enforce these: it has powers of suspending a broadcaster from the air for a period and of awarding damages of up to NZD 5,000 for breaches of privacy.[39] Print media has no equivalent tribunal, although the Press Council, a voluntary body, hears complaints about breaches of ethical standards. It has no coercive power, but makes determinations upholding or dismissing complaints that are expected to be published.[40] Additionally, broadcasters have developed a third industry-led body to regulate the previously unregulated area of online news and current affairs content. The New Zealand Online Media Standards Authority (OMSA) came into being on 1 July 2013. It is an industry-funded, self-regulatory body which oversees online

33. Defamation law derives from a mixture of the common law and a statute – the Defamation Act 1992.
34. Criminal liability also arises under the Trespass Act 1982.
35. Human Rights Act 1993, s. 61(2).
36. *Doe v. Australian Broadcasting Corporation* [2007] VCC 281.
37. *C v. Holland* [2012] 3 NZLR 672.
38. Crimes Act 1961, ss 216G-N.
39. See below para. 234.
40. See below para. 214.

news and current affairs content standards.[41] The OMSA has established a Code of Standards for all news and current affairs content published online by its members.[42]

International law is now seen as a vital source impacting the development of laws affecting media in New Zealand. For example, the Universal Declaration of Human Rights, the European Convention on Human Rights, the International Covenant on Civil and Political Rights, and the United Nations Convention on the Rights of the Child, have all influenced privacy law,[43] while the International Covenant on Civil and Political Rights Article 18 freedom of religion has been cited as the reason why the law of blasphemy has been retained.[44] Furthermore, it should be noted that New Zealand looks to features of the domestic laws of countries with similar common law systems in developing its media laws. For example, developments in the United Kingdom, Australia and Canada have influenced New Zealand privacy law, breach of confidence and to a lesser extent, defamation law.[45]

New Zealand now has a written bill of rights in the form of the New Zealand Bill of Rights Act 1990 (NZBORA), which contains a form of freedom of expression. This is discussed in more detail in Part I. below.

41. Online Media Standards Authority 'Broadcasting Industry to Launch Online News and Current Affairs Self-Regulatory Body' (media release, 14 Feb. 2013); Online Media Standards Authority 'New Online Media Standards Authority to Launch on 1 Jul. 2013' (media release, 7 May 2013).
42. See www.omsa.co.nz, accessed 12 Dec. 2014.
43. See Gault P & Blanchard J in *Hosking v. Runting* [2005] 1 NZLR 1, at [6] [19] and Tipping J, at [241].
44. *Mendelssohn v. Attorney-General* [1999] 2 NZLR 268 (CA) especially at [16]–[18].
45. See Gault P & Blanchard J in *Hosking v. Runting* [2005] 1 NZLR 1, at [7].

Part I. Freedom of Speech

9. Section 14 of the NZBORA 1990 (Bill of Rights Act) provides:

> Everyone has the right to freedom of expression, including the freedom to seek, receive and impart information and opinions of any kind in any form.

Common law judges had been making reference to such a principle for some time before its enactment.[46] However, its incorporation in the Bill of Rights Act gives it greater currency and ensures that it is more likely to be expressly raised before the courts in cases involving media law.

No rights in the Bill of Rights Act are absolute. This is recognized in section 5 of the Act:

> [T]he rights and freedoms contained in this Bill of Rights may be subject only to such reasonable limits prescribed by law as can be demonstrably justified in a free and democratic society.

There are many rules limiting freedom of speech, including defamation, contempt of court and invasion of privacy. Under the Bill of Rights Act, Parliament and the courts must try to ensure that these limitations on freedom of expression are, in the words of section 5, 'reasonable' and such as can be 'demonstrably justified in a free and democratic society'. The Bill of Rights Act is not supreme law, and contains no judicial strike-down power, thus operating as an interpretative direction for the judiciary and other state servants.[47] The enactment of the Bill has elevated the rights

46. See Paul Rishworth (ed.), *The New Zealand Bill of Rights* (OUP 2003), Ch. 12. See also the discussion by Thomas J in the Supreme Court in *Brooker v. Police* [2007] NZSC 30 at [171]–[231], as to the role and purpose of bills of rights.
47. The key provisions are:

> *4. Other enactments not affected–*
> No court shall, in relation to any enactment (whether passed or made before or after the commencement of this Bill of Rights),–
> (a) Hold any provision of the enactment to be impliedly repealed or revoked, or to be in any way invalid or ineffective; or
> (b) Decline to apply any provision of the enactment–
> by reason only that the provision is inconsistent with any provision of this Bill of Rights.
>
> *5. Justified limitations–*

consciousness of the general New Zealand public, the media and the legal fraternity. New Zealand courts balance rights in the European style and have not adopted the hierarchical approach to protecting speech which dominates the approach in American law.[48]

Whenever any rights in the Bill are impacted by the operation of other legislation, the Bill must be taken into account in some fashion. The leading case *Hansen v. R*[49] mandates that the rights in the Bill are given effect through statutory construction. The question of whether limits to rights can be demonstrably justified in a free and democratic society has been thrust to the centre of the Bill of Rights analysis.[50] It is answered by using the Canadian approach of asking whether the limiting measure serves a purpose sufficiently important to justify curtailing the right or freedom, and then querying whether it is rationally connected to its purpose, impairs the right no more than is reasonably necessary to achieve that purpose and is in due proportion to the importance of the objective.[51]

There is no statutory requirement in New Zealand to carry out a Bill of Rights analysis in relation to actions between private citizens. New Zealand's Bill was intended to have only vertical effects: it applies to the three branches of Government and bodies exercising public functions,[52] and thus in general only protects private citizens from the state.[53] In spite of this, it is clear that the New Zealand judiciary gives the Bill horizontal effect when resolving disputes between private citizens and when developing the common law, including media law.[54] Because this process does not produce directly enforceable rights, the horizontal effect is usually regarded as weakly or strongly indirect.[55] It is given content in two ways, though sometimes in combination: the judges argue they are simply bound by the Bill as the judicial arm of the state, or that they are implicitly required to take account of the values expressed in the Bill.

Section 14 of the Bill of Rights Act operates in a number of ways. First, judges should take cognizance of it when they are developing the rules of common law. Second, many statutory provisions impose limitations on freedom of speech. Parliament should, when passing such statutes, consider whether they comply with the

---

> Subject to section 4 of this Bill of Rights, the rights and freedoms contained in this Bill of Rights may be subject only to such reasonable limits prescribed by law as can be demonstrably justified in a free and democratic society.
>
> 6. *Interpretation consistent with Bill of Rights to be preferred–*
>
> Wherever an enactment can be given a meaning that is consistent with the rights and freedoms contained in this Bill of Rights, that meaning shall be preferred to any other meaning.

48. András Koltay, *Freedom of Speech* 109 (Complex Publisher Ltd, 2013).
49. [2007] 3 NZLR 1.
50. See Claud*a Geiringer, 'The Principle of Legality and the Bill of Rights Act: A Critical Examination of R v. Hansen*, 6 N. Z. J. Pub. & Intl. L. 59 (2008).
51. *R v. Oakes* [1986] 1 SCR 103. See Tipping J in Hansen, n. 9 above, [104] and Anderson J, [272].
52. The New Zealand Bill of Rights Act 1990, s. 3.
53. See Rishworth, *Human Rights*, 1 N. Z. L. Rev. 87 (2005).
54. *Simunovich Fisheries Ltd v. Television New Zealand Ltd* [2008] NZCA 350, [89].
55. Jane Norton, '*Hosking v Runting* and the Role of Freedom of Expression', 10 AULR 245, 249 (2004).

Bill of Rights Act. The Attorney-General is obliged to inform Parliament if any provision in a Bill before Parliament is incompatible with the Bill of Rights.[56] However, once a statute has been passed, even if a court concludes that the statute imposes an unreasonable limit on the freedom, it has no option but to enforce it. The Bill of Rights Act itself provides that statutes that are inconsistent with the freedoms contained in it are not thereby rendered invalid.[57] However, statutes often require interpretation, and the Act provides that in interpreting them the courts should, as far as possible, give them a meaning which is 'consistent' with the Bill of Rights freedoms.[58] Third, many rules, of both common law and statute, confer discretionary powers on the court (or other officials). For example, the Criminal Procedure Act 2011 confers power on a judge in a criminal trial to suppress the name of the accused (or anyone else involved in the proceedings). In exercising this power, the court must have regard to the importance of freedom of expression contained in the Bill of Rights Act.

56. Bill of Rights Act 1990, s. 7.
57. Bill of Rights Act 1990, s. 4.
58. Bill of Rights Act 1990, s. 6.

Chapter 1. Overview of Bill of Rights Cases

§1. Defamation

10. One of the most important defamation cases in New Zealand's legal history is *Lange v. Atkinson*,[59] where the Court of Appeal held that a defence of qualified privilege exists to protect discussion about politicians. This conclusion, which enhances freedom of discussion about people in the political arena, is derived from a number of different sources, including common, statutory and international law. However, section 14 of the Bill of Rights is referred to at length in the Court's 1998 judgment.

Section 14 often makes an appearance in defamation cases. For example, it has been used to emphasize the principle that the limits of honest opinion (or fair comment) are broad.[60] However, sometimes the court does not accept an invitation to extend the law, on the ground that it already strikes the right balance, in other words, that the limitation it imposes on freedom of speech is justifiable. Thus, it has been held that section 14 does not require any change in the approach to assessing damages in defamation cases.[61]

§2. Contempt of Court

11. In contempt cases, the court has had to balance freedom of expression against the need to preserve the integrity of the courts. The question has arisen in three contexts.

In the New Zealand cases, while section 14 of the Bill of Rights Act receives generous mention, the balancing process has resulted in a rather more restrictive outcome than in some other countries. Freedom of expression is recognized by requiring that only a 'real risk' of prejudice to a fair trial should curtail publication. Once it is clear that there is a real risk, publication should be restrained 'until the risk is past'. The law of contempt does not as a rule permanently bar publication, but rather 'suspends' it until the trial, and with it the risk of prejudice, is over. This is the balance between the two important rights.[62]

In the most recent significant contempt case, the Full Court of the High Court also referred to this balancing process:[63]

> The law of contempt is based on public policy and requires the balancing of two public interest factors both of which are affirmed in the New Zealand Bill of Rights Act 1990. The first is the right to freedom of expression affirmed by

59. *Lange v. Atkinson* [1998] 3 NZLR 424 (CA); [2000] 3 NZLR 385 (CA).
60. *Awa v. Independent News Auckland Ltd* [1997] 3 NZLR 590 (CA) at 595–596 per Blanchard J.
61. *Quinn v. Television New Zealand Ltd* [1995] 3 NZLR 216 (HC) at 227 per Anderson J; *Television New Zealand Ltd v. Haines* [2006] 2 NZLR 433 (CA).
62. *Solicitor-General v. W & H Specialist Publications Ltd* [2003] 3 NZLR 12 (HC) at 16–17.
63. *Solicitor-General v. Fairfax New Zealand Ltd* HC Wellington CIV-2008-485-705, 10 Oct. 2008, at [78].

> s 14 and the second is the right to a fair hearing guaranteed as a minimum standard of criminal procedure under s 25(a) …

and confirmed that where freedom of expression and fair trial rights cannot both be fully assured, some temporary curtailment of freedom of expression in order to guarantee a fair trial is lawful.[64]

The question has arisen whether the ancient common law offence of 'scandalizing the Court' has survived the Bill of Rights Act. The High Court of New Zealand has held it remains in existence here, being a justifiable limitation on freedom of speech.[65] Courts can only effectively discharge the function of upholding the rule of law if they command the authority and respect of the public. The rights guaranteed by the Bill of Rights Act depend on the rule of law.

§3. Privacy

12. New Zealand courts have considered whether the common law should protect the privacy of the individual. Unlike freedom of expression, privacy is not a right expressly protected by the Bill of Rights Act. Moreover, the two notions are in some respects inconsistent with each other. High Court judges differed on the question, and when it arose in the Court of Appeal in *Hosking v. Runting*,[66] the Court of Appeal divided 3:2. The dissenters, Keith and Anderson JJ, found that privacy, a concept of uncertain definition, was not a justifiable limitation on freedom of expression.[67] However the majority (Gault P, Blanchard and Tipping JJ) took a different view of the matter, and found that the protection from publication of some information on aspects of private lives was a justifiable limitation. Nonetheless, their Honours were concerned to impose a qualification that publication of even the most private information must be subject to a public interest override in a particular case. They said a defence of 'legitimate public concern' would ensure that the scope of privacy protection would not exceed such limits on freedom of expression as are justified in a free and democratic society.

When recognizing a further privacy tort of intrusion into seclusion in 2012, Whata J also referred to the New Zealand Bill of Rights in two ways, first, to support a possible new tort,[68] and second, by preserving the possibility of a legitimate public concern defence.[69]

---

64. *Solicitor-General v. Fairfax New Zealand Ltd* HC Wellington CIV-2008-484-705, 10 Oct. 2008 at [81] per Randerson and Gendall JJ.
65. *Solicitor-General v. Smith* [2004] 2 NZLR 540 (HC) at 568. However, the Law Commission has recently supported abolition of the offence: *Contempt in Modern New Zealand*, LCIP 36, May 2014.
66. *Hosking v. Runting* [2005] 1 NZLR 1 (CA).
67. *Hosking v. Runting* [2005] 1 NZLR 1 (CA) at [267].
68. *C v. Holland* [2012] 3 NZLR 672, [87].
69. *C v. Holland* [2012] 3 NZLR 672, [96].

§4. STATUTE

13. There are still few instances of a court interpreting a statutory provision about media law in the manner prescribed by section 6 of the Bill of Rights Act.[70] It happened in *Moonen v. Film and Literature Board of Review*,[71] where the question involved the Films, Videos, and Publications Classification Act 1993. Section 3 of that Act deems a publication to be objectionable if it 'promotes or supports' conduct of proscribed types. It was held that those words convey more than just 'describing' the conduct; the work must have the 'effect' of promoting or supporting it. This more stringent interpretation was required to impose no more than a reasonable limitation on freedom of expression.

On other occasions, arguments based on section 6 of the Bill of Rights Act have failed. Thus, it has been argued that section 8 of the Defamation Act 1992 should be liberally construed to allow a defendant to plead the truth of a meaning that is different from, and lesser than, that alleged by the plaintiff. However that argument has not been supported,[72] and the Court of Appeal confirmed this conservative approach to meanings.[73]

Nevertheless, there is ample scope in media law for arguments based on a Bill of Rights-centred interpretation of ambiguous or unclear statutory provisions. For example, in *Gravatt v. Auckland Coroner's Court*,[74] suppression under the Coroners Act 2006[75] of the identities of health professionals responsible for the care of a patient who had died of meningococcal disease was successfully challenged. Whata J held none of the statutory grounds were triggered, and the reasons provided by the Coroner for suppression were too generalized and had failed to demonstrate why the principles of open justice and freedom of expression should be outweighed.

It is notable that the BSA has been at the forefront of development of an integrated approach to the NZBORA, and in 2011, adopted a new, simpler methodology when applying broadcasting standards under the Broadcasting Act 1989.[76] The Authority now justifies its reasoning and the complaint outcome throughout the decision and concludes with a short summary, which may sometimes refer to the Bill of Rights Act specifically.[77]

---

70. See *Browne v. Canwest TV Works Ltd* [2008] 1 NZLR 654 (HC), [28].
71. *Moonen v. Film and Literature Board of Review* [2000] 2 NZLR 9 (CA). The approach to the bill in *Moonen* has generally been superseded by that in *R v. Hansen* [2007] NZSC 7, [2007] 3 NZLR 1. However, in the censorship context, *Moonen* is still applied by the Classification Office.
72. *Julian v. Television New Zealand Ltd* HC Auckland CP367 SD/01, 25 Feb. 2003 at 26. Compare *Manning v. TV3 Network Services Ltd* [2003] NZAR 328 (HC) at 340 per Young J.
73. *Television New Zealand Ltd v. Haines* [2006] 2 NZLR 433 (CA).
74. [2013] NZHC 390, [2013] NZAR 345.
75. Coroners Act 2006, s. 74.
76. See *BSA Annual Report 2012*, 16; *Axford, Bate and Oldham and Television New Zealand Ltd* BSA 2011-115.
77. See e.g.: *WS and MediaWorks TV Ltd* BSA 2014-100.

§5. Exercise of Powers

14. Many statutes give New Zealand courts power to make orders of various kinds. Sometimes the power must be exercised in accordance with stated statutory criteria; at other times, the court has an unfettered discretion. Likewise, the courts have powers at common law (or, more correctly, in equity) to issue orders, such as injunctions, which are discretionary. It is now clearly established that, in exercising such powers, the courts should ensure that their decisions comply not only with any statutory criteria there may be, but also with the rights and freedoms in the Bill of Rights Act. In the New Zealand context, any orders they make should be no more than a reasonable and justifiable limitation on freedom of expression.

Accordingly, it is now well established that, in considering an application for suppression of name under section 200 of the Criminal Procedure Act 2011, the courts start with the presumption of openness: there must be strong reasons for the suppression order.[78] Section 14 operates in this context as more than just a criterion to be taken into account in the decision-making process; it creates a presumption which is the starting point of the exercise. This was recognized in one case, where Randerson J had to interpret section 68 of the Evidence Act 2006, which itself contains a new presumption against forcing journalists to disclose their sources. He said:[79]

> While the statute does not give any specific guidance as to the relative weight to be attached to the elements which must be assessed under s 68(2), the trend of authority both in New Zealand and in the United Kingdom is to attach substantial weight to freedom of expression in a broad sense as well as in the narrow sense of encouraging the free-flow of information and the protection of journalists' sources.

Similarly, section 14 has influenced the cases involving applications for injunctions against the media. It has bolstered the principle, already established at common law, that interim injunctions should be only rarely granted in defamation cases; otherwise, one would be engaging in a form of censorship.[80] In the leading case,[81] the principle of freedom of expression codified in section 14 was cited for the proposition that injunctions against the media should be a rarity in all cases where that freedom is at stake. In another case in the Court of Appeal, Young J observed that 'in cases of genuine doubt, section 14 should tip the balance in favour of freedom of expression and this is especially so in a prior restraint context'.[82]

Nor are the courts the only bodies whose powers must be exercised conformably with the Bill of Rights Act. The Film and Literature Board of Review must apply it

78. *Lewis v. Wilson & Horton Ltd* [2000] 3 NZLR 546 (CA) at 558–559 per Elias CJ.
79. *Police v. Campbell* [2010] 1 NZLR 483 (HC) at [92].
80. *Auckland Area Health Board v. Television New Zealand Ltd* [1992] 3 NZLR 406 (CA) at 407 per Cooke P.
81. *TV3 Network Services Ltd v. Fahey* [1999] 2 NZLR 129 (CA) at 134 per Richardson P. See also *Chatwin v. APN News and Media Ltd* [2014] NZHC 11.
82. *Television New Zealand Ltd v. Rogers* [2007] 1 NZLR 156 (CA) at [125].

in making classifications,[83] as must the BSA in hearing complaints. The police are bound by it in many of their operations. Most significantly for the media, the courts have held that freedom of expression is an important consideration when the police obtain a search warrant to search a media office. The Court of Appeal has formulated a set of guidelines for the issue and exercise of such warrants that nicely balance the interests involved.[84] Furthermore, a number of discretionary decisions by civil servants responsible for running New Zealand's prisons where media have been refused the right to interview individuals convicted of prominent crimes may be the subject of successful judicial review applications focused on the Bill of Rights Act. Recently the High Court stated:[85]

> Where no concerns of prison security are raised, and where the communication is to a reputable journalist, then that is a circumstance where the rights in s 14 of NZBOR should almost always prevail.

---

83. *Moonen v. Film and Literature Board of Review* [2000] 2 NZLR 9 (CA).
84. *Television New Zealand Ltd v. Attorney-General* [1995] 2 NZLR 641 (CA) at 646 per Cooke P. See now also s. 136(1)(i) of the Search and Surveillance Act 2012 and *Hager v. Attorney-General* [2014] NZHC 3293.
85. *Watson v. Chief Executive of the Department of Corrections* [2015] NZHC 1227, [68]. See also *Television New Zealand Ltd v. Attorney-General* (2004) 8 HRNZ 45 (CA), and *Taylor v. Chief Executive of the Department of Corrections* [2013] NZHC 2953.

Part II. Regulation of Print Media

Chapter 1. The Journalists' Profession

15. There are no special rules or conditions that apply to individuals who wish to work as journalists in New Zealand. While it is now more common for journalists to be trained in some way or to hold journalism diplomas or degrees,[86] it is not a condition of entry into the profession, and many experienced journalists trained 'on the job' by entering a newsroom at a young age because of interest in newsgathering.

Journalists are regulated as part of the news media in New Zealand by a combination of self-regulation, and specific and general laws. The law also gives news media a special legal status under various legal privileges and exemptions.[87] Corporate governance also impacts on how journalists behave in the form of industry charters and ethical codes.

§1. Statutory Recognition of Journalists

16. No single New Zealand statutory provision defines a journalist for legal purposes, although a number of statutes do contain different definitions. For example, the Evidence Act 2006 provides for journalist source confidentiality to be claimed before a court, if a person is a journalist. A journalist means a person who in the normal course of that person's work may be given information by an informant in the expectation that the information may be published in a news medium, and a news medium means a medium for the dissemination to the public or a section of the public of news and observations on news.[88] This can be contrasted with the definition in the Privacy Act 1993 which is relevant to a media exemption from the Act. The Privacy Act does not apply to the media in general in relation to gathering, preparing and broadcasting or publishing news for public broadcast. Section 2 of the Privacy Act 1993 provides:

---

86. For example: http://www.canterbury.ac.nz/future-students/qualifications-and-courses/subjects/journalism/m and http://www.massey.ac.nz/massey/learning/colleges/college-business/school-of-communication-journalism-and-marketing/study/postgrad/master-of-journalism-and-postgraduate-diploma-in-journalism/master-of-journalism-home.cfm, accessed 28 Jul. 2015.
87. The news media meets 'new media', Law Commission Report 128, March 2013, Ch. 2, http://r128.publications.lawcom.govt.nz/, accessed 29 Jul. 2015.
88. Evidence Act 2008, s. 68(5).

> *Agency*… does not include… in relation to its news activities, any news medium…
>
> *News activity* means–
>
> (a) the gathering of news, or the preparation or compiling of articles or programmes of or concerning news, observations on news or current affairs, for the purposes of dissemination to the public or any section of the public;
>
> (b) the dissemination, to the public or any section of the public, of any article or programme of or concerning:
>
> (i) news:
>
> (ii) observations on news:
>
> (iii) current affairs.

This definition was revealed to be limited when the High Court recently held the exception does not apply to a journalist who collected information about a person during interviews carried out for the purpose of research for a book about the person. The journalist was employed by a newspaper but was held to be publishing the book in a private capacity. Further, the journalist was not engaged in a news activity, because the definition refers to the compiling of articles or programmes, not books.[89]

The New Zealand Law Commission has examined the nexis between journalists and new media such as bloggers, and recommended that all statutes which give privileges or exemptions specifically to the news media should be amended to include a new and consistent definition of 'news media', which would include new media.[90] Under this definition, news media would have to meet specified statutory criteria:

- a significant element of their publishing activities involves the generation and/or aggregation of news, information and opinion of current value;
- they disseminate this information to a public audience;
- publication is regular and not occasional; and
- the publisher must be accountable to a code of ethics and to the NMSA.

Bloggers could therefore meet this definition and take advantage of journalistic privileges and exemptions if they are prepared to develop a code of ethics. However, this proposed new definition has not been given effect by government.[91]

89. *Dotcom v. Attorney-General* [2014] NZHC 1343, [57]–[77].

90. 'The news media meets new media', NZLC R 128 (2013), http://r128.publications.lawcom.govt.nz/, accessed 28 Jul. 2015.

91. New Zealand Ministry of Justice, *Government Response to Law Commission Report 'News Media Meets New Media'* (October 2013) http://www.justice.govt.nz/publications/global-publications/n/news-media-meets-new-media-government-response-to-law-commission-report, accessed October 2013.

§2. Common Law Recognition of New Media

17. The definition of journalist in the Evidence Act 2006 referred to above was tested recently in relation to new media, in a defamation claim.[92] In this case, a controversial blogger used the Evidence Act 2006 to resist a discovery order sought by the plaintiff in proceedings for publication of various posts on a blog. The plaintiff wished to test the defendant's defence of honest opinion, and sought discovery of emails that the defendant had acknowledged belonged to the plaintiff. The blogger claimed journalist source protection in relation to the emails, arguing that at the time of the relevant blog posts, he was a journalist in terms of the Evidence Act.[93] Asher J found that at the time of the posts, the blogger and his blog did fit the definition of a journalist and a news medium although the style of journalism might be criticized and could be dramatic and abusive, and the expression was vigorous and coherent. There was no evidence of consistent inaccuracy or deceit in the blog posts,[94] it was published regularly and the blogger derived revenue from it. Overall, the blog was not of such low quality that it was not reporting news. However, the blogger was ultimately ordered to comply with the discovery order because the blog posts related to a private dispute and it seemed likely the emails were obtained illegally by the sources. Ultimately, the Judge found that the protection in the Act was not available to the blogger.[95] This case demonstrates that new media such as bloggers may be recognized by the law as part of news media and regulated accordingly.

92. *Slater v. Blomfield* [2014] 3 NZLR 835. See also *Director of Human Rights Proceedings v. Slater* [2014] NZHRRT 53.
93. Evidence Act 2006, s. 68(5).
94. This finding was seen as controversial because of a book written by an investigative journalist about the activities of the blogger: *Slater v. Blomfield* [2014] 3 NZLR 835, [3]–[4].
95. Evidence Act 2006, s. 68(2). See para. 20 below.

Chapter 2. Journalists' Rights

§1. Role of Journalists as Watch-Dogs of Society

18. In liberal democracies like New Zealand, media and journalists are independent watch-dogs of the exercise of state and private power. They also search out and publish information to the public about those in power, they represent the public and they facilitate public debate. This quasi-constitutional role allows citizens to exercise their power to vote in elections on an informed basis and to remain vigilant between elections. Journalists are thus essential to functioning democracies. However, their activities serve both this public interest and a commercial interest, and this dual role requires significant public trust.[96]

§2. Journalists' Independence

19. Journalists and the media earn and maintain public trust by observing practices and values which are at the heart of journalistic practice. Professional codes of ethics became common in New Zealand in the 1970s, and a number of journalistic organizations have developed them. Industry codes are prominent, such as those developed by Fairfax Media,[97] and APN News and Media.[98] The journalists union, the Engineering, Printing and Manufacturing Union (EPMU) also has a well-known code.[99] The latter covers such requirements as honesty, privacy and respecting the grief of individuals, accuracy and the need to identify as a journalist. One of the most important standards is independence and integrity. Journalists must maintain robust independence from people and organizations being investigated and reported on. Personal interests should not influence professional duties, and gifts and advantages should be rejected or disclosed. Codes may be enforceable directly through office supervision or disciplinary procedures, but are not enforceable by members of the public under the general law.[100] The New Zealand Press Council self-regulatory code also provides for the independence of the profession,[101] as does the Code of Standards of the Online Media Standards Authority.[102]

96. 'The news media meets new media', NZLC IP 27, (2011), http://lawcom.govt.nz/our-projects/regulatory-gaps-and-new-media?id=725, accessed 28 Jul. 2015, Ch. 4.
97. See http://www.fairfaxmedia.co.nz/pressroom/NZ/fairfax-media-new-zealand-journalism-charter, accessed 29 Jul. 2015.
98. See http://www.apn.com.au/header/corporate-governance1/, accessed 29 Jul. 2015.
99. See http://www.epmu.org.nz/journalist-code-of-ethics/, accessed 29 Jul. 2015.
100. See EPMU Code of Ethics, d-f, http://www.epmu.org.nz/journalist-code-of-ethics/, accessed 29 Jul. 2015.
101. See New Zealand Press Council Principle 6, Conflicts of Interest, http://www.presscouncil.org.nz/principles, accessed 29 Jul. 2015.
102. OMSA Code, Responsible Content, Standard 5, http://www.omsa.co.nz/how-we-work/code/, accessed 29 Jul. 2015.

§3. Protection of Journalistic Sources

20. As a rule, a person must answer all questions put to him or her when giving evidence in a court of law. Failure to do so is contempt of court and can result in a penalty: there is even power to detain the offender in custody.[103] Certain categories of professional people are exempted from this obligation and may not disclose information about their clients without their clients' consent, for example, doctors, lawyers, patent attorneys and ministers of religion.[104] Journalists do not fall within these categories. They have no special privilege. If a court requires them to disclose information, or the sources from which they obtained information, they must do so. However, New Zealand journalists have all the general protections available to any other witness. For instance, as a rule witnesses cannot be compelled to answer any question that tends to expose them or their spouses to any criminal charge.[105]

While the journalist has no special privilege as such, New Zealand courts nevertheless have a discretion and may decide in a particular case not to press a question, particularly one relating to sources of information. Such a discretion exists at common law[106] and is occasionally used in favour of the media.[107]

I. Evidence Act 2006

21. New Zealand also has statutory provisions which specifically address the issue. Section 68 of the Evidence Act 2006 contains a new presumption of non-compulsion for journalists where disclosure of sources is at risk.[108] Despite the presumption, journalists do remain ultimately compellable where a judge finds there is

103. Criminal Procedure Act 2011, s. 165. See *Beckett v. Jaffe* HC Auckland M658/89, 5 May 1989 (under the old legislation).

104. Evidence Act 2006, ss 53–67.

105. This is a common law rule. Statute has imposed certain qualifications on it.

106. See: *Attorney-General v. Mulholland* [1963] 2 QB 477 (CA) esp at 492 per Donovan LJ; *Senior v. Holdsworth* [1976] QB 23 especially at 42 per Scarman LJ. See also *M v. L* [1990] 1 NZLR 747 (CA).

107. *R v. Cara and Kelman* HC Auckland CRI-2004-004-6560, 2 Jun. 2004. See also: *Rakhimi v. District Court of Waitakere* HC Auckland M944-IM01, 20 Jul. 2001; *Broadcasting Corporation of NZ v. Alex Harvey Industries Ltd* [1980] 1 NZLR 163 (CA); *European Pacific Banking Corporation v. Television New Zealand Ltd* [1994] 3 NZLR 43 (CA).

108. Section 68 (reversing a previous presumption in s. 35 of the Evidence Amendment Act 1980) provides:

Protection of journalists' sources

(1) If a journalist has promised an informant not to disclose the informant's identity, neither the journalist nor his or her employer is compellable in a civil or criminal proceeding to answer any question or produce any document that would disclose the identity of the informant or enable that identity to be discovered.

(2) A Judge of the High Court may order that subsection (1) is not to apply if satisfied by a party to a civil or criminal proceeding that, having regard to the issues to be determined in that proceeding, the public interest in the disclosure of evidence of the identity of the informant outweighs–

(a) any likely adverse effect of the disclosure on the informant or any other person; and

greater public interest in disclosure. The High Court first applied the provision in 2009.[109] The case arose from an interview with an alleged medal thief carried out by broadcaster John Campbell on a current affairs programme in February 2009. The interview had actually taken place earlier in the day in a hotel, where the alleged thief had been recorded on audio only, and an actor had been used to broadcast the interview that evening using a transcript of the real interview. The police then applied for an order under section 68 of the Evidence Act 2006, compelling John Campbell and five of his production team to produce relevant information at depositions and at trial relating to the alleged burglary. The Court concluded that the public interest in the media's role is of considerable weight, but so is the need to investigate and prosecute crime. The Court made useful findings as to the new provision.[110] The starting point is no obligation on the journalist to disclose, but with potential for that prima facie immunity to be displaced. The party seeking displacement must make the case, but the requirement that the judge has to be satisfied the public interest in disclosure is outweighed is not a standard of proof requirement. Being satisfied in this context simply means that the judge has made up his or her mind, that is, they have behaved judicially.

The balancing exercise is not a conventional exercise of discretion, but rather an evaluative judgment made up of fact and degree. Protection should not be overridden easily, but no high threshold is to be assumed, such as requiring truly exceptional or compelling circumstances. Neither does the statute specify how weight is to be attributed. However, freedom of expression is to be given substantial weight, both in a narrow sense relating to protecting sources and a broad sense. The Court used case law and a general reference to the NZBORA 1990 to support this. Hence, the presumptive right to protection is not to be displaced lightly and only after careful weighing.

A number of issues are relevant in the weighing exercise. It will be relevant to consider whether other means are available to obtain the information. The status of the evidence in the context of the prosecution case will also be considered. It need not be crucial, but must at least be important. The nature of the charge will also

---

(b) the public interest in the communication of facts and opinion to the public by the news media and, accordingly also, in the ability of the news media to access sources of facts.

(3) The Judge may make the order subject to any terms and conditions that the Judge thinks appropriate.

(4) This section does not affect the power or authority of the House of Representatives.

(5) In this section–

informant means a person who gives information to a journalist in the normal course of the journalist's work in the expectation that the information may be published in a news medium;

journalist means a person who in the normal course of that person's work may be given information by an informant in the expectation that the information may be published in a news medium;

news medium means a medium for the dissemination to the public or a section of the public of news and observations on news;

public interest in the disclosure of evidence includes, in a criminal proceeding, the defendant's right to present an effective defence.

109. *Police v. Campbell* [2010] 1 NZLR 483 (HC).

110. *Police v. Campbell* [2010] 1 NZLR 483 at [84]–[103].

impact on the degree of public importance in disclosure. Public interest in disclosure includes the defendant's right to present an effective defence. However, adverse effects arising from disclosure on the informant or others must also be considered. Further, chilling effects arguments, both contextual in a given case, and affecting the media generally, must be addressed. Even if public interest in disclosure prevails, an order will not automatically follow as the power to make the order is discretionary. Terms and conditions may be attached. The case suggests that although there is now a presumption in favour of media contained in the new statutory provision, the courts are still inclined to carry out a fact-specific weighing exercise when applying it.

II. New Media

22. More recently, the new provision was further tested in relation to new media, in a defamation claim,[111] where a blogger attempted to use the Evidence Act 2006 to resist a discovery order. The blogger claimed journalist source protection in relation to certain emails, arguing that at the time of the relevant blog posts, he was a journalist in terms of the Evidence Act.[112] Although this case demonstrated that the journalist source privilege can apply to new media such as blogs, the blogger was ultimately ordered to comply with the discovery order because the blog posts related to a private dispute, and it seemed likely the emails were obtained illegally by the sources. This diminished the importance of protecting the sources in terms of public interest, and there would be no real chilling effect from ordering disclosure which might affect media sources generally. Additionally, the extreme nature of the attack in the blog and the allegation of malice involving the sources meant there was public interest in disclosure of the sources. Ultimately, after a specific fact-weighing exercise, the protection in the Act was not available to the blogger.[113]

III. The Newspaper Rule

23. A special rule known as the 'newspaper rule' existed for many years. If a news medium was sued[114] and admitted publication, a court would not order it to disclose its sources of information before trial, whether by interrogatory or order for discovery. The term 'source' extended beyond the mere names of informants and could cover such things as interview notes.[115] The reason often given for this rule was that it is unfair to allow a plaintiff to delve around to see who else he or she can sue. However, New Zealand authority[116] holds that its real basis was the public

111. *Slater v. Blomfield* [2014] 3 NZLR 835. See also *Hager v. Her Majesty's Attorney-General* [2015] NZHC 3268.
112. Evidence Act 2006, s. 68(5).
113. Evidence Act 2006, s. 68(2).
114. Most of the cases were defamation cases, although in *Broadcasting Corporation of NZ v. Alex Harvey Industries Ltd* [1980] 1 NZLR 163 (CA) it was extended to slander of goods.
115. *Brill v. Television One* [1976] 1 NZLR 683 (SC).
116. *Broadcasting Corporation of NZ v. Alex Harvey Industries Ltd* [1980] 1 NZLR 163 (CA).

interest in protecting the media's sources of information so as to encourage the free-flow of information to them. This authority confirmed: (i) that the rule would be applied as a matter of course except in the most exceptional circumstances; and (ii) that it applied only at the pre-trial stage and not when questions are asked during the trial itself. Nor was it applied in cases other than defamation and injurious falsehood. In New Zealand, the rule was codified in what is now r 8.46 of the High Court Rules. This provides that if the defendant pleads that the words or matters complained of are honest opinion on a matter of public interest, or were published on a privileged occasion, no interrogatories as to the defendant's sources of information or grounds of belief may be allowed unless the interrogatories are necessary in the interests of justice.[117] The rule was amended with effect from 1 November 2004 to address the criticism that it was previously too generous in stating an absolute prohibition.[118] There is now uncertainty about the status of the newspaper rule because it has been held to have been subsumed by section 68 of the Evidence Act.[119]

117. The rule also applies to discovery.
118. *Lange v. Atkinson* [2000] 3 NZLR 385 (CA) at 404, per Tipping J.
119. *Slater v. Blomfield* [2014] 3 NZLR 835, [29]–[30].

Chapter 3. Journalists' Liability

§1. General Information on the Liability System

24. Normally, for criminal offences, the principal liability is visited on the media company. A company, being an artificial person, can only act through individuals. Sometimes there can be a difficult question of whether the intention of an individual can be attributed to the company. Depending on the extent of their participation and on the way the relevant statute defines the ingredients of the offence, individuals such as the reporter, and in particular the editor, may be personally liable to a penalty as well.[120]

Civil claims such as defamation, privacy, breach of copyright and breach of confidence may impose civil liability on media companies and journalists when people aggrieved by the publication sue to obtain remedies for the injury done to them.

§2. Defamation and Libel

25. Defamation is principally a civil wrong that gives the injured party a right to claim substantial damages. Until 1 February 1993, it was also punishable as a specific criminal offence, since repealed by the Defamation Act 1992.[121] In New Zealand, a distinction is no longer drawn between libel and slander, and the same rules apply to all defamatory statements.[122]

I. Definition

26. Although the Defamation Act 1992 refined certain elements of the law of defamation and offers some special remedies, it is still basically a common law subject. Four definitions of what is defamatory are often used by New Zealand courts although the cases are English and the language somewhat dated:

(a) a statement that might tend to lower the plaintiff in the estimation of right-thinking members of society generally;[123]
(b) a false statement about a man to his discredit;[124]

---

120. In *Solicitor-General v. Fairfax* HC Wellington CIV-2008-485-705, 10 Oct. 2008, contempt proceedings were brought against both the company which published the *Dominion Post* newspaper and the editor, Tim Pankhurst.
121. Crimes Act 1961, ss 211–216; repealed by s. 56(2) of the Defamation Act 1992. See *Single v. Church* DC Napier CP22/93, 10 May 1994, one of the last prosecutions for criminal defamation. It was unsuccessful. Any new forms of criminal libel would probably be inconsistent with the rights and freedoms in the New Zealand Bill of Rights Act 1990, and therefore require a report to Parliament under s. 7 of the Bill.
122. Defamation Act 1992, s. 4. See *Wells v. Haden* [2008] DCR 859 at [60]–[62].
123. *Sim v. Stretch* [1936] 2 All ER 1237 at 1240 per Lord Atkin.
124. *Youssoupoff v. MGM Pictures Ltd* (1934) 50 TLR 581 at 584 per Scrutton LJ.

(c) a publication without justification that is calculated to injure the reputation of another by exposing him to hatred, contempt or ridicule;[125]
(d) a statement about a man that tends to make others shun and avoid him.[126]

It is not actionable to make disparaging statements about a dead person in New Zealand.[127]

II. Intention Not Necessary

27. A person publishing defamatory words may be liable even if he or she did not intend to defame anyone. What matters is not what the defendant intended the words to convey, but rather what they do convey to a reasonable reader or listener. In New Zealand, publishers have been sued for defamation for using a photograph of a woman with her grandchildren in a book about sex that was later declared indecent.[128] A hard New Zealand case[129] is a warning to the media of the consequences of negligence by a journalist resulting in the publication of defamatory visual material. A senior and experienced reporter allowed the publication of a photograph of an innocent individual incorrectly described in a newspaper as a 'Gang Chief' claimed by police to be a career criminal and a leader of career criminals. The journalist accepted responsibility for the mistake, but argued that the system at the newspaper for dealing with photographs was inadequate. He was eventually dismissed for serious misconduct and pursued a personal grievance action arguing the decision was not a fair and reasonable one. The matter found its way to the Court of Appeal which upheld the decision to dismiss on the basis that it was open to the employer, acting fairly and reasonably, to have reached the view that the journalist's conduct meant he had lost the confidence of his superiors that he could be relied on in the future, notwithstanding his previous unimpeachable employment record with the newspaper. The Court had regard to the nature of the business of publishing newspapers and the need to rely on reporters for the veracity of information published, which was seen as fundamental to the reputation and credibility of the newspaper.

III. The Meaning of the Statement

28. Before a court can say whether words are defamatory, it must decide what the words mean.[130] Generally, it will take the natural and ordinary meaning of the words, that is, the meaning that would be attributed to them by ordinary readers and

125. *Parmiter v. Coupland* (1840) 6 M & W 105 at 108 per Parke B.
126. *Youssoupoff v. MGM Pictures Ltd* (1934) 50 TLR 581 at 587 per Slesser LJ.
127. *Small v. Globe Printing Co* [1940] 2 DLR 670.
128. *Taylor v. Beere* [1982] 1 NZLR 81; see also *Kirk v. AH & AW Reed* [1968] NZLR 801.
129. *W & H Newspapers Ltd v. Oram* [2001] 3 NZLR 29 (CA).
130. Meanings should be determined as early as possible, because defences and discovery may depend on these: *Young v. Television New Zealand Ltd* [2014] NZCA 50, [73]–[74].

listeners. But sometimes it will decide that the words bear a further meaning (an innuendo), which would be appreciated only by a limited number of people in possession of special knowledge.

A. Natural and Ordinary Meaning

29. When the plaintiff does not plead an innuendo, the words complained of must be construed in their natural and ordinary sense. The 'reasonable men' test is articulated as a 'reasonable person' test. The principles were stated by the New Zealand Court of Appeal in 1996:[131]

(a) The test is objective; under the circumstances in which the words were published, what would the ordinary, reasonable person understand by them?
(b) The reasonable person reading the publication is taken to be one of ordinary intelligence, general knowledge and experience of worldly affairs.
(c) The Court is not concerned with the literal meaning of the words or the meaning which might be extracted on close analysis by a lawyer or academic linguist. What matters is the meaning which the ordinary reasonable person would as a matter of impression carry away in his or her head after reading the publication.
(d) The meaning includes what the ordinary reasonable person would infer from the words used in the publication …
(e) But the Court will reject those meanings which only emerge as the product of some strained or forced interpretation or groundless speculation …

A statement might convey more to the reasonable person than it actually says expressly: the words might have overtones and convey inferences that are apparent to an ordinary person. Some of the most hurtful imputations are contained 'between the lines'. For example, in New Zealand, a newspaper ran a series of articles critical of a certain religious sect, alleging that it had driven one of its Motueka members to suicide. A photograph next to one of the articles showed an officer of the sect in Christchurch escorting an eminent visiting American member. It was held that a reasonable reader would associate the officer with the particular events described in the article: that officer recovered damages, although as a Christchurch person he was remote in distance from Motueka, where those events had occurred.[132]

Inferences might arise from publications that grammatically state the opposite to the meaning intended. A weekly business newspaper referred in a column to a bankrupt who was said to be living beyond his means, using the words: 'Of course, all

131. *Young v. Television New Zealand Ltd* [2014] NZCA 50, *New Zealand Magazines v. Hadlee (no 2)* [2005] NZAR 621 (CA); *Gerdelan v. The Problem Gambling Foundation* HC Auckland CIV-2003-404-03497, 16 May 2005. See also *Charleston v. News Group Newspapers* [1995] 2 AC 65, [1995] 2 All ER 313 (HL).
132. *Christchurch Press Co Ltd v. McGaveston* [1986] 1 NZLR 610 (CA).

this opulence was funded, not by our bankrupt bon vivant, but by his employer … '.[133] This was held to be capable of the meaning that it was probably false that the plaintiff's opulent lifestyle was funded by his employer.

Even denials that facts exist might lead an ordinarily alert reader to suspect that they do and can be defamatory. A useful example is provided by *New Zealand Magazines v. Hadlee*.[134] An article in a women's magazine took the form of an interview with a prominent woman, containing photographs and a heading: 'Tell me it isn't true, M'. The article's opening paragraph began: 'It's time to set the record straight and shut up the gossips – M is not having an affair with H!' The interview that followed contained several denials by M of the rumours. The majority of the Court of Appeal held that in reading the article a notional, reasonable reader could feel there was 'no smoke without fire'. A defamatory rumour coupled with a denial of a rumour might still leave the matter capable of a defamatory meaning. It is thus dangerous to use such common devices as: 'Mr X today denied rumours that … '.[135]

1. Bane and Antidote Doctrine

30. New Zealand courts apply the 'bane and antidote doctrine' whereby the bane of an article must be taken together with a later antidote. In *McGee v. Independent Newspapers Ltd*,[136] McGee claimed he was defamed by published reports following his arrest in Bangkok suggesting he was connected to an alleged international investment scam, the sting of which branded him as a fraudster. McGee had in fact been convicted and sentenced for working in Thailand without a permit. The defendants argued that the publications contained this latter information which was an antidote to the suggested sting. The Court assessed all the publications, and in particular, treated two broadcasts by TVNZ as parts of a story emerging over a two-day period. As the plaintiff had relied on the stories as a whole to establish identification, the Court thought that what was sauce for the goose was sauce for the gander.[137] This saying means that if the plaintiff can benefit from a contextual approach, so can the defendant. The Court therefore considered the two stories as a coherent whole in looking at meanings and whether information in the later story could provide an antidote to the sting. However, it was found that the story could still support the alleged meaning, as could all of the publications.

B. Innuendo

31. An innuendo arises where the words the defendant has used bear no sinister connotations by themselves and to the ordinary reader would appear perfectly

133. *Pauanui Publishing Ltd v. Montgomerie* [2004] NZAR 702 at 707. The bankruptcy had been annulled shortly before.
134. *New Zealand Magazines v. Hadlee* [2005] NZAR 621 (CA).
135. See *Savige v. News Ltd* [1932] SASR 240.
136. *McGee v. Independent Newspapers Ltd* [2006] NZAR 24.
137. *McGee v. Independent Newspapers Ltd* [2006] NZAR 24 at [50].

innocent. However, to certain readers who have what might be colloquially called 'inside information', in other words, who have knowledge of certain extraneous facts that do not appear in the passage concerned, these words take on a colour that is damaging to the plaintiff. It seems not to matter how many people know the special facts, for even if there is only one such person the plaintiff has been defamed to that person. All that is required is that there be proof 'that there are people who know the special facts and so might understand the words in a defamatory sense'.[138] The fewer the people with special knowledge, the lower the damages are likely to be.

The publisher's ignorance of the special facts is irrelevant to liability. It has also been decided that to support an innuendo the extrinsic facts must have been in existence at the time the statement was published; otherwise, the writer of originally innocuous words would become responsible for any connotations they might acquire through later changes in circumstance.[139]

C. Relationship between Types of Meaning

32. Section 37 of the Defamation Act 1992 makes it a requirement that pleadings set out the natural and ordinary meaning attributed to the words, so that the defendant (and the court) can know precisely what is being complained of.[140] Special innuendo meanings must also be pleaded and the person or class to whom that meaning is known must also be specified, together with any other relevant facts and circumstances. Pleading requirements have not been allowed to become a strait-jacket, however. In *Howard-Smith v. Truth Weekender Ltd*, it was held to be unnecessarily pedantic to require the plaintiff to join the dots between particular words in the publication and the alleged meanings.[141]

A question unanswered in New Zealand is whether a plaintiff, having in his or her pleadings specified a particular meaning of the words complained of, can at the trial fall back on some other meaning. The Court of Appeal has indicated that this might not be possible unless the pleadings make it clear that this right is reserved.[142]

A plaintiff who relies on both natural and ordinary meaning and innuendo was said to have two causes of action at common law. However, section 7 of

---

138. See *Fullam v. Newcastle Chronicle & Journal Ltd* [1977] 1 WLR 651, [1977] 3 All ER 32 (CA), where the plaintiff had to plead that the relevant facts were known to some of the newspaper's readers and to identify those readers.
139. *Grappelli v. Derek Block (Holdings) Ltd* [1981] 1 WLR 822, [1981] 2 All ER 272 (CA); *Simons Proprietary Ltd v. Riddell* [1941] NZLR 913 at 932–933 per Blair J.
140. Careful pleading is required: *Dorbu v. Cooke* HC *Auckland* CIV-2008-404-005222, 30 Apr. 2009.
141. Unreported HC Auckland, CIV-2010-404-843, Associate Judge Bell, [13]–[21]. However, plaintiffs in person who do not comply with s. 37 and who do not attempt to meet pleading deficiencies may have their claim struck out: see *Lau v. ACP Media Ltd* [2013] NZHC 1165.
142. *Broadcasting Corporation of New Zealand v. Crush* [1988] 2 NZLR 234 at 239 per Cooke P.

the Defamation Act 1992 now provides that a single publication constitutes one cause of action, no matter how many imputations are contained in it.[143]

D. Context

33. The meanings of words can be coloured by their surroundings. Words may be defamatory or not according to the context in which they appear. For example, the overall style of a publication may be significant in deciding how words in it are likely to be understood by readers.[144]

It is always dangerous to read one part of an article in isolation from the rest, for a passage that by itself appears innocent may take on defamatory connotations when the whole article is read. The converse is true also.[145] Similarly, *breakouts*, the journalistic practice of prominently isolating an extract from the body of an article, should not be read on their own.[146] Thus, a person suing in respect of a passage in an article should specify any other parts of the article that clarify or qualify the passage of which the plaintiff complains. Nevertheless, this must not be allowed to obscure the rule that the plaintiff must in the pleadings isolate the words of which he or she complains; it is not enough to set out the whole of a newspaper article in the pleadings without identifying the precise passages alleged to be defamatory.[147]

Sometimes an article that seems inoffensive by itself assumes a defamatory meaning when read in conjunction with other articles or news items, whether in the same newspaper or in earlier or even (possibly) later issues of the newspaper.[148] There is authority to the effect that a plaintiff can sue in respect of a series of articles, where the Court assessed all the publications, and in particular, treated two broadcasts by TVNZ as parts of a story emerging over a two-day period. It considered the two stories as a coherent whole in looking at meanings.[149]

Media may also be successfully sued in respect of an article that is defamatory when read in the light of prior news items published or broadcast by other media. If such items can be regarded as part of the general knowledge of the community,

143. Television broadcasts are not to be broken into audio and visual components so as to create two causes of action. The entire audio-visual message is one publication: *Jaques v. Morgan* [1995] DCR 220 at 229–230.
144. *Willis v. Katavich* HC Auckland CP547/85, 21 Aug. 1989.
145. *Charleston v. News Group Newspapers Ltd* [1995] 2 AC 65 at 71–73 and 74, [1995] 2 All ER 313 (HL) per Lord Bridge and Lord Nicholls. It may be that *Charleston* illustrates the very limit of such principles. In an Australian case, Kirby J disagreed with the reasoning in *Charleston*, where he said: 'To the extent that dicta in *Charleston* or other cases suggest that the courts should attribute to the recipients of matter published in the mass media a close and careful attention to the entirety of the item published, I would not follow that opinion … The ordinary reader will draw conclusions from general impressions. He or she will not reread or review the matter complained of.' *Chakravarti v. Advertiser Newspapers Ltd* (1998) 154 ALR 294, at 336–337.
146. *Pauanui Publishing v. Montgomerie* [2004] NZAR 702.
147. *Scott v. Fourth Estate Newspapers Ltd* [1986] 1 NZLR 336. The approach is not too pedantic, however: see *Howard-Smith v. Truth Weekender Ltd* Unreported HC Auckland, CIV-2010-404-843, Associate Judge Bell, [13]–[21].
148. See *Pilcher v. Knowles* (1900) 19 NZLR 368 (SC); *Simons Proprietary Ltd v. Riddell* [1941] NZLR 913; and *Ballantyne v. Television New Zealand Ltd* [1992] 3 NZLR 455.
149. *McGee v. Independent Newspapers Ltd* [2006] NZAR 24.

they are arguably part of the context in which the latest contribution has been published.[150] This suggests that great care should be exercised. A jury may also be referred to a later article to identify the person referred to in defamatory terms in an earlier article.[151] This is an alarming prospect in these days of news saturation by various media. But before a defendant can be successfully sued, it has to be clear that in some way the defendant has said something defamatory of the plaintiff. If a statement has contributed to a lowering of an individual's reputation, but nothing in that statement was in any way false and defamatory of the plaintiff, it cannot be defamatory. However, it may be different if that statement has in some way referred to and adopted the earlier ones.

IV. Repetition of Stories

34. Even if all media do is to repeat words that someone else has spoken or written, there can still be liability if those words are defamatory. As a general rule, if journalists report defamatory words used by someone in an interview, or in a speech or at a meeting, the journalist and their employer will be open to a defamation action. This could be very hard on the news media, so a limited amount of statutory protection has been extended in respect of words reported at various types of meeting where matters of public interest are being discussed.

V. Links in a Chain of Publication

35. If a defamatory statement appears in a publication, all those concerned with it are liable – for a newspaper for example, this will be the company, the editor, the reporter, even the sub-editors and layout editors. In practice, usually only the company is sued, for the others may not be pursuing.[152] But a newspaper will be just as much liable even if the writer of the offensive material was not a member of the newspaper staff at all: if, for example, he or she was the writer of a letter to the editor, because even in such a case the newspaper is the channel through which the defamatory subject-matter was communicated to the public.[153]

Similar principles apply to radio and television companies as their situation is basically no different. However, some aspects of broadcasting have no real equivalent in the newspaper world. These are the live interview and talkback show, where

150. *Hyams v. Peterson* [1991] 3 NZLR 648.
151. *Peters v. Cushing* [1999] NZAR 241. See also *Buchanan v. Jennings* [2002] 3 NZLR 145 (CA).
152. In *Montgomerie v. Pauanui Publishing Ltd* HC Auckland CP71/95, 3 Mar. 1997 an award of NZD 30,000 was broken into NZD 20,000 payable by the publishing company and NZD 10,000 by Jenni McManus personally, who, as business editor of *The Independent*, was author of one article. In *McManus v. Beckham* [2002] 4 All ER 497 (CA), the plaintiff successfully sued the original maker of a verbal statement, who was the celebrity Posh Spice, rather than the media who had republished the statements she made. This was because the defendant was aware what she said or did was likely to be reported in the media.
153. See for example: *Willy v. Fairfax New Zealand Ltd* HC Wellington CIV-2008-085-1429, 22 Jul. 2009.

there is always the risk that the interviewee, without any complicity on the part of the broadcasting officials, may make an impromptu remark that is defamatory of some person. However, even here the broadcasting station will normally be held liable, for it has assisted in publishing the remark, that is, in disseminating it to the public.[154] Live interviews are risky, and by staging one, the company is providing an opportunity for ill-considered statements, so it is necessary to use some monitor or delay system to censor such statements before they are heard by listeners. In some situations, a talkback show host or interviewer might also be personally liable, although this would be so only if that person had made comments personally,[155] or could be said to have been in some way responsible for the statements made by the interviewee.[156]

Printers are generally thought to be liable for material printed by them, because they contribute to its publication. However, with the advent of modern printing techniques, it has become increasingly unfair to saddle printers with such liability, for often they cannot be expected to detect defamatory remarks in material run off by them.[157] This was recognized when the Defamation Act was passed in 1992. Processors and distributors can use the defence of innocent dissemination in section 21 of the Act. Printers come within the definition of 'processor' in section 2 of the Act, which provides that it means a person who prints or reproduces, or plays a role in printing or reproducing, any matter.

VI. Repetition, Republication and the Internet

36. Most New Zealand newspapers now publish internet editions,[158] while broadcasters maintain websites too.[159] Journalists and the media generally are heavy users of internet information gathering and dissemination facilities. It is beyond doubt that defamation can occur via the internet, based on ordinary principles. It has been held in New Zealand that the fact that the defamation appeared in 'cyberspace' makes no difference to the application of defamation law.[160] In *Nationwide News Pty v. The University of Newlands and Forrester*,[161] the Court of Appeal examined a claim based on publication in New Zealand of the internet edition of an

154. *Russell v. Radio i Ltd* SC Auckland A590/74 (1976); *Australian Broadcasting Corporation v. Comalco Ltd* (1986) 68 ALR 259.
155. *Church of Scientology Inc v. Anderson* [1980] WAR 71.
156. *Australian Consolidated Press Ltd v. Bond* (1984) 56 ACTR 14. For the liability of a person who gives an interview which he or she knows will be widely published, see *McManus v. Beckham* [2002] 4 All ER 497. There is no liability if publication is due to a wrongful act that could not be foreseen: *Coulthard v. State of South Australia* (1995) ATR 81-326.
157. See *Thompson v. Australian Capital Television Pty Ltd* (1996) 141 ALR 1 per Brennan CJ at 8–9 and Gaudron J at 14.
158. See for example: the *Fairfax* site: www.stuff.co.nz and the *NZ Herald:* www.nzherald.co.nz.
159. See for example: *Television New Zealand*: tvnz.co.nz and *TV3:* www.tv3.co.nz.
160. *O'Brien v. Brown* [2001] DCR 1065: 'I know of no forum in which an individual has the freedom to say what he likes and in any manner he wishes about another individual citizen with immunity from suit for all consequences. Merely because the publication is being made to cyberspace does not alter this', per Judge Ross at 1074.
161. *Nationwide News Pty Ltd v. University of Newlands* CA202/04, 9 Dec. 2005.

Australian newspaper, *The Australian*. *Sadiq v. Baycorp (NZ) Ltd*[162] involved credit information published on a website. Internet publication in defamation cases is no longer unusual.[163]

New Zealand journalists will be personally responsible for any defamatory material they send via email, whether they know it is defamatory or not.[164] Employers may be vicariously liable for publication by any employees using the internet, but will have a defence of innocent dissemination if it is available to the employee. However, it is unlikely that the statutory defence of innocent dissemination could be used to suggest that an employee is merely processing or distributing information on a computer by simply playing a role in reproducing it. It would be difficult to argue that the conditions of section 21 of the Defamation Act 1992 are met because it is now well known that defamatory material circulates on the internet. Employees would be unable to make a convincing 'lack of knowledge' argument, and this weakness would be passed on to an employer if vicarious liability applies.

A. *Hyperlinking to a Defamatory Web Page*

37. More complex questions have arisen for media in relation to publication on the internet on which the stance taken by New Zealand law is as yet unclear. One question is whether media can be held to be publishing material from other websites by giving the URL address of the website, or by linking to it in some way. In a recent case, four articles in newspapers and on media websites referred to an ongoing debate about an acquittal in a prominent retrial and to statements made about it on a Facebook group and on another website.[165] The media articles generally did not repeat what was said on the sites, but contained hyperlinks to them and to an online petition. The creator of one of the sites was also quoted. The court rejected an application by media for separate consideration of the question of publication arising from hyperlinks. Fairfax referred to the Canadian decision of *Crookes v. Newton* to suggest that on the matter of hyperlinks New Zealand law was clear and the claim should fall away. However, the New Zealand High Court did not agree that New Zealand law will inevitably follow *Crookes*, so the question remains open. Therefore, media hyperlinking in a story to a website containing defamatory material may amount to media actually publishing what is on the website.

B. *Third-Party Publication on the Internet*

38. As noted above, it is well established that media are liable for repeating statements made by others.[166] When applied to media websites, it is clear that

162. *Sadiq v. Baycorp (NZ) Ltd* HC Auckland, CIV-2007-404-6421, 31 Mar. 2008.
163. Other examples are *Salmon v. McKinnon* [2007] NZCA 516 (email), and *Read v. Minister of Economic Development* HC Auckland CIV-2007-404-2655, 12 Sep. 2007 (website).
164. They would not be liable for anything seen on their computer screens by others passing by; however, as this would be unintentional publication.
165. *Karam v. Fairfax New Zealand Ltd* Unreported, High Court, Auckland, CIV-2010-404-005021, Associate Judge Osborne, 10 May 2012.
166. See para. 36 above.

responsibility for publication could flow from any invited comments posted about stories which are defamatory. A recent non-media case has clarified when media could be liable as a publisher of third-party comments online. In *Wishart v. Murray*[167] allegedly defamatory comments by anonymous third parties were posted on a Facebook page established by the defendant, who had also used Twitter to publicize the page. The Court of Appeal held that a publisher should be required to have actual, not imputed knowledge of the nature of the third-party comments.[168] The Court considered that an 'ought to know' test places a web host who does not know of the defamatory comment in a worse position than a host who actually does know, because the latter does not become a publisher until a reasonable time for removal of the statement has passed and will not be a publisher at all if the statement is removed in a reasonable time. In contrast, a host lacking knowledge would be a publisher from the moment of posting but is unable to avoid that outcome by removing the comment. Further, an 'ought to know' test could be in breach of the NZBORA requirement in section 14 to balance the right to reputation against freedom of expression, tipping the balance too far in favour of reputation. The imputed knowledge test was also seen as too uncertain, and finally, a web host would probably not have access to an innocent dissemination defence if found to be a publisher. The requirement for publication in these circumstances is therefore now based on a test of actual knowledge, with the opportunity to escape liability by removing the offending material within a reasonable time. In hosting their own websites and inviting comment, anonymous or otherwise, media must now incorporate the actual knowledge test into publication practice.

C. ISP Liability

39. The law in New Zealand (and overseas) is also unclear for Information Service Providers (ISPs), which as part of their business pass on information on the internet to subscribers. ISPs appear to have a stronger argument than media that they are mere conduits. Other recent case law has raised the novel question whether search engines themselves can be publishers.[169] In *A v. Google New Zealand Ltd*,[170] the High Court thought the matter was too novel to be dealt with summarily, but expressed a view that there may be a need to consider whether there has been 'a stamp of human intervention' in each case.[171]

Overall, the New Zealand judgments so far in this area indicate a reluctance to create exceptions to the existing law for the internet, and a preference for holding parties liable where there is knowledge of defamatory material, with access to the defence of innocent dissemination or other appropriate defences. There has never been liability for accidental publication. But publication on the internet is not in that

167. [2013] NZHC 540 (19 Mar. 2013).
168. *Murray v. Wishart* [2014] 3 NZLR 722.
169. *Metropolitan Internation Schools Ltd v. Designtechnica Corp* [2011] 1 WLR 1743, [2009] EMLR 27 held Google was not responsible for publication as a search engine. See also *Trkulja v. Yahoo!* Inc LLC [2012] VSC 88.
170. Unreported, HC Auckland, CIV: 2011-404-002780, 12 Sep. 2012, Associate Judge Abbott, [68].
171. *Ibid.*, [71]–[75]. See para. 40 below.

category. Levels of knowledge and control do vary depending on how material has been published and by whom. Those features are significant in the assessment of whether there should be liability in defamation in relation to the internet.[172]

D. Innocent Dissemination Defence

40. A further outstanding issue is whether, if liability arises from a form of publication online, a defence of innocent dissemination would be available, particularly for ISPs. Section 21 of the Defamation Act 1992, which contains the defence, appears ill-suited to adapt to such technological developments, because its wording is confined to 'processors' and the limited definition in the Act refers to being involved in 'reproduction'. The provision should be amended even though there have been no cases involving ISPs, as it is genuinely unclear whether the existing legislation covers the technology.[173] However, even if the legislation was altered, ISPs would need to exercise care because the defence of innocent dissemination is lost where knowledge of possible defamation exists. New Zealand does not have a specific defence for website operators as in the United Kingdom Defamation Act 2013,[174] nor any form of general safe harbour protection such as that which derives from European directives.[175] It is likely that in the future, the law will have to specifically address the matter of defences for mere conduit, caching and hosting internet services.

E. Place of Publication on the Internet

41. The question of when and where material available on the internet is published for the purposes of defamation has also apparently been answered, at least in Australia and the United Kingdom in *Dow Jones v. Gutnick*,[176] and New Zealand appears inclined to take the same approach. In that case, the High Court of Australia found that material on the World Wide Web is not available in comprehensible form until downloaded onto the computer of a person who has used a web browser to pull the material from the web server, and that it is where that person downloads the material that the damage to reputation may be done. *Gutnick* has had some degree of acceptance in New Zealand.[177] However, the Supreme Court has not ruled

172. See also *Rafiq v. Google New Zealand Ltd* [2014] NZHC 551.
173. See Law Commission *Electronic Commerce Part Two* (NZLC R58, 1999) at [262]–[270]; Law Commission *Electronic Commerce Part Three* (NZLC R68, 2000) at [80].
174. Defamation Act 2013 (UK), s. 5. See also ss 10 and 13. On the new Defamation Act generally, see Alistair Mullis & Andrew Scott, *Tilting at Windmills: The Defamation Act 2013*, 77(1) Modern L. Rev. 87 (2014).
175. The Electronic Commerce (EC Directive) Regulations 2002 are derived from EC Directive 2000/31/EC ('The E-Commerce Directive'), Regulations 17, 18 and 19. See *Kaschke v. Gray* [2010] EWHC 690 (QB), *Karim v. Newsquest Media Group* [2009] EWHC 3205 (QB), and *Metropolitan International Schools Ltd v. Designtechnica Corporation* [2009] EMLR 27, [2009] EWHC 1765.
176. *Dow Jones & Company Inc v. Gutnick* (2002) 194 ALR 433.
177. *Nationwide News Pty Ltd v. University of Newlands* CA202/04, 9 Dec. 2005.

out the possibility that it might revisit the principles relating to publication on the internet in appropriate circumstances in the future.[178]

F. Proof of Publication on the Internet

42. A further question is how it is to be proved that publication has occurred on the internet. Under English law, a plaintiff in a libel action based on internet publication cannot rely on a presumption of law that there has been substantial publication, as exists in relation to publication in the mass media.[179] The plaintiff bears the burden of proof. It must be shown that at least one person, other than the plaintiff, saw, read or heard the communication, usually by downloading it.[180] However, publication can be inferred in relation to generally accessible websites, bulletin boards and other web-based services with many subscribers.[181] In New Zealand, once again, the law is unclear;[182] however, it appears likely the English approach would be followed.

G. The Multiple Publication Rule

43. The English *Loutchansky* decisions[183] confirmed that multiple publications could arise from initial publication on the internet. This is particularly significant in relation to articles which are republished in internet media websites, and which remain available in electronic archives. For media which maintain an online presence, and which leave that content to function as an online archive, potential liability has increased. Under *Loutchansky*, online publishers potentially face new legal action each time an article is clicked on, even if this occurs many years after it was first published. In the UK, the multiple publication rule has now been replaced with a 'single publication rule' in the Defamation Act 2013,[184] at least where the republication is by the same publisher. The issue has been addressed in New Zealand, where the multiple publication rule remains.

---

178. *University of Newlands Ltd v. Nationwide News Pty Ltd* [2006] NZSC 16. The *Gutnick* principle has clearly been accepted in contempt cases: *Solicitor General v. Krieger* [2014] NZHC 172; *Siemer v. Solicitor General* [2010] 3 NZLR 767, breach of suppression: *Police v. Slater* [2011] DCR 6, and in criminal cases: *R v. Standard 304 Ltd* [2010] NZAR 194; *Batty v. Choven* [2006] NZAR 127, (2005) CRNZ 214 approved.
179. *Al Amoudi v. Brisard* [2006] EWHC 1062 [2007] 1 WLR 113, [2006] 3 All ER 294, (QB).
180. A similar approach is *taken in Australia, eg: MacDonald v. ABC* [2014] NSWSC 206, [27]. See also *Crookes v. Newton*, 2011 SCC 47, [2011] 3 S.C.R. 269.
181. See *Karam v. Parker* Unreported, HC Auckland, CIV-2010-404-003038, 29 Jul. 2011, Associate Judge Sargisson, [50]–[56].
182. *Nationwide News Pty Ltd v. University of Newlands* CA202/04, 9 Dec. 2005.
183. *Loutchansky v. Times Newspapers Ltd (Nos 4 and 5), Loutchansky v. Times Newspapers Ltd (Nos 2, 3 and 5)* [2002] QB 783, [2002] 1 All ER 652.
184. Defamation Act 2013 (UK) s. 8. For criticism of the single publication rule, see Alistair Mullis & Andrew Scott, *Tilting at Windmills: The Defamation Act 2013,* 77(1) Modern L. Rev. 87 (2014), and the Inforrm blog: Libel Reform Debate Part 3: The Multiple Publication Rule: http://inforrm.wordpress.com/2010/07/06/libel-reform-debate-part-3-the-multiple-publication-rule/, accessed 4 Apr. 2014.

VII. Defamation of Overseas Persons

44. There is nothing to stop a foreign plaintiff from suing in New Zealand,[185] nor is it beyond the bounds of possibility, if copies of the publication reached his or her own country, that the plaintiff could obtain leave from his or her own court to bring the action there and enforce in New Zealand the judgment thus obtained.[186] However, the courts control 'forum shopping' using the 'forums conveniens' principle, whereby whether the chosen country is a suitable forum because there has been or will be a real and substantial tort within the jurisdiction, and whether there is another jurisdiction more suitable, are determinative.[187] If these conditions are not met, claims will be struck out as an abuse of process. Currently, there is no suggestion that levels of foreign claims are of concern in New Zealand. New Zealand courts are concerned to control the ability of New Zealand plaintiffs to sue foreign defendants in this country when overseas publications are downloadable here on the internet.[188]

VIII. Defamation of the Plaintiff

45. In order to succeed in a defamation action, a plaintiff must show that he or she was defamed, that is, the defamatory statement referred to the plaintiff. This does not mean that the plaintiff has to be referred to by name. A New Zealand example is a reference in a satirical programme to a character called 'Beamish Teeth' was found to be to Mr Hamish Keith, chairman of the council of the National Art Gallery.[189]

In other cases, no name at all may be used, but circumstances connect the plaintiff with the publication. In one New Zealand case when sexist material was included in an 'advertisement' for Coronet Peak Skifield, it was held that this reflected on the Mount Cook Group Ltd, the operator of the skifield, who were entitled to damages and an injunction for the inference was that they must have approved or condoned the advertisement.[190]

185. *Cooper v. Independent News Auckland Ltd,* DC Auckland NP552/96, 21 Apr. 1997. An English inquiry agent recovered NZD 5,000 for defamation that arose when he visited New Zealand.

186. For the reverse case of a New Zealander applying for leave to commence an action in this country against a foreigner: see *Eyre v. Nationwide News Pty Ltd* [1967] NZLR 851.

187. United Kingdom courts have barred visiting plaintiffs because they could receive substantial justice in the United States, and some United States courts have concluded that media defendants would not receive justice if the United States court grants orders enforcing English libel judgments: *Berezovsky v. Forbes* [1999] EMLR 278; *King v. Lewis and others* [2004] All ER (D) 91 (February).

188. *Nationwide News Pty Ltd v. University of Newlands* CA202/04, 9 Dec. 2005.

189. *Television New Zealand v. Keith* [1994] 2 NZLR 84.

190. *Mount Cook Group Ltd v. Johnstone Motors Ltd* [1990] 2 NZLR 488. But in *Bradley v. Wingnut Films Ltd* [1993] 1 NZLR 415, Gallen J rejected an argument that the appearance of a family grave plot for fourteen seconds in a schlock horror film could be identified with the plaintiff, the suggestion being that he had consented to its use and approved of and made financial gain from the film. The Judge held that people would not necessarily identify the tombstone with the plaintiff – it was simply part of the background of the scene in the film.

Where corporations sue, it is important to do so using the correct name in order to establish that the defamatory statement was 'of and concerning the plaintiff'.[191]

Sometimes the identity of the person is revealed only by reading two or more articles together.[192] In New Zealand, television items sixteen months apart have been connected to determine that the first statement was aimed at the plaintiff,[193] and in another case,[194] the plaintiff relied on a number of stories broken over time as a whole to establish identification.

A. *Group Defamation*

46. As to the question whether anyone can sue if derogatory statements are made about a group of people, in New Zealand, the test to be applied is the same as for defamation of a single person: an individual who is part of the group referred to can only sue if the words can be understood to relate to that individual. If a statement is made generally of a large group or class – for instance the statement that 'all lawyers are sharks' – a member of the group will not normally be entitled to damages, because most readers treat such sweeping statements as exaggerations, and not as meaning that every single member of the class is being attacked.

However, in some instances aspersions cast on a group of people may be actionable by an individual member of the group. First, the smaller the group, the greater the likelihood that a plaintiff will be able to show that the words were directed at him or her.[195] Even in the case of a large group, individual members could sue if the language of the statement complained of was so explicit as to leave no doubt that every member of the group was being pointed to.[196] Sometimes statements about a group reflect particularly on one or more members of it.[197]

B. *Corporate Bodies*

47. In the eyes of the law, human beings are not the only persons who can sue in New Zealand: entities such as companies, trade unions and incorporated societies are recognized as persons also. Like any other persons, they may be defamed and may bring an action if they are.[198] A corporation, having no feelings, can recover

191. [2012] NSWSC 1136. See also *Euromoney Institutional Investor Plc v. Aviation News Ltd & Anor* [2013] EWHC 1505 (QB).
192. *Hayward v. Thompson* [1982] QB 47, [1981] 3 All ER 450. See also *Baltinos v. Foreign Language Publications Pty Ltd* (1986) 6 NSWLR 85. Contrast, however, *Astaire v. Campling* [1966] 1 WLR 34, [1965] 3 All ER 666 (CA).
193. *Peters v. Cushing* [1999] NZAR 241.
194. *McGee v. Independent Newspapers Ltd* [2006] NZAR 24.
195. *Ballantyne v. Television New Zealand Ltd* [1992] 3 NZLR 455.
196. *Hyams v. Peterson* [1991] 3 NZLR 648 (plaintiff referred to as a member of 'the Gang of 20').
197. *Christchurch Press Co Ltd v. McGaveston* [1986] 1 NZLR 610.
198. However, an English Judge warned against the proliferation of 'satellite' actions whereby proprietors of companies who have been defamed also bring actions on behalf of the company: *Jameel*

damages only if it can show that financial or commercial loss has occurred or is likely to occur.[199]

C. *Local Councils*

48. There is also authority holding that a city council, a democratically elected body corporate, may not sue.[200] There are doubts as to how far this principle extends and whether the ingredient of popular election is central.[201]

IX. Defamation and Negligence

49. New Zealand courts hold steady in cases involving media defendants in refusing to adopt the principle in the English case *Spring v. Guardian Assurance*[202] that a negligence action can be used to protect reputation.[203] The matter appears to be settled – the behaviour of the media in researching, filming or interviewing, or reporting news or current affairs, is not subject to any duty based on the tort of negligence if damage to reputation results. In the main, defamation covers the ground.

X. Remedies

50. A number of remedies are available to a plaintiff who has been defamed or fears that he or she is about to be defamed. Some of these were introduced by the Defamation Act 1992.

A. *Damages*

1. Compensatory Damages

51. If the plaintiff in a defamation action receives a favourable verdict, he or she will normally be awarded money damages. The amount is settled by the jury if there is one and by the judge if there is not. In theory, the plaintiff should receive enough

---

v. Times Newspapers Ltd [2004] EWCA Civ 983 at [36] per LJ Sedley. Section 1 of the Defamation Act 2013 (UK), after stating a threshold serious harm requirement for all plaintiffs, s. 1(2) clarifies that 'harm to the reputation of a body that trades for profit is not 'serious harm' unless it has caused or is likely to cause the body serious financial loss'.

199. *Mount Cook Group Ltd v. Johnstone Motors Ltd* [1990] 2 NZLR 488, at 497; s. 6 of the Defamation Act 1992.
200. *Derbyshire County Council v. Times Newspapers Ltd* [1993] AC 534, [1993] 1 All ER 1011 (HL), overruling *Bognor Regis Urban District Council v. Campion* [1972] 2 All ER 61.
201. *Tairawhiti District Health Board v. Perks* [2002] NZAR 533.
202. *Spring v. Guardian Assurance* Plc [1995] 2 AC 296, [1994] 3 All ER 129.
203. *Midland Metals Overseas Pte Ltd v. The Christchurch Press Company* [2002] 2 NZLR 289.

to compensate him or her for the injury to his or her reputation. Sometimes there will be an economic loss, actual or prospective. Whether or not the economic loss exists, there is always a degree of mental hurt. Juries are instructed to return a single lump sum award; by the very nature of things, this lump sum is not arrived at by any precise arithmetical calculation but is more often nominated instinctively.[204] Knowledge of the amounts awarded in like cases in the past plays a part.

a. Nominal Damages

52. Defamation is actionable per se and therefore nominal damages are available once the plaintiff establishes liability. Nominal damages only are comparatively rare, but *Ti Leaf Productions Ltd v. Baikie*[205] is an example and concerned damage to the reputation of a film company which was said to flow from both defamation and contract, but which was only nominal. The plaintiff argued successfully that the defendant had breached a tenancy agreement not to make negative comments about the plaintiff to the media during the making of a film. However, although nominal damages of NZD 500 were awarded, the plaintiff was not able to establish that the publication to the defendant's Member of Parliament and others had caused withdrawal of support from investors and the eventual abandonment of the project, taking into account the modest pace of production, the amount expended on pre-production and the absence of adequate planning for the film.[206]

b. Aggravated Damages

53. Sometimes compensatory damages are awarded for mental hurt caused by aggravating factors in the nature of the defamation or the defendant's conduct. These damages (called 'aggravated damages') are truly compensatory, but they are easily confused with punitive damages whose purpose is to punish. In any event, it appears that companies cannot claim aggravated damages. The Defamation Act 1992 only allows corporate clients to recover economic loss, which does not and cannot include aggravated damages.[207] In New Zealand, aggravated damages continue to be awarded and sometimes separately itemized.[208]

2. Punitive or Exemplary Damages

54. In addition to compensatory damages, in rare cases a jury is also entitled to award a sum by way of 'exemplary' or 'punitive' damages for the sole purpose of

204. *Television New Zealand Ltd v. Quinn* [1996] 3 NZLR 24 at 42–43 per McKay J.
205. *Ti Leaf Productions Ltd v. Baikie* HC Christchurch CP9-97, 3 Oct. 2000, affirmed *Ti Leaf Productions Ltd v. Baikie* (2001) 7 NZBLC 103,464 (CA).
206. Expenses of NZD 5,000 were awarded to the plaintiff, as they had flowed in part from the defendant's actions.
207. *Midland Metal Overseas Pte Ltd v. The Christchurch Press Ltd* [2002] NZLR 289 (CA) at 293–294 and 302–303.
208. [2011] 2 NZLR 361.

punishing the defendant and deterring him or her from like conduct in the future. These 'damages' focus on the behaviour of the defendant rather than the hurt to the plaintiff. Punitive awards are reserved for serious cases where the defendant has acted in flagrant disregard of the rights of the plaintiff. It was established by a case in 1982 that punitive damages are available for defamation in New Zealand.[209] Section 28 of the Defamation Act 1992 has now made the 'flagrant disregard' test a statutory requirement,[210] but it is not an easy test to satisfy.[211] Punitive should be awarded rarely and at moderate levels.[212]

3. Relevant Factors in Awarding Damages

55. Leaving punitive damages aside, many factors will influence the court in the size of the damages award it eventually makes. The following matters are relevant.

a. Bad Reputation

56. If the plaintiff already had a bad reputation, the defendant's attack may not have caused much extra damage and damages may not be high. The courts may now admit evidence of specific instances of misconduct by the plaintiff, to establish that the plaintiff's reputation is generally bad in the aspect to which the proceedings relate.[213]

b. The Defendant's Conduct

57. The defendant's conduct at the time of and subsequent to the publication is relevant. If the defendant publishes an apology, for instance, this is taken into account.[214] If, however, the defendant maintains a high-handed hostile attitude that can be said to increase the plaintiff's hurt, this can have the reverse effect. Such matters as republication of the defamation or insulting cross-examination of the plaintiff in court will be relevant in this regard. An unsuccessful plea of truth can sometimes have this effect.[215]

---

209. *Taylor v. Beere* [1982] 1 NZLR 81.
210. The test was failed in *Cooper v. Independent News Auckland Ltd* DC Auckland NP552/96, 21 Apr. 1997 and in *Penn v. Ansley* DC Christchurch NP1628/95, 1 Oct. 1997 (upheld in *Ansley v. Penn* HC Christchurch, A36/98, 28 Aug. 1998).
211. See for example: *Chinese Herald Ltd & ors v. New Times Media Ltd & ors* [2004] 2 NZLR 749, where the case came near the threshold, but punitive damages were not awarded: [63]. The compensatory damages awarded were seen as sufficient to punish the defendants and to deter them and others. Cf: *Siemer v. Stiassny* [2011] 2 NZLR 361.
212. *Television New Zealand Ltd v. Quinn* [1996] 3 NZLR 24. The proceedings were filed before the Defamation Act 1992 came into effect, but Lord Cooke noted that there was little difference between the old law and the 'flagrant disregard' test in the new Act (at 36).
213. Defamation Act 1992, s. 30.
214. Section 29, Defamation Act 1992. Likewise if he or she qualifies the original statement.
215. *Columbus v. Independent News Auckland Ltd* HC Auckland CP600/98, 7 Apr. 2000.

c. Defendant's State of Mind

58. Media which make an honest mistake will be in a much better position than media which deliberately publish derogatory comments.[216] In *Columbus*, it was found that the *New Zealand Truth* knew the true situation, yet published the untrue story with the mercenary aim of increasing circulation figures.[217]

d. Extent of Publication

59. A small district newspaper that publishes a defamation in its own district may be better off than a national network that diffuses the information throughout New Zealand.[218] Internet publication is global and has a greater reach.[219]

(e) Character of Statement.

The nature of the defamatory statement is of prime importance. The grosser the attack, the higher the damages.[220]

f. Plaintiff's Conduct

60. Plaintiff's conduct may be relevant. If he or she had provoked the defendant into defaming him or her, this may be reflected in damages. Misleading the court during the litigation may be in this category.

g. Prior Claim

61. It will be taken into account that the plaintiff has recovered or claimed damages or compensation in respect of publication of the same, or substantially the same, matter.[221]

h. Other Matters

62. The Defamation Act 1992 now allows the court to take into account: (a) the nature, extent, form and manner, and time of any correction, retraction, apology, or statement in rebuttal or explanation; (b) the terms of any injunction or declaration that the court proposes to grant; and (c) any delay for which the plaintiff was

216. *Bryce v. Rusden* (1886) 2 TLR 435.
217. See *Columbus v. Independent News Auckland Ltd* HC Auckland CP600/98, 7 Apr. 2000 at [64].
218. *Shadbolt v. Independent News Media (Auckland) Ltd* HC Auckland CP207/95, 7 Feb. 1997 (*Truth* newspaper distributed throughout New Zealand).
219. *Columbus v. Independent News Auckland Ltd* HC Auckland CP600/98, 7 Apr. 2000 at [61]–[62].
220. In *Columbus,* Anderson J thought the jury could take into account the fact that the defamatory statements were made in conjunction with remarks deprecating the plaintiff's vocal act, even though those statements were not sued on and would probably have attracted a defence of honest opinion: see *Columbus v. Independent News Auckland Ltd* HC Auckland CP600/98, 7 Apr. 2000 at [63].
221. Defamation Act 1992, s. 31.

responsible in bringing the proceedings to a conclusion.[222] These matters are in addition to matters already allowed in mitigation.

4. The Size of Damages Awards

63. Awards of damages in defamation cases are at times high. The largest single jury award to date was NZD 675,000.[223] However, in an extraordinary case,[224] a judge in the High Court made an order for the highest award of damages to date in a New Zealand defamation case,[225] of over NZD 900,000. This case does not suggest levels of damages for defamation are rising dangerously or are out of control in New Zealand because of the behaviour of the defendant, whereby he deprived himself of an opportunity to defend the actual proceedings. Very recently, the High Court made a total award of NZD 525,000, for approximately fifty statements published online in the context of discussion about a prominent murder retrial. The award demonstrates how numerous publications online can significantly increase damages awards.[226]

B. Injunction

64. Although not common, injunction to prevent publication is a possible remedy in defamation cases. An injunction was granted, for instance, to stop the continued display of a defamatory poster[227] and of a billboard sign.[228] The jurisdiction is 'of a delicate nature' and 'ought only to be exercised in the clearest cases'.[229] In the leading case,[230] the Court of Appeal affirmed its view that an interim injunction will not be granted readily in a defamation case because of the need to preserve freedom of expression. The Court emphasized that restraint should only be exercised for clear and compelling reasons and noted that where the competing rights of freedom of expression and the right to a fair trial cannot be balanced, it might be appropriate to curtail media expression temporarily.[231]

---

222. Section 29. See *Shadbolt v. Independent News Media (Auckland) Ltd*, HC Auckland CP207/95, 7 Feb. 1997; *Television New Zealand v. Ah Koy* [2002] 2 NZLR 616; and *Tipple v. Buchanan* HC Christchurch CIV-2001-409-000801, 20 Jul. 2005.
223. *Columbus v. Independent News Auckland Ltd* HC Auckland CP600/98, 7 Apr. 2000.
224. *Korda Mentha v. Siemer* HC Auckland CIV-2005-404-1808, 23 Dec. 2008.
225. [2011] 2 NZLR 361.
226. [2014] NZHC 737.
227. *Mount Cook Group Ltd v. Johnstone Motors Ltd* [1990] 2 NZLR 488.
228. *CB Norwood Distributors Ltd v. Nottingham* HC Hamilton CP 34/95, 13 Jun. 1995.
229. *Wm Coulson & Sons v. James Coulson & Co* (1887) 3 TLR 846 at 846 per Lord Esher MR.
230. *TV3 Network Services Ltd v. Fahey* [1999] 2 NZLR 129. See also *Hodgson v. Siemer* HC Auckland CIV-2005-404-1808, 5 May 2005.
231. The courts are more prepared to maintain injunctions where the news media are not involved and the matter at issue is in the nature of a private dispute: *Alexander v. Rountree et al* CA229/00, 15 Feb. 2001.

C. Defamation Act 1992

65. The Defamation Act 1992 contains certain other remedies, the rationale for some of them being that damages are not always the most appropriate remedy for defamation. These are correction recommendations, declarations, and retraction or reply.[232]

XI. Defamation Defences

A. Privilege

66. There are certain occasions on which New Zealand law regards the right of one person to speak his or her mind or to convey information as being of more importance than the right of another to their reputation. Several kinds of privilege are recognized. Absolute privilege applies to judicial proceedings, parliamentary proceedings and state communications.

1. Parliamentary Privilege Act 2014

67. Part 3 of the Parliamentary Privilege Act 2014 deals with the communication of proceedings in Parliament and subpart 1 provides a process whereby a person can seek a stay of civil (including defamation) or criminal proceedings based on communication by that person of proceedings in Parliament or of a document relating to those proceedings, or communication of an authorized parliamentary communication.[233] The person may apply to the Speaker for a certificate stating that the communication was made under the authority of the House or of a Committee of the House, or was an authorized parliamentary communication, and, when filed in the relevant court, the proceedings will be stayed and finally determined. Subpart 2 of the Parliamentary Privilege Act 2014 provides for a form of qualified immunity from civil or criminal liability for certain communications.[234] The immunity defence is conditional however, in that it is not available if the defendant abused the opportunity to communicate the information by acting in bad faith or with a predominant motive of ill will or both. This form of qualified immunity is available for delayed communication to the public of proceedings in Parliament,[235] and for fair and accurate reports of proceedings in Parliament, and fair and accurate extracts

232. Defamation Act 1992, ss 24–26.

233. Parliamentary Privilege Act 2014, s. 17. Communication includes communication to or for any people, in any form, on any basis, and using any medium or media, as well as live or delayed original communication and delayed recommunication, and live or delayed communication to the public: s. 5(1). Examples usefully given in the Act include email, internet posting, radio or television broadcast and webcast or podcast. Communication to the public means to or for the public or a class of the public: s. 5(1).

234. Parliamentary Privilege Act 2014, s. 18.

235. Parliamentary Privilege Act 2014, s. 19.

from or summaries of documents communicated under the House's or a Committee's authority and documents relating to proceedings in Parliament.[236] The qualified immunity does not limit or affect other laws relating to absolute or qualified privilege and in particular, the relevant provisions in the Defamation Act 1992 which are discussed below.[237]

2. Parliamentary Papers

68. If reports, papers, notes or proceedings are published under the authority of the House of Representatives, no defamation action may be brought in respect of that publication.[238] If any action is commenced, it will be stayed on production of the appropriate evidence that the House authorized the publication. Publication to the House by presenting or laying a document before it is protected[239] as is an official or authorized record of proceedings of the House.[240] Correct copies of the authorized publications are likewise privileged.[241] Tabling documents in the House does not confer privilege on journalists because tabling merely conveys content to Members; only authorization of publication carries privilege with it.[242]

Live broadcasts by any broadcaster of proceedings in the House are clearly protected by statute.[243]

3. The Position of the Media

69. With the exception of the stay process now set out in the Parliamentary Privilege Act 2014 and described above,[244] the media's privilege is generally a qualified privilege only.

a. Common Law Qualified Privilege

70. If an occasion is one of qualified privilege, a speaker or writer is immune from defamation proceedings unless it can be shown that he or she was actuated by ill will in making the statement concerned or took improper advantage of the occasion of publication. The destructive effect of this ill will is the difference between qualified and absolute privilege.

---

236. Parliamentary Privilege Act 2014, s. 20.
237. Parliamentary Privilege Act 2014, s. 21. See para. 74 below.
238. Defamation Act 1992, s. 13(3)(a). See *Lange v. Atkinson* [1998] 3 NZLR 424 at 437. The definition of 'proceedings in Parliament' in the Defamation Act has now been aligned with that in s. 10 of the Parliamentary Privilege Act 2014: s. 13(4).
239. Defamation Act 1992, s. 13(3)(b).
240. Defamation Act 1992, s. 13(3)(c).
241. Defamation Act 1992, s. 13(3)(d). But not a summary or extract, which come under qualified privilege: Sch. 1, Part 1, cl. 3.
242. See Joseph [1994] NZLJ 292 at 293.
243. Defamation Act, s. 13(2).
244. See para. 67 above.

i. Duty and Interest

71. Qualified privilege exists at common law in New Zealand in circumstances authoritatively defined by the House of Lords:[245]

A privileged occasion is ... an occasion where the person who makes a communication has an interest or a duty, legal, social or moral, to make it to the person to whom it is made, and the person to whom it is made has a corresponding interest or duty to receive it.

This vague test envisages a kind of reciprocal relationship between communicator and recipient that renders the communication of the information more vital than the interest of some third person in his or her reputation. The relevant interest can include self-interest, but there does not have to be a 'pressing need' for the defendant to protect the relevant interest.[246] In New Zealand, publication in media by the police of photographs of suspected offenders has been held to be within the defence.[247]

To attract this type of privilege, the publication must be made only to those persons who have an 'interest or duty' to receive it, which is known as the 'shared interest test'. Usually excessive publication will not be privileged. There may be cases where, on the facts, the public would have a sufficient interest to know, and media a sufficient duty to publish, to attract the privilege, but they are rare. Specialist publications which communicate matters of particular interest to a target audience, such as consumer magazines, have been recognized to be within this category.[248]

ii. Constitutional Qualified Privilege or Political Expression

72. Common law qualified privilege has recently bifurcated to develop a special form which, although generally available, is of particular benefit to media. This defence arose from a series of decisions known as the *Lange* decisions.[249] The New Zealand Court of Appeal decided that qualified privilege may protect a statement which is published generally, and covers statements which directly concern the functioning of representative and responsible government. The defence failed only if the plaintiff proved that the defendant was predominantly motivated by ill will towards the plaintiff or otherwise took improper advantage of the occasion of publication.[250] Ill will is established if it is shown the defendant did not believe what was published, or published the matter recklessly, not caring whether or not the words are true. The decision was appealed to the Privy Council,[251] which allowed the appeal and remitted the matter back to New Zealand for further hearing.

245. *Adam v. Ward* [1917] AC 309 at 334 per Lord Atkinson.
246. *Papaconstituntinos v. Holmes a Court* [2012] HCA 53 (5 Dec. 2012).
247. *Attorney-General v. Wright* [2007] NZAR 740 (HC).
248. *Julian v. Television New Zealand Ltd* HC Auckland CP367-SD01, 25 Feb. 2003; *BMW NZ Ltd v. Pepi Holdings Ltd* HC Christchurch CP16 & 28–94, 5 Sep. 1996; *Weepu v. Greymouth Evening Star* HC Greymouth CP4–91, 19 Mar. 1997; *Lange v. Atkinson* [1997] 2 NZLR 22 (HC); *Pauanui Publishing Ltd v. Montgomerie* [2004] NZAR 702.
249. *Lange v. Atkinson* [1997] 2 NZLR 22 (HC).
250. *Lange v. Atkinson* [1998] 3 NZLR 424 (CA).
251. *Lange v. Atkinson* [2000] 1 NZLR 257 (PC).

This time the Court of Appeal affirmed its previous decision, and summarized its conclusions about the defence of qualified privilege as it applies to political statements which are published generally as follows:[252]

(1) The defence of qualified privilege may be available in respect of a statement which is published generally.
(2) The nature of New Zealand's democracy means that the wider public may have a proper interest in respect of generally published statements which directly concern the functioning of representative and responsible government, including statements about the performance or possible future performance of specific individuals in elected public office.
(3) In particular, a proper interest does exist in respect of statements made about the actions and qualities of those currently or formerly elected to Parliament and those with immediate aspirations to such office, so far as those actions and qualities directly affect or affected their capacity (including their personal ability and willingness) to meet their public responsibilities.
(4) The determination of the matters which bear on that capacity will depend on a consideration of what is properly a matter of public concern rather than of private concern.
(5) The width of the identified public concern justifies the extent of the publication.
(6) To attract privilege the statement must be published on a qualifying occasion.

Therefore, the privilege is a generic one attaching to discussion about Members of Parliament past, present or future. In New Zealand, once a factual matrix passes through the subject-matter gateway, section 19 of the 1992 Act provides protection against press irresponsibility by mandating loss of the defence if ill will or misuse of the opportunity to publish exists.[253]

This defence has the potential to grow into a true public interest defence and appears to be doing so. As many predicted, the subject-matter of the defence is apparently open to expansion. The Court of Appeal has in obiter dicta suggested the subject-matter of the defence can cover local as well as national politicians.[254] A number of High Court decisions also suggest the defence may become a public interest defence in future.[255] This growing body of High Court decisions suggesting openness to a public interest defence is yet to be tested by a superior court in New Zealand. However, the law appears to be consolidating around the issue, with public interest defences being filed in response to new claims. New Zealand's progress lags behind that in the UK where the passage of the Defamation Act 2013 has

---

252. *Lange v. Atkinson* [2000] 3 NZLR 385 (CA) at 390–391 and 400.
253. See 75. below.
254. *Vickery v. McLean* [2006] NZAR 481 (CA) at [17] per Tipping J.
255. *Osmose v. Wakeling* [2007] 1 NZLR 841, *Lee v. The New Korea Herald Ltd* HC, Auckland, CIV 2008-404-5072, 9 Nov. 2010; *Dooley v. Smith* [2012] NZHC 529; *Smith v. Dooley* [2013] NZCA 42; *Dooley v. Smith* [2013] NZSC 155, *Cabral v. Beacon Printing & Publishing* [2013] NZHC 2684; *Karam v. Parker* [2014] NZHC 737.

given statutory form to a similar common law defence,[256] and in Canada where the Supreme Court of Canada (SCC) modified the common law of defamation by creating a public interest defence which it called 'responsible communication on matters of public interest'.[257]

iii. Defence against Attack

73. Defence against attack is another form of common law qualified privilege whereby a person attacked is entitled to publish a rebuttal, and provided he or she goes no further than reasonably necessary for the purpose of self-defence and is not actuated by malice, any imputations cast are privileged. This applies no matter how public the dispute may be. Normally in these cases not only the writer, but also apparently any media that publishes the reply, are protected by the privilege. However, there are limits to the generosity of this privilege. If the defendant goes beyond what is necessary for defence and 'proceeds to offence',[258] he or she exceeds his or her privilege. Similarly, the privilege does not extend to statements that are gratuitous.[259] If the defendant makes counter-charges against the original attacker's character unconnected with the substance of the attack, that is deemed to be going too far. In any event, such charges are usually actuated by ill will, and this negates qualified privilege.[260]

A plaintiff may, instead of attacking the defendant, invite a response on a particular matter, and in replying the defendant may say something defamatory of the plaintiff. An honest reply will attract qualified privilege where the defendant stays within the subject-matter raised by the plaintiff and does not use a forum wider than that chosen by the plaintiff.[261]

b. Statutory Qualified Privilege

74. The Defamation Act 1992 contains far-reaching statutory privileges. These statutory privileges cover what may be loosely called 'reports': each of them gives protection to media that merely relay to the public words spoken by someone else. The statute lists a number of kinds of proceedings, reports of which are privileged.[262] The privilege, being a qualified one, is negated by the defendant being motivated by ill will towards the plaintiff or otherwise taking improper advantage of publication.[263]

---

256. Defamation Act 2013, (UK) s. 4(6).
257. *Grant v. Torstar Corp* 2009 SCC 61, 22 Dec. 2009 at [7] and [65].
258. *News Media Ownership v. Finlay* [1970] NZLR 1089 (CA).
259. *Radio 2UE Sydney Pty Ltd v. Parker* (1992) 29 NSWLR 448 (gratuitous remarks made by radio journalist during interview).
260. *Chinese Herald Ltd v. New Times Media Ltd* HC Auckland CP366-SW00, 31 Oct. 2003.
261. *Doyle v. Stemson* HC Hamilton CP122–92, 22 Aug. 1995; see also *Hill & Lewis v. Wellington Newspapers Ltd* HC Wellington CP163–89, 5 Nov. 1990.
262. Defamation Act 1992, s. 16 and sch. 1. Cf Defamation Act 2013 (UK), s. 7, and Defamation Act 1996, sch. 1.
263. Defamation Act 1992, s. 19(1). See para. 75 below.

Statutory qualified privilege is of two kinds, a stronger and a weaker. Stronger qualified privilege attaches to the specified statements without explanation or contradiction.[264] Weaker qualified privilege is subject to the requirements set out in section 18 of the Act.

c. Loss of Privilege

75. Qualified privilege exists to allow a person to fulfil a duty or satisfy an interest without fear of recrimination. If he or she goes further than is necessary for this purpose, for instance by publishing to a wider public than necessary, or by saying more than needed, he or she will find that the privilege will not extend to the publication. Privilege may also be lost if the defendant published the statement for an improper purpose.

The defence of qualified privilege will fail if the plaintiff proves that the defendant was predominantly motivated by ill will towards the plaintiff or otherwise took improper advantage of the occasion of publication.[265] The mere existence of ill will or spite is by itself insufficient to defeat privilege; otherwise, an editor would never be safe in publishing any item about a person the editor did not like. The claim to privilege is defeated only if the defendant's animosities are his or her reason for publishing in that way. The desire to injure must be the dominant motive.[266] Taking improper advantage of the occasion of publication covers any improper motive for publication.[267]

The burden of proving ill will is on the plaintiff who alleges it, and it involves the plaintiff in the task of trying to establish the defendant's motive for publication. The following are the kinds of factors that might induce a court to make a finding of ill will or improper purpose: undue sensationalism in the report and its headlines; the addition of comment or irrelevant matter;[268] disproportionate prominence to the report itself or certain aspects of it; publication of the report at a seemingly irrelevant time[269] (for instance some time after the event); and repetition of publication[270] or unnecessarily wide publication.[271] Sometimes the language of the publication may itself be evidence of ill will or improper purpose,[272] but considerable caution is required; writers and presenters must be allowed a degree of

264. Defamation Act 1992, ss 16 and 19.
265. Defamation Act 1992, s. 19.
266. *Horrocks v. Lowe* [1975] AC 135 at 149.
267. *Horrocks v. Lowe* per Lord Diplock; *Brooks v. Muldoon* [1973] 1 NZLR 1 at 10 per Haslam J.
268. *Horrocks v. Lowe* [1975] AC 135 at 151. Sometimes, however, matter may be so totally irrelevant that it is not within the privileged occasion at all: see *Dunford Publicity Studios Ltd v. News Media Ownership Ltd* [1971] NZLR 961; *Adam v. Ward* [1917] AC 309 at [327]; and *Monaghan v. Muldoon* HC Wellington A368–80, 13 May 1983.
269. See the discussion by Hannen J in *Salmon v. Isaac* (1869) 20 LT 885 at 886; and *Bunker v. James* (1980) 26 SASR 286 at 290 and 302.
270. *Hill v. Balkind* [1918] NZLR 740 (SC).
271. *Culling v. Wheeler* (1906) 8 GLR 477 (SC).
272. See *Collerton v. Maclean* [1962] NZLR 1045; *Calwell v. Ipec Australia Ltd* (1975) 135 CLR 321; and *Verry v. Gibson* DC Napier PLT725–94, 9 Feb. 1996.

latitude as to how they express themselves.[273] Evidence of such things as personal animosity between the plaintiff and the writer[274] and failure to apologize may also be relevant, although the latter is at best tenuous evidence[275] – it may demonstrate no more than sincerity of belief.

It is important to recall that the new form of common law qualified privilege (constitutional qualified privilege or political discussion) may be lost if there is ill will or the taking of improper advantage of an occasion of publication.[276] A plaintiff will establish ill will if it can be shown that the defendant did not really believe what he or she wrote or was reckless whether it be true or false. In New Zealand, a more expansive approach is taken to what constitutes misuse of the occasion. If the publisher is unable or unwilling to disclose any responsible basis for asserting a genuine belief in truth, the jury may well be entitled to draw the inference that no such belief existed. Furthermore, a publisher who is reckless or indifferent to the truth of what is published cannot assert a genuine belief that it was true. Carelessness will not of itself be sufficient to negate the defence, but its existence may well support an assertion by the plaintiff of a lack of belief or recklessness. Reckless indifference to truth is almost as blameworthy as deliberately stating falsehoods. Indifference to truth is recognized as not the same thing conceptually as failing to take reasonable care with the truth, but they are seen in practical terms as tending to shade into each other.[277]

Furthermore, what constitutes recklessness is something which takes its colour from the nature of the occasion and the nature of the publication. In New Zealand, therefore, it can be a form of misusing the occasion where a reckless defendant has failed to give such responsible consideration to the truth or falsity of the statement as a jury would consider should have been given in all the circumstances. Thus, the privilege is likely to be lost if the defendant takes what in all the circumstances can fairly be described as a cavalier approach to the truth of the statement.

Additionally, but more than this, no consideration and insufficient consideration can also create an inference of misuse of the occasion. The privilege granted must be responsibly used. Irresponsibility has been described as recklessness by the Court and what amounts to a reckless statement was seen to depend significantly on what is said and to whom and by whom.[278] Put simply, some circumstances require more responsibility than others, and the media defendant is required to make a judgment as to this.

---

273. *Laughton v. Bishop of Sodor and Man* (1872) LR 4 PC 495 at 508. See also *Pinniger v. John Fairfax & Sons Ltd* (1979) 26 ALR 55: exuberant reporting is not malice; neither is the use of one or two unhappy expressions: *Patterson v. Smith* HC Wellington CP85–92, 16 Feb. 1994; nor exaggeration: *Cunningham v. Clarke* HC Wellington CP93–88, 23 Mar. 1990.
274. *Simpson v. Robinson* (1848) 12 QB 511; *Reeves v. Saxon* CA134–89, 17 Dec. 1992 at 31; compare *Doyle v. Stemson* HC Hamilton CP122/92, 22 Aug. 1995.
275. *Peters v. Cushing* [1999] NZAR 241; *Young v. Television New Zealand Ltd* [2014] NZCA 50, [67].
276. Defamation Act 1992, s. 19. *Lange v. Atkinson (Lange No 2)* [2000] 3 NZLR 385 at 400. See para. 72 above. See also *Attorney-General v. Leigh* [2011] NZSC 106, [16]–[23].
277. *Lange v. Atkinson (Lange No 2)* [2000] 3 NZLR 385 at 401.
278. *Lange v. Atkinson (Lange No 2)* [2000] 3 NZLR 385.

Ill will and taking improper advantage should be addressed separately.[279] In one case, letters to media and opposition to the way a special trust was being run were not evidence of ill will, but of genuine concern about governance, and the fact that the defendant had taken care to check the facts before authorizing a newspaper to publish his comments meant there had been no recklessness and hence no taking improper advantage.[280]

B. Honest Opinion

76. At common law, any individual has the right to express an opinion on it. Provided this opinion is honestly held, and the speaker got his or her basic facts right, it does not matter how unusual or extreme or damaging the opinion may be. The 1992 Act renamed the defence 'honest opinion'.[281] In New Zealand, this defence has succeeded when a newspaper described the uncle of an entertainer, Billy T James, as a 'body-snatcher'.[282]

Honest opinion is the bastion of the writers of letters to the editor in the daily papers, of the editors themselves in their leaders, of the writers of literary and art reviews, and now, of the posters of comments on websites and blogs.[283] However, the defence has been confined within limits, and a number of conditions must be complied with before the defence will succeed.[284]

First, the opinion must be based on true facts. There are two requirements here. One requirement is that the commentator must indicate the facts on which he or she is commenting. It is normally sufficient that the commentator merely gives some indication of the facts on which he or she is giving an opinion.[285] Very little if anything will be necessary if the opinion is on facts already well known to the public. Comment can now be supported by reference to shared experiences and events reported by others, even online.[286]

Second, the facts on which the commentator relies must be true. The facts must be proved true or not materially different from the truth.[287] The defendant does not need to assert the truth of all the facts asserted in support of the opinion.[288] Any facts sufficient to justify the statement will be sufficient.[289]

Third, the opinion must obviously be opinion. A classic example is a restaurant review.[290] Additionally, an opinion may be a conclusion or inference of fact drawn

279. As required by *Lange v. Atkinson (Lange No 2)* [2000] 3 NZLR 385.
280. *Dooley v. Smith* [2013] NZCA 428, [73]–[91]. *Du Claire v. Palmer* [2012] NZHC 934, [120]–[123].
281. Defamation Act 1992, s. 9.
282. *Awa v. Independent News Auckland Ltd* [1997] 3 NZLR 590 (CA).
283. *Karam v. Parker* [2014] NZHC 737.
284. *Du Claire v. Palmer* [2012] NZHC 934, [48].
285. *Kemsley v. Foot* [1952] AC 345 at 357 per Lord Porter.
286. A generous approach was taken in *Karam v. Parker* [2014] NZHC 737.
287. *Mitchell v. Sprott* [2002] 1 NZLR 766 at 773. Defamation Act 1992, s. 11. See *Lee v. New Korea Herald Ltd* Unreported, HC, Auckland, CIV-2008-404-005072, 9 Nov. 2010, Heath J, [48].
288. *Mitchell v. Sprott* [2002] 1 NZLR 766.
289. *Mitchell v. Sprott* [2002] 1 NZLR 766.
290. *Gacic v. John Fairfax Publications Pty Ltd* [2013] NSWSC 1920.

from the primary facts on which the commentator is relying.[291] Whether the defendant's statement is one of fact or opinion depends on how the words look to an ordinary, reasonable reader.[292]

Fourth, the opinion must be genuine, in the sense of being honest, which still allows strong, exaggerated or even prejudiced views to be expressed. The defendant must prove that the genuine belief existed and was subjectively held by the defendant.[293] The Act requires a plaintiff who intends to allege that an opinion is not the genuine opinion of the defendant, or that there was reasonable cause to believe the opinion was not the genuine opinion of the author where the author was not the defendant, to serve a notice to that effect within ten working days after the plaintiff was served with the defendant's statement of defence.[294] The New Zealand Court of Appeal has emphasized that a fair-minded person includes one holding prejudiced, obstinate or even racially insensitive views.[295] However, when criticism is so vicious and so unreasonable that no honest person could really believe it, sheer invective is unlikely to be protected by the defence.[296]

Where the person sued is not the person who expressed the opinion, the Defamation Act 1992 provides rules to cover this situation:[297]

> In any proceedings for defamation in respect of matter that includes or consists of an expression of opinion, a defence of honest opinion by a defendant who is not the author of the matter containing the opinion shall fail unless,–
>
> (a) Where the author of the matter containing the opinion was, at the time of the publication of that matter, an employee or agent of the defendant, the defendant proves that–
> (i) The opinion, in its context and in the circumstances of the publication of the matter that is the subject of the proceedings, did not purport to be the opinion of the defendant; and
> (ii) The defendant believed that the opinion was the genuine opinion of the author of the matter containing the opinion.[298]

This covers articles written by journalists employed by media. The employer has to positively believe in genuineness.

The Act also provides:

291. *Willis v. Katevich* HC Auckland CP547–85, 21 Aug. 1989; *Keith v. Christchurch Press Co Ltd* HC Christchurch A259/71, 4 Aug. 1972.
292. *Mitchell v. Sprott* [2002] 1 NZLR 766 at 772. It is the defendant's statement, not the imputations pleaded by the plaintiff as arising from it, which must be the focus of the honest opinion defence: *Haines v. Television New Zealand* [2004] NZAR 513 (HC) at [61]–[68].
293. Defamation Act 1992, s. 10(1).
294. Section 39. See *APN New Zealand Ltd v. Simunovich Fisheries Ltd* [2008] NZSC 101.
295. *Awa v. Independent News Auckland Ltd* [1997] 3 NZLR 590 (CA) at 595.
296. *Cornwell v. Myskow* [1987] 1 WLR 630.
297. Defamation Act 1992, s. 10.
298. Section 10(2)(a).

(b) Where the author of the matter containing the opinion was not an employee or agent of the defendant at the time of publication of that matter, [the defence shall fail unless] the defendant proves that–
   (i) The opinion, in its context and in the circumstances of the publication of the matter that is the subject of the proceedings, did not purport to be the opinion of the defendant or of any employer or agent of the defendant; and
   (ii) The defendant had no reasonable cause to believe that the opinion was not the genuine opinion of the author of the matter containing the opinion.[299]

This provision covers the freelance writer or an ordinary member of the public writing a letter to the editor or posting a comment on a news website. Extremely odd or biased views will be opinions under this provision, provided the defendant has no reasonable cause to believe the opinions are not genuinely held.[300] The defendant need not prove the opinion was in fact a genuine opinion, only that there was reasonable cause to believe this was so.

The High Court has clarified when a publisher is to be treated as the author of an opinion for the purposes of the honest opinion defence, and how the opinion may be shown to be genuine.[301] Media defendants must adduce some evidence to satisfy the requirements of section 10, and calling the author would appear to be the normal approach. This will be possible where the author is an employee or agent of the defendant. Where an outside contributor is involved, his or her evidence will be useful to establish authorship if he or she can be tracked down. A representative of the media company who holds a decision-making position relevant to the publication of the article or letter should give evidence as to belief in genuineness or lack of cause to believe the opinion was not genuine.[302]

C. Truth

77. Once a plaintiff has established that defamatory remarks were made, the defendant is then allowed, if he or she can, to prove that the remarks were true. If the defendant succeeds in this, he or she has a complete defence. The Act requires the defendant to plead particulars specifying which statements are statements of fact, and the facts and circumstances relied on to show they are true.[303] The defences of truth and honest opinion must be pleaded separately.[304]

---

299. Section 10(2)(b).
300. *Karam v. Fairfax New Zealand Limited* [2012] NZHC 887, [47]–[49].
301. *Hubbard v. Fourth Estate Holdings* HC Auckland CIV-2004-404-5152, 13 Jun. 2005.
302. *Vague v. Banks* [2002] DCR 782.
303. Defamation Act 1992, s. 38. *Wasan International Co Ltd v. Lee* HC Auckland CIV-2003-404-004113, 26 May 2004.
304. Defamation Act 1992, s. 40. *Karam v. Parker* Unreported, HC,Auckland, CIV-2010-404-003038, 29 Jul. 2011, Associate Judge Sargisson.

Although the defendant has to prove truth only on the balance of probabilities, the courts have tended to require a fairly high standard of accuracy.[305] The Act embodies this approach in providing that a defence of truth shall succeed if the defendant proves the imputations published were true or not materially different from the truth.[306] The Court of Appeal has said: 'It is a complete answer to the plaintiff's claim if the defendant proves that the defamatory words are true in substance, even if not strictly accurate in minor detail.'[307]

It is not enough for the defendant to know that his or her statements are true; he or she must be able to prove them to be true in a court of law by legally admissible evidence. Sometimes to prove something true may involve media in disclosing their sources, which they may not be prepared to do.[308] The statements of third parties cannot be pleaded to support truth.[309]

If the plaintiff in the statement of claim sets out the meaning of the words of which he or she complains, the defendant cannot allege that the words bear a different meaning and proceed to prove them true in that different meaning.[310] The plaintiff, by attributing a particular meaning to the words, has drawn the battle-lines. He or she will stand or fall by that meaning, and the defendant cannot try to justify the words in some other meaning. This means the defendant may plead the truth of the publication only in the sense complained of by the plaintiff.[311]

D. Consent

78. If the plaintiff has consented to the publication of a statement, he or she cannot sue for defamation in respect of it. Section 22 of the Act states: 'It is a defence to proceedings for defamation if the defendant alleges and proves that the plaintiff consented to the publication of the matter that is the subject of the proceedings.' This applies whether the plaintiff has been specifically asked for his or her consent and has given it verbally or in writing, or whether the plaintiff himself or herself voluntarily asked media to publish something. In such cases, the consent will be a defence if it has not been withdrawn before publication.

However, the proof of consent should be clear and convincing,[312] and the defendant will have to prove not just that the plaintiff consented (which may itself be difficult if the consent was given orally), but also that he or she consented to this very matter being published in this way.[313]

305. *Reeves v. Saxon* CA134–89, 17 Dec. 1992, Cooke P, Gault J & Thomas J. The Court has regard to the gravity of the case and the seriousness of the allegations, particularly where the allegation is one of fraud (at 16).
306. Defamation Act 1992, s. 8(3)(a).
307. *Lange v. Atkinson* [1998] 3 NZLR 424 at 435 (CA).
308. See Elias J in *Lange v. Atkinson* [1997] 2 NZLR 22 (CA) at 33.
309. *APN NZ and TVNZ v. Simunovich Fisheries Ltd* [2010] 1 NZLR 315.
310. *Templeton v. Jones* [1984] 1 NZLR 448 (CA); *Broadcasting Corporation of New Zealand v. Crush* [1988] 2 NZLR 234 (CA); *Bell v. Grondin* HC Whangarei CP55–91, 7 Sep. 1993 at 5.
311. *Broadcasting Corporation of New Zealand v. Crush* [1988] 2 NZLR 234 (CA).
312. *Mihaka v. Wellington Publishing Co (1972) Ltd* [1975] 1 NZLR 10 (SC) at 17 per Haslam J.
313. *Mihaka v. Wellington Publishing Co (1972) Ltd* [1975] 1 NZLR 10 (SC).

E. Limitation

79. The Limitation Act 2010[314] now applies to claims based on events occurring on or after 1 January 2011.[315] The Act applies to claims for money and provides a scheme where such claims can be made within a primary limitation period and what is now known as a late knowledge period. For defamation claims, claims should be made within a primary period of two years after publication; however, claims can still be made within two years of the claimant having late knowledge of the claim. It is a defence if the defendant proves that the claim is filed at least two years after the late knowledge date.[316]

F. Apology

80. A public apology and correction will sometimes mollify the plaintiff to the point where he or she decides not to pursue the claim. Second, publication of an apology is often an element in a negotiated settlement. Third, an apology is always something to be taken into account by a jury when assessing damages.[317] If they find that the apology was genuine, made promptly and given prominence, they may well conclude that the injury to the plaintiff's reputation is slight and that damages should be reduced accordingly.[318]

§3. PRIVACY

81. Privacy laws that impact on the media exist in New Zealand in the form of: laws impacting on spying and photography; trespass laws; two actions in tort; the privacy principles developed by the BSA; the legislative requirements for the collection, storage and use of personal information set out in the Privacy Act 1993; the requirements of the Harassment Act 1997; and a number of miscellaneous legal requirements. These laws affect not only how the media carry out their news-gathering function, but also how they store and use the information to which they have access.

I. Spying and Photography

82. Generally speaking, in New Zealand there is no law against spying on, or taking photographs of, a person's property from any place outside it.[319] As far as

314. See generally *Todd on Torts* (6th ed., 2013, Thomson Reuters), Stephen Todd General Editor, 26.5.12, and A. Beck [2010] NZLJ 337.
315. Limitation Act 2010, s. 2.
316. Limitation Act 2010, s. 11(2) and (3)(a).
317. Defamation Act 1992, s. 29.
318. *Truth (NZ) Ltd v. Bowles* [1966] NZLR 303 (CA).
319. *TVNZ v. KW* HC Auckland CIV-2007-485-1609, 18 Dec. 2008 at [62]–[63]. *Bernstein v. Skyviews Ltd* [1978] QB 479, *Victoria Park Racing and Recreation Grounds Co Ltd v. Taylor* (1937) 58 CLR 479.

aircraft are concerned, the Civil Aviation Act 1990 provides that no action for trespass lies in respect of aircraft flying over property at a reasonable height.[320] Drones are beginning to be regulated by the Civil Aviation Authority, with certification requirements and new rules effective from 1 August 2015. Conditions of operation will be determined in each case for individual licenses.[321] Privacy has been highlighted as a concern in this process. In any event, complying with civil aviation requirements does not confer immunity from legal action under the general law.

While generally it is not unlawful to take photographs of a person's property from outside their land, if media activities are of such a nature as to cause substantial embarrassment or discomfort to a householder, and to interfere with the enjoyment of land, the common law wrong of nuisance would be committed and damages or an injunction could be obtainable.[322]

II. Trespass

83. Unauthorized entry on to another's land is a trespass and is wrongful. The occupier of the land may bring a civil action for damages and, in some circumstances, a criminal prosecution may also result. However, ordinary visitors or callers have an implied permission to come on to a property to speak to those in possession of the land. New Zealand reporters commit no trespass by going to a house and knocking on the door, or to business premises and presenting at the counter, with intent to ask the occupier questions. If told to leave they must do so. It is different, however, if they initially entered the property not intending to communicate with the occupier, but simply to 'snoop'. They would then be trespassers from the moment of entry. If reporters and/or camera crew enter premises for purposes going beyond the extent of any implied licence, they are likely to be trespassers.[323] It is also a trespass if reporters enter by trickery, for example, by misrepresenting their intentions or identity.[324] Further, if, having entered for one purpose, media deviate from that purpose and move outside the terms of the licence, that then becomes a trespass. It is quite legitimate for a reporter to go on to private property with the purpose of interviewing someone, but not if the purpose is to enable film to be taken of the person whether or not she or he consented to be interviewed.[325]

320. Civil Aviation Act 1990, s. 97(2).
321. See http://www.caa.govt.nz/rules/pending_rules.htm, accessed 23 Jun. 2015.
322. *Bernstein v. Skyviews Ltd* [1978] QB 479 at 489. See also *Victoria Park Racing and Recreation Grounds Co Ltd v. Taylor* (1937) 58 CLR 479 at 493.
323. *TV3 Network Services Ltd v. Fahey* [1999] 2 NZLR 129 at 135(entering a doctor's surgery with a hidden camera could scarcely come within the normal licence as a patient with an appointment).
324. *TCN Channel Nine Pty Ltd v. Ilvariy Pty Ltd* [2008] NSWCA 9. See also *Whyte v. TCN Channel Nine Pty Ltd* [2006] FMCA 841.
325. *TV3 Network Services Ltd v. Broadcasting Standards Authority* [1995] 2 NZLR 720 (HC); *Taka v. Police* [1996] 2 NZLR 449 (HC) at 452.

A. Meetings

84. Local authority meetings are governed by statute, and the press, as a rule, have a right to be present. However, most other meetings are not subject to a statutory regime, and the right of reporters to attend is not statutorily protected (e.g., election meetings and meetings of the shareholders of a company). To many such meetings, the press are invited. Even if no express invitation is issued, it may be legitimate in many cases to assume that there is an implied invitation, for example, a meeting of the shareholders of a public company.[326] If there is an invitation, express or implied, reporters commit no trespass by attending. However, such an invitation may be withdrawn, either generally or in respect of specific individuals, at any time during the course of the meeting, and people remaining in defiance of a requirement to leave become trespassers. It has been held that if a reporter has been invited (expressly or impliedly) to attend a meeting of shareholders of a company, only the shareholders can validly withdraw the invitation. The chair, although in control of the meeting, does not alone have the authority to do so.[327]

B. Civil Remedies for Trespass

85. If a person is a trespasser, the person lawfully in occupation of the premises may eject him or her, using no more force than is reasonably necessary. If more force is used in the heat of the moment than is really necessary, or if it should turn out that the person ejected was lawfully on the premises, the ejection will amount to an assault. In addition to this type of 'self-help', the occupier[328] can also sue the trespasser for damages. Usually these will be slight, but if the wrong is committed in an objectionable way, or for objectionable reasons, significant damages may be awarded.[329]

C. Criminal Penalties for Trespass

86. Trespass can also be a criminal offence. There are a number of minor statutory provisions.[330] However, general provisions of considerable importance are contained in the Trespass Act 1980. A person who is found trespassing on private land may be required by the occupier, or a member of the police, to give name and address.[331] Perhaps the most important provisions of the Trespass Act 1980 are those that deal with 'warning off'. A person commits an offence 'who trespasses on any place and, after being warned to leave that place by an occupier of that place,

326. *Police v. Rennie, The Press* (30 Nov. 1988).
327. *Police v. Rennie, The Press* (30 Nov. 1988).
328. To maintain an action for trespass, the plaintiff must show that he or she is in exclusive possession of the land: *Moore v. McMillan* [1977] 2 NZLR 81.
329. *TCN Channel Nine Pty Ltd v. Ilvariy Pty Ltd* [2008] NSWCA 9.
330. Summary Offences Act 1981, ss 30, 31.
331. Trespass Act 1980, s. 9.

neglects or refuses to do so'.[332] If the land is in possession of a public agency, 'warning off' must take account of the NZBORA 1990.[333] It has been said that this applies whenever the police give a warning.[334] The provision is apt only to cover the case where a person is warned off property and does not leave on that occasion. It does not cover the case of the person who leaves on being warned but comes back at a later date. That person's case is provided for by another section of the same statute.[335] A few specific statutes confer a power similar to that in the Trespass Act 1980 to warn people off particular types of property.[336]

III. The Common Law Tort of Invasion of Privacy

A. A Tort of Invasion of Privacy by Publication of Information

87. The existence of a tort of invasion of privacy was considered substantively by the Court of Appeal in the leading case *Hosking v. Runting*,[337] which arose from an attempt to prevent publication of photos of celebrity broadcaster Mike Hosking's twin daughters. The images were taken by a freelance photographer while the children were being pushed in a pram by their mother on a Christmas shopping trip, on a public footpath, in a busy shopping mall. Although it rejected Hosking's specific privacy claim, the Court of Appeal, in a 3:2 majority judgment, confirmed that a tort of privacy does exist in New Zealand and attempted to describe the basic form it takes. The joint judgment of the majority stated two fundamental requirements for a claim:

- the existence of facts in respect of which there is a reasonable expectation of privacy;[338] and
- publicity given to those private facts that would be considered highly offensive to an objective reasonable person.[339]

Hosking established a limited tort of breach of informational privacy in New Zealand. It was intended to protect against publication or threatened publication of intimate and personal facts.

332. Trespass Act 1980, s. 3. The word 'place' has replaced the words 'private land', which appeared in the earlier legislation. See *Bright v. Police* [2009] NZCA 187, aff on appeal, [2009] NZSC 85.
333. *Police v. Beggs* [1999] 3 NZLR 615 (HC); appeal dismissed, [2002] NZAR 917; *Bright v. Police* [NZCA] 187; aff on appeal, [2009] NZSC 85 at [48].
334. *Ross v. Police* (2002) 6 HRNZ 734. The police have guidelines which they apply in these circumstances.
335. Trespass Act 1980, ss 4 and 5.
336. Civil Aviation Act 1990, s. 54.
337. *Hosking v. Runting* [2005] 1 NZLR 1 (CA).
338. However, after initially stating this requirement, the joint judgment refers only to a requirement for 'private facts'.
339. *Hosking v. Runting* [2005] 1 NZLR 1 (CA) at [117].

1. The Elements of the Tort

a. A Reasonable Expectation of Privacy

88. A broad view is taken of the reasonable expectation element. Reasonable expectation of privacy can cover events that took place in public,[340] and apply to facts which were public but became private again over time.[341] Reasonable expectation of privacy is assessed at the time of publication because the interference arises by publicity, although the passage of time since the facts arose, and changed circumstances, may impact on the reasonable expectations actually held.[342]

b. Private Facts

89. Domestic matters such as behaviour, particularly sexual or intimate behaviour, or personal or family circumstances such as medical records will be private. However, there is a general area of uncertainty. Some public facts, for example, criminal convictions, can become private over time.[343] Private facts do not need to be absolutely secret. In New Zealand, private facts are those unknown to the world at large at the time of publication, but possibly known to some people or a class of people.[344] Images on videotape portraying graphically intimate and personal details of someone's personality and demeanour are also capable of being private facts, although if the video is produced to be shown in public, the expectation will not attach.[345] Therefore, although information may be capable of being private facts, a reasonable expectation may not exist in those facts in the circumstances of the case.

c. Privacy in a Public Place

90. Taking a photograph of a person in a public place without their consent does not as a general rule constitute publication of private facts.[346] However, the fact that the plaintiff is in a public place should not automatically determine the issue. The fact that something occurred in a public place does not mean that it should be widely publicized where it was not a matter of public concern.[347]

As in the United Kingdom, it has been accepted in New Zealand that in exceptional cases, a reasonable expectation of privacy can arise even though the facts have been recorded in a public place.[348] There is little guidance in New Zealand yet

340. *Andrews v. TVNZ* [2009] 1 NZLR 220 (HC); *Andrews v. TVNZ* [2009] 1 NZLR 220 (HC).
341. *Brown v. Attorney-General* [2006] NZAR 552.
342. *Andrews v. TVNZ* [2009] 1 NZLR 220 (HC) at [30].
343. *Tucker v. News Media Ownership Ltd* [1986] 2 NZLR 716 (HC).
344. *Andrews v. TVNZ* [2009] 1 NZLR 220 (HC) at [28].
345. *Rogers v. TVNZ* [2008] 2 NZLR 277 at [100]–[102].
346. *Bernstein v. Skyviews Ltd* [1978] QB 479; *Victoria Park Racing and Recreation Grounds v. Taylor* (1937) 58 CLR 479; *Sports and General Press Agency v. 'Our Dogs' Publishing* [1916] 2 KB 880 affirmed [1917] 2 KB 125 (CA); *Australian Consolidated Press Ltd v. Ettingshausen* (1991) 23 NSWLR 443 (SC); *Cruise and Kidman v. Southdown Press Pty Ltd* (1993) 26 IPR 125; *Marris v. TV3 Network Services Ltd* HC Wellington CP754/91, 14 Oct. 1991.
347. *Bradley v. Wingnut Films Ltd* [1993] 1 NZLR 415 (HC) at 424.
348. *Hosking v. Runting* [2005] 1 NZLR 1 (CA) at [164]; *Andrews v. Television New Zealand* [2009] 1 NZLR 220.

as to what constitutes an exceptional case. English courts appear prepared to protect some mundane activities carried on in public, particularly if those activities involve children. The New Zealand Court of Appeal considered whether the special vulnerability of children required a particular approach in relation to depictions of them, but rejected such a course.[349] It is considered that the elements required for the tort contain sufficient flexibility to give real weight to children's vulnerability and, further, that the private lives of children would seldom be of concern to the public.[350] It has also been recognized that the children of celebrities may have diminished expectations of privacy in relation to some aspects of private family life unless the evidence establishes risk associated with the public figure role.[351] This was established before and contrasts with, the English approach.[352]

Therefore, although New Zealand law has recognized the possibility of exceptional cases, the specific claim failed in *Hosking* because it was not seen as exceptional enough. The Hosking children were being pushed in their pram in a public street, and the Court held that the images did not show anything that any member of the public could not have seen on the relevant day.[353] In contrast, being filmed saying intimate things to a loved one following a serious car accident has been found to be an exceptional situation in New Zealand.[354]

d. Publicity

91. What constitutes sufficient publicity given to the private information varies according to the facts. It is clear that publication of information in a newspaper or a television or radio broadcast, or on a webpage, satisfies the test.[355] However, it is unlikely publication to only one person will do.[356] In *Hosking*, the joint judgment rejected the approach in defamation where publication to a single third party is sufficient, and stated that the concern of the tort of privacy is with widespread publicity of very personal and private matters.[357]

e. Identification

92. It is unclear whether publication requires identification of the person. In one case, it was held that lack of identification did not prevent a breach being established

349. *Hosking v. Runting* [2005] 1 NZLR 1 (CA) at [139]–[147].
350. *Hosking v. Runting* [2005] 1 NZLR 1 (CA) at [147].
351. *Hosking v. Runting* [2005] 1 NZLR 1 (CA) at [124]. *Venables v. News Group Newspapers Ltd* [2001] Fam 430, [2001] 1 All ER 908 was used as an example). In *Hosking*, the plaintiffs argued, unsuccessfully, that the publication of the photographs of the Hosking children would increase their risk of being kidnapped. The Court did not accept that as realistic: *Hosking v. Runting* [2005] 1 NZLR 1 (CA) at [163].
352. See *Murray v. Big Pictures (UK) Ltd* [2008] 3 WLR 1360, [2008] EMLR 12, *Weller v. Associated Newspapers* [2014] EWHC 1163 (QB.
353. *Hosking v. Runting* [2005] 1 NZLR 1 at [164] and [260].
354. *Andrews v. TVNZ* [2009] 1 NZLR 220 (HC).
355. *L v. G* [2002] DCR 234.
356. *X v. Attorney-General* [1994] NZFLR 433 (HC).
357. *Hosking v. Runting* [2005] 1 NZLR 1 (CA) at [125]. Tipping J did not attempt to define publication in any way.

because the rights protected by the tort of invasion of privacy relate not to issues of perception and identification by members of the public to whom information is disclosed, but to the loss of the personal shield of privacy of a person to whom the information relates.[358] However, in that case, the extent of identification was a relevant factor in the assessment of damages.

More recently, it has been stated as an assumption that in most circumstances a plaintiff will need to establish he or she has been identified in the publication, either directly or by implication.[359] While no New Zealand court is prepared to close the door completely on the idea of a personal shield of privacy, it remains possible to argue that an exceptional case might exist where lack of identification should not prevent liability from arising. Given that damages would be reduced in such cases, these claims would be rare.

f. Plaintiff Culpability

93. It has been suggested by one New Zealand court that the morality and behaviour of the plaintiff can be taken into account, with appropriate varying effects on any reasonable expectation of privacy, even to the extent of its total destruction.[360] This has not been applied in any other case or endorsed by a higher court.

g. Offensive and Objectionable Nature

94. In contrast to the United Kingdom, New Zealand privacy plaintiffs also have to show that disclosure or publication of the relevant information would have been highly offensive to a reasonable person. It was not until *Hosking* that the New Zealand courts clarified this requirement by emphasizing that the concern is with publicity which is highly offensive, and not the facts themselves.[361] However, *Hosking* did not make clear that the test is one with both subjective and objective elements, so the matter has to be highly offensive to the reasonable person in the shoes of the plaintiff, a desirable position. The Court of Appeal has said:

> Whether disclosure would be highly offensive must be tested from the perspective of that person but subject to an objective overlay. The fragile sensibility of the claimant cannot prevail so a reasonable person test is introduced to that extent.[362]

Additionally, the burden of this element is a high one, and the court may be able to use the plaintiff where he or she is found to be a person of ordinary sensibilities but otherwise a fictitious reasonable person should be used. Further, the character of

358. *L v. G* [2002] DCR 234 at 246, [2002] NZAR 495 (DC).
359. *Andrews v. Television New Zealand* [2009] 1 NZLR 220 (HC) at [52].
360. *Andrews v. Television New Zealand* [2009] 1 NZLR 220 (HC) at [46]–[47].
361. *Hosking v. Runting* [2005] 1 NZLR 1 (CA) at [117].
362. *Television New Zealand v. Rogers* [2007] 1 NZLR 156 at [67].

disclosure must be examined because tone and extent of a publication may be determinative.[363]

Undoubtedly, in some cases, the subjective/objective test is not an easy one to apply. It has been suggested that the test is problematic if the plaintiff is manifestly not an ordinary person. Nonetheless, the courts have managed to apply it.[364] The mixed approach expresses a view of privacy as a human right which is available to all, even those who are outcast from society, or who otherwise live lives out of the ordinary. It is important that the approach is applied correctly, with equal weight given to both objective and subjective points of view.

h. Defence of Legitimate Public Concern in Publication

95. After some doubt about the matter,[365] *Hosking* clarified that this element is for the defendant to make out and not the plaintiff.[366] The defence ensures freedom of expression is taken into account,[367] and it means the judiciary has the pragmatic function, disliked intensely by the media, of determining what should and should not be published.[368] The defence is referred to as one of legitimate public concern covers matters properly within the public interest, not simply of general interest.[369] This clearly covers matters referred to in the United Kingdom cases such as public health, economy and safety, the detection of crime, and national security generally.[370] In New Zealand, the decisions of the BSA are also instructive, although by no means definitive. They show that broadcasts dealing with accountability of public figures alleged to have acted incorrectly, inconsistently or illegally, the apprehension of criminals, misbehaviour of public servants or failure of government departments, and public health issues, will almost always be matters of public interest.

Courts permit a degree of journalistic latitude so as not to destroy the context of a story.[371] The legitimate public concern necessary will rise or fall depending on the level of invasion of privacy,[372] and if there is intrusiveness, it should not be disproportionate to its relevance to the story.[373] The conversation about the place of public interest in the New Zealand privacy tort has not advanced a great deal. The public interest question, where the clash between freedom of expression and privacy is always engaged, is probably the most difficult aspect of privacy for the courts, and the emerging jurisprudence is tentative.

363. *Andrews v. Television New Zealand* [2009] 1 NZLR 220 at [49]–[50].
364. *Brown v. Attorney-General* [2006] NZAR 552 (HC) at [80]–[81].
365. See *P v. D* [2000] 2 NZLR 591 (HC).
366. *Hosking v. Runting* [2005] 1 NZLR 1 (CA) at [129], [257] and [259].
367. *Hosking v. Runting* [2005] 1 NZLR 1 (CA) at [130].
368. *Hosking v. Runting* [2005] 1 NZLR 1 (CA) at [132].
369. *Andrews v. Television New Zealand* [2009] 1 NZLR 220 (HC) at [81].
370. *Malone v. Metropolitan Police Commissioner* [1979] Ch. 344 at 376.
371. *Andrews v. Television New Zealand* [2009] 1 NZLR 220 (HC) at [82]–[83].
372. *Andrews v. Television New Zealand* [2009] 1 NZLR 220 (HC) at [84].
373. *Andrews v. Television New Zealand* [2009] 1 NZLR 220 (HC) at [89]–[90]. Here, the treatment of intrusiveness suggests that the tort is about more than informational privacy.

i. Remedies

96. In New Zealand, the primary remedy for the newly recognized privacy tort has been identified as damages, but injunctive relief is also possible.[374] The test for the grant of injunctions in privacy cases appears similar to that applying for defamation claims: prior restraint is to be available where there is compelling evidence of most highly offensive intended publicizing of private information, and there is little legitimate public concern in the information.[375]

As to damages, only two cases, both in our lowest court, have resulted in damages awards so far and levels have remained modest, in contrast to recent developments in the United Kingdom.[376] One New Zealand claimant was awarded the highest figure of NZD 25,000 in the District Court for breaches of privacy and confidence,[377] and the award in the other case was a mere NZD 2,500.[378] Arguably, the losses compensated in breach of privacy cases are very similar to those in defamation, and the different damages levels should draw closer over time. Aggravated damages are also available in privacy claims and possibly exemplary damages as well.

B. A Tort of Intrusion into Seclusion

97. Future cases involving intrusive behaviour in the obtaining of private information may not need to be argued using the *Hosking* tort and may not depend on publicity or threatened publicity. In 2012, the New Zealand High Court recognized that a tort of intrusion into seclusion also exists in this jurisdiction.[379] The case involved a claim arising from facts that had nothing to do with media – this was secret intimate video filming of the claimant in a bathroom, with no publication. The High Court concluded that existing protections for intentional intrusion into personal space and affairs are coherent but not comprehensive.

The New Zealand tort of intrusion upon seclusion currently requires an intentional and unauthorized intrusion into seclusion (meaning intimate personal activity, space or affairs), involving an infringement of a reasonable expectation of privacy that is highly offensive to a reasonable person. The possibility of a public interest defence was left open, and there is clearly potential for the action to develop into a tort remedying general intrusions into privacy arising from news gathering.

The tort has been considered in a neighbour dispute, where the plaintiff objected to the operation of a camera installed on the roof of a garage adjacent to a driveway running to his property.[380] The camera filmed the plaintiff's land and public land and

374. *Hosking v. Runting* [2005] 1 NZLR 1 (CA) at [149]–[150].

375. *Hosking v. Runting* [2005] 1 NZLR 1 at [158]. This approach has been endorsed in recent academic commentary: David Rolph, *Irreconcilable Differences? Interlocutory Injunctions for Defamation and Privacy*, 17 Media & Arts L. Rev. 170 (2012).

376. *Gulati v. MGN Ltd* [2015] EWHC 1482 (Ch).

377. *Brown v. Attorney-General* [2006] DCR 630.

378. *L v. G* [2002] DCR 234, [2002] NZAR 495 (DC.

379. *C v. Holland* [2012] 3 NZLR 672.

380. *Faesenkloet v. Jenkin* [2014] NZHC 1637.

could therefore capture images of people using the driveway although this did not amount to clear images. In this case, it was accepted that invasion in the context of the tort could extend to a public place. However, the claim failed because there could be no reasonable expectation of privacy given the public ownership and use of the driveway, and on the facts, the intrusion by the camera was not objectively highly intrusive. The Court also suggested there may be no need for two separate torts.

More recently, the High Court granted an urgent injunction against unknown persons to prevent publication of hacked emails, and referred briefly to *Holland* as authority demonstrating that courts will respond to novel facts of unwanted invasions of privacy.[381] Computer or phone hacking is analogous to accessing a bank account, which has been recognized in Canada as a form of intrusion into seclusion.[382]

As with any new form of civil action, the *Holland* tort requires clarification and delineation, but could clearly apply to media news-gathering activities which are particularly intrusive, such as secret filming and spying, and accessing of private information such as bank accounts and that held on personal computers and mobile phones.

IV. Privacy and the BSA

98. Under the Broadcasting Act 1989, the BSA has jurisdiction to deal with complaints that a broadcaster has breached some aspect of privacy of the individual.[383] Privacy complaints can be made by any party, not just by those affected,[384] and go directly to the Authority.[385] They must be received within sixty working days, beginning on the first working day after the programme was broadcast.[386] The BSA can award compensation up to NZD 5,000 on upholding a privacy complaint.[387] It has done this in two decisions in the last ten years,[388] in recognition of the most extreme breaches that occurred. The largest recent order was NZD 1,500 compensation and NZD 1,000 costs to the Crown.[389]

---

381. *Slater v. APN New Zealand Ltd* [2014] NZHC 2157, [6]. However, media who had received information from the hacker and had not been involved in the hacking were not restrained from publishing any information currently held. Slater later abandoned the claim against media after receiving an undertaking not to publish any of the material in which there was no genuine interest – this was stated by the court to cover information about the plaintiff's wife and children, his medical records, the death of his mother and information of a similar nature.
382. *Jones v. Tsige* 2012 ONCA 32.
383. See 234, which details the wider jurisdiction of the Authority.
384. *Archer v. TVNZ* 1997-043-044; *TV3 Network Services Ltd v. ECPAT New Zealand Inc* [2003] NZAR 501 (HC).
385. Broadcasting Act 1989, s. 8(1).
386. There is no discretion to accept complaints out of time: s. 9.
387. Broadcasting Act 1989, s. 13(1)(d).
388. *EF v. CanWest Radioworks Ltd* BSA 2006-112, 30 May 2007 (disclosing medical details); *LM v. TVNZ* BSA 2007-138, 18 Sep. 2008 (broadcast of breast augmentation without consent).
389. *MA v. TVNZ Ltd* BSA 2010-084.

Privacy complaints can arise under section 4(1) of the Broadcasting Act 1989, which provides that:

> Every broadcaster is responsible for maintaining in its programmes and their presentation, standards which are consistent with– ... (c) the privacy of the individual.

There is no definition of privacy in the Act. However, in 1992 the BSA issued an advisory opinion under section 21(1)(d) of the Act that highlighted relevant privacy principles.[390] The privacy principles can be wider than the tort of privacy and are to be given a fair, large and liberal interpretation.[391]

The privacy principles will now be described,[392] together with brief summaries of selected BSA decisions that may be important and of interest to the media. Space demands that the selection is by no means comprehensive, and the BSA's annual reports and website[393] should be consulted for a full picture of its decisions.[394]

A. *The Privacy Principles*

1. Principle 1

99. It is inconsistent with an individual's privacy to allow the public disclosure of private facts, where the disclosure is highly offensive to an objective reasonable person.[395]

Although the Principle refers to 'private facts', the BSA has adopted an expansive approach to this concept. In a recent decision, the Authority held that private facts do not actually have to be facts.[396] Therefore, as with the privacy tort, information covered by the broadcasting regime can be private, whether it is true or not. Private facts are those which will significantly expose or embarrass an individual in some way if disclosed, whether they can be ascertained publicly or not.[397] A message on an answer phone primarily directed at friends and acquaintances, but in part addressed to the media, was not considered to be private facts.[398] This was even

390. There are now eight, promulgated in August 2006.
391. *TV3 Network Services Ltd v. Broadcasting Standards Authority* [1995] 2 NZLR 720 (HC).
392. See Broadcasting Standards Authority 'Privacy Principles' (2010) http://bsa.govt.nz/standards/privacy, accessed 2 May 2014. See also Privacy Practice Note: Privacy as a Broadcasting Standard: June 2010: http://bsa.govt.nz/images/assets/Practice-Notes/Privacy-Practice-Note.pdf, accessed 7 May 2014.
393. See Broadcasting Standards Authority: http://bsa.govt.nz/.
394. See also Steven Price, *Media Minefield: A Journalists' Guide to Media Regulation in New Zealand* (NZJTO, Wellington, 2007) at ch 5; and Stephen Penk & Rosemary Tobin (eds) *Privacy Law in New Zealand* (Brookers, Wellington, 2010) Ch. 9.
395. See Practice Note: Privacy Priniple 1: The Public Disclosure of Private Facts – June 2011: http://bsa.govt.nz/standards/practice-notes/privacy-principle-1-practice-note accessed 7 May 2014.
396. *Hill v. Radio One* BSA 2013-074.
397. *Radford v. TVNZ* 2003-017 (an unpaid debt was a private matter between the complainants and repossession agents). See also *M v. TV3 BSA* 2000-132, 28 Sep. 2000.
398. *Lindley v. TV3* BSA 2002-122-123, 23 Oct. 2003.

though it was later edited by the media for its own purposes, because the message was in the nature of a public statement which anyone could access.

This approach begs the question of what is in the public arena. The decisions indicate it covers information on public record (such as a death or marriage certificate),[399] criminal convictions,[400] the name of a person charged with an offence even where that person's name is later suppressed by a court,[401] ownership details relating to transfer of land and motor vehicles,[402] and information disclosed in open court.[403] Similarly, a person's name, address, telephone number and appearance were regarded as public facts, being publicly ascertainable.[404] The public arena is now taken to include publication on social media sites.[405]

It is generally accepted that health and personal and sexual relationships will be subject to an assumption of inherent privacy.[406] The location of the incident will be relevant as, conventionally, filming, photographing or interviewing a person in a public place has been taken to render facts public rather than private.[407] Graffiti has been held to be public by its very nature.[408] However, the mere fact that something occurs or exists in public does not necessarily make it something the public should know about; therefore, there may be exceptions to the general principle. Involuntary and intimate details can be revealed in public and yet still be seen as private facts.[409]

Culture may also make a fact a private one.[410] Information previously disclosed in the media itself may appear to be in the public domain.[411] However, re-broadcasting footage or whole programmes shown some years earlier may be risky if it is reasonable for the subject to assume the film will not be repeated many years after the first broadcast.[412] Lapse of time is also relevant. It is difficult to identify a unifying rationale for the making of exceptions, but if disclosure of the information will significantly expose or embarrass an individual in some way, this is a strong indication that something about the information is inherently private, or retains the characteristics of privacy, whether it can be publicly ascertained or not.[413]

399. *Hansen v. TVNZ* 1993-044; *Muldoon v. TV3 Network Services Ltd* BSA1994-112, 17 Nov. 1994.
400. *O'Neill v. TV3 Network Services Ltd* BSA 1994-093, 6 Oct. 1994.
401. *SF v. The Radio Network Ltd* BSA 2001-094-095, 16 Aug. 2001.
402. *Cook v. TVNZ* 1991-001; *Rutherford v. TVNZ* 1991-033.
403. *Mrs S v. TV3 Network Services Ltd* BSA1994-001, 19 Jan. 1994.
404. *Arnesen v. TVNZ* BSA 1997-100/101, 7 Aug. 1997.
405. *Middleton v. TVNZ* BSA 2013-040.
406. *Ms P v. TV3 Network Services Ltd* 1994-021.
407. *Moore and Television New Zealand Ltd* BSA 2013-093. Public place includes places to which members of the public have access, such as the lobby of an apartment building: *de Villiers v. TVWorks Ltd* BSA 2012-103.
408. *Beytagh v. TVNZ* BSA 2001-001, 29 Jan. 2001.
409. *DS v. TVNZ Ltd* BSA 2011-144.
410. *M v. Radio 531 PI* BSA 2001-028, 26 Apr. 2001.
411. *Stables v. RadioWorks Ltd* BSA 2012-108.
412. *MQ v. TVNZ Ltd* BSA 2011-033, *TJ and Television New Zealand Ltd* 2013-092.
413. See also Wiebe Zwaga, Michael Stace & Colmar Brunton, *Real Media, Real People: Privacy and Informed Consent in Broadcasting* 24–26 (BSA, Wellington, 2004).

a. Public Disclosure

100. While it is clear enough that the tort of invasion of privacy requires wide disclosure,[414] in contrast, the Authority has noted that disclosure to one person may contravene its privacy principles.[415] However, as with the tort, this is subject to the approach taken to identification, discussed next.

b. Identification

101. Connected with the requirement of public disclosure and with that of private facts is a separate requirement of the Authority that a person is able to be identified or is identifiable.[416] The broadcast must positively identify an individual whose privacy is said to have been breached.[417]

The Authority applies the definition given to 'individual' in the Broadcasting Amendment Act 2000, which is the same meaning as it is given in section 2(1) of the Privacy Act 1993. 'Individual' therefore means a natural person, other than a deceased natural person.[418]

There must be some aspect of the broadcast which discloses identity to enable a breach of privacy to be established. Where visuals are clear or pixelation has failed, the requirement is usually met.[419] There is no requirement that the individual be named or even actually shown. In most cases,[420] the starting point is that a person is not identified if identifiable only by a limited number of people such as family and close friends.[421]

Furthermore, identification appears to mean that the individual need not be identifiable within New Zealand but must simply be identifiable somewhere. The privacy principles must be adhered to by those who broadcast in New Zealand regardless of whether individuals portrayed in a broadcast live in New Zealand. The privacy principles do not differentiate between nationals and non-nationals.[422]

c. Offensive or Objectionable to a Reasonable Person

102. The approach appears to be a combined test based on whether the disclosure is highly offensive to objective reasonable people 'in the shoes of the individual whose privacy is alleged to have been breached'.[423] 'Offensive' in the context of the television code means 'hurtful, harmful, injurious' and 'ordinary people' are average people, without exceptional knowledge or experience. 'Reasonable' means

414. See para. 91 above.
415. *Ms P v. TV3 Network Services Ltd* BSA 1994 -021, 28 Apr. 1994.
416. This was not required for the tort in *L v. G* [2002] DCR 234, [2002] NZAR 495 (DC).
417. *Jobe v. TVNZ* BSA 2002-205, 17 Dec. 2002.
418. *Phillips v. TVNZ* BSA 2001-018, 8 Mar. 2001; *Turia v. TVNZ* BSA 2000-165, 9 Nov. 2000; *Giles v. TVNZ* BSA 2002-073, 13 Jun. 2002. See also *Middleton v. TVNZ Ltd* BSA 2013-040.
419. *Moore v. TVWorks Ltd* BSA 2009-036, 8 Jul. 2009.
420. *Khan v. TVNZ* BSA 2001-236, 17 Dec. 2001.
421. *Moore v. TVWorks Ltd* 2009-036; *MA v. TVNZ Ltd* BSA 2010-084,.
422. *TV3 Network Services Ltd v. Ecpat New Zealand Inc* [2003] NZAR 501.
423. *MA v. TVNZ Ltd* BSA 2010-084, [38]–[39]. See also *FS v. TVNZ Ltd* BSA 2012-036.

to have sound judgment, to be sensible.[424] The matter has to be highly offensive.[425] Public figures are expected to be more robust, since they generally put themselves in the public eye.[426]

2. Principle 2

103. Principle 2 states:

> It is inconsistent with an individual's privacy to allow the public disclosure of some kinds of public facts. The 'public' facts contemplated concern events (such as criminal behaviour) which have, in effect, become private again, for example through the passage of time. Nevertheless, the public disclosure of public facts will have to be highly offensive to an objective reasonable person.

Disclosure of convictions for criminal offences is a recurring category where the passage of time is relevant. In one case,[427] an eight-year-old murder conviction was not private because it had been widely covered by the media at the time and nothing had occurred to make the events private again. However, in another case,[428] the passing of twelve years was enough to make an allegation of a sexual offence a private matter.

The factors which will be relevant are the nature of the offence, the public's right to know, the extent and continuation of publicity, and the individual's right to put their past behind them.[429] The Criminal Records (Clean Slate) legislation is also relevant to decisions about the privacy of criminal convictions.[430]

3. Principle 3

104. Principle 3 states:

(a) It is inconsistent with an individual's privacy to allow the public disclosure of material obtained by intentionally interfering, in the nature of prying, with that individual's interest in solitude or seclusion. The intrusion must be highly offensive to an objective reasonable person.
(b) In general, an individual's interest in solitude or seclusion does not prohibit recording, filming, or photographing that individual in a public place ('the public place exemption').

---

424. *TVNZ v. KW* HC Auckland CIV-2007-485-1609, 18 Dec. 2008 at [68].
425. *Commissioner for Children et al v. Television New Zealand* BSA 1999-93-101, 15 Jul. 1999.
426. *Laws v. TV3 Network Services Ltd* BSA 1997-024 6 Mar. 1996.
427. *Earlly v. Radio Pacific Ltd* BSA 1994-043, 23 Jun. 1994.
428. *Drury and Daisley v. TV3 Network Services Ltd* BSA 1996-130, 10 Oct. 1996.
429. *Reekie v. TVNZ* HC Auckland CIV-2009-404-3728, 8 Feb. 2010.
430. *Reekie v. TVNZ* HC Auckland CIV-2009-404-3728, 8 Feb. 2010 at [53].

(c) The public place exemption does not apply when the individual whose privacy has allegedly been infringed was particularly vulnerable, and where the disclosure is highly offensive to an objective reasonable person.

This principle covers not only intrusive filming and recording but also any form of 'prying' practice. 'Prying' has been interpreted as 'inquiring impertinently into the affairs of another person'.[431] Solitude is the 'state of being alone' and this has never been satisfied.[432] It is very difficult to be alone in the required sense in an overcrowded world.[433]

Seclusion is a different matter. It 'suggests a state of screening or shutting off from outside access or public view'.[434] This creates a zone of physical or sensory privacy to which a complainant's rights of ownership or possession may also be relevant, because they determine reasonable expectations regarding seclusion. However, behaviour can also establish such a zone. For example, victims of the Christchurch earthquakes in February 2011 were found to have an interest in seclusion because of their vulnerability. However, the taking of live footage by media during the quake aftermath did not amount to prying in such circumstances.[435]

Principle (iii) is usually breached where filming is surreptitious, as where the complainant has no knowledge of the existence of cameras, or the camera is hidden.[436] However, the principle can apply to situations where filming is not secret. In one case, a ride-along film crew breached the principle when it accompanied police to a private property and filmed the owner in his driveway and in parts of his house while he admitted to police that he possessed a small amount of cannibas.[437] Further, it is not necessary for an individual to be present to have their interest in seclusion intruded upon.[438] There will be a serious breach where a party has been assured that they will not be filmed or quoted and that their comments are 'off the record'.[439]

It appears more difficult for public figures to argue that there has been an intrusion.[440] Public figure, are expected to be robust in the face of persistent attempts to interview. Public figures need not be celebrities but may be ordinary people in a public role.[441]

The principle generally is not breached where the intrusion occurs in or from a public place.[442] However, location of the intrusion will not always determine the

431. *Macdonald v. The Radio Network Ltd* 2004-047, 6 May 2004.
432. *TVNZ v. KW* HC Auckland CIV-2007-485-001609, 18 Dec. 2008.
433. *Tashkoff v. Televsion New Zealand Ltd* BSA 2009-095, 21 Dec. 2009.
434. *CanWest TVWorks Ltd v. XY* [2008] NZAR 1 (HC) at [42].
435. *Malskaitis v. TVWorks* BSA 2011-039.
436. *BQ and CR v. TVNZ* BSA 2002-193-194, 28 Oct. 2002, *Dr Z v. TVNZ Ltd* BSA 2012-074.
437. *MA v. TVNZ Ltd* BSA 2010-084.
438. *J and J McDonagh v. TVNZ* BSA 1996-007, 13 Feb. 1996, *Balfour v. TVNZ* 2005-129; *Balfour v. TVNZ Ltd* BSA 2012-040.
439. *Hood v. TVNZ* BSA 2007-028, 14 Aug. 2007.
440. *Laws v. TV3 Network Services Ltd* BSA 1996-024, 6 Mar. 1996.
441. *The Diocese of Dunedin et al. v. TV3* BSA 1999-125-137, 9 Sep. 1999; *Bowers, Patel and the Universal Church of the Kingdom of God* BSA 2012-050.
442. *JS v. TVWorks Ltd* BSA 2011-122.

issue. Listening secretly to a private conversation taking place in public and reporting the overheard details,[443] and broadcasting remarks not intended for broadcast made during a break in filming an interview,[444] have been held to be forms of intentional prying. Further, the more intrusive the manner of obtaining the footage, the more likely the location will be irrelevant.[445]

4. Principle 4

105. This states:

> The protection of privacy includes the protection against the disclosure by the broadcaster, without consent, of the name and/or address and/or telephone number of an identifiable individual, in circumstances where the disclosure is highly offensive to an objective reasonable person.[446]

It is not enough to merely disclose the details; disclosure must also be highly offensive.[447] The principle has recently been applied to negligent or careless disclosure, where harassment occurred after release of details without consent during a matchmaking programme. Where harassment is foreseeable even though unintended, the principle may be breached.[448]

Any name and address released has to be linked to an identifiable person.[449] The principle will not apply to information already in the public domain.[450] There is no expectation of anonymity if a person is communicating by email with a broadcaster.[451] Email is regarded as a public forum and consent to disclose will usually be implied. A person emailing a talkback radio station should therefore expect that any part of their correspondence can be disclosed by the host, including names, unless it is made explicit in the emails that the correspondent did not wish to be identified.

Harassment by email, especially in a large volume, is recognized as having the potential to be as distressing and unpleasant as harassment by other means and the principle now applies to email addresses.[452] Disclosure of email addresses can also fall within Principle 1.[453]

---

443. *Black v. The Radio Network* BSA 1998-003, 29 Jan. 1998.
444. *Crowley v. TVNZ* BSA 2000-139, 29 Jan. 1998.
445. *CD v. TV3 Network Services Ltd* BSA 2000-142-143, 12 Oct. 2000.
446. Practice Note: Privacy Principle 4: Disclosure for the Purposes of Encouraging Harassment, June 2011, http://bsa.govt.nz/standards/practice-notes/privacy-principle-4-practice-note, accessed 7 May 2014.
447. *Spring v. The Radio Network Ltd* BSA 2007-108, 21 Apr. 2008.
448. *NJ and APNA Networks Ltd* BSA 2010-066.
449. *South Pacific Pictures v. RadioWorks Ltd* BSA 2008-017, 4 Jul. 2008.
450. *Baines v. The Radio Network Ltd* BSA 2006-094, 27 Nov. 2006.
451. *Malone v. The Radio Network Ltd* BSA 2006-034, 28 Jun. 2006.
452. *Marshall v. RadioWorks Ltd* BSA 2010-146, [13].
453. See para. 99 above.

5. Principle 5

106. This states:

> It is a defence to a privacy complaint that the individual whose privacy is allegedly infringed by the disclosure complained about gave his or her informed consent to the disclosure. A guardian of a child can consent on behalf of that child.

'Informed consent' is based on an awareness of being interviewed, of knowing the true context of the interview and of being aware of the purposes to which the interview is to be put – the planned use.[454] However, this does not mean the person consenting needs to appreciate what exposure might follow from the broadcast of the material.

Consent may be actual or inferred from words and behaviour.[455] The onus to establish inferred consent is on the broadcaster.[456] Consent is inferred where callers take part in radio competitions or voluntarily call radio stations and participate in exchanges with announcers on air,[457] or email them.[458] Operating businesses which maintain telephone numbers to make information available to potential customers may also imply consent to broadcast of calls made by announcers to obtain information.[459] Only the individual concerned can consent.[460]

6. Principle 6

107. This principle states:

> Children's vulnerability must be a prime concern to broadcasters, even when informed consent has been obtained. Where a broadcast breaches a child's privacy, broadcasters shall satisfy themselves that the broadcast is in the child's best interests, regardless of whether consent has been obtained.

A number of decisions in the late 1990s emphasized the need to protect the privacy of children,[461] and the Authority developed this special code provision in response. The principle imposes a separate liability on broadcasters which must be satisfied in addition to obtaining consent. The onus on broadcasters reflects the high degree of

454. *TVWorks Ltd v. Du Fresne* [2008] NZAR 382 (HC).
455. *Diocese of Dunedin v. TV3 Network Services Ltd* BSA 1999-125/137.
456. *Bowen v. TVNZ* BSA 1997-032, 10 Apr. 1997.
457. *Malcolm v. The Radio Works Ltd* BSA 2003-007, 13 Feb. 2003.
458. *Malone v. The Radio Network Ltd* BSA2006-034, 28 Jun. 2006.
459. *Simpson v. The Radio Network Ltd* BSA 1999-058, 27 May 1999.
460. *O'Connell v. TVWorks Ltd* BSA 2007-067, 25 Jun. 2008.
461. *Smits v. Television New Zealand Ltd* BSA 1998-005-006, 12 Feb. 1998; *Commissioner for Children et al v. TVNZ* BSA 1999-093-101, 15 Jul. 1999; *Burnell et al v. TVNZ* BSA 1999-087-089, 15 Jul. 1999.

importance, recognized by courts and international treaties, of protecting children in light of their particular vulnerability.[462] In considering the best interests of the child, broadcasters should address the nature and context of the information to be disclosed, the age and maturity of the child, and the potential effects of disclosure on the well-being of the child.

7. Principle 7

108. This states:

> For the purpose of these Principles only, a 'child' is defined as someone under the age of 16 years. An individual aged 16 years or over can consent to broadcasts that would otherwise breach their privacy.

Specifying the age of children as below 16 has significantly simplified matters for complaints involving consent.[463] Age limits aside, the Authority has actually applied the 'spirit and intent' of the best interests principle to a 16-year-old victim of sexual abuse due to her particular vulnerability and apparent incapacity.[464]

8. Principle 8

109. Principle 8 states:

> Disclosing the matter in the 'public interest', defined as of legitimate concern or interest to the public, is a defence to a privacy complaint.

This principle establishes a public interest defence, as exists for the civil action for invasion of privacy. The question to be asked is a balancing one of when the right to privacy should give way to the public's right to know. Matters properly within public concern are of legitimate concern to the public and not just merely interesting on a human level.[465] Matters of public interest have been stated to include:[466]

- criminal matters, including exposing or detecting crime;
- issues of public health or safety;
- matters of politics, government, or public administration;
- matters relating to the conduct of organizations which impact on the public;
- exposing misleading claims made by individuals or organizations;
- exposing seriously anti-social and harmful conduct.

462. *JB v. TVNZ* BSA 2006-090, 22 Feb. 2007.
463. *Hastings District Council v. TVWorks Ltd* BSA 2009-088, 2 Mar. 2010.
464. *Bulathsinghala v. Television New Zealand* BSA 2004-129, 8 Nov. 2004.
465. *TV3 Network Services Ltd v. Broadcasting Standards Authority* [1995] 2 NZLR 720 (HC) at 733.
466. *Balfour v. TVNZ* BSA 2005-129, 21 Mar. 2006.

In general, the material being broadcast must be of importance and concern to the New Zealand public. A very clear example is live footage of victims in the aftermath of the Christchurch earthquake in February 2011.[467] However, the ultimate determination is dependent on the facts in each case. For example, there was no public interest whatsoever in disclosing the identity of a child at the centre of a bitter custody dispute.[468] A connection must be made between all footage used and the public interest in a broadcast because the Authority looks for public interest in the specific part of the broadcast complained about, not the whole programme.[469] Hence, sensationalism and irrelevance may destroy public interest in an otherwise legitimate story.[470]

B. The BSA and Reality Shows

110. The BSA has identified three things in particular that broadcasters involved in TV reality shows can do to avoid privacy complaints arising.[471] These are also useful guidelines to apply generally, not just in relation to reality television production and broadcast. They are:

- make sure the subject of the filming or interview is not identifiable;
- get informed consent;
- do not assume that exposing minor crime will be justified in the public interest.

V. The Privacy Act 1993

A. Principles and Operation

111. In 1993, the New Zealand Parliament passed comprehensive privacy legislation. The Act follows closely the OECD *Guidelines on the Protection of Privacy and Transborder Flows of Personal Data* (1980), which also shaped the Australian federal privacy legislation, and as such was part of an international response to concerns about the collection, storage and use of personal information and the flow of information across international borders. The Act sets out twelve Information Privacy Principles, which are to operate as guidelines for agencies that collect, store and use personal information about identifiable individuals.[472] Paraphrased, the Principles are:

(1) Collection of information about an individual must be necessary for a lawful purpose connected in some way with something the body collecting the information does.

467. *Malskaitis v. TVWorks* BSA 2011-039.
468. *JB v. TVNZ* BSA 2006-090, 22 Feb. 2007.
469. *MA v. TVNZ Ltd* BSA 2010-084.
470. *Balfour v. TVNZ* BSA 2005-129, 21 Mar. 2006.
471. *MA v. TVNZ* BSA 2010-084.
472. See generally the Office of the Privacy Commissioner website: https://www.privacy.org.nz/.

(2) The information must come from the individual except in certain specified circumstances, such as where the information is already public, or the maintenance of the law would be impeded, or it is not practically possible to do so.
(3) Where the information comes from the individual, reasonable steps must be taken to tell that person what is happening, why it is happening, who is getting the information, who will hold the information, and the individual's right to have access to and correct the information. (These are the main requirements only, and there are circumstances where this principle does not have to be followed, which are almost identical to those described where information does not have to be collected directly from the individual, above.)
(4) Information must not be collected in a way that is unlawful, unfair or intrusive.
(5) The information has to be stored securely to prevent loss, unauthorized access or other misuse.
(6) Individuals are to be able to find out whether personal information is held about them and have access to it if it can be retrieved readily. (Sections 27–29 allow the agency to refuse to disclose. The grounds relate to likely prejudice to security, defence and international relations, the possibility of giving away trade secrets or unreasonably prejudicing a party's commercial position, and other situations including where an individual's position is threatened in some way by disclosure, in the areas of health, confidence, legal professional privilege, rehabilitation following a criminal offence, or because the request is frivolous or vexatious, or the information cannot be retrieved easily.)
(7) An individual can request correction to the information, or, if the agency refuses to correct, it must attach a statement setting out the request in the requester's words to the information.
(8) The information has to be checked if reasonable, before legitimate use, for accuracy, completeness, immediacy and relevance.
(9) The information is not to be kept longer than necessary.
(10) The information may not be used for a purpose other than that for which it was collected except in particular situations, including the need to enforce the law, imminent and serious threat to public health and safety, or to the individual's life or health or that of someone else.
(11) The information is not to be disclosed to anyone else or to another agency unless the agency holding it reasonably believes: it was collected for disclosure; it came from a public source; disclosure is to the individual; the individual has authorized disclosure; disclosure is needed to maintain or enforce the law, protect the Revenue, or facilitate court proceedings; there is a serious threat to public health or safety, to the individual's life or the life of another; disclosure is necessary to sell or dispose of a business as a going concern; the individual will not be identified.
(12) An individual will not be identified with a label unique to him or her (such as an ID number) unless it is necessary for an agency to function. Agencies shall not share ID numbers. Care must be taken if an individual is given an ID number to ensure it is assigned accurately. An individual cannot be compelled

to supply their ID number unless it is needed for one of the purposes for which it was issued.

The principles are drafted in general language with a number of exceptions provided for. A particular industry may draw up its own code of practice to limit or expand the principles because of specialist needs. The code is approved by the Privacy Commissioner and, when issued by him or her, takes on the force of law. It then operates instead of the privacy principles and is enforceable. An important example is the Health Information Privacy Code 1994.[473] Industries can also voluntarily develop their own codes and abide by these.

The Act also provides for the appointment of the Privacy Commissioner to whom complaints can be made.[474] Under Part 8 of the Act, a complaint may be made that one of the privacy principles has been breached. But under section 66(1)(b), it is required that the action complained of:

(i) Has caused, or may cause, loss, detriment, damage, or injury to that individual; or
(ii) Has adversely affected, or may adversely affect, the rights, benefits, privileges, obligations, or interests of that individual; or

Has resulted in, or may result in, significant humiliation, significant loss of dignity, or significant injury to the feelings of that individual.

These requirements mean that there must be some actual, significant effect on a complainant before a complaint will be entertained.[475] Mere annoyance is insufficient to support a complaint to the Privacy Commissioner. The onus is on the complainant to establish the loss or humiliation.[476]

Complaints are dealt with by a process of investigation and conciliation. The Commissioner may call compulsory mediation conferences. If the complaint cannot be settled, the Commissioner may refer it to the Director of Human Rights Proceedings who can commence proceedings in the Human Rights Review Tribunal, established under the Human Rights Act 1993. The complainant may self-refer if the Commissioner does not do so. The Tribunal has the normal powers of a court and can order that the interference with privacy cease, award damages up to NZD 200,000[477] or costs, or make such other order as it sees fit. Damages up to NZD 40,000 have been awarded,[478] but awards are more often below NZD 5,000.[479]

473. Revised in 2008. Seven codes are currently in force. Privacy Commissioner 'Codes of Practice' https://www.privacy.org.nz/the-privacy-act-and-codes/codes-of-practice/, accessed 30 Jun. 2015.
474. The current Commissioner is John Edwards: http://privacy.org.nz/about-us/who-we-are/.
475. However, adverse consequences or harm as set out in s. 66(1)(b) are not required when s. 66(2) operates, which describes limited actions that constitute an interference with privacy when access to personal information is requested: *Winter v. Jans* [2004] BCL 465 (HC).
476. *Lehmann v. CanWest Radioworks Ltd* [2006] NZHRRT 35 (21 Sep. 2006).
477. Human Rights Act 1993, s. 92Q.
478. *Hamilton v. The Deanery 2000 Ltd* [2003] NZHRRT 28 (29 Aug. 2003).

B. The Position of the Media under the Privacy Act

112. The Act applies to personal information,[480] and this is information about any live person who can be identified.[481] The legislation covers both public and private bodies ('agencies'). Government departments and bodies are therefore covered, both national and local, such as the Inland Revenue Department, Social Welfare, the police, the Department of Justice, and local councils and health authorities. Private institutions such as banks are also subject to the Act, as are employers and commercial firms such as retailers, insurance companies, building societies, credit agencies and direct marketing agencies. Even individuals are covered.

However, most importantly, the Act does not apply to the media in general in relation to gathering, preparing and broadcasting or publishing news for public broadcast.[482] Section 2 of the Privacy Act 1993 provides:

> *Agency* ... does not include ... in relation to its news activities, any news medium ...
>
> *News activity* means–
>
> (a) the gathering of news, or the preparation or compiling of articles or programmes of or concerning news, observations on news or current affairs, for the purposes of dissemination to the public or any section of the public;
> (b) the dissemination, to the public or any section of the public, of any article or programme of or concerning:
> (i) news:
> (ii) observations on news:
> (iii) current affairs.

In one case,[483] the Tribunal held that publication of the plaintiff's name as part of the 'Rich List' did not breach its right to privacy. This was because, in compiling the list, the defendant was acting in relation to a 'news activity' and the contents of the list were 'news' or 'current affairs'. The defendant was carrying out a news-gathering activity, and therefore the Privacy Act 1993 had no application to it.

A broad approach to the definition has been accepted at High Court level.[484] In another case, a man complained that the filming of his rescue in a national park by a search and rescue team for a documentary about the work of such teams interfered with his privacy even though the film was not used when he refused consent.

479. *Winter v. Jans* [2004] BCL 465 (HC); *Harder v. Proceedings Commissioner* [2000] 3 NZLR 80 (CA).
480. See *Harder v. Proceedings Comm*issioner [2000] 3 NZLR 80 (HC).
481. However, note that under s. 29 an agency can refuse to give access to personal information relating to you where it involves the unwarranted disclosure of the affairs of another individual or a deceased person: Privacy Act 1993, s. 29(1)(a).
482. Which is why the Act could have applied to Radioworks' broadcast campaign seeking a debtor which was not news-gathering: see *Lehmann v. CanWest Radioworks Ltd* BSA 2002-077-080, 13 Jun. 2002.
483. *Talley Family v. National Business Review* (1997) 4 HRNZ 72.
484. *Lau v. ACP Media Ltd* [2013] NZHC 1165.

The Commissioner found the exemption applied because the film crew was preparing a programme concerning current affairs, and this was done for the purpose of disseminating the information to the public through the documentary.[485]

Consumer television programmes may come under the exception, even though they have a large entertainment component. In another opinion,[486] the Privacy Commissioner considered a complaint by a television technician who had been covertly filmed for a consumer programme 'Target', when called to a house to repair a television set, and edited footage taken during the filming was later broadcast. The Commissioner determined that the series came within the category of news/current affairs and that, as a news medium, the programme producer fell within the exception to 'agency'. No complaint could therefore be considered under the Act.[487]

However, the High Court has recently held that the exception does not apply to a journalist who collected information about a person during interviews carried out for the purpose of research for a book about the person. The journalist was employed by a newspaper but was held to be publishing the book in a private capacity. Further, the journalist was not engaged in a news activity, because the definition refers to the compiling of articles or programmes, not books.[488] It appears the definition may be too narrow in this respect.

The test to be applied to photographs is apparently established by consideration of the purpose for taking the photographs and how they are used. The Commissioner has indicated that a photographer documenting political demonstrations for publication in a newspaper or magazine would be a news medium carrying out a news activity. However, the same person taking photographs for inclusion in a brochure advertising a company's goods or services would not be. The Commissioner has also concluded that photographs taken of people's homes and published in a newspaper as part of the editorial content came within the exemption.[489]

C. The Privacy Act and the Official Information Act

113. Requests to public sector agencies are requests for official information even if what is asked for is personal information about someone else. The Privacy Act 1993 does not apply unless the information is about the person requesting it. Other requests are subject to the Official Information Act 1982 and should be dealt with

---

485. *Case Note 62972* [2005] NZPrivCmr 1.
486. *Case Note 38197* [2003] NZPrivCmr 24. See also *Case Note 18148* [1997] NZPrivCmr 15; and *C v. Countrywide Bank* CRT20/97.
487. The Commissioner pointed out that a complaint to the BSA was possible: see IV above.
488. *Dotcom v. Attorney-General* [2014] NZHC 1343, [57]–[77]. Blogger Cameron Slater is currently claiming the media exemption in a Privacy Act complaint made against him by Matthew Blomfield: *Director of Human Rights Proceedings v. Slater* [2014] NZHRRT 53. Although Slater has been found to be a journalist in the context of a defamation action and s. 68 of the Evidence Act 2006, it is uncertain the Privacy Act exemption will be interpreted in the same way: *Slater v. Blomfield* [2014] 3 NZLR 835.
489. Commissioner Bruce Slane in an address to the Photo Library Association, reported in *Private Word* No 21 (January 1998) at 4.

under that Act, which takes a contrasting approach to the Privacy Act 1993 because it is based on a principle that information should be made public unless there is good reason to withhold it.

However, if a journalist asks for comment on an issue rather than for specific information held, the request may not be a request for official information even if it is made to a public sector agency because the agency will have to create the information to respond to the inquiry. These requests have to be dealt with under the Privacy Act 1993.

D. Health Sector Information

114. A further area of difficulty identified by the media is obtaining information from the health sector, in particular about accident victims. The Privacy Commissioner issued the Health Information Privacy Code in 1994, which covers all medical and health information collected and held by health agencies and was last revised in 2008.[490] The rules in the code are generally more stringent than the information privacy principles. Rule 11 emphasizes individual patient autonomy. Disclosure of health information relating to an individual patient is permitted only with the patient's consent. However, a number of exceptions can apply where it is not practicable or desirable to obtain consent. The condition of accident victims is one. An exception is contained in the code, which allows for the release of very basic details of injuries by health agencies where it is not practicable or desirable to seek authorization. Disclosure is permitted if:[491]

> the information to be disclosed briefly describes only the nature of injuries of an individual sustained in an accident and that individual's identity and the disclosure is:
>
> (i) by a person authorised by the person in charge of a hospital;
> (ii) to a person authorised by the person in charge of a news medium;
>
> for the purpose of publication or broadcast in connection with the news activities of that news medium and the disclosure is not contrary to the express request of the individual concerned or his or her representative.

Another exception allows disclosure of basic details relating to the progress and condition of a patient on a daily basis. This also allows release of the information to friends of the patient. Both exceptions can be vetoed by the patient or his or her agent.[492]

---

490. See Privacy Commissioner 'Health Information Privacy Code' (2008) http://privacy.org.nz/the-privacy-act-and-codes/codes-of-practice/health-information-privacy-code/, accessed 8 May 2014.
491. Health Information Privacy Code 1994, r. 11(2)(f).
492. Health Information Privacy Code 1994, r. 11(1)(e).

VI. Other Provisions

A. Harassment

115. It is normally not a legal wrong for media to badger or question a person persistently with a view to extracting information from them. However, New Zealand courts could apply UK case law such that the developing tort of harassment which could impact on media if such questioning is carried out in an extreme fashion.[493]

The Harassment Act 1997 includes an offence of criminal harassment, and establishes a civil regime that provides for the making of civil restraining orders where harassment is at a lower level. The offence of criminal harassment includes watching, loitering near, or preventing or hindering access to or from a person's home or workplace, following, stopping, or accosting that person, entering or interfering with a person's property, and making contact with a person (whether by telephone, correspondence, or in any other way).[494] While it is clear that acts of members of the media may well fall within the definition of harassment, it is highly unlikely that the criminal offence will be applicable because of the requirement that there be a mental intent to cause fear in the victim or recklessness as to that result.[495] It is perhaps a little more likely that the media might find themselves subject to applications for civil restraining orders, as provided in Part 3 of the 1981 Act. Restraining orders may be made if the respondent has engaged in or is engaging in behaviour that amounts to harassment, and given all the circumstances, the behaviour reasonably causes or threatens to cause the applicant distress to such an extent that an order should be made.[496] Previously harassment has required a pattern of behaviour rather than a single incident, but amendment under the Harmful Digital Communications legislation means it now covers acts done on any one occasion that continue to have effect over a protracted period, for example, where offensive material about a person is placed online and remains there for some time.[497] A court must consider the order necessary to protect from further harassment, the application must be on notice, and ultimately, a court can use its discretion to reject unfounded or vexatious applications. There is also a defence of lawful purpose.[498] The burden of proving the lawfulness of the purpose lies on the respondent. 'Lawful purpose' is not defined. However, the defence is at least intended to protect legitimate behaviour such as picketing, protesting or media investigations.

It is an offence under the Summary Offences Act 1981 to follow a person or watch loiter near a person's house or place of business, but only if this is done with intent to frighten or intimidate.[499]

493. *Khorasandjian v. Bush* [1993] QB 727.
494. Summary Offences Act 1981, s. 4.
495. Section 8(1)(a).
496. Harassment Act 1997, ss 9 and 16. It has been held that the civil regime can be applied against bloggers who pursue online campaigns against other individuals: *Flannagan v. Sperling* DC CIV 2012-090-986 (4 Jun. 2013); *Brown v. Sperling* [2012] DCR 753.
497. Harmful Digital Communications Act 2015 s. 32.
498. Harassment Act 1997, s. 17.
499. Summary Offences Act 1981, s. 21.

B. Victims' Rights Act 2002

116. The Victims' Rights Act 2002 contains a principle that the police and other persons dealing with victims should treat them with courtesy, compassion and respect for their personal dignity and privacy.[500] The principle can be relevant to the media in name suppression cases where it may be argued to support application for name suppression of victims. The Court of Appeal has recognized that a judge may be required to take the principle into account in considering name suppression under the Criminal Justice Act 1985.[501] However, because the Victims' Rights Act 2002 does not create legal rights of any kind,[502] application of the principle becomes part of the exercise of judicial discretion in the name suppression context, and appears unlikely to displace the principle of open justice. However, in other contexts, breach of the principle might add weight to a complaint to the BSA or the Press Council.

C. Interception Devices

117. As a result of the Crimes Amendment Act 1979, it is an offence punishable by imprisonment for up to two years intentionally to intercept any private communication by means of an interception device.[503] An 'interception device' is any electronic, mechanical, electromagnetic, optical or electro-optical instrument, apparatus, equipment, or other device that is used or is capable of being used to intercept a private communication.[504] Thus, bugging devices, tape recorders and telephone taps are included, as well as hidden cameras and internet spyware. A 'private communication' means a communication (whether oral or written) made under circumstances that may reasonably be taken to indicate that any party to the communication desires it to be confined to the parties to the communication.[505] It does not include such a communication occurring in circumstances in which any party ought reasonably to expect that the communication may be intercepted by some other person not having the express or implied consent of any party to do so.[506] Most importantly, however, the prohibition does not apply where the person intercepting the private communication is a party to it,[507] or where the interception takes place with the consent of one of the parties.[508] Thus, there would appear to be

500. Victims' Rights Act 2002, s. 7.
501. *Re Victim X* [2003] 3 NZLR 230 (CA) at [47]–[55].
502. Victims' Rights Act 2002, s. 10.
503. Crimes Act 1961, s. 216B.
504. Crimes Act 1961, s. 216A(1). Listening to and recording a conversation on a mobile telephone is 'interception': *Edelsten v. Investigating Committee of NSW* (1986) 7 NSWLR 222 (SC) (although the Australian legislation is rather different).
505. Crimes Act 1961, s. 216A(1).
506. Crimes Act 1961, s. 216A(1).
507. Crimes Act 1961, s. 216B(2). *R v. Leete* (2002) 19 CRNZ 464 (CA).
508. Crimes Act 1961, s. 216A(2)(b).

nothing wrong with a person's tape recording a telephone conversation to which that person is a party.[509]

It is an offence to disclose the contents, or even the existence of, an illegally intercepted communication, without the consent of a party, if the person disclosing it knows that it has come to his or her knowledge as a direct or indirect result of an illegal interception.[510] The contents of such communications are not admissible in evidence in court proceedings.[511] Once again, however, there appears to be nothing to render inadmissible tape recordings of conversations taken by a party to them.

Even if an interception has been lawfully made, it is an offence knowingly to disclose the contents, or even the existence of it, if the person concerned has acquired knowledge of it as a direct or indirect result of the interception.[512]

These provisions were tested recently when, prior to the November 2012 election, the Prime Minister, John Key, referred the matter of an audio recording he said was illegally obtained to the police. Mr Key and a political alley, Mr Banks, had held a meeting in a café to which media were invited in the week running up to election day. After media had been asked to go outside, Mr Key discovered a recording device had been left on the table. A cameraman, Bradley Ambrose, who owned the device, obtained a recording remotely from it, which he later released to a newspaper when Mr Key accused him of deliberately recording the conversation. Police were asked to investigate whether Mr Bradley had intentionally intercepted a private communication using an interception device.[513] The newspaper refused to release the recording on the basis that it could be breaching the provision prohibiting disclosure of such communications.[514] Mr Bradley sought a declaration that the discussion between Mr Banks and Mr Key was not a private one. The judge refused to adjudicate on the grounds that insufficient facts were before her and the police had not completed their investigation.[515] The police eventually announced they would not prosecute Mr Ambrose who had written a letter of regret, but delivered a warning to him and to the media that his actions were probably illegal and any publication of the tape would be also. However, the tape had been leaked long since by prominent media law bloggers linking to it, arguing that the meeting could never have been private, and any media publishing the tape would not be in breach of the criminal law either. The application of the law remains obscure.

A provision is contained in the Crimes Act 1961 which is intended to apply to 'hacking', whereby individuals attempt to access computer systems without authority to demonstrate their skill at overcoming any measures in place protecting the

509. The Privacy Act 1993 may also not cover such circumstances: see *Harder v. Proceedings Commissioner* [2000] 3 NZLR 80 (CA). Such a complaint could be dealt with under the broadcasting codes as an unfair practice: see *Criminal Bar Association of NZ Inc v. TV3 Network Services Ltd* BSA-1997-128/129, 25 Sep. 1997.
510. Crimes Act 1961, s. 216C(1).
511. Misuse of Drugs Amendment Act 1978, s. 25.
512. Crimes Act 1961, s. 312K; Misuse of Drugs Amendment Act 1978, s. 26. There is, of course, an exception where the person communicates the information in the course of his or her duty.
513. *Crimes Act 1961* (NZ) ss 216A–B.
514. *Crimes Act 1961* (NZ) s. 216C.
515. *Ambrose v. Attorney-General* [2012]NZAR 23.

system, but without any intention to cause harm.[516] There must be intention to gain access, directly or indirectly, to the computer system. However, the offence does not include unauthorized behaviour by authorized persons,[517] nor is there any offence by a law enforcement agency which has accessed a computer system under authority of any interception warrant or a search warrant.[518] It is an offence to intentionally or recklessly destroy, damage or alter any computer system if a person knows or ought to know that danger to life is likely to result.[519] Further, it is an offence to intentionally or recklessly, and knowing there is no authorization, damage, delete, modify or otherwise interfere with or impair any data or software in any computer system, to cause any data or software in any computer system to be damaged, deleted, modified or otherwise interfered with or impaired, or to cause any computer system to fail or deny service to any authorized users.[520]

D. *Telephone*

118. It is no wrong merely to telephone a person to attempt to obtain information from them, although if the calls were persistent this conduct could possibly, in a most exceptional case, be classified as a nuisance for which damages or an injunction would lie in a civil action.[521] In addition it is, by the Telecommunications Act 2001, an offence to use a telephone for the purpose of 'disturbing, annoying or irritating' any person.[522] It is doubtful whether persistent contact for the genuine purpose of acquiring information could ever be said to fall within this section, for intention to offend is necessary. However, in a very extreme case, a court can be persuaded that there was the necessary element of wilfulness. In 1994, a newspaper publisher was charged with misusing a telephone by making a number of telephone calls in the early hours of the morning to the home of the owner of a rafting company which had been involved in a tragedy. The publisher was found guilty, but was discharged without conviction.[523] It is also an offence to give a fictitious message on the phone, which could cover blagging of the kind that has become notorious in the UK Leveson Inquiry.[524]

516. Crimes Act 1961, s. 252(1).
517. Crimes Act 1961, s. 252(2).
518. Crimes Act 1961, s. 252(3).
519. Crimes Act 1961, s. 250(1).
520. Crimes Act 1961, s. 250(2).
521. However, malice may be an essential ingredient: see *Stoakes v. Bridger* [1958] QWN 6, noted in 32 ALJ 205, and ownership of the property where the calls were received would be an issue: see *Khorasandjian v. Bush* [1993] QB 727, [1993] 3 WLR 476; *Hunter v. Canary Wharf* [1997] AC 655, [1997] 2 WLR 684 (HL).
522. Telecommunications Act 2001, s. 112(2)(a). The Act refers to a 'telephone device', which can apply to emails: *Jacks v. Hastings District Court* [2005] NZAR 736 (CA) and to texts: *Fernandos v. Police* HC Auckland CRI-2010-404-280, 12 Nov. 2010.
523. *The Press*, 20 Oct. 1994. See also *Spooner v. Police* (1992) 8 CRNZ 666 (HC).
524. Telecommunications Act 2001, s. 112(2)(b). See BBC News: 'Gordon Brown Allegations: What is Blagging?' 12 Jul. 2011, http://www.bbc.co.uk/news/uk-14120244, accessed 8 May 2014.

In addition to the prohibitions on interception devices contained in the Crimes Amendment Act 1979, the Telecommunications Act 2001 imposes specific restrictions on interference with a telephone network. A person may only connect equipment to a network, or to anything connected to a network, that is owned or operated by an operator who has agreed to the connection.[525] An operator must not agree to the connection of a telephone analyser to a network that is owned or operated by an operator unless the connection is to enable a person to whom the operator provides telecommunications services to obtain call associated data that relates to telecommunications between the person and other persons, to maintain the network, or to detect, investigate or prosecute relevant offences.[526] There is specific provision that damages may be awarded[527] or an injunction granted by the High Court.[528]

E. Photographs

119. The tort of invasion of privacy may in some circumstances not cover the taking of photographs of a person in a public place or of their property. There is also no statute law against photographing a person without his or her consent. Normally, even the publication of a photograph taken without consent is not wrongful, although in some circumstances it could be. For instance, it might be defamatory. The Copyright Act 1994 conveys a moral right to privacy of photographs and films on a person who has commissioned the work for a private and domestic purpose, where the copyright itself is owned by the person who has made the work and not the person who has commissioned it.[529] Such photographs or films are not to be copied and issued, exhibited or shown in public, or broadcast or included in a cable programme. There are exceptions relating to incidental copying, parliamentary and judicial proceedings, royal commissions and statutory inquiries, acts done under statutory authority, and anonymous or pseudonymous works.[530] Infringement of this right is actionable by the person entitled, who can sue for damages and an injunction.[531]

F. Documents and Letters

120. It is of course an offence to steal a document. Moreover, receipt of a document that has been stolen or obtained through the commission of some other imprisonable offence constitutes the crime of receiving if the recipient knows it was

525. Telecommunications Act 2001, s. 106(1).
526. Telecommunications Act 2001, s. 107(1).
527. Telecommunications Act 2001, s. 110.
528. Telecommunications Act 2001, s. 111.
529. Copyright Act 1994, s. 105. See *R v. Barai* [2004] DCR 71.
530. Copyright Act 1994, s. 105(3).
531. Copyright Act 1994, s. 125. See *Radford v. Hallensteins Bros Ltd* [2009] DCR 907.

dishonestly obtained.[532] It is enough to constitute knowledge that the recipient believes that the document has been dishonestly obtained; wilful blindness may be evidence of belief. Receipt of a document belonging to someone else will normally also amount to the tort of conversion, and detention of it to the tort of detinue. Possible remedies are damages and an order that the document be returned to the owner. If what is acquired is not the original, but a photocopy of it, the law of copyright provides similar remedies.

It is an offence punishable by imprisonment of up to six months for a person to open a postal article that is not addressed to them.[533] Penalties are imposed on anyone who, on receiving a postal article meant for someone else, does not forward it to the intended recipient or any postal operator.[534] It is also an offence for a person to divulge without good and sufficient cause any information obtained from a postal article not intended for him or her.[535]

G. *Radiocommunications*

121. It is an offence for a person to receive a radiocommunication and, knowing that it was not intended for that person, to make use of it or of any information in it, or to reproduce it or the information in it.[536] Neither may a person disclose the existence of the radiocommunication.[537] The offence does not apply to any radiocommunications intercepted by a member of the police, a Customs officer, or any other specified classes of law enforcement official for the purpose of avoiding prejudice to the maintenance of the law, including the detection, prevention, investigation, prosecution and punishment of offences, or by an officer or employee of the New Zealand Security Intelligence Service, for the purpose of obtaining intelligence relevant to security, or by the Government Communications Security Bureau, for the purpose of obtaining foreign intelligence.

H. *Clean Slate Legislation*

122. The Criminal Records (Clean Slate) Act allows an individual who has committed a minor criminal offence to go on with life without a criminal record. An individual is deemed to have no criminal record if asked about it, and may answer as if they do not have a record, if they are eligible.[538] Such a person is also entitled to have their record not disclosed by government departments and law enforcement agencies.[539] A person is eligible if it is seven years since they were last sentenced

532. Crimes Act 1961, s. 246.
533. Postal Services Act 1998, s. 23.
534. Postal Services Act 1998, s. 19.
535. Postal Services Act 1998, s. 20(2).
536. Radiocommunications Act 1989, s. 133A(1).
537. Radiocommunications Act 1989, s. 133A(1).
538. Criminal Records (Clean Slate) Act 2004, s. 14. A person may answer the question truthfully if they wish.
539. Criminal Records (Clean Slate) Act 2004, ss 15–16.

for an offence, no custodial sentence has ever been imposed, no mental impairment order has been made, the individual has not been convicted of a specified offence,[540] has paid all fines or compensation and is not disqualified from holding a driver's licence.[541]

It is an offence to unlawfully disclose information required to be concealed. If a person has access to criminal records and discloses the record of an eligible person knowing they cannot do this lawfully under the Act, or being reckless as to whether or not this can be done, such a person is liable on summary conviction to a fine of up to NZD 20,000.[542] It is also a summary offence to require or request an individual, without lawful authority, to disregard the 2004 Act, when answering questions about their criminal record, or to require them to disclose or give consent to disclosure of their criminal record.[543] Protection is not absolute. An individual must state if they have a criminal record, and so must a government department, law enforcement agency and their employees, in certain circumstances. These are: where the information is needed for the prevention and detection function of a law enforcement agency, or for the administration of sentences by a law enforcement agency, or for functions of the secret service, or where the record is relevant to criminal or civil proceedings, or where the eligible individual has applied for an arms licence, or has applied for a position involving New Zealand's national security, or as a judge, JP, or community magistrate, as a member of the police, prison officer, probation officer, or security officer, or has applied to act in a role involving the care and protection of children or young people (outside of education), or the record is relevant to an investigation into the ill-treatment or neglect of a child or young person, or the record is relevant to certain government-approved historical research.[544]

The Act is intended to affect the behaviour of employers in the main. The extent of its application to the media is uncertain. It seems reasonably clear that the media may not put any sort of pressure on an individual when asking them questions about their own criminal record. In one case,[545] a judge said:

The scheme under the Act is clearly directed toward eligible individuals being permitted to avoid disclosure of his or her previous convictions when asked about or requested to provide information on them.

The Act may also be raised in other contexts, such as in BSA complaints, particularly in support of arguments that a public conviction has become private again over time.[546]

It also seems clear that a person with official access to criminal records must not disclose in breach of the 2004 Act and this may affect what information the media

540. This is a varied selection of sexual offences such as rape, incest, procuring young girls, unlawful anal intercourse, as defined in s. 4.
541. Criminal Records (Clean Slate) Act 2004, s. 7. See *Reekie v. TVNZ* HC Auckland CIV-2009-404-3728, 8 Feb. 2010.
542. Criminal Records (Clean Slate) Act 2004, s. 17.
543. Criminal Records (Clean Slate) Act 2004, s. 18, punishable by a fine of up to NZD 10,000.
544. Criminal Records (Clean Slate) Act 2004, s. 19.
545. *Kerr v. Dominion Post* HC Wellington CIV-2007-485-2243, 12 Feb. 2008.
546. See *Gough v. Television New Zealand Ltd* BSA 2012-095. See IV above (BSA PP; *Reekie v. Television New Zealand Ltd* HC Auckland CIV-2010-404-4893, 3 Nov. 2010.

can have access to in this respect. However, it is likely that the law will not apply when the media do not use official sources of information about criminal convictions.[547]

547. Justice and Electoral Select Committee Report on the Criminal Records (Clean Slate) Bill (2003) at 2.

Chapter 4. Right to Reply

122.1. There is in New Zealand law no general right of reply for a person mentioned in print media to correct errors or defend his or her reputation. Persons harmed in such a manner may use general tort law such as the law of defamation, under which the Defamation Act 1992 makes provision for judges to recommend a correction order,[548] or the complaints processes of the industry-run New Zealand Press Council, described below.[549] The Harmful Digital Communications Act 2015 contains a power for a District Court judge to make a correction or right of reply order, but this legislation only applies to digital communications.[550]

548. See para. 65 above.
549. See para. 214 below.
550. See para. 282 below.

Chapter 5. Access to Public Information

§1. PUBLIC DOCUMENTS AND MEETINGS

I. Official Information

A. *The Official Information Act 1982*

123. The Act applies to information held by Ministers of the Crown and more than 200 government departments and other organizations listed in schedules to the Ombudsmen Act 1975 and the Official Information Act 1982 itself.[551] These lists include virtually all departments and governmental organizations. All Crown entities are now included.[552] Of particular importance to the media is the inclusion of Television New Zealand (TVNZ) and Radio New Zealand Ltd, the Māori Television Service and every subsidiary of the Māori Television Service, and the BSA.

The number of state organizations remaining outside the Act is very small. They include courts and (in relation to their judicial functions) tribunals.[553] Royal commissions and commissions of inquiry are also excluded, as well as the Judicial Conduct Commissioner and related officials. However, Cabinet and Cabinet committee records are covered by the Act, and 'every request for Cabinet records must be considered on its merits against the criteria in the Act'.[554]

'Official information' is any information held by a Minister or one of the listed departments and organizations,[555] (henceforth, the word 'organization' will be used to cover all these things.) Information held by officers, employees or members of an organization, or independent contractors engaged by it, is deemed to be held by the organization. However, this does not apply to information held only by virtue of the person's connection with some other body not governed by the Act.[556]

The Ombudsmen have defined 'information' as 'that which is appraised or told: intelligence, news'.[557] There is no express requirement that the information be in written or other permanent form. It probably covers even information held only in the memory of officials. Moreover, with the few exceptions mentioned, official information is all information held by these organizations, even such things as internal office manuals. Indeed, the Act specifically refers to these, and lays down a 'duty' to disclose them.[558] The Act is also retrospective to the extent that it covers information that came into existence before it was passed.[559]

---

551. Official Information Act 1982, s. 2, definitions of 'department', 'official information' and 'organisation'.
552. Ombudsmen Act 1975, sch. 1, Part 2.
553. Official Information Act 1982, s. 2(6)(a) and (b).
554. *Cabinet Manual* (2008), cl. 8.30. http://cabinetmanual.cabinetoffice.govt.nz/node/72#8.30, accessed 9 Mar. 2015. The *Cabinet Manual* also contains guidelines for the writing of memoirs by Ministers and for the release of information by former Ministers: cls 8.112–8.115.
555. Official Information Act 1982, s. 2(1).
556. Official Information Act 1982, s. 2(3)–(5).
557. Case 10, *First Compendium of Case Notes of the Ombudsmen.*
558. Official Information Act 1982, s. 22.
559. Case 10, *First Compendium, of Case Notes of the Ombudsmen.*

1. The Principle of Availability

124. It is a main purpose of the Act 'to increase progressively the availability of official information to the people of New Zealand'.[560] Section 5 lays down 'the principle of availability' as follows:

> *5. Principle of availability*
> The question whether any official information is to be made available, where that question arises under this Act, shall be determined, except where this Act otherwise expressly requires, in accordance with the purposes of this Act and the principle that the information shall be made available unless there is good reason for withholding it.

Generally speaking, therefore, a member of the public, including media, will be supplied with the information he or she requests unless there is good reason for withholding it. It is wrong to categorize information as being of a type that should always be released or always withheld.

2. Conclusive Reasons for Withholding Information

125. Section 6 of the Act lays down five conclusive reasons for withholding official information. If any one of these reasons exists, the organization is conclusively justified in withholding the information. These reasons exist if the making available of that information would be likely:

(a) to prejudice the security or defence of New Zealand or the international relations of the government of New Zealand; or
(b) to prejudice the entrusting of information to the government of New Zealand on a basis of confidence by–
  (i) the government of any other country or any agency of such a government; or
  (ii) any international organisation; or
(c) to prejudice the maintenance of the law, including the prevention, investigation, and detection of offences, and the right to a fair trial;[561] or
(d) to endanger the safety of any person; or
(e) to damage seriously the economy of New Zealand by disclosing prematurely decisions to change or continue government economic or financial policies relating to–

560. Official Information Act 1982, s. 4(a). Another purpose of the Act is 'to protect official information to the extent consistent with the public interest and the preservation of personal privacy'.
561. A good example is Case W38403, *11th Compendium of Case Notes of the Ombudsmen*, where information from a Crown Health Enterprise about the treatment of a patient on trial for murder was refused. Under this provision, the Ombudsmen have consistently upheld the right to withhold the identity of an informant (say, to the Police): *Nicholl v. Department of Work and Income* [2003] 3 NZLR 426 (HC) at 430; Case W45324, *14th Compendium of Case Notes of the Ombudsmen*; *Stoves v. Commissioner of Police* (2009) 19 PRNZ 334 (HC).

(i) exchange rates or the control of overseas exchange transactions;
(ii) the regulation of banking or credit;
(iii) taxation;
(iv) the stability, control, and adjustment of prices of goods and services, rents, and other costs, and rates of wages, salaries, and other incomes;
(v) the borrowing of money by the Government of New Zealand;
(vi) the entering into of overseas trade agreements.

In March 2009, TVNZ sought from police a copy of the footage of an incident that had been recorded by a taser camera. The police refused to supply the information relying on the conclusive reason that the making available of that information would be likely to prejudice the maintenance of the law, including the right to a fair trial. The subject of the taser film was at the time of the request for the information facing trial. The Ombudsman upheld the decision of the police on the basis of protecting the subject's fair trial rights and found that pixelation would not have protected his privacy. However, the Ombudsman expressed a view that after trial proceedings concluded, the application of section 6(c) would be weakened.[562]

3. Other Reasons for Withholding Information

126. Section 9 of the Act lays down 'other reasons' for withholding information. These reasons are not conclusive: they may be outweighed in a particular case by other considerations that render it desirable in the public interest to make the information available.[563] The organization must assess the weight of these competing interests and strike a balance.[564]

These other reasons exist if the withholding of the information is necessary to:[565]

(a) protect the privacy of natural persons, including that of deceased natural persons; or
(b) protect information where the making available of the information–
  (i) would disclose a trade secret; or
  (ii) would be likely unreasonably to prejudice the commercial position of the person who supplied or who is the subject of the information; or
(ba) protect information which is subject to an obligation of confidence or which any person has been or could be compelled to provide under the authority of any enactment, where the making available of the information–
  (i) would be likely to prejudice the supply of similar information, or information from the same source, and it is in the public interest that such information should continue to be supplied; or

562. *Ombudsman's Finding on Complaint by Television New Zealand Ltd Against Police* (February 2010): http://www.ombudsman.parliament.nz/system/paperclip/document_files/document_files/241/original/first_taser_cam_case.pdf?1344201714, accessed 21 Mar. 2015.
563. Official Information Act 1982, s. 9(1).
564. *10th Compendium of Case Notes of the Ombudsmen* vol 2 at 6.
565. Official Information Act 1982, s. 9(2).

(ii) would be likely otherwise to damage the public interest;

(c) avoid prejudice to measures protecting the health or safety of members of the public; or

(d) avoid prejudice to the substantial economic interests of New Zealand; or

(e) avoid prejudice to measures that prevent or mitigate material loss to members of the public; or

(f) maintain the constitutional conventions for the time being which protect–

  (i) the confidentiality of communications by or with the Sovereign or her representative;

  (ii) collective and individual ministerial responsibility;

  (iii) the political neutrality of officials;

  (iv) the confidentiality of advice tendered by Ministers of the Crown and officials; or

(g) maintain the effective conduct of public affairs through–

  (i) the free and frank expression of opinions by or between or to Ministers of the Crown or members of an organisation or officers and employees of any department or organisation in the course of their duty; or

  (ii) the protection of such Ministers, members of organisations, officers, and employees from improper pressure or harassment; or

(h) maintain legal professional privilege; or

(i) enable a Minister of the Crown or any department or organisation holding the information to carry out, without prejudice or disadvantage, commercial activities; or

(j) enable a Minister of the Crown or any department or organization holding the information to carry on, without prejudice or disadvantage, negotiations (including commercial and industrial negotiations); or

(k) prevent the disclosure or use of official information for improper gain or improper advantage.

It should be noted that withholding is justified under section 9 only if it is 'necessary' for one of the stated reasons. Where ground (a) (privacy) is a possible reason for withholding, consideration should be given to Information Privacy Principle 11 in the Privacy Act 1993. If the matter is taken to the Ombudsmen, they must consult with the Privacy Commissioner.[566] It is important to note, however, that under the Official Information Act 1982 even if the privacy ground is established, there must still be an inquiry as to whether other considerations outweigh it and whether it is desirable in the public interest to release the information.[567] Where TVNZ unsuccessfully sought from police a copy of the footage of an incident that had been recorded by a taser camera,[568] withholding the taser film was upheld on the basis of privacy. However, in another case where media sought information from a university containing details of expenditure on items used by a staff member at his private residence, although the Ombudsman found there was a privacy interest in the information in particular because it related to the staff member's terms and conditions of

566. Official Information Act 1982, s. 29B.

567. *11th Compendium of Case Notes of the Ombudsmen,* at 68.

568. *Ombudsman's Finding on Complaint by Television New Zealand Ltd Against Police*, see n. 562 above.

employment, the public interest in expenditure of public money outweighed this.[569] However, this only required that sufficient information be released, and therefore a statement giving approximate values and context was made available.

In a case where media had sought tape and transcript records of pilot communications to Christchurch Air Traffic Control prior to a plane crashing and killing Crop & Food research staff, the Ombudsman found no obligation of confidence arose either from the Convention on International Civil Aviation, or from the air traffic controllers' collective agreement.[570] A realistic assessment must be made of the nature of the information and the likely consequence of disclosure.[571] An Ombudsman has held that journalists' sources may be protected under this ground.[572] Privacy and confidentiality may overlap.[573]

Even if one of the grounds in section 9(2) exists, it must still be considered whether there is a countervailing public interest in disclosure.[574] In 2012, the Chief Ombudsman concluded that the Earthquake Commission (EQC) did not have to reveal the cost estimates for repair work when it gave a scope of works to individual property owners following the Christchurch earthquakes in 2010 and 2011. Under the Act, withholding of the information was necessary to enable EQC to carry on negotiations with contractors, without prejudice or disadvantage,[575] and the public interest in government openness and transparency did not outweigh this.[576]

4. Administrative Reasons

127. Section 18 of the Act provides that an organization may also refuse a request for information for certain, largely administrative, reasons: that the information will soon be publicly available;[577] that a document does not exist or cannot be found; that the information cannot be made available without substantial collation or research;[578] that it is not held by the organization to whom the request was

---

569. Case C7014, *14th Compendium of Case Notes of the Ombudsmen*, at 106.
570. Cases W50570 and W50585, *14th Compendium of Case Notes of the Ombudsmen*, at 129.
571. *Wyatt Co (NZ) Ltd v. Queenstown Lakes District Council* [1991] 2 NZLR 180 (HC).
572. Case W3043, *10th Compendium*, at 135.
573. The Ombudsman indicated in the taser case referred to n. 568 above that the result under s. 9(2)(ba) (confidentiality) would have been the same because the police have confidentiality obligations in carrying out filming for law enforcement duties.
574. For a good example of commercial sensitivity being overridden by the public interest in disclosure, see Case W1728, *10th Compendium of Case Notes of the Ombudsmen*; and for a case of privacy considerations being overridden by public interest, see Case W3376, *10th Compendium of Case Notes of the Ombudsmen* at 95.
575. Official Information Act 1982, s. 9(2)(j).
576. Ombudsman Casenote for Cases 313674, 316626 and 318456, February 2012.
577. See Case W31968, *11th Compendium* at 144: the annual report of TVNZ was properly withheld; it was soon to be tabled in Parliament under the State-Owned Enterprises Act 1986.
578. However, as the result of an amendment to the Official Information Act in 2003, the organization should, if possible, attempt to find ways of handling the matter. This could be, for example, by imposing a charge, extending the time limit, or consulting the requestor about other ways of framing the request: ss 18A, 18B.

made and there is no ground for believing it is held by any other organization; or that the request is frivolous or vexatious;[579] or the information requested is trivial.

5. Procedures

128. Anyone who is a New Zealand citizen, or who is a permanent resident of New Zealand or is resident in New Zealand, can request information from an organization.[580] There is no need to give a reason why the information is required.[581] There is no statutory requirement that the request need be in writing: a telephone call will do. The information requested must be specified with 'due particularity'.[582] If the person wants the request to be treated as urgent, reasons must be given.[583] Organizations are under a statutory obligation to give assistance to inquirers;[584] they must also transfer to the appropriate organization requests relating to information not held by them.[585]

The organization must let the inquirer know as soon as reasonably practicable, and in any case not later than twenty working days after the receipt of the request, whether the request is granted.[586] In the case of requests involving much work (e.g., because of the quantity of information involved), the time of twenty working days may be extended.[587] If the request relates to information to which sections 6, 7 or section 9(2)(b) apply, the organization may simply give notice that it neither confirms nor denies the existence of the information.[588]

6. Granting of Request

129. If the request is granted and the information is supplied, the organization may make a reasonable charge.[589] It may also be stipulated that the charge be paid in advance. The Ministry of Justice has issued guidelines on charging; the Ombudsmen regard charges fixed in accordance with them as reasonable.[590] If the

579. See case W36125, *11th Compendium* at 150, where a requester who had had an acrimonious relationship with the police made a request in intemperate terms. While this was some evidence that the request was vexatious and frivolous, the Ombudsmen persuaded the parties that the requester should represent the request in reasonable terms.
580. See further the Official Information Act, s. 12(1).
581. *Television New Zealand Ltd v. Ombudsmen* [1992] 1 NZLR 106 (HC) at 118 per Heron J.
582. Official Information Act 1982, s. 12(2). This is not a reason for refusal; the organization must attempt to assist the requester. Case W3541, *10th Compendium.*
583. Official Information Act 1982, s. 12(3).
584. Official Information Act 1982, s. 13.
585. Official Information Act 1982, s. 14.
586. Official Information Act 1982, s. 15.
587. Official Information Act 1982, s. 15A. The Act does not envisage multiple extensions; organizations should set a realistic time (*10th Compendium* vol 2 at 20).
588. Official Information Act 1982, s. 10.
589. Section 15(1A), (2) and (3).
590. *10th Compendium* vol 2 at 20.

information is in a document, it may be made available by: letting the requester inspect the document; providing a copy; giving an excerpt or summary of the contents; or giving oral information about its contents.[591] If the information is contained in a film or a recording, arrangements may be made to let the requester hear or view the sounds and images.[592] If the document is in code or shorthand or if the information is on a sound recording, a transcript may be provided.[593] However, normally the organization must make the information available in the way preferred by the person requesting it.[594] If it is supplied in a different way, the requester must be given the reason.[595]

If the document contains some information that can be supplied and some that cannot, deletions may be made.[596]

It is a serious error to assume that if information is supplied to an inquirer under the Act, it is necessarily safe for that person to publish it to the world. If the information supplied contains some defamatory material, or some confidential material, or material in contempt of court, for instance, publication in the media may well render the publisher liable to court action. Likewise, much of the information supplied is likely to be subject to copyright, and reproduction of it in the media could well be a breach of copyright. The Act itself recognizes this. It provides that the supply of information under it does not, for the purposes of the law relating to defamation, breach of confidence, or infringement of copyright, constitute an authorization or approval of publication.[597] However, the Act does protect the author of the information, and the person who supplied it to the organization, from the consequences of such publication.[598]

There appears also to be power in an organization to impose conditions on publication when supplying information, although the only reference to this in the Act is an oblique one. It provides that the Ombudsman may review such a decision.[599]

7. Refusal of Request: The Ombudsmen's Jurisdiction

130. If a request for information is refused, the organization must give the applicant the reason for the refusal and, if the applicant requests it, the grounds in support of that refusal, unless giving the grounds would prejudice the interests protected.[600]

591. Official Information Act 1982, s. 16(1).
592. Official Information Act 1982, s. 16(1)(c).
593. Official Information Act 1982, s. 16(1)(d).
594. Official Information Act 1982, s. 16(2).
595. Official Information Act 1982, s. 16(3). In Case W30757, *11th Compendium* at 75, a request for the curricula vitae of shortlisted applicants for a job was satisfied by the Ombudsmen recommending that the requester be given summaries, deleting names.
596. Official Information Act 1982, s. 17. When a request was made for papers that led to a decision to withdraw troops from Bosnia, there were many deletions in the documents supplied. The Ombudsmen accepted most of them, but said a little more information could be made available: Case W35756, *11th Compendium* at 61.
597. Official Information Act 1982, s. 48.
598. Official Information Act 1982, s. 48(1)(b). See *Attorney-General v. Davidson* [1994] 3 NZLR 143 (CA); Press Statement, Stuart Grieve QC 'Tony Veitch' (22 May 2009).
599. Official Information Act 1982, s. 28(1)(c).
600. Official Information Act 1982, s. 19.

The applicant may complain to the Ombudsmen against the refusal.[601] The Ombudsmen will then investigate and review the decision; they may require the organization to furnish information relating to the investigation.[602] If an Ombudsman concludes after investigation that the request should not have been refused, or that the decision was unreasonable or wrong, the Ombudsman will report this to the organization, with an appropriate recommendation.[603] The most common recommendation will be that the information be released. However, in certain exceptional instances, such as where the Prime Minister certifies that security is at stake, a recommendation for release cannot be made.[604]

When a recommendation is made to an organization, it has a public duty to observe it after twenty working days unless, before the expiry of that time, the Governor-General by Order-in-Council otherwise orders.[605] Such an Order-in-Council is to be published in the *Gazette* and laid before the House of Representatives as soon as practicable after it is made. The Order-in-Council must set out the reasons for which it is made and the grounds in support of those reasons.[606] An application may be made to the High Court to review the making of the Order-in-Council on the ground that it was beyond the powers conferred in the Act or otherwise wrong in law.[607]

In addition to the compendia of case notes, and opinions, the Ombudsmen have a set of Guides on various aspects of the Act.[608] These Guides are extensive and dispel many common misapprehensions. In particular, the legislation guides provide detailed analysis of the statutory criteria, and discuss the interface between the Official Information Act 1982 and the Privacy Act 1993.[609]

8. Directory of Official Information

131. The Official Information Act 1982 provides[610] that the Ministry of Justice must produce a publication that includes, in respect of each government department and organization, a description of its structure and functions, a description of the categories of documents held by it, a description of all manuals and similar sets of policies and guidelines, and a statement of information that needs to be available to people who want official information from the department or organization, including the officers to whom requests for information should be sent. This publication,

601. Official Information Act 1982, s. 28(1)–(3). Undue delay is deemed a refusal (s. 28(5)).
602. Official Information Act 1982, s. 29A.
603. Official Information Act 1982, s. 30.
604. Official Information Act 1982, s. 31.
605. Official Information Act 1982, s. 32.
606. Official Information Act 1982, s. 32A.
607. Official Information Act 1982, s. 32B.
608. See http://www.ombudsman.parliament.nz/resources-and-publications/guides, accessed 27 Mar. 2015.
609. See http://www.ombudsman.parliament.nz/resources-and-publications/guides/official-information-legislation-guides, accessed 27 Mar. 2015.
610. Official Information Act, s. 20; this duty used to lie on the State Services Commission.

the *Directory of Official Information*, is a comprehensive and exceedingly useful work. Members of the public have a right of access to this publication.[611]

9. Local Government Information

132. Local Government Official Information and Meetings Act was passed in 1987. Parts 1–6 of the Act make bodies such as city and district councils subject to a regime of openness which mirrors that in the Official Information Act 1982.

10. Local Authorities

133. The local authorities to which the disclosure provisions apply are listed in the first schedule to the Act. They include such bodies as regional councils, community boards, airport authorities, irrigation boards, licensing trusts, and a number of particular local authorities. Council controlled organizations in which the local authority has a controlling interest of 50% or more within the disclosure regime of the 1987 legislation.[612]

'Official information' is any information held by a local authority.[613] However, the term does not include information: contained in library or museum material kept for reference or exhibition purposes; held by the authority as an agent; contained in correspondence between the authority and an Ombudsman relating to an Ombudsman's investigation; or contained in correspondence between the Ombudsman and the Privacy Commissioner relating to an investigation under the Privacy Act 1993.[614] It also covers information to which the authority has access by virtue of a contract.[615] Apart from this, the definition parallels that in the Official Information Act 1982.

The purpose of the 1987 Act and its principle of availability are the same as in the Official Information Act 1982, that is, information held by local authorities is to be made available unless there is good reason for withholding it.[616] Conclusive reasons for withholding exist if disclosure would be likely:[617]

(a) to prejudice the maintenance of the law, including the prevention, investigation and detection of offences, and the right to a fair trial; or
(b) to endanger the safety of any person.

The other reasons (those that may be outweighed by considerations making it desirable in the public interest to make the information available) are contained in

611. See http://www.justice.govt.nz/publications/corporate/directory-of-official-information, accessed 19 Mar. 2015. The current version is dated 2013.
612. Local Government Act 2002, s. 74.
613. Local Government Official Information and Meetings Act 1987, s. 2(1).
614. Local Government Official Information and Meetings Act 1987, s. 2(1).
615. Local Government Official Information and Meetings Act 1987, s. 2(5) and (6).
616. Local Government Official Information and Meetings Act 1987, s. 5.
617. Local Government Official Information and Meetings Act 1987, s. 6.

section 7 of the 1987 Act which provides that information may be withheld if and only if the withholding is necessary to:

(a) protect the privacy of natural persons, including that of deceased natural persons; or
(b) protect information where the making available of the information–
  (i) would disclose a trade secret; or
  (ii) would be likely unreasonably to prejudice the commercial position of the person who supplied or who is the subject of the information; or
(ba) in the case only of an application for a resource consent, or water conservation order, or a requirement for a designation or heritage order, under the Resource Management Act 1991, to avoid serious offence to tikanga Māori, or to avoid the disclosure of the location of waahi tapu; or
(c) protect information which is subject to an obligation of confidence or which any person has been or could be compelled to provide under the authority of any enactment, where the making available of the information
  (i) would be likely to prejudice the supply of similar information, or information from the same source, and it is in the public interest that such information should continue to be supplied; or
  (ii) would be likely otherwise to damage the public interest; or
(d) avoid prejudice to measures protecting the health or safety of members of the public; or
(e) avoid prejudice to measures that prevent or mitigate material loss to members of the public; or
(f) maintain the effective conduct of public affairs through
  (i) the free and frank expression of opinions by or between or to members or officers or employees of any local authority, or any persons to whom section 2(5) of this Act applies,[618] in the course of their duty; or
  (ii) the protection of such members, officers, employees, and persons from improper pressure or harassment; or
(g) maintain legal professional privilege; or
(h) enable any local authority holding the information to carry out, without prejudice or disadvantage, commercial activities; or
(i) enable any local authority holding the information to carry on, without prejudice or disadvantage, negotiations (including commercial and industrial negotiations); or
(j) prevent the disclosure or use of official information for improper gain or improper advantage.

The 'administrative reasons' for refusal are the same as in the Official Information Act 1982.[619]

618. Section 2(50) has actually been repealed.
619. Local Government Official Information and Meetings Act 1987, s. 17. See also ss 17A and 17B added in 2003.

The procedure for making requests, and the obligations of the local authority with respect to the granting and refusal of requests, are the same in all material respects as the obligations of a national organization under the Official Information Act 1982.[620] The Ombudsmen likewise have a duty to review decisions by local authorities when a complaint is made to them.[621] The compendia of case notes of the Ombudsmen contain cases where they have reviewed decisions of local authorities.

If an Ombudsman makes a recommendation to a local authority to release information, the authority must comply with it unless, before the expiry of twenty working days, the local authority decides otherwise by resolution at a meeting and records that decision in writing.[622] Such a decision must be published in the *Gazette* and publicly notified in the district as soon as practicable. The decision must set out the reasons for the decision, the ground in support of those reasons, and any advice on which the decision is based.[623] An application to review this decision may be made to the High Court, but only on the grounds that it was ultra vires or otherwise wrong in law.[624]

11. Information to Which There is a Right of Access

134. Outside the Official Information Act, there is information that the public has a right to see. The government publication, the *Gazette,* contains official information and announcements on a wide variety of topics. Likewise the *Appendix to the Journals of the House of Representatives* contains a very large number of parliamentary papers, that is, reports and other documents tabled in Parliament and published by order of the House of Representatives. They are available in libraries. In addition, many government agencies are proactively publishing a lot of information on their websites. The Government is encouraging more such proactive release, as well as facilitating the lawful re-use of such material by recipients.[625]

Other such information has the important feature that publication of it carries qualified privilege against defamation proceedings. By virtue of the Defamation Act 1992,[626] privilege is accorded to:

> A fair and accurate copy of or extract from any register that is kept in pursuance of any Act and that is open to inspection by the public, or of any other document which is required by the law of New Zealand to be open to inspection to the public.

620. Local Government Official Information and Meetings Act 1987, ss 10–18. The local authority may charge for the supply of information: s. 13(1A).
621. Local Government Official Information and Meetings Act 1987, ss 27–39.
622. Official Information Act 1982, ss 32.
623. Official Information Act 1982, s. 33.
624. Official Information Act 1982, s. 34.
625. 'The New Zealand Government Open Access and Licensing Framework (NZGOAL)': https://www.ict.govt.nz/guidance-and-resources/open-government/new-zealand-government-open-access-and-licensing-nzgoal-framework/, accessed 27 Mar. 2015.
626. Defamation Act 1992, sch. 1, Part 2, cl. 12.

This information includes public records, decisions of tribunals, public registers, information held by local authorities under the Local Government Act 2002, and the Resource Management Act 1991, and information that can be disclosed under the accountability regime under the State-Owned Enterprises 1986.[627]

12. Information with No Right of Public Access

135. Certain rules of law, statutory or part-statutory, forbid the disclosure of certain types of information. These specific rules take precedence over the Official Information Act 1982 as far as they extend. This includes requirements under the New Zealand Security Intelligence Service Act 1969, the Intelligence and Security Committee Act 1996, and the Inspector-General of Intelligence and Security Act 1996.

The Serious Fraud Office Act 1990 provides that every member of the Serious Fraud Office 'shall observe the strictest secrecy' in relation to: information obtained in the exercise of the Director's powers; information derived from or based upon any such information; and 'information relating to the exercise or *possible* exercise of any power conferred by Part 2 of this Act'. Part 2 confers powers of investigation 'where the Director has reasonable grounds to believe that an offence involving serious or complex fraud may have been committed'.[628]

For the most part information in the hands of the police is confidential, and may not be disclosed by them. The police code of conduct provides that every member of the police must observe confidentiality in relation to police business and any information coming into the member's possession by virtue of his or her office. Members may release information only in accordance with applicable legislation and recognized standards, policies and directives. They may not access or use confidential, personal or sensitive information for personal purposes or advantage, or divulge such information to another person outside of official duties or as otherwise required by law. Nor can police access personal information for the purpose of satisfying curiosity. Official and private information can only be released in accordance with applicable legislation and police procedures, and by police authorised to deal with requests for information.[629]

There are other more specific statutory provisions. Under the Misuse of Drugs Amendment Act 1978,[630] the International Terrorism (Emergency Powers) Act 1987,[631] and the Crimes Act 1961,[632] the police are given power under warrant and

627. For more detailed information, see the *Directory of Official Information* (December 2013): www.justice.govt.nz/publications/corporate/directory-of-official-information, accessed 19 Mar. 2015.
628. Serious Fraud Office Act 1990, s. 7. *M v. Television New Zealand Ltd* HC Christchurch CP52/94, 28 Apr. 1994. See also *Johnston v. PriceWaterhouse* [2001] NZAR 9 (HC); and *R v. Aspinall* CA295/06, 19 Sep. 2006.
629. Policing Act 2008, s. 20, *Police Code of Conduct* https://admin.police.govt.nz/ about/code-of-conduct.html, accessed 31 Aug. 2010.
630. Misuse of Drugs Amendment Act 1978, ss 14–19.
631. International Terrorism (Emergency Powers) Act 1987, s. 10.
632. Crimes Act 1961, ss 216B and 312B.

in emergency to intercept private communications. No person who intercepts such a communication, or who acquires knowledge of it as a result of that interception, may disclose the substance or purport of that communication to anyone. Fines may be imposed.[633]

It is an offence to hold any communication with any prisoner in the custody of a police employee that may prejudice the maintenance of the law, the safe custody of the prisoner, the safety of any other person, or the security of any prison, or to attempt to deliver anything to that prisoner, without the permission of the police employee.[634] It is an offence to hold any communication with a prisoner who is inside a prison if that communication may prejudice: the maintenance of the law; the safe custody of the prisoner; the well-being of any victim of an offence committed by that prisoner; the safety of any person, or the security of any prison; or to make any visual recording (whether by photograph, film, videotape or otherwise) or sound recording of a prisoner if the making of such a recording would have the same prejudicial effects, except with authority under the Corrections Act 2004 or the express authority of the prison manager or the Chief Executive.[635] It is also an offence to communicate, or attempt to communicate, with any prisoner in the custody of a security officer without the permission of an officer or constable.[636]

The Corrections Regulations 2005 lay down detailed rules regulating prison visits.[637] In making a decision on a request for an interview with a prisoner, the Chief Executive must take into account the right of the prisoner under the NZBORA 1990 to freedom of expression.[638]

13. Information from Officials Who Should Not Disclose

136. Numerous statutes and regulations provide that people holding specific jobs may not disclose information acquired in the course of those jobs. Examples include officials conducting an inspection under the Securities Act 1978,[639] and employees of the Reserve Bank.[640] A financial institution must not disclose that it has made, or is contemplating making, a suspicious transaction report.[641]

In addition to the requirements of the Privacy Act 1993, and the privacy exception to the Official Information Act 1982, there is sometimes express statutory provision that officers should not disclose such information. For instance, no member of the Ombudsmen's staff may disclose any information acquired in the course of his or her employment.[642] Health agencies (including hospitals, doctors, medical

633. Misuse of Drugs Amendment Act 1978, s. 23; International Terrorism (Emergency Powers) Act 1987, s. 18; Crimes Act 1961, s. 312K.
634. Policing Act 2008, s. 52.
635. Corrections Act 2004, s. 141(1)(e) and (f). Attempts are also offences.
636. Corrections Regulations 2005, reg 88.
637. Corrections Regulations 2005, reg 101. Corrections Act 2004, s. 99(i).
638. *Watson v. Chief Executive of the Department of Corrections* [2015] NZHC 1227.
639. Securities Act 1978, s. 67A.
640. Reserve Bank of New Zealand Act 1989, s. 105.
641. Financial Transactions Reporting Act 1996, s. 20.
642. Ombudsmen Act 1975, s. 21.

schools and other providers of health and disability services) are bound by the Health Information Privacy Code 1994. All employees of the Department of Statistics, and any other departments engaged in the collection and processing of official statistics, are required to subscribe a statutory declaration of secrecy.[643]

Officials who breach these statutes are liable to the penalties prescribed in them. Media and journalists to whom such information was disclosed might also be liable to a penalty in some cases. If they actively elicited the information, they might be guilty of inciting the commission of an offence, or of aiding and abetting its commission. In such a case, they would be a party to the offence.[644]

II. Private Documents with a Right of Access

137. Obviously, there is normally no right of public access to documents of private individuals and organizations; it is entirely at the discretion of the individual or organization whether it will show them to a reporter, or indeed to anyone else. However, there are a small number of exceptions. A building society must supply a copy of its rules to anyone who asks, and a small fee is payable.[645] Under the Companies Act, companies are required to hold certain documents at their offices and produce them.

III. Meetings of Local Authorities

138. Local authorities' meetings are regulated by the Local Government Official Information and Meetings Act 1987, which provides that these meetings must be open to the public. The local authorities to which the Act applies are listed in its schedules. There are two schedules: those local authorities listed in the second schedule are subject to the Official Information Act; those listed in the first are not.[646] As far as the holding of meetings is concerned, however, the same regime applies to both groups.

The bodies concerned are creatures of statute and local in character. The large number of councils and boards that operate on a national level (such as the Producer Boards and the Broadcasting Commission) are not regulated by the Act; their meetings are not open as of right to the press or the public.[647]

---

643. Statistics Act 1975, s. 21.
644. Crimes Act 1961, s. 66.
645. Building Societies Act 1965, s. 20.
646. However, those authorities in the first schedule are subject to the disclosure regime in the Local Government Official Information and Meetings Act 1987 which mirrors that in the Official Information Act 1982.
647. Exceptions are the New Zealand Conservation Authority, the New Zealand Fish and Game Council, and the National Animal Ethics and Welfare Advisory Committees which are in Part 2 of the second schedule.

A. Publicity Provisions

139. The Act lays down the basic rule that 'every meeting of the local authority shall be open to the public'.[648] Bona fide members of the news media are deemed to be members of the public, and they are entitled to attend for the purpose of reporting.[649] The word 'meeting' is broadly defined. However, a meeting at which no resolutions or decisions are made is not a meeting for the purposes of the Act,[650] and if members of a local authority gather informally to discuss matters (e.g., at a 'workshop'), but do not take any decisions, the gathering does not qualify as a meeting and the media are therefore not entitled to be present.[651] The term 'local authority' includes committees and subcommittees of the whole local authority.[652]

Members of the news media may attend 'for the purpose of reporting'.[653] The Act does not expressly allow cameras, but it could be argued that each branch of the media should be allowed to record the proceedings in its own way. Some local authorities make provision in their Standing Orders for filming of their proceedings by television.

Members of the public are entitled, without fee, to inspect within two working days of a meeting all agenda and associated reports that have been circulated to members.[654] The agenda must be available for inspection at the authority's offices and public libraries, and must be accompanied either by the associated reports or an indication of where those reports may be inspected.[655] Members of the public may ask for a copy of any part of the agenda or an associated report; a fee may be charged.[656] If a meeting is an extraordinary meeting, it may not be possible to meet these requirements; the agenda and reports must in such a case be made available as soon as is reasonable.[657]

A matter not explicit in the Act is the extent to which reporters, having inspected the agenda and associated reports before the meeting, can safely publish material in them before the meeting. Since the material is open to the public under the Act, it is difficult to see why it should not be published. However, in so doing reporters must beware of the law of defamation.

---

648. Local Government Official Information and Meetings Act 1987, s. 47. The provision creates a presumption, which is, however, subject to power to exclude (s. 48) and to remove parties in order to maintain order (s. 50): *Bright v. Police* [2009] 3 NZLR 132, [2009] NZAR 324 (CA); aff [2009] NZSC 85 at [22].
649. Local Government Official Information and Meetings Act 1987, s. 49(a).
650. Local Government Official Information and Meetings Act 1987, s. 45(2).
651. However the Ombudsmen have advised that local authorities need to be careful where a 'workshop' has been called to discuss an issue 'not to create a perception when the issue is brought to a meeting for deliberation and discussion that the matter has been predetermined'. The requirements of the 1987 Act cannot be avoided simply by calling what is in reality a meeting by a different name: see the Annual Reports of the Ombudsmen for the years ending 30 Jun. 2002 and 30 Jun. 2003 at A3.
652. Local Government Official Information and Meetings Act 1987, s. 2(1).
653. Local Government Official Information and Meetings Act 1987, s. 49(a).
654. Local Government Official Information and Meetings Act 1987, s. 46A(1).
655. Local Government Official Information and Meetings Act 1987, s. 46A(2).
656. Local Government Official Information and Meetings Act 1987, s. 46A(5).
657. Local Government Official Information and Meetings Act 1987, s. 46A(6).

The chair may exclude particular persons for bad behaviour.[658] The criminal provisions in the Trespass Act 1980 can be used once the right to be at the meeting has been displaced by exercise of the power to exclude. The person must then be warned under section 3(1) of the Trespass Act 1980. If he or she refuses to do so, he or she becomes a trespasser.[659]

A local authority has a much wider power to exclude. In essence, the local authority (which includes a committee or subcommittee) may exclude the public from its meetings on the same grounds on which it may withhold official information from a person requesting it.[660] Likely prejudice to the maintenance of the law and the likely endangering of the safety of any person are conclusive reasons for the public being excluded. In addition, such things as protection of individual privacy, protection of trade secrets and protection of information supplied in confidence are 'good reasons' for exclusion of the public, unless outweighed by other considerations that render it desirable in the public interest to have the information made available. Other reasons are:[661]

- that the public conduct of the meeting would be likely to result in the disclosure of information the public disclosure of which would be contrary to statute or in contempt of court or Parliament;
- that the purpose of that part of the meeting is to consider a recommendation made to the local authority by an Ombudsman relating to the release of official information;
- that the exclusion of the public is necessary to enable the local authority to deliberate on its decision or recommendation in certain types of proceedings (namely, proceedings where a right of appeal lies to a court or tribunal against the authority's decision or where the authority is statutorily required to make a recommendation, and proceedings in relation to an application or objection under the Marine Farming Act 1971).

The public can be excluded only by resolution. The resolution must be put while the meeting is open to the public, and its text must be available to any member of the public who is present; it will form part of the minutes.[662] This procedure is important; it is not enough for the public body merely to 'go into committee'.

No member of the public has a right to minutes of a meeting (or part of a meeting) from which the public was excluded. However, any request to see such minutes is deemed to be a request for official information;[663] this means that the minutes

658. Local Government Official Information and Meetings Act 1987, s. 50.
659. *Bright v. Police* [2009] 3 NZLR 132, [2009] NZAR 324 (CA), aff, [2009] NZSC 85, at [39]–[40], [47]–[48].
660. Local Government Official Information and Meetings Act 1987, s. 48.
661. Local Government Official Information and Meetings Act 1987, s. 48(1)(b), (c) and (d).
662. Local Government Official Information and Meetings Act 1987, s. 48(4). See case C7554 in the *14th Compendium of Case Notes of the Ombudsmen* where the recorded minutes were wrong and the Council acted contrary to law by not making the resolution available to the public.
663. Local Government Official Information and Meetings Act 1987, s. 51(3). Publication of defamatory matter in the minutes or agenda under this process is privileged: s. 52. However, publication by media of such information would not be and the ordinary defences available to media would have to be used.

should be disclosed unless one of the statutory 'good reasons' for not disclosing them exists.

If a local authority does exclude the public, there remains the question of the status of an account of the private proceedings 'leaked' by a member of the authority to the media. The principles of breach of confidence may entitle the local authority to an injunction restraining publication and possibly to other remedies as well.[664] The local authority may well censure or discipline the member guilty of the indiscretion. The report would also clearly not be privileged.

B. Other Local Bodies

140. District Health Boards (DHBs) and the various health advisory committees[665] have a meeting regime very similar to that of local authorities. Meetings of all kinds must be publicly notified.[666] Community trusts were first established in 1988 when the trustee banks were restructured. They hold funds on trust for charitable purposes. The trustees of a community trust must hold a public meeting in the region of the trust no later than 31 October in each year. At the meeting, the trustees must report on the operation of the trust during the preceding financial year, and the financial statements for that year.[667]

IV. Parliament

A. The Power of Parliament to Punish

141. Parliament retains power to punish persons guilty of improper conduct towards it.[668] Not only Members of Parliament are subject to this jurisdiction; members of the public (and this includes the news media) can also be summoned before the House and dealt with. The 'improper conduct' thus punishable by Parliament is often referred to as 'contempt of Parliament'.[669] The term is sometimes used as if it were equivalent to 'breach of privilege', although contempt is in fact wider. The House can punish not only for breach of specific privileges, but also for acts that do not violate a specific privilege but rather interfere with the proper performance of the House's functions. However, it is not incorrect to deal with contempt under the heading of 'privilege', for it is in fact a privilege of the House to punish for contempt. The House may impose a fine of up to NZD 1,000 for contempt.[670]

664. See *Neagle v. Rimmington* [2002] 3 NZLR 826 (HC).
665. Community and public health advisory committees, disability support advisory committees and hospital advisory committees.
666. The meeting provisions are contained in the New Zealand Public Health and Disability Act 2000, sch. 3 (DHBs) and sch. 4 (committees).
667. Community Trusts Act 1999, s. 14.
668. Parliamentary Privilege Act 2014, s. 8.
669. The whole subject is fully discussed in McGee, *Parliamentary Practice in New Zealand* (3d ed., 2005) at Ch. 47.
670. Parliamentary Privilege Act 2014, s. 22.

The courts will not provide relief from a punishment administered by Parliament, unless it has attempted to create a new kind of privilege unrecognized by the law. Once a return is produced to the effect that X has been dealt with for contempt, a court will refuse to inquire further.[671]

The procedure for dealing with offenders in New Zealand is laid down in the Standing Orders of the House of Representatives.[672] If there is a finding of contempt, the House has far-reaching powers. If a news organization is involved, the offending reporter and editor (and indeed anyone else connected with the publication) may be called to account. The House has power to imprison. This power has never been exercised in New Zealand. Statute now provides that the House may impose a fine of up to NZD 1,000 for contempt.[673] Censure and exclusion from the precincts of the House are further possibilities. In one case, a reporter was punished by suspending him from Bellamy's.[674] Nowadays, in New Zealand the normal procedure is for the apology of the offender to be accepted, perhaps with a condition that the apology be published in the news medium concerned.

The Privileges Committee observes the rules of natural justice. Persons appearing before it may be represented by lawyers, and cross-examination of witnesses by such lawyers is also allowed.[675]

B. Reporting Parliament

1. The Right to Report Proceedings of Parliament

142. In New Zealand, Parliament meets in open session, and accurate reports of debates have never been objected to. There is a New Zealand equivalent of Hansard, and the press have always been permitted to report proceedings in the House.

The Parliamentary Privilege Act 2014 provides that the communication of a fair and accurate report of parliamentary proceedings, or a fair and accurate extract or summary of documents communicated under the House's or a committee's authority, or of a document just relating to proceedings in Parliament, and communicated under the House's or a committee's authority or the authority of any statute, are protected by qualified immunity. The immunity is not simply from any defamation claim, as previously, but from any civil and criminal proceedings as long as there is no ill will or bad faith.[676]

---

671. See the discussion by the High Court of Australia in *R v. Richards, ex parte Fitzpatrick & Brown* (1954) 92 CLR 157. The powers of the Courts may now be even more limited by the operation of ss 4 and 7 of the Parliamentary Privilege Act 2014.
672. Standing Orders (2014) ch 8: http://www.parliament.nz/resource/en-nz/00HOHPBReferenceStOrders4/eb7c8b9e4a6c7aa88a47d14dc4100513b2557e60, accessed 11 Mar. 2015.
673. Parliamentary Privilege Act 2014, s. 22.
674. Bellamy's is the New Zealand Parliament's restaurant and bar.
675. See McGee, *Parliamentary Practice in New Zealand* (3d ed., 2005) at 666–667.
676. Parliamentary Privilege Act 2014, s. 20, s. 18, and see Ch. 3.

The Standing Orders make reference to the press gallery.[677] Filming and photography within the parliamentary complex can take place but must have the prior approval of the Speaker for each event.[678] This includes all corridors, foyers, general work areas and offices. There are exceptions, however, such as the Press Gallery in the Chamber.[679]

The House does have the right to exclude 'strangers', that is, members of the public, including media representatives.[680] Any Member of Parliament can move that strangers be ordered to withdraw, and if the motion is carried they must leave. Broadcasting ceases also.[681] Any Member of Parliament who disclosed what had passed at a secret session would be guilty of a breach of privilege, as would a media organization that published the disclosures.

In addition to the right of the House to move that strangers be ordered to withdraw, the Speaker or Serjeant-at-Arms has a discretion to order strangers to withdraw if they interrupt proceedings or otherwise misconduct themselves.[682] The Speaker also controls admissions to the House, and may issue rules setting out who may be admitted to the various areas.[683]

The Standing Orders make no express reference to any power in the House or the Speaker to order that parts of a debate in open session not be reported, but the leading textbooks assume such a power.[684]

2. The Right to Broadcast Parliamentary Proceedings

143. Since 1936, the proceedings of the New Zealand Parliament have been broadcast on radio, during all hours of sitting.[685] At one time cameras were not allowed in Parliament. The Standing Orders now provide that the proceedings of the House 'are available for television coverage', and the Clerk or a provider of official television coverage or any person filming from the gallery, must comply with certain rules.[686]

The content of television coverage is still restricted.[687] For example, cameras must cover the Member speaking until they have finished. Coverage is normally

677. Standing Orders 2014, cl. 42.

678. Part B, *Protocol for interviewing members, filming and photographing in Parliament Buildings*: May 2011, *Filming and Photography in the Parliamentary Complex,* accessed 11 Mar. 2015.

679. Part A, *Protocol for interviewing members, filming and photographing in Parliament Buildings*: May 2011, *Filming and Photography in the Parliamentary Complex,* accessed 11 Mar. 2015. See also Appendix D of Standing Orders 2014, which deals with official filming of the House: http://www.parliament.nz/resource/en-nz/00HOHPBReferenceStOrders4/eb7c8b9e4a6c7aa88a47d14dc4100513b2557e60, accessed 11 Mar. 2014.

680. SO 41.

681. SO 42.

682. SO 43.

683. SO 44.

684. McGee, *Parliamentary Practice in New Zealand* (3d ed., 2005) at 638.

685. SO 46(1).

686. SO 46(2-3) and Part A of Appendix D.

687. See Part A of Appendix D Standing Orders 2014: http://www.parliament.nz/resource/en-nz/00HOHPBReferenceStOrders4/eb7c8b9e4a6c7aa88a47d14dc4100513b2557e60, accessed 11 Mar. 2015. *Rules for filming and conditions for use of official television coverage.*

medium-range head and shoulders. The default shot is on the Speaker. Interjections are not to be covered unless the Member speaking engages with the interjector.

Live coverage is broadcast through Parliament TV.[688] The live footage is made available to broadcasters on a number of conditions.[689] Broadcasts in any medium must comply with any legal obligations, reports using extracts or purporting to be summaries must be fair and accurate, and the coverage must not be used for election campaigns or advertising without permission, for commercial sponsorship or advertising, or for satire, denigration or ridicule. The latter requirements were contentious.[690]

3. Select Committees

144. Normally, proceedings of select committees during the hearing of evidence are open to the public[691] unless the evidence is private or secret. Witnesses are given the opportunity to make written submissions before appearing to give oral evidence.[692] However, some of the evidence to be given to a select committee may, by leave, be heard or received in private.[693] If so, strangers will be required to withdraw, and the evidence heard in private is confidential to the committee until it reports to the House.[694] In exceptional cases, a select committee may declare evidence to be secret. Secret evidence is delivered into the custody of the clerk following the committee's report to the House, and may not be disclosed to anyone unless the House so authorizes.[695]

The rules about reporting select committees are dealt with below.

4. Information Held on Parliamentary Information and Security Systems

145. The Parliamentary Privileges Committee has recently established a number of principles dealing with parliamentary information systems. There is now a presumption that information held on parliamentary information and security systems should not be released. Second, material relating to individual members should only be released where that member specifically agrees to its release.

A third key principle provides that journalists working in the parliamentary precinct should retain complete control over the release of any information that relates to them. Therefore, material relating to a journalist or group of journalists who work in the parliamentary precinct is covered.

---

688. See http://www.parliament.nz/en-nz/about-parliament/see-hear/ptv, accessed 13 Mar. 2015.
689. See SO 46(4), Part B of Appendix D to the Standing Orders 2014.
690. See, for example, 'It's Official: Politicians Just Can't Take a Joke' *New Zealand Herald* (27 Jun. 2007): www.nzherald.co.nz/nz/news/article.cfm?c_id=1&objectid=10448159, accessed 24 Aug. 2010.
691. SO 222 (1).
692. SO 215.
693. SO 218(1).
694. SO 218(2) and 218(3).
695. SO 219.

The final principle provides that information requests that do not relate to an individual member are dealt with by the Speaker of the House of Representatives as the ultimate decision-maker.

In moving that the protocol be adopted by the House, Attorney-General, the Hon Christopher Finlayson stated: 'We must, whether we are members of the executive or members of this House, remember at all times that we have a press gallery in Parliament so that they can keep an eye on us, not so that we can keep an eye on them.'[696]

5. Contempt of Parliament

146. The current Standing Orders of the House of Representatives, which came into force in 2014, provide definitions and examples of contempt of the House. The relevant Standing Orders provide as follows:

409. Contempt of House

The House may treat as a contempt any act or omission which–

(a) obstructs or impedes the House in the performance of its functions, or
(b) obstructs or impedes any member or officer of the House in the discharge of the member's or officer's duty, or
(c) has a tendency, directly or indirectly, to produce such a result.

SO 409(2) provides:

In deciding whether or not to treat any act or omission as a contempt, the House may consider–

(a) the conduct of any person taking part in parliamentary proceedings:
(b) the nature of any action taken against any person on account of that person's actions when taking part in parliamentary proceedings.

Standing Order 410 contains examples of contempt. A variety of types of contempt are most relevant to the media. For example, it is a contempt to publish material reflecting on the House or a Member of Parliament. Moderate criticism has never been prohibited; and there is much more tolerance than was once the case. But criticism that the House finds to be based on inaccurate assumptions may be held contemptuous and subjecting the House to ridicule has on several occasions resulted in a finding of contempt. In New Zealand in 1968, submissions were made to a committee of the House on the question of homosexuality. The submissions mentioned that statistics showed that 5% of men had such tendencies, or 4 out of 80, the number of Members of Parliament in the House. A newspaper reported this statement under the headline 'Statistical Claim is Made that Four MPs in New Zealand are

696. (2014) 700 NZPD 19325 Privilege – Consideration of Report of Privileges Committee, Question of Privilege Regarding Use of Intrusive Powers Within the Parliamentary Precinct.

Probably Homosexual'. This was held to be a contempt. The Committee of Privileges found that this was not an allegation against any particular Member(s), but that it did amount to a reflection against Parliament as a whole.[697]

It is a punishable contempt to cast aspersions on an individual Member of Parliament: to say, for instance, that the Member is using his or her position to make a profit; or that the Member is corrupt; or that, as chairman of a committee, he or she is biased.[698] However, personal attacks on Members do not themselves amount to contempt. It is no bar to a finding of contempt of Parliament that the maker of the statement might also be liable to a defamation action in the courts.[699] In 1998, a newspaper advocating smoking bans suggested in an editorial that one Member of Parliament was under the control of an organization outside the House in the way he voted. On the matter being raised in the House, the newspaper immediately proffered an unqualified apology. The Privileges Committee, to which the matter had been referred, recommended that the apology be accepted.[700]

The Speaker is in a special position. 'Being the embodiment of Parliament, reflections upon [the Speaker's] character or conduct directly attack the very institution of Parliament itself.'[701] Thus, statements attacking the Speaker are more risky than others. In 1985, a newspaper article stated that the appointment of a Member as Speaker had deprived his electorate of a representative voice in Parliament. This was held to be an inaccurate statement that could be construed as a contempt. However, the Privileges Committee decided that the matter was not of such gravity as to warrant a full hearing.[702]

Given the more open atmosphere these days, and the value placed on freedom of expression, proceedings for this kind of contempt will not be common, and will be reserved for serious transgressions.[703]

The Standing Orders lay down rules about select committees. It is permissible to report the proceedings of a select committee, and the evidence heard by it, when it is open to the public. However, beyond that one cannot go. SO 239(1) provides as follows:

> (1) The proceedings of a select committee or a subcommittee other than during the hearing of evidence are not open to the public and remain strictly confidential to the committee until it reports to the House.

SO 240(1) provides:

---

697. (1968) 189 AJHR 239.
698. See (1986) 475 NZPD 5333.
699. (1978) 418 NZPD 1294: Speaker's Ruling.
700. (1998) 570 NZPD 10582.
701. (1975) 400 NZPD 3295.
702. (1985) 464 NZPD 5596.
703. In 2014, the House expressed uncertainty about the application of parliamentary privilege to official social media usage for disseminating information about what Parliament is doing and facilitating wider public participation. A Question of Privilege Regarding Use of Social Media to Report on Parliamentary Proceedings, was referred to the Privileges Committee: (2014) 699 NZPD 18073.

> A report or a draft of the report of a select committee or a subcommittee is strictly confidential to the committee until it reports to the House.

It is a contempt to publish in contravention of these Standing Orders.

There is also a rule about confidentiality of select committee proceedings. However, the following proceedings may be disclosed:

(a) those proceedings that do not relate to any business or decision still before the committee;
(b) those proceedings in respect of matter of process or procedure that do not–
  (i) relate to decisions on matters of process or procedure that are still before the committee, or
  (ii) include any substantive proceedings relating to business before the committee, or
  (iii) reflect, or divulge the contents of, a report or draft report or the committee's potential findings.

(4) A committee making an interim report or a special report to the House may resolve that some or all proceedings relating to the report remain confidential to the committee until it reports finally to the House.[704]

A serious view is taken of the 'leaking' of draft reports. In 2001, a newspaper set out in some detail the findings of the Education and Science Committee on its inquiry into the teaching of reading. At the time of publication, the Committee had not reported to the House. A Member of Parliament acknowledged that she had released the report to the newspaper in breach of the confidentiality rules. The matter was referred to the Privileges Committee. The House accepted the apologies of both the Member and the editor of the newspaper. The newspaper article was couched in conditional and speculative terms rather than directly asserting what was in the draft report but style of reporting made no difference.[705]

If media do publish matter under consideration by a select committee before it has reported, there is precedent for the House to resolve that a letter be sent to the media asking it to explain how it became possessed of the information,[706] and even for it to call the reporters concerned before the Committee of Privileges for questioning on their sources of information.[707] However, in one such case, the reporters refused to answer the question, and the committee decided not to press the point.[708]

There is nothing to stop the media discussing a matter under consideration by a select committee, and even speculating on the outcome. However if that speculation is based on information that could only have come from an illegitimate leak, there could be difficulty.[709]

---

704. SO 239(3) and (4).
705. (2001) 597 NZPD 13842.
706. AJHR (1903) 172.
707. (1977) 412 NZPD 1588 and 1878.
708. (1977) 412 NZPD 1588 and 1878. See also (1989) 500 NZPD 12179, where the Privileges Committee decided not to call the journalists concerned because of the likelihood that they would not be prepared to disclose their sources.
709. See (1977) 412 NZPD 1588 and 1878.

The Standing Orders provide that a select committee may make a written submission to it available to the public at any time after receiving it.[710] However, the expectation is that a select committee controls the distribution of evidence given to it, and a witness who distributes a submission before it is presented to the select committee may not be popular.[711]

Inaccurate reports may be dealt with as a contempt; this includes not only false reports but also reports that are so incomplete as to be misleading. Contentious opinion does not qualify as a false account. There must be factual error.[712]

It is and always has been a contempt to refuse to answer a question, or to provide information, required by the House or a committee. In 1992, a courier firm that refused to answer questions put to it by a select committee about its clients was held in contempt, and was effectively banned from doing business within the precincts of Parliament.[713] It is also a contempt to mislead a committee.[714]

Since the list of examples in SO 410 is not exhaustive, other things may from time to time be held to be contempts. Premature disclosure of a matter on Parliament's agenda may well be one of these. It has been said, for example, that it is a breach of privilege to publish a question that is going to be asked of a Minister in the House before it actually is asked.[715] Disclosure of the contents of a bill before it is introduced into the House would be another example.

§2. Court Hearings and Documents

I. The Right to Report in the Principal Courts

A. *Chambers Applications*

147. A hearing in chambers means a hearing that takes place in circumstances in which the general public is not admitted, except with the leave of the judge, and includes any conference that is held.[716] By definition, matters heard in chambers are not heard in open court, and the public have no right of admittance.[717] They may be held by telephone or video link.[718] However, to say that a case is heard in chambers does not necessarily mean that it is heard in the judge's private rooms. At common law, the position is that information about what occurs in chambers can be made available to the public on request, and any judgment or order made in chambers should be made available. However, while a judge is sitting in Chambers, no filming may take place.[719] By virtue of the District Court and High Court Rules it is

710. SO 217(1).
711. See the *Review of Standing Orders I. 18B* (2003) at 39.
712. (2000) 589 NZPD 7497.
713. (1992) 528 NZPD 10628.
714. (2002) 598 NZPD 14744.
715. (1966) 346 NZPD 990 and 1000.
716. High Court Rules, r. 1.3, Interpretation, hearing in chambers.
717. *R v. Bow County Court* [1999] 2 All ER 582 (QB).
718. High Court Rules, r. 7.34(2).
719. In-Court Media Coverage Guidelines (2012), Standard Conditions for Film at [4].

now clear in relation to civil cases that particulars of the hearing or the decision or both (including the reasons for the decision) may be published, unless the judge or Registrar otherwise directs.[720]

B. Trials

148. Hearings of both civil actions and criminal prosecutions must take place in public.[721] The Criminal Procedure Act 2011 provides that every criminal hearing is open to the public, subject to special powers to clear the court, and mandated clearance where crimes of a sexual nature are involved.[722] The rule has two aspects. In the first place, the hearing must take place in open court, and members of the public (including reporters)[723] are entitled as of right to be present. The NZBORA 1990 reaffirms this principle; it provides that a person charged with an offence has a right to 'a fair and public hearing by an independent and impartial court'.[724] In the second place, the media have at common law a right to report court proceedings (although inroads have been made by statute in modern New Zealand). This right can be seen as part of the right of freedom of expression, now contained in section 14 of the NZBORA 1990. It has been placed in that setting in a number of cases,[725] and has been described as a right of the public, rather than just one of the accused or any group of individuals.[726]

However, the law has modified its insistence on publicity. Some exceptions have grown up at common law, but the main inroads have been by statute. The statutory intervention has occurred principally in relation to family and criminal proceedings; by and large civil hearings are still subject to the common law.

C. Cameras in the Courts

149. Until quite recently, it was not permitted to televise court proceedings. However, New Zealand now has *The In-court media coverage guidelines 2012*.[727]

720. District Courts Rules 2009, r. 3.23; High Court Rules, r. 7.35. See *Sagapolu v. Commonwealth Securities Ltd* (2002) 16 PRNZ 191 (HC), and *M v. Television New Zealand Ltd* HC Christchurch CP52/94, 28 Apr. 1994.
721. The leading authority is *Scott v. Scott* [1913] AC 417 (HL). See also *M v. R* [2013] NZCA 113, [23].
722. Criminal Procedure Act 2011, s. 196. See *R v. ABC* [2014] NZHC 8, [8].
723. 'I find it difficult to imagine a case which can be said to be held publicly if the press have been actively excluded': *R v. Denbigh Justices* [1974] QB 759 at 765 per Lord Widgery CJ.
724. New Zealand Bill of Rights Act 1990, s. 25(a).
725. For example: *Television New Zealand Ltd v. R* [1996] 3 NZLR 393 (CA).
726. *Police v. O'Connor* [1992] 1 NZLR 87 (HC) at 98 per Thomas J.
727. The rules may be obtained from a High Court office. They are also available on the Ministry of Justice website: https://www.courtsofnz.govt.nz/business/media-centre/media-centre/In-Court-Media-Coverage-Guidelines-2012-2.pdf, to be replaced by a new draft in 2015: http://www.courtsofnz.govt.nz/In-Court-Media-Review/In-Court-Media-Review/In-Court-Media-Coverage-Guidelines-2015-180315.pdf, accessed 2 Jun. 2015, and Protocol for application of the Guidelines to the District Court Summary jurisdiction: http://courtsofnz.govt.nz/business/media-centre/media-centre/In-Court-Media-Coverage-Summary-Jurisdiction.pdf. See also Supreme Court

These are not rules or regulations: they are advisory to the judges and create no rights or expectations.

The *Guidelines* apply expressly only to the Court of Appeal, High Court and District court. They provide that witnesses (except the accused and official witnesses) in criminal cases can apply to have their identity protected and are entitled to this as of right. The accused and official witnesses in criminal trials and all witnesses in civil trials can apply not to be filmed, photographed or recorded, and the court has discretion in these cases. In deciding, the court takes into account the following:

- need for a fair trial;
- the desirability of open justice;
- the principle that the media have an important role in the reporting of trials as the eyes and ears of the public;
- the importance of fair and balanced reporting of trials;
- court obligations to the victims of offences;
- the interests and reasonable concerns and perceptions of victims and witnesses;
- whether covering the trial is likely to affect adversely the quality of the evidence to be given by the witness;
- whether the presence of a video camera, a photographer or a sound recorder is likely to lead to the witness not turning up to give evidence;
- whether being filmed, photographed or recorded may cause undue stress or anxiety to the witness;
- whether being filmed, photographed or recorded may lead to intimidation or harassment of the witness;
- whether the witness's privacy interests outweigh the public interest in publishing or broadcasting that witness's evidence, given the likely significance of the evidence;
- any other relevant matters.

The accused may be filmed when giving evidence (subject to any protection, the judge may grant under the witness protection provisions). He or she may also be filmed in the dock for the first fifteen minutes of a day, except when a verdict is being taken or a sentencing is underway. The judge may grant permission to film the accused during sentencing. Film may be taken of the accused at other times only with the accused's consent in writing through his or her lawyer, and if the judge does not prohibit it. There is to be no visual coverage of members of the jury or of the public who are in attendance. Counsel's papers must not be filmed, and exhibits must not be filmed without the judge's permission. No film may be taken in the absence of the judge. A judge can impose any further conditions he or she thinks appropriate.

Only one camera may be situated in the courtroom, regardless of how many people are given authority to film. In the event there is a dispute between those

---

Media Guidelines (2004) http://courtsofnz.govt.nz/business/media-centre/media-centre/Supreme-Court.pdf, and Ministry of Justice *Media Guide for Reporting the Courts and Tribunals* (ed 3.1, 2013) http://www.justice.govt.nz/publications/global-publications/m/media-guide-for-reporting-the-courts-and-tribunals-edition-3.1 . Some Coroner's Courts have adopted similar guidelines.

authorized to film as to whose camera will be situated in the courtroom, the judge rules. The Guidelines take account of tweeting and other electronic forms of communication.[728] Information communicated electronically generally must not be published until at least ten minutes have elapsed and electronic communication must be as unobtrusive as possible.

Film taken must not be used while the trial continues, other than in the programme or website nominated in the application form. Broadcast must be delayed for at least ten minutes, unless it is of an appeal, a judge's summing up, a jury's verdict or a sentencing, when it can be live. Film must be used having regard to the importance of fair and balanced reporting of trials and may not be used out of context.

There are virtually identical guidelines regulating still photography and radio coverage. In fact, all matters are at the discretion of the judge. If the guidelines or any conditions imposed are breached, the judge can terminate the coverage.[729] The Courts also take into account behaviour of media outside the court and have somewhat questionably restricted permission to film inside the court if media harass participants outside the courtroom.[730]

The Supreme Court has its own guidelines.[731] All applications to televise or otherwise record proceedings are deemed to be approved unless a party indicates, within three days of being advised by the Registrar of the application, that they object. The Registrar must immediately communicate any objection to the news media applicant and to all other parties to the proceedings, who have three days to respond to the objections, after which the court or a judge determines the application. If an application is made and there is insufficient time for parties to be given notice or respond, or to enable the court properly to consider the application, the Registrar must refer the matter to a judge for decision. The physical arrangements for any televising or recording of proceedings are determined by the Registrar after appropriate consultation.

The Guidelines have been reviewed recently, and draft new Guidelines have been issued.[732] The changes made are not major. The differences in the new rules require that all media coverage of courtroom proceedings must now provide accurate, as well as fair and balanced reporting, and must not be used out of context. Applications will have to be filed with the Registrar of the court at least five working days before the trial is due to start (instead of ten), except in relation to a first appearance in a criminal matter. Prior to filing, the application will now have to be served on counsel for the parties and any unrepresented party, and counsel and unrepresented

728. See the problems arising from new technology apparent in *R v. Bain* HC Christchurch CRI-1994-012-217294, 13 Nov. 2008.

729. *R v. Banks* [2014] NZHC 1155.

730. *R v. Petricevic, Roest, Urwin, Steigrad and Davidson*, HC, Auckland, CRI-2008-004-029179, 13 Jul. 2011 (Minute).

731. Supreme Court Media Guidelines (2004) http://courtsofnz.govt.nz/business/media-centre/media-centre/Supreme-Court.pdf, accessed 20 May 2014.

732. See http://www.courtsofnz.govt.nz/In-Court-Media-Review/In-Court-Media-Review/In-Court-Media-Coverage-Guidelines-2015-180315.pdf, accessed 3 Jul. 2015; http://www.courtsofnz.govt.nz/In-Court-Media-Review/In-Court-Media-Coverage_-_consultation-paper_.pdf, accessed 20 May 2014.

parties should be asked by the appropriate member of the Registry to provide electronic addresses for communication at the outset of their involvement in criminal or civil proceedings. Parties receiving the application will have three working days to respond rather than two. Complainants in sexual cases will be notified about the application but will have less influence on the outcome than in the past. There will be a presumption that no one under 18 can be filmed, photographed or recorded; however, the judge can permit this but must have regard to the effect of publicity and stress on the child and their welfare. The draft rules now also specify that authority to cover a trial may be revoked if witnesses and parties are being subjected to unreasonable media pressure outside the courtroom.

Significantly, the draft 2015 rules provide as part of the standard conditions for film, that filming of any party, witness, counsel or the judge must not involve a close-up showing less than the head and shoulders of the person filmed, and must not focus on any particular feature of the person being filmed such as fingers, hands, mouth or eyes. Further, no filming can take place if the camera does not have an operator, and the camera should be switched off at all such times.[733] Finally, concern for the observance of formality is expressed in the requirement that media applicants and their representatives must at all times conduct themselves in court with courtesy and decorum.

II. Statutory Exceptions to the Publicity Principle

150. The legislature has passed a number of statutes restricting publicity in relation to certain types of proceeding and has recently reformed the relevant procedure for criminal trials.[734] Some of the provisions empower the judge to clear the court. Others empower the judge to prohibit reports of proceedings or the identities of parties. Generally, statutory provisions in the main protect either (a) the parties' sensibilities or (b) the public interest, or both. In each case, refusal to comply with the law is an offence carrying a fine or imprisonment. The statutory provisions are classified as follows.

A. *Criminal Trials*

151. In criminal trials, the publicity principle is strong: there must be compelling reasons to make exceptions.[735] However, in a criminal trial, there may be interests, whether of the public at large or of the individuals concerned, that prevail over and outweigh the need for publicity.[736]

---

733. Inclusion of these new conditions was prompted by the case *R v. Banks* [2014] NZHC 1155. The requirement about close-ups is standard for photography as well.

734. See Law Commission *Suppressing Names and Evidence* (NZLC IP13, 2008) and (NZLC R109, 2009) and the Criminal Procedure Act 2013, Part 5, subpart 3, Public access and restrictions on reporting. The principles have essentially remained the same and therefore previous case law is still relevant.

735. *Television New Zealand Ltd v. R* [1996] 3 NZLR 393 (CA) at 395 per Keith J.

736. See especially, *R v. B* [2008] NZCA 130, [2009] 1 NZLR 293 at [3].

1. Right to Clear Court

152. In any proceedings in respect of an offence, any court exercising criminal jurisdiction may order that all or any persons leave the court for the whole or part of the proceedings if it is satisfied the order is necessary to avoid:

undue disruption to the conduct of the proceedings, prejudicing the security or defence of New Zealand, a real risk of prejudice to a fair trial, endangering the safety of any person, or prejudicing the maintenance of the law, including the prevention, investigation and detection of offences; and a suppression order is not sufficient to avoid that risk.[737]

Certain persons are entitled to remain in court despite an exclusion order. They are the judge and jury, the prosecutor, the defendant, any lawyer engaged in the proceedings, any officer of the court and the police employee in charge of the case.[738] No media may be required to leave the court unless the interests of security or defence so require.[739] Media are members of the media who are subject to a code of ethics and the complaints procedure of the BSA or the Press Council, or such other persons reporting on the proceedings as permitted by the court.[740]

Notwithstanding that such an exclusion order is made, the announcement of the court's verdict or decision and the passing of sentence must take place in public. However, in exceptional circumstances, the court may decline to state in public the facts or reasons for its decision or the considerations it has taken into account in reaching it.[741]

The court must be cleared when a complainant gives evidence of a sexual nature, but media, as defined above, are one of the parties entitled to remain.[742]

2. Right to Prohibit Publication[743]

153. Although reporters are normally entitled to remain in court, there is a wide power in the court to forbid them to report the whole or any part of: (i) the evidence adduced, or (ii) the submissions made.[744] An order can be made if the court is satisfied publication would be likely to cause undue hardship to any victim of the offence, create a real risk of prejudice to a fair trial, endanger the safety of any person, lead to the identification of a person whose name is suppressed by order or

737. Criminal Procedure Act 2011, s. 197(2). See *R v. ABC (Redacted)* [2014] NZHC8, [8].

738. Criminal Procedure Act 2011, s. 197(1).

739. Criminal Procedure Act 2011, s. 198(1).

740. Criminal Procedure Act 2011, s. 198(2). See *Capital and Merchant Finance Ltd (In Receivership and Liquidation) v. Stace Hammond* [2013] NZHC 2121, [8], where journalists of *Fairfax Media* were said to fit the description.

741. Criminal Procedure Act 2011, s. 197(3).

742. Criminal Procedure Act 2011, s. 199.

743. 'Publication' covers any report or account of the relevant proceedings: Criminal Procedure Act 2011, s. 195. This is not limited to media reports and accounts and can apply to bloggers and other new media: *Slater v. Police [*2011] Unreported, HC Auckland, CRI-2010-404-000379, 10 May 2011, [67]–[71].

744. In *George v. Police* HC Invercargill AP12/90, 23 Feb. 1990, an order was made in the High Court suppressing certain remarks by the District Court Judge who had heard the case.

by law, prejudice the maintenance of the law, including the prevention, investigation, and detection of offences, or prejudice the security or defence of New Zealand.[745]

However, as under the previous law, and in particular in the light of section 14 of the NZBORA 1990, the reasons for such orders should be compelling, and the orders must be no wider than necessary. In *R v. Vaki*,[746] Heath J refused to suppress the evidence of an accomplice witness. Although the witness said he was afraid for his personal safety, the Judge found that there was an absence of specific evidence to justify this belief.

A court must give reasons for making, varying or revoking a suppression order, but if satisfied that exceptional circumstances exist, it may decline to state in public all or any of the facts, reasons or other considerations that it has taken into account in reaching its decision.[747]

A non-publication order may be made for a limited period or permanently. In the former case, it may be renewed.[748] An order can be reviewed by the court at any time.[749] The legislation now provides that members of the media who are subject to a code of ethics and the complaints procedure of the BSA or the Press Council, or such other persons reporting on the proceedings as permitted by the court, can bring an application for review to the court.[750] Third parties also have a right at common law to informally seek amendment or discharge, which operates in tandem with the media's right to seek review.[751]

The Criminal Procedure Act 2011 provides for much greater penalties for breach of suppression. There are two types of offences for breach – these are based on a distinction between intentional and unintentional breach. Therefore, if an order is breached knowingly or recklessly, the penalty is imprisonment of up to six months for an individual and a fine of up to NZD 100,000 for a body corporate. Unintentional breach attracts a penalty of a fine up to NZD 25,000 for an individual and up to NZD 50,000 for a body corporate.[752] Unintentional breach cannot apply to third-party hosts of websites or other electronic retrieval systems, unless the person has placed the specific information there themselves.[753]

3. Case Management Memorandums and Sentencing Indications

154. The Criminal Procedure Act 2011 put in place a case management process that now requires the prosecution and defence to enter into discussions outside the courtroom to determine whether the matter should proceed to trial and how this might best and most efficiently be done.[754] The discussions do not take place in open

745. Criminal Procedure Act 2011, s. 205.
746. *R v. Vaki* [2003] NZAR 605 (HC).
747. Criminal Procedure Act 2011, s. 207.
748. Criminal Procedure Act 2011, s. 208.
749. Criminal Procedure Act 2011, s. 208(3).
750. Criminal Procedure Act 2011, s. 210. See *Siemer v. Solicitor-General* [2013] 3 NZLR 441, [187].
751. See *Siemer v. Solicitor-General* [2013] 3 NZLR 441, [183].
752. Criminal Procedure Act 2011, s. 211.
753. Criminal Procedure Act 2011, s. 211 (3).
754. Criminal Procedure Act 2011, s. 55.

court, but the memorandum should come to the case review hearing and will be able to be reported in the usual way, unless some restriction is imposed.

A defendant may request before the trial that the judge give a sentencing indication,[755] and in order to do so, the court must be supplied with the facts, the detail of any previous convictions and relevant impact statements from victims. Prosecutor and defendant may be heard on the matter. Sentencing indications must be made in open court and become part of the court record.[756] However, if the matter proceeds to trial in spite of a sentencing indication being given, the fact that a request was made for the indication is not admissible in the proceedings.[757] This means nothing related to the sentencing request will be able to be reported until after the trial and any appeal period has expired.

4. Name Suppression

155. A number of statutory provisions prohibit the publication of the names of certain persons involved in criminal proceedings. The prohibitions are as follows.

a. Automatic Suppression

156. It is an offence to publish the names of certain persons, in a report of court proceedings. No direction need be given by the court; the names are automatically suppressed. The first category is child complainants and witnesses who are under the age of 18 years.[758] The court must make an order allowing publication if the complainant is over 18 and has applied to the court, the court is satisfied the complainant fully understands the effect of doing so, and no separate discretionary order has been made suppressing the defendant's identity. Nothing in the provision prevents publication of the name of the defendant or the nature of the charge.

Second, there is automatic suppression of the identity of the defendant in specified sexual cases.[759] No one may publish the name, address, or occupation of a person accused or convicted of the offences of incest or sexual conduct with a dependent family member. The provision states specifically that the purpose of the automatic suppression is to protect the complainant.[760] This statutory explanation emphasizes that the suppression is not imposed to protect the defendant.[761] The court must make an order allowing publication if the complainant is over 18 and has requested it and the court is satisfied the complainant fully understands the effect of doing so and no separate discretionary order has been made suppressing the defendant's identity.[762]

755. Criminal Procedure Act 2011, s. 61.
756. Criminal Procedure Act 2011, s. 62. See *R v. s.* [2014] NZHC 944.
757. Criminal Procedure Act 2011, s. 65.
758. Criminal Procedure Act 2011, s. 204. The inclusion of child complainants is new.
759. Criminal Procedure Act 2011, s. 201.
760. Criminal Procedure Act 2011, s. 201(2).
761. *Police v. Slater* [2011] DCR 6, *Slater v. Police* [2011] Unreported, HCt Auckland, CRI-2010-404-000379, 10 May 2011.
762. Criminal Procedure Act 2011, s. 201.

There is similar provision for automatic suppression of the identity of the complainant in specified sexual cases,[763] and for the court to allow publication under the same conditions.

The fourth person whose name is automatically suppressed is a person in respect of whom an application has been made for an order to authorize the taking of a blood or DNA sample unless (in the case of an adult) the judge permits publication or the person has been charged with the relevant offence.[764]

Such suppressions are truly automatic, and apply unless the judge expressly makes an order permitting publication. If an automatic suppression is in place, it prohibits publication not just of the person's name, but also of any particulars 'likely to lead' to the person's identification.[765] 'Likely to lead' signifies an appreciable risk that publication will have that effect.[766] In one case, police charged a blogger for the first time with breach of a number of suppression orders.[767] Some of the charges were based on the posting of pictorial clues and binary code on the blogger's website which would allow the identification of a variety of people. The binary information and the pictogram were capable of being 'particulars'. An aggregation of information could lead to the identification of the person by a process of elimination – this was like interpreting a particular code or solving a puzzle.[768]

It is permissible to publish the name or particulars of a person who has escaped from custody or failed to attend any court, if the police have requested publication for the purpose of facilitating recapture or arrest.[769]

In cases of serious crimes where an undercover police officer gives evidence, the Commissioner of Police may file a certificate in the court, in which case the true name and address of the witness will not be given in court.[770]

Section 13A of the New Zealand Security Intelligence Service Act 1969 provides that it is an offence to publish the fact that any person is a member of the SIS. Thus, if an SIS member gives evidence in a trial, that person's identity and his or her membership of the service must not be linked.

b. Discretionary Suppression

157. The Evidence Act 2006 re-enacted substantially provisions allowing witnesses, in exceptional cases, to be granted total anonymity, even from the accused.[771] If the court makes such an order, no one may publish the name of the

763. Criminal Procedure Act 2011, s. 203. The crimes are the serious sexual offences in 128–142A or 144A of the Crimes Act 1961. This does not apply where the victim has been killed during the alleged offending: *R v. McDonald* Unreported, HCt Christchurch, CRI-2014-009-2921, 18 Mar. 2015 (Declaration).
764. Criminal Investigations (Bodily Samples) Act 1995, ss 14 and 19.
765. Criminal Procedure Act 2011, s. 194.
766. *R v. W* [1998] 1 NZLR 35 (CA) at 40 per Richardson P.
767. *Police v. Slater* [2011] DCR 6, *Slater v. Police* [2011] Unreported, HCt Auckland, CRI-2010-404-000379, 10 May 2011 (decided under the old law).
768. *Police v. Slater* [2011] DCR 6, [139].
769. Criminal Procedure Act 2011, s. 209.
770. Criminal Procedure Act 2011, s. 209(1).
771. Evidence Act 2006, ss 110–119.

witness or any particulars likely to lead to identification. The penalties for contravening such an order are much heavier than for other types of suppression order; a deliberate breach is punishable by imprisonment for up to seven years, and a non-deliberate breach by a fine that in the case of an individual, carries a maximum of NZD 2,000 and in the case of a body corporate NZD 10,000. Nothing, moreover, is to affect the power of the court to impose penalties for contempt.[772]

The Criminal Procedure Act 2011 provides that a court may make an order forbidding publication of the name, address or occupation of any person who is called as a witness, or is a victim of the offence, or is connected with the proceedings, or with the person accused of, convicted of, or acquitted of the offence.[773] A victim is a person against whom an offence is committed by another person, and a person who suffers physical injury, or loss of, or damage to, property due to an offence committed by someone else.[774] The grounds on which the court must be satisfied to make such an order, and the nature of the discretion, are the same as for discretionary name suppression.[775]

The most important statutory provision about suppression of name is now section 200 of the Criminal Procedure Act 2011, which gives the court a discretionary power to suppress publication of the names of persons involved in proceedings in respect of offences. The main provisions of the section are:

(1) A court may make an order forbidding publication of the name, address, or occupation of a person who is charged with, or convicted or acquitted of, an offence.
(2) The court may make an order under subsection (1) only if the court is satisfied that publication would be likely to–
  (a) cause extreme hardship to the person charged with, or convicted of, or acquitted of the offence, or any person connected with that person; or
  (b) cast suspicion on another person that may cause undue hardship to that person; or
  (c) cause undue hardship to any victim of the offence; or
  (d) create a real risk of prejudice to a fair trial; or
  (e) endanger the safety of any person; or
  (f) lead to the identification of another person whose name is suppressed by order or by law; or
  (g) prejudice the maintenance of the law, including the prevention, investigation, and detection of offences; or
  (h) prejudice the security or defence of New Zealand
(3) The fact that a defendant is well known does not, of itself, mean that publication of his or her name will result in extreme hardship for the purposes of subsection (2)(a).

772. Evidence Act 2006, s. 119. These anonymity orders should be sparingly made and the statute requires the judge to have regard to the principle that witness anonymity orders are justified only in exceptional circumstances. *Pahau v. District Court at New Plymouth* HC New Plymouth CIV-2009-443-285, 3 Aug. 2009.

773. Criminal Procedure Act 2011, s. 202.

774. Criminal Procedure Act 2011, s. 5, and Victims Rights Act 2002, s. 4.

775. Criminal Procedure Act 2011, s. 202(2).

(4) Despite subsection (2), when a person who is charged with an offence first appears before the court the court may make an interim order under subsection (1) if that person advances an arguable case that one of the grounds in subsection (2) applies.
(5) An interim order made in accordance with subsection (4) expires at the person's next court appearance, and may only be renewed if the court is satisfied that one of the grounds in subsection (2) applies.
(6) When determining whether to make an order or further order under subsection (1) that is to have effect permanently, a court must take into account any views of a victim of the offence conveyed in accordance with section 28 of the Victims' Rights Act 2002.

The section does not apply to civil proceedings; any power to suppress names in civil proceedings derives from the inherent jurisdiction of the court.

The court has a discretion to order suppression. However, the provision contains specific grounds to be used by the court before making an order.[776] Nevertheless, the starting point will still be the principle of openness, and the onus is on the person requesting suppression to make out a clear case.[777] Therefore, in some cases, suppression will not be ordered even though one of the grounds has been made out. The court must additionally answer a wider question of proportionality, which means addressing the public interest generally in open reporting and in terms of the specific facts of the case.[778]

The new provisions make it easier to obtain interim name suppression orders on first appearance and somewhat harder thereafter.[779] The court must be satisfied that publication of a name is likely to result in one or more of the outcomes set out in the statutory list before it can make a suppression order. It has been held in relation to the similar provision allowing name suppression for witnesses, victims and connected persons[780] that 'likely' means a real risk that cannot be discounted as remote or fanciful.[781]

5. Power of Registrars

158. A Registrar may now make an interim order on the first appearance of the defendant if adjourning the proceedings and if both parties agree. Such orders expire after twenty-eight days and the Registrar can only exercise the power once for each charge. Registrars can also renew orders until the defendant's next court appearance.[782] The power to make an order is discretionary and, as for judges, a Registrar is required to turn his or her mind to the required balancing exercise, but because

776. Law Commission *Suppressing Names and Evidence* (NZLC R109, 2009), R 5 and Ch. 3.
777. *Robertson v. New Zealand Police* [2015] NZCA 7.
778. *R v. Wilson* [2014] NZHC 32, [27]–[28].
779. See Criminal Procedure Act 2011, s. 200(4) and (5).
780. Criminal Procedure Act 2011, s. 202.
781. *Beacon Media Group v. Waititi* [2014] NZHC 281, [17] and [21].
782. Criminal Procedure Act 2011, s. 206.

the provision is intended to make it easier to obtain interim injunctions, is not likely to require a great deal of information in order to be satisfied of the need for suppression.[783]

6. Defences

159. Few excuses will be accepted for breach of a suppression order. It has, for instance, been held that ignorance of the existence of a suppression order (e.g., because the reporter has come into court late) is no defence to someone who publishes a name in contravention of it.[784] Nor has accident been accepted as a defence. In one case, a television channel was fined when it inadvertently allowed a suppressed name to be heard during the broadcast of a recorded telephone conversation.[785] However, such circumstances will be relevant to the severity of the penalty imposed.[786]

Nevertheless, breach of a suppression order is an offence of strict, but not absolute, liability. This means that the prosecution can establish prima facie liability by proving that there was publication of the suppressed name. However, the media organization will have a defence if it can establish on the balance of probabilities that it took all reasonable care that a reasonable person would take in the circumstances.[787] Before the defence is made out, due diligence must be proved; ignorance because of carelessness or failure to check will not be enough. In *Solicitor-General v. Fairfax and Pankhurst*,[788] the High Court concluded there was reckless failure to ascertain the correct position as to orders made in several bail hearings which both the editor and the publisher were aware. Journalists from *Fairfax* had been at a number of the hearings, and the orders were clear as to their nature and scope. They had been in place for several weeks before publication.

Where a genuine mistake has occurred, a timely apology and explanation to the court may avoid punishment for breach. In 2012, the *Herald* accidentally breached an order in a story about an attempted murder. After the editor and journalist

---

783. Criminal Procedure Act 2011, s. 200(4).
784. *Police v. Thames Star Co Ltd* (1965) 11 MCD 343.
785. *Police v. Television New Zealand Ltd, The Press* (23 Sep. 1994). See also *The Press*, 3 Feb. 1995. *The Press* itself was in a similar situation when a suppressed name was revealed in a letter to the editors.
786. In one case (unreported), where a reporter had missed the suppression order when he left the court for ten minutes after the completion of the evidence, the newspaper was not fined but was ordered to pay NZD 50 costs.
787. *Karam v. Solicitor-General* HC Auckland AP50/98, 20 Aug. 1999. See also: *Police v. Television New Zealand Ltd* [1990] DCR 504; *Police v. News Media Auckland Ltd* [1998] DCR 134; *Bailey v. Hinch* [1989] VR 78 (SC). The Law Commission recommended that the offence remain one of strict liability: Law Commission *Suppressing Names and Evidence* (NZLC R109, 2009) at R 30, 71.
788. *Solicitor-General v. Fairfax and Pankhurst* HC Wellington CIV-2008-485-70, 10 Oct. 2008 (redacted version).

appeared before the High Court to explain the mistake, and an apology was made to the victim's family, the Crown decided not to proceed further.[789]

7. Breach, Evasion and Attempted Evasion

160. Breaches of suppression orders are now punished according to presence of knowledge or lack of intention. If an order is breached knowingly or recklessly, the penalty is imprisonment of up to six months for an individual and a fine of up to NZD 100,000 for a body corporate. Unintentional breach attracts a penalty of a fine up to NZD 25,000 for an individual and up to NZD 50,000 for a body corporate.[790] Intentional breach on social media is beginning to be made an example of, with a number of recent prominent cases.[791] In 2013, a Christchurch man was sentenced to two months' community detention with a curfew and ordered to complete 140 hours of community service for breaching a suppression order. He had filmed two men accused of assaulting a well-known cricketer outside court and posted the footage on YouTube.[792]

Once an order is made, it is not only publication of the name that is prohibited but also any evasion or attempted evasion of the order. The Act provides simply that 'name' also includes any particulars likely to lead to the person's identification.[793] In theory, this could cover breach by jigsaw publication, although difficulties of attribution and proof make this unlikely. 'Any particulars' was held in one case under the previous law to cover the use of binary and phonetic code in a pictogram on a blog, and this would also be the case under the new law.[794]

8. Effect of Parliamentary Privilege

161. On occasion, Members of Parliament have openly stated in the House the names of persons whose names have been suppressed by a court. There is no doubt that those Members are protected from legal action by the absolute privilege of Parliament. However, it was unclear whether media's qualified privilege to report Parliament had any application outside the law of defamation.[795] Part 3 of the Parliamentary Privilege Act 2014 now provides a process whereby a person can

789. See 'No punishment for Herald's name suppression breach', *NBR*, 27 Nov. 2012, nbr.co.nz/article/herald-gun-over-suppression-breach-ca-p-132987, accessed 26 May 2014.

790. Criminal Procedure Act 2011, s. 211.

791. See e.g.: 'Judge warns on name breach', *Timaru Herald* 9 Oct. 2013, http://i.stuff.co.nz/timaru-herald/news/9259909/Judge-warns-on-name-breach, accessed 23 May 2014.

792. See 'Ryder Assault Case: Man Sentenced Over Suppression Breach', *ONE News*, 10 Jul. 2013, http://tvnz.co.nz/national-news/ryder-assault-case-man-sentenced-over-suppression-breach-5504598, accessed 23 May 2014.

793. Criminal Procedure Act 2011, s. 194.

794. *Slater v. Police* [2011] DCR 6 [129]–[136]. *Slater v. Police* Unreported, HCt, Auckland, CRI-2010-404-000379, [138]–[140].

795. See, however, the dictum of Lord Denning in *Attorney-General v. Times Newspapers Ltd* [1973] QB 710 (CA) at 741: 'Whatever comments are made in Parliament, they can be repeated in the newspapers without any fear of an action for libel or proceedings for contempt of court.' The New

seek a stay of civil or criminal proceedings based on communication by that person of proceedings in Parliament or of a document relating to those proceedings, or communication of an authorized parliamentary communication.[796] The person may apply to the Speaker for a certificate stating that the communication was made under the authority of the House or of a Committee of the House, or was an authorized parliamentary communication, and, when filed in the relevant court, the proceedings will be stayed and finally determined. Subpart 2 of the Parliamentary Privilege Act provides for a form of qualified immunity from civil or criminal liability for certain communications.[797] The immunity defence is conditional however, in that it is not available if the defendant abused the opportunity to communicate the information by acting in bad faith or with a predominant motive of ill will or both.

9. Naming before a Court Appearance

162. New Zealand courts have criticized media that have occasionally named an arrested person before the person appears in court because such an action prejudices the court's power to suppress. In a recent case, a newspaper published the names of two men arrested following an assault on a prominent cricketer before their first appearance in court. The judge dealt with this by granting an interim order to preserve fair trial, and requiring removal of all reference to the names online.[798]

10. Impact of the Internet

163. A number of general points can be made about suppression orders and the internet. First, if the accused's name is widely known in connection with the matter before any suppression order is made, this may be a reason for not making an order: the law will not engage in an exercise in futility.[799] Second, if after a suppression order has been made the name is leaked by someone in New Zealand to an overseas publication, that person in New Zealand undoubtedly commits a breach of the order. Third, the fact that after a suppression order has been made the name appears on an overseas website will not usually be a ground for revoking the order. Maintenance of the order in New Zealand will still ensure that a significant number of people

---

Zealand Press Council followed this dictum in 2004 in Case no. 983, 984. It noted, however, that its job is 'not to set legal precedents'. See also *Wason v. Walter* (1868) LR 4 QB 73.

796. Parliamentary Privileges Act 2014, s. 17. Communication includes communication to or for any people, in any form, on any basis, and using any medium or media, as well as live or delayed original communication and delayed recommunication, and live or delayed communication to the public: s. 5(1). Examples usefully given in the Act include email, internet posting, radio or television broadcast and webcast or podcast. Communication to the public means to or for the public or a class of the public: s. 5(1).

797. Parliamentary Privileges Act 2014, s. 18.

798. 'Ryder Incident Not "Jesse Hate Crime" – Lawyer', *Stuff* website, 4 Apr. 2013, http://i.stuff.co.nz/sport/cricket/8505995/Ryder-incident-not-Jesse-hate-crime-lawyer, accessed 26 May 2014.

799. *Lewis v. Wilson & Horton Ltd* [2000] 3 NZLR 546 (CA) at 568, *Tucker v. News Media Ownership Ltd* [1986] 2 NZLR 716 (HC) at 736.

remain unaware of the person's identity.[800] Moreover, to allow an order to be defeated in this way would encourage similar stratagems in future.[801] Fourth, if the name has appeared on an overseas website, the New Zealand media must be careful not to publish information which could lead their audience to it: to do so might be to 'attempt to evade' the order. Finally, there might be an argument that an overseas organization which places a name suppressed in New Zealand on its website commits an offence against New Zealand law. This is because an act necessary to the completion of the offence (i.e., publication) occurs in New Zealand.[802] But the difficulties of enforcement render this possibility of academic interest only.

The internet has impacted considerably on suppression orders. Under the new Act, the offence provision does not apply to a person who hosts material on websites or other electronic retrieval systems that can be accessed by a user unless the specific information has been placed or entered on the site or system by that person.[803] It is current practice for Crown Law to contact such parties where possible and seek removal on an informal basis in any event.

11. Relationship with Inherent Jurisdiction

164. There was probably an inherent power[804] at common law for a judge in a criminal case to clear the court, to suppress publication of names and evidence and to postpone publication. The existence of this inherent power has been examined exhaustively recently by the Supreme Court, which found by majority that it definitively exists in a case involving publication of a suppressed judgment on a website.[805] This power is referred to as an inherent power to make non-party suppression orders. In the case itself, an entire judgment had been suppressed in order to protect the right to a fair trial. The Court observed that the power to bind non-parties by suppression may cover judgments and things such as evidence which one party wants to adduce but which has been held inadmissible, and facts such as a defendant's prior criminal record.[806] Although the case involved the previous law, the Court also commented on the Criminal Procedure Act regime and the relationship of the new provisions with the inherent powers. It noted that the new scheme is not a code and so has not ousted any inherent power, except perhaps to the extent that the newly specified grounds for exercising the discretion under the Act might do so.[807]

In criminal proceedings, therefore, the statutory powers of suppression are not exhaustive, and co-exist with inherent powers that the courts will still be prepared

800. See Steven Price, *Fact Suppression*, Media L. J. Blog, 29 Nov. 2009, http://www.medialawjournal.co.nz/?p=323, accessed 26 May 2014.
801. *R v. X* HC Wellington M109/02, 25 Jul. 2002. Contrast *Abbott v. Wallace* [2002] NZAR 95 (HC).
802. Crimes Act 1961, s. 7.
803. Criminal Procedure Act 2011, s. 211(3).
804. See the distinction between inherent power and inherent jurisdiction explained by the Supreme Court in *Siemer v. Solicitor-General* [2013] 3 NZLR 441,[113].
805. *Siemer v. Solicitor-General* [2013] 3 NZLR 441.
806. *Siemer v. Solicitor-General* [2013] 3 NZLR 441, [146].
807. *Siemer v. Solicitor-General* [2013] 3 NZLR 441, [137(d)] and [169], referring to ss 200, 202 and 205 of the Criminal Procedure Act 2011. The statutory power to clear the court has specifically ousted the inherent power, however: Criminal Procedure Act 2011, s. 197(4).

to resort to it in situations not precisely covered by the statute.[808] Other pre-Criminal Procedure Act examples include a case where a Judge ordered that there be no photographs of the security arrangements at a trial: this order was made in the inherent jurisdiction.[809] In another, the High Court held that the District Court could prohibit publication of photographs or combinations of particular words under its inherent power to prevent abuse of process.[810]

12. General Matters Concerning the Statutory Rules

a. Penalties

165. If a valid order prohibiting publication of evidence or suppressing a name is made, an offence is committed by a news medium that publishes. A fine, or even in some cases imprisonment, can result. In most instances, the maximum penalty is specified in the relevant section, but in some sections, of which section 86 of the Evidence Act 2006 is an example, publication is merely said to amount to contempt of court. In such cases, the maximum penalty is likely to be three months' imprisonment or a fine of NZD 1,000.[811]

b. Media's Right to Be Heard

166. At common law, when a judge is asked to make an order, such as an order suppressing a name, the media have a sufficient interest to be heard on the application.[812] Further, under the Criminal Procedure Act 2011, media have been given general statutory standing to initiate and be heard in relation to any application for a criminal suppression order, and any application to renew, vary or revoke a suppression order.[813] Standing has been given to persons who are reporting on the proceedings and who are either subject to or employed by an organization that is subject to a code of ethics, and the complaints procedures of the BSA or the Press Council; and any other person reporting on the proceedings with the permission of the court.

c. Who is Liable?

167. In the case of a breach of an order made under statutory authority, it is normally the media corporation that is prosecuted. In a number of cases, however, editors have been proceeded against personally.[814] In May 2006, the police charged the editor of *The Press* and two of its journalists for breach of automatic name suppression for the alleged victim of a sexual assault. The charges against the individuals

808. *R v. R* [2015] NZCA 287.
809. *R v. Grant* HC Christchurch T35/01, 18 Jun. 2001.
810. *Paraha v. Police* [2008] NZAR 581 (HC).
811. Crimes Act 1961, s. 401. See also *Siemer v. Solicitor-General* [2010] NZSC 54.
812. See: *Fairfax NZ Ltd v. C* [2008] NZCA 39, [2008] 2 NZLR 368; *Police v. PIK* [2008] DCR 853; *Bain v. R* [2009] NZSC 59, (2009) 19 PRNZ 524.
813. Criminal Procedure Act 2011, s. 210, s. 210(1).
814. *Dominion Post*, 7 Apr. 2006.

were later dropped but the paper's publisher, *Fairfax Media*, pleaded guilty and was ordered to pay reparation to the victim of NZD 500.[815] It is clear courts are reluctant to convict individuals, but wish to encourage responsibility where possible. In March 2014, *Fairfax Media* was convicted and fined NZD 2,250 for breach of a suppression order made by a Coroner. The editor of the *Waikato Times* was also charged, but was granted a discharge without conviction and ordered to pay NZD 500 to the subject of the order for the emotional harm the breach had caused.[816]

B. Civil Cases

168. Civil proceedings are not regulated by statute to the same degree as criminal proceedings, and the inherent power still applies to them.[817]

1. In camera

169. If it is absolutely necessary for the administration of justice, the court may sit behind closed doors; it is then said that the hearing is in camera.[818] Privacy must be essential to administer justice, and the power is to be exercised only in exceptional cases.[819] The instances where this requirement has been fulfilled are few. They include: cases involving ill or mentally ill persons;[820] those concerned with secret processes or commercially sensitive matters where publicity would destroy the whole subject-matter;[821] and cases heard during time of insurrection when the admission of the public could lead to a riot.[822] Even then, only so much of the trial should be in camera as is necessary to attain justice.[823]

Considerable uncertainty surrounds the question of how far reports of matters heard in camera may be published. However, the question is not often going to arise, for if the proceedings take place in camera with the media absent they will only have access to what went on if the judge releases it (in which case it is safe) or if it is leaked by one of the parties (in which case its accuracy may be suspect, and it may be dangerous for that reason).

815. John Henziel, 'Newspaper Fined for Suppression Breach', *The Press*, 22 Jul. 2006 at A7; 'Police Drop Charges against Editor', *The Press*, 19 May 2006 at A3.
816. 'Fairfax Fined for Suppression Breach', *Stuff* website, 26 Mar. 2014, http://www.stuff.co.nz/national/9871017/Fairfax-fined-for-suppression-breach, accessed 28 May 2014.
817. *Siemer v. Solicitor-General* [2013] 3 NZLR 441, [173(d)]. There are, of course, a few statutory exceptions: see, for example, the Accident Compensation Act 2001, s. 160 and the Harassment Act 1997, s. 39.
818. See *Scott v. Scott* [1913] AC 417 (HL). This is still the leading case.
819. *B v. Auckland District Law Society* Unreported, HCt Auckland, 2 May 2000, M 1539-SD99, Paterson J.
820. *Tucker v. News Media Ownership Ltd* [1986] 2 NZLR 716 (HC).
821. See *Skope Enterprises Ltd v. Consumer Council* [1973] 2 NZLR 399 (SC).
822. *R v. Lewes Prison Governors Ex parte Doyle* [1917] 2 KB 254.
823. *Re London and Norwich Investment Services Ltd*, *The Times* (16 Dec. 1987).

2. Reports

170. The common law allows certain restrictions on the reporting of matters in open court. In New Zealand, the courts have held that the High Court does have an inherent jurisdiction to make an order, binding on the public and the media, suppressing publication of a name.[824] There are now quite a large number of cases where the names of parties have been suppressed in civil cases.[825] Many of them involve intimately personal family circumstances. The New Zealand Supreme Court has recently affirmed that courts have an inherent power to make non-party suppression orders in civil proceedings, although it emphasized that what is being referred to is the inherent power of the court rather than inherent jurisdiction.[826] In spite of this, open justice remains the starting point.

III. Access to Court Records

171. Media are increasingly and successfully seeking access to court records in New Zealand.[827] These decisions reflected the increasing influence of the NZBORA 1990 as an impetus towards more openness generally, as well as developments in areas of the law such as privacy. Criminal procedure generally has been comprehensively revised, and new provisions covering access are contained in the Criminal Procedure Act 2012, with accompanying Rules.[828] As regards civil proceedings, the District Courts Rules 2014 contain powers of search of court documents that parallel those laid down in respect of the High Court by the High Court Rules.[829] The Family Court has its own rules governing access,[830] and adoption records are subject to special provision.[831]

The criminal jurisdiction is covered by the Criminal Procedure Rules 2012,[832] while the civil jurisdiction is covered by the High Court Rules 2009.[833] As far as possible, the two sets of rules are the same. What follows is a description of the main features of the rules, with differences between civil and criminal jurisdiction highlighted.

The Civil Rules apply to all civil proceedings in the High Court including interlocutory applications.[834] The Criminal Rules cover the trial, sentencing, bail proceedings, proceedings or applications under miscellaneous acts such as the Criminal

824. *Taylor v. Attorney-General* [1975] 2 NZLR 675 (CA).
825. See e.g.: *A v. Attorney-General* Unreported, HC, Auckland, CIV-2011-404-1529, 13 Apr. 2011.
826. *Siemer v. Solicitor-General* [2013] 3 NZLR 441, *Siemer v. Solicitor-General* [2012] 3 NZLR 43.
827. See e.g.: *Rogers v. Television New Zealand Ltd* [2007] NZSC 91, [2008] 2 NZLR 277.
828. Criminal Procedure Rules 2012, Part 6, RR 6.1–6.10.
829. District Courts Rules 2014 Part 3, rr 3.1–3.12.
830. Family Court Rules 2002, rr 426–429, by virtue of the operation of R 3.2 of the District Court Rules 2014 on R 430 of the Family Court Rules 2002.
831. Adoption Act 1955, s. 23, R 430(a) of the Family Court Rules 2002.
832. Criminal Procedure Rules 2012, Part 6, Access to court documents, rr 6.1–6.10, (called Criminal Rules).
833. High Court Rules 2009, Part 3, subpart 2, Access to court documents, rr 3.5–3.16 (called Civil Rules).
834. Civil Rules, r. 3.5.

Investigations (Bodily Samples) Act 1995, the Criminal Procedure (Mentally Impaired Persons) Act 2003, the Extradition Act 1999, the Parole Act 2002, and appeals under the Criminal Procedure Act 2011 or the Bail Act 2000.[835]

There are three underlying principles for the rules. First, prior to judgment or verdict, allegations made in pleadings and indictments are unproven, and permission of the Court should be required where non-parties seek access to ensure parties are protected from publication of statements that may ultimately be found to lack substance. Second, during committal, at trial or at full hearing, open justice should be given effect by a generous and responsive approach, to enable media to perform their legitimate functions of reporting court proceedings. Third, the verdict or judgment is the formal and definitive record of the decision of the court. Access to other material by non-parties, such as excluded evidence, requires permission of the court.

There is a general right of access to the formal court record in both sets of rules.[836] Everyone has a general right to access the permanent court record under the Criminal Procedure Rules 2012. Access is to the permanent court record, any published list providing notice of a hearing, any judgment, order or minute of the court given, including any record of the reasons given by a judicial officer, and any judicial officer's sentencing notes. However, a court may direct that judgments, orders or sentencing notes not be accessed without the permission of the court. In the civil jurisdiction, 'formal court record' includes a register or index, court lists, judgments, orders or minutes of the court including records of reasons.[837]

During a criminal court proceeding, access is only available by request. This applies from the commencement of the proceeding by the filing of a charging document until all applicable appeal periods have expired. Access will be granted unless the parties to the proceedings object, in which case the request must be referred to the judge.[838]

In civil proceedings, it is possible to access filed pleadings, notices and applications, affidavits, depositions and other admitted written statements or documents, and transcriptions of oral evidence. This regime extends for twenty working days after judgment in civil proceedings or until the discontinuance of the proceedings.[839] In all other cases, access is by informal written request to the Registrar identifying the document and giving reasons.

In criminal cases, a judge dealing with any aspect of an access request must consider the nature of the application, the reasons for it and each of the following matters that is relevant to the application, request or objection:[840]

- the right of the defendant to a fair hearing;
- the orderly and fair administration of justice;

835. Criminal Rules, r. 6.1, definition of 'criminal proceeding'.
836. Criminal Rules, r. 6.4; Civil Rules, r. 3.7. In the Civil Rules, this includes certain applications under the Administration Act 1969.
837. Civil Rules, r. 3.5.
838. Criminal Rules 2012, r. 6.6.
839. Civil Rules, r. 3.9.
840. Criminal Rules, r. 6.10.

- the protection of confidentiality, privacy interests (including those of children and other vulnerable members of the community), and any privilege held by, or available to, any person;
- the principle of open justice, namely, encouraging fair and accurate reporting of, and comment on, trials and decisions;
- the freedom to seek, receive and impart information;
- whether a document to which the application or request relates is subject to any restriction under the rules; and
- any other matter that the judge thinks just.

In civil cases, the list of relevant considerations is the same but the first is deleted.[841]

Access is in any event always subject to any enactment, court order or direction which restricts access, and payment of a prescribed fee.[842] Further, permission of a judge is always required in criminal cases for access to: written statements or transcripts, videotaped or electronic records of interviews, and photographs or electronic images, of complainants or parties who give or intend to give, propensity evidence; videotaped or other records of interviews with a defendant; documents identifying a person whose identity is suppressed by enactment or court order; and statements or documents or records of anything said while the public were excluded from the proceedings. Permission is required in civil cases in relation to the following enactments:

- Adoption Act 1955.
- Alcoholism and Drug Addiction Act 1966.
- Arbitration Act 1996.
- Care of Children Act 2004.
- Civil Union Act 2004.
- Family Proceedings Act 1980.
- Family Protection Act 1955.
- Intellectual Disability (Compulsory Care and Rehabilitation Act 2003.
- Marriage Act 1955.
- Mental Health (Compulsory Assessment and Treatment) Act 1992.
- Property (Relationships) Act 1976.
- Protection of Personal and Property Rights Act 1988, and
- Status of Children Act 1969.

In the civil jurisdiction, Registrar's decisions are subject to review by a judge upon application.[843] Any decisions made by a judge are subject to appeal. The rules provide that decisions about access to court documents made in criminal proceedings are made in the civil jurisdiction of the relevant court.[844]

841. Civil Rules, r. 3.16. The rule also applies to Registrars.
842. Criminal Rules, r. 6.9; Civil Rules, r. 3.12.
843. Civil Rules, r. 3.15.
844. Criminal Rules, r. 6.3.

In a non-media civil case, the High Court held that the threshold for non-parties to obtain access to court documents is now considerably lower and reflects a progressive movement towards making the 'open justice' principle paramount, indeed, almost presumptive.[845] However, it seems media cases provoke a more cautious approach,[846] and judges have the ability to impose conditions on access. Where there has been no substantive hearing or court decision, such as when a proceeding has been discontinued, or may never be completed, the public interest in media getting access to the file will be hard to engage.[847] Open justice therefore had less significance where the dispute might not ever be heard by the court. An absence of detail about the reason for the request also does not assist – in one case, the reason for seeking access was described as being 'to write stories' and this did not weigh greatly in the balancing process.[848] Access will also be refused where material on the file relates to decisions made in other forums, and it is unclear that publication of those decisions has been allowed.[849]

In the criminal jurisdiction, the first decision reported under the 2012 criminal rules declined.[850] In two applications, media sought access to a psychologist's report, and to all documents on the present court file, prior to completion of the trial. Both applications were declined, the first because the psychologist's report contained much confidential material and the second, very broad application, because there was other confidential material throughout the file. Unfocussed, fishing expeditions of this kind are unlikely to succeed.

The Court of Appeal draws on the High Court Rules to inform its decisions on non-party access to documents filed in that court.[851]

IV. Other Courts and Tribunals

172. In New Zealand, there are a number of 'special courts' and a very large number of other tribunals with judicial and quasi-judicial functions. These courts and tribunals have widely differing rules about publicity.

A. *The Special Courts*

1. Family Court

173. The Family Court is a division of the District Court. It has jurisdiction over all family matters, and hears matters under a variety of Acts, including the Adoption

845. *BNZ Investments v. CIR* (2010) 24 NZTC 23,997 at [15], [34], [35] and [40]–[42].
846. *ASB Bank Ltd v. Versalko* HC Auckland CIV-2009-404-5449, 22 Apr. 2010.
847. *Danone Asia Pacific Holdings PTE Ltd v. Fonterra Co-operative Group Ltd* [2014] NZHC 393.
848. *Murray v. Ministry of Justice* [2014] NZHC 2959.
849. *Murray v. Ministry of Justice* [2014] NZHC 2959.
850. *Chief Executive of the Department of Corrections v. Robertson* [2014] NZHC 1526 and *Chief Executive of the Department of Corrections v. Robertson* [2014] NZHC 1621.
851. *Patterson v. Commissioner of Inland Revenue* [2013] NZCA 4, [2013] NZAR 136; *Schenker AG v. Commerce Commission* [2013] NZCA 114. The Court has its own rules: the Court of Appeal (Access to Court Documents) Rules 2009.

Act 1955, the Care of Children Act 2004, the Property (Relationships) Act 1976, the Family Proceedings Act 1980, the Protection of Personal and Property Rights Act 1988, the Children, Young Persons, and Their Families Act 1989, and the Domestic Violence Act 1995. Initially, a policy of privacy prevailed in the Family Court. On 1 July 2005, after twenty-five years of private legal proceedings, the Court was opened up to the media and hence to the public gaze, first under the Care of Children Act 1980, with other jurisdictions following suit later.[852] Accredited news media reporters now have a right to attend hearings, although the judge can at any time request them to leave, in which case they must do so.[853] It is permissible to publish a report of proceedings, although there must be no names or particulars that might identify the child concerned or a vulnerable person as defined in the Act. Identifying information includes any name or particulars likely to lead to the identification.[854] The court can give leave to publish reports that do not comply with these identification constraints.[855]

The Family Court Act 1980 provides for a fine of up to NZD 2,000 for breach of the non-reporting provision.[856] But, it also provides that nothing in the relevant provision 'shall limit the power of any Court to punish any contempt of court'.[857]

Most of the relevant legislation relating to the Family Court refers to 'reports of proceedings'. 'Report' in not limited to detailed or sensitive information, but means any particularized information pertaining to a proceeding. However, publishing anonymized information that did not identify those connected to a proceeding is not prohibited. Further, publishing the legal status of a person (such as identifying a person as the custodial parent of an identified child) is not prohibited as long as the report does not link that status with the hearing.[858]

Family Court records may only be searched by a person other than a party if the Court permits the person to do so. Application must be made in writing identifying the documents of interest and giving reasons for seeking access.[859] Access can be sought until records are transferred to Archives New Zealand.[860]

2. Disputes Tribunals

174. Disputes Tribunals, formerly known as Small Claims Tribunals, are a division of the District Court. A tribunal is presided over by a specially appointed

852. Family Courts Act 1980, ss 11A–11D. See Ursula Cheer, John Caldwell & Jim Tully, 'The Family Court, Families and the Public Gaze', *Families Commission Blue Skies Report* (No. 16/07, Mar. 2007) at 4.
853. Family Courts Act 1980, s. 11A. There is no definition of 'accredited media'. However, the Court operates a practice of applying the provision to organizations or reporters subject to a code of ethics or professional standards and a relevant complaints procedure: Law Commission *Suppressing Names and Evidence* (NZLC R109, 2009) at 45. See also Criminal Procedure Act 2011, s. 198.
854. Family Courts Act 1980, s. 11C. *Ridge v. Parore*[2013] NZHC 2335.
855. Family Courts Act 1980, s. 11B.
856. Family Courts Act 1980, s. 11B(6).
857. Family Courts Act 1980, s. 11B(7). *Solicitor-General v. Smith* [2004] 2 NZLR 540 (HC).
858. *Television New Zealand Ltd v. Solicitor-General* [2009] NZFLR 390 (CA) at [1]–[2]. The case dealt with s. 27A of the Guardianship Act 1968, now repealed.
859. Family Courts Rules 2002, r. 429.
860. Family Courts Rules 2002, r. 426.

referee.[861] It hears disputed claims for amounts up to NZD 15,000.[862] The tribunal can also hear claims in respect of loss or damage to property. The tribunal's primary function is to attempt to bring the parties to an agreed settlement, which will then form the basis of an order.[863] If that is not possible, the tribunal may make an order to resolve the dispute,[864] which it will do according to the substantial merits and justice of the case rather than to strict legal niceties.[865] The essence of the tribunal's procedure is informality; parties appear in their own right and may not have representatives unless the tribunal gives special permission.[866] All proceedings are held in private,[867] and no one other than those involved may be present, although the court does have power to allow a person to sit in if that person has 'a genuine and proper interest either in those proceedings or in the proceedings of Tribunals generally'.[868] The records of the tribunal may be searched only by a person with an interest in the matter concerned.[869] The Disputes Tribunals Act 1988 is silent on the position of the media.

In 2013, the Government announced proposals to improve Disputes Tribunals, one aim being more transparency.[870] The proposals suggest that hearings be open to the public and the media except when the referee is mediating an agreement or privacy is needed, and that decisions be published online unless there is good reason not to do so. A bill containing the proposed changes was to be introduced in 2014 although this does not appear to have occurred yet.

3. Coroner

175. The Coroners Act 2006 reformed and formalized the Coronial system so that up to twenty legally qualified full-time Coroners replaced fifty-five mostly part-time Coroners, and they are supported by a dedicated service unit in the Ministry of Justice. As previously, the Act nowhere uses the term 'court' in connection with a Coroner's proceedings. However, it is clear that the term is properly used in this context.[871] The most prominent Coroner's function is to hold inquests into manner of death. He or she must hold such an inquest in cases where the death appears to have been suicide or a death in official custody or care.[872] He or she may hold an inquest in the case of other reported deaths.[873] The Solicitor-General and the High

861. Disputes Tribunals Act 1988, s. 5.
862. Disputes Tribunals Act 1988, s. 10, amended in 1998. If both parties agree the maximum may be increased to NZD 20,000: s. 13.
863. Disputes Tribunals Act 1988, s. 18(1).
864. Disputes Tribunals Act 1988, s. 18(5).
865. Disputes Tribunals Act 1988, s. 18(6).
866. Disputes Tribunals Act 1988, s. 38(2).
867. Disputes Tribunals Act 1988, s. 39(1).
868. Disputes Tribunals Act 1988, s. 39(3).
869. Disputes Tribunals Rules 1989, r. 35.
870. See 'Disputes Tribunals' Threshold to Increase', Government Press release, 10 Dec. 2013.
871. *Coroner's Court v. Newton* [2006] NZAR 312 (CA) at [40].
872. Coroners Act 2006, ss 4 and 80(a).
873. Coroners Act 2006, s. 80(b).

Court may also order an inquiry if a Coroner has failed or refused to open one.[874]

The inquest is a judicial hearing, presided over by a warranted judicial officer.[875] An inquest is open to the public and therefore to reporters,[876] but the Coroner may exclude any persons, or people from all or part of an inquest,[877] and may exclude a witness until he or she gives evidence.[878] The expression 'part of an inquest' is very wide and might perhaps include the decision.

If there is reasonable cause to believe that a death was self-inflicted, no person may without a Coroner's authority make public before the completion of an inquiry 'any particular relating to the manner in which the death occurred'.[879] The provision means that in a case of apparent suicide the media may not, even in a news item and regardless of the public interest of the matter, say how the person died unless they have the Coroner's permission. There are two ostensible reasons for this prohibition: the sensibilities of the deceased's family, and the fear of copycat suicides. The prohibition remains controversial in media circles, as in some cases it can be difficult to know whether there is 'reasonable cause to believe' that death was self-inflicted. It may also be difficult or impossible to report certain deaths of major public interest properly, for example, autocides or murder-suicides.

The legislation also provides that if a Coroner has found a death to be self-inflicted, the name, address and occupation of the deceased may be reported and the fact that the Coroner has found the death to be self-inflicted.[880] The only grounds on which a coroner may authorize the making public of any other particulars of the death are that publication is unlikely to be detrimental to public safety, which is very broad. In deciding whether to authorize such publicity, a coroner must have regard to the characteristics of the person who is, or is suspected to be, the dead person concerned, matters specified in any relevant practice notes issued by the chief coroner, and any other matters the coroner considers relevant. It is hoped practice notices will promote consistency in exercise of the discretion. There is certainly room for openness.[881]

A coroner may also prohibit publication of: any evidence given or submissions made in any part of the proceedings of an inquiry (e.g., at an inquest); and the name, and any name or particulars likely to lead to the identification of any witness or witnesses, if satisfied that it is in the interests of justice, decency, public order or personal privacy to do so.[882]

---

874. Coroners Act 2006, s. 95.
875. *Burns v. Legal Services Board* [1995] 1 NZLR 594 (HC).
876. Coroners Act 2006, s. 86. Some coroners have drawn up guidelines for expanded media coverage to include television, radio and still photography. As with other courts, expanded coverage is at the discretion of the coroner.
877. Coroners Act 2006, s. 86.
878. Coroners Act 2006, s. 87.
879. Coroners Act 2006, s. 71.
880. Coroners Act 2006, s. 71(2).
881. This was possible under the previous legislation. On 13 Jul. 2010, Christchurch Coroner Richard McElrea allowed the publication of an inquest into a suicide under the previous legislation by permitting media to say that the death was suicide but ruled that it should not be mentioned in a headline.
882. Coroners Act 2006, s. 74.

In one case, it was found that a Coroner had erred in law in making orders suppressing the names of a doctor and other medical workers who had been involved in a case which resulted in the death of a young man from meningococcal disease in 2009. A generalized fear about being named is insufficient, and latent potential for unfair media criticism is too opaque to justify limiting freedom of expression. The decision makes it clear that a robust and focussed analysis is to be applied where speech can be suppressed by the exercise of the statutory discretion.[883]

The penalty for improper publication is a fine of up to NZD 1,000 in the case of an individual and NZD 5,000 in the case of a company.[884]

In 2013, the Minister for Courts asked the Law Commission to carry out a targeted review of the coronial system. The Commission reported in 2014, making a number of significant recommendations for change.[885] It recommended, first, that the statutory prohibitions on reporting be replaced with a narrow prohibition which prevents reporting, either directly or indirectly, of the method of a death, and any description of a death that describes it as a suicide. However, nothing should prevent a person from stating that a death is a suspected suicide. Second, the Commission recommended that urgent exemptions to such prohibitions could be sought from the Chief Coroner, who would be supported by an expert panel if necessary. The system would give priority to such requests for exemption. Third, decisions of the Chief Coroner would be subject to urgent review procedures. Fourth, fines for breach would increase to NZD 20,000 for a body corporate and NZD 5,000 in all other cases. This offence would not apply to website hosts unless they are responsible for the information being on the site.

Finally, it was recommended that the Minister of Health, together with media representatives, those representing mental health interests, and any other interested parties, should prepare revised standards for suicide reporting. The standards would apply to mainstream and new media, but would be applied by a non-legislative regime. The Minister of Health would also have a duty to maintain implementation of the standards and promotion and dissemination of them. The proposals essentially take a co-regulatory approach backed by specific offences and fines. The Government accepted all fourteen recommendations made and introduced amending legislation in 2014 which provides, among other amendments, that it will be possible to report that a death is a suspected suicide, while exemptions from reporting restrictions will be able to be granted by the Chief Coroner under special conditions.[886]

4. Youth Court

176. The Youth Court is presided over by a District Court judge. The Court deals with offences committed by young persons (persons older than 14 but younger than

883. *Gravatt v. The Coroner's Court at Auckland* [2013] NZHC 390.
884. Coroners Act 2006, s. 139.
885. *Suicide Reporting*, LC R 131, March 2014.
886. Coroners Amendment Bill 239-1, s. 38: http://www.legislation.govt.nz/bill/government/2014/0239/latest/DLM6223504.html, accessed 25 Feb. 2015.

17). Every young person charged with an offence (other than murder, manslaughter or a minor traffic offence) comes before the Youth Court in the first instance.[887] Most are dealt with entirely by this Court. However, in the case of more serious offences, the young person may go for trial by jury in the District Court or High Court after pre-trial processes in the Youth Court; trial by jury is obligatory in the case of murder and manslaughter and at the option of the young person in other cases.[888] If the case is dealt with by the Youth Court, the judge has a wide variety of powers, including fine, admonition, the ordering of reparation, and placing the young person under the supervision of the Director-General of Social Welfare. The judge may also, in the case of a young person of 15 or older, convict the young person and order that he or she come before the District Court for sentence or decision.[889]

As far as practicable, the sittings of the Court are to be arranged so that persons attending are not brought into contact with persons in attendance at any other court, and the young persons and their parents do not congregate together while waiting for a case to be heard.[890] The Court is not open to the public. The only persons entitled to be present at a hearing are those involved (e.g., the parties, their lawyers, parents and guardians, and social workers) and accredited news media reporters. No one else may attend unless specially permitted by the Court.[891] However, the media have few reporting rights. Save with the consent of the Court, it is not lawful to publish *any* report of proceedings.[892] (This prohibition does not apply to reports in professional or technical publications for circulation to specialists, such as the legal profession, nor to statistical information and bona fide research about proceedings under the Coroners Act 2006.)[893] Moreover, in *no* case (i.e., to say, even with consent), is it lawful to publish in any report of proceedings under the Act:[894]

(a) The name of any child or young person or the parents or guardians or any person having the care of the child or young person; or
(b) The name of any school that the child or young person is or was attending;
(c) Any other name or particulars likely to lead to the identification of the child or young person or of any school that the child or young person is or was attending; or
(d) … the name of any complainant.

Anyone who infringes these prohibitions is liable to a fine not exceeding NZD 2,000 or, in the case of a body corporate, to a fine not exceeding NZD 10,000. The prohibition on publishing the name of the young person's school is occasionally forgotten by the media. In some cities, fairly full reports are sometimes published, obviously with the court's consent (although of course the parties are anonymous).

887. Children, Young Persons, and Their Families Act 1989, s. 272.
888. Children, Young Persons, and Their Families Act 1989, ss 274 and 275.
889. Children, Young Persons, and Their Families Act 1989, s. 283.
890. Children, Young Persons, and Their Families Act 1989, s. 331.
891. Children, Young Persons, and Their Families Act 1989, s. 329.
892. Children, Young Persons, and Their Families Act 1989, s. 438(1).
893. Children, Young Persons, and Their Families Act 1989, s. 438(2).
894. Children, Young Persons, and Their Families Act 1989, s. 438(3).

In other cities, almost no reports are published. In the past, some judges have required to see a draft report before permitting publication. While this is within the judge's power (a power to approve publication of a document must entail power to approve it in a certain form), some among the media are unhappy with what they perceive to be judicial editing of their copy.

5. Courts Martial

177. Courts martial have jurisdiction over members of all three services, whether they are in the regular forces or are territorials or trainees (although in the last two cases, persons are not subject to the jurisdiction unless they are actually in the service at the time).[895] A court martial can punish for a wide range of offences, including both offences of a 'civil' nature (for instance theft and assault)[896] and the large number of special military offences laid down by the Armed Forces Discipline Act 1971.[897] These latter range from such serious matters as aiding the enemy and mutiny to insubordinate behaviour and behaving in a disgraceful manner. There is a tiered approach to dealing with offences. Commanding officers have a limited power to deal summarily with lesser offences,[898] but the matter may be tried by a court martial where the accused elects.

The Court Martial Act 2007 establishes a court of record called the Court Martial of New Zealand and that Act is to be read in conjunction with the Armed Forces Discipline Act 1971 because the Court Martial was established as a replacement for the ad hoc courts martial provided for previously under the Armed Forces Discipline Act 1971.[899] That Act establishes a court of record called the Summary Appeal Court of New Zealand which hears appeals from decisions made summarily,[900] and sits in divisions each comprising one judge assigned by the chief judge. Penalties can be heavy, including long periods of imprisonment.[901]

The Court Martial must hold its proceedings in closed court while the judge sits alone to rule on any question of law or procedure, the military members deliberate on the finding, and the judge and the military members deliberate on the sentence. The Court Martial may also hold its proceedings in closed court on any other deliberation.[902] Orders restricting publication of reports or accounts of the proceedings, including evidence or submissions, or of names, or to exclude certain parties, can be made. However, accredited news media reporters may only be excluded from the proceedings if the Court considers that a statement may be made or evidence given that might lead to the disclosure of information that would or might be directly or indirectly useful to the enemy or any foreign country, or be otherwise harmful to

895. Armed Forces Discipline Act 1971, Part I. See also the Court Martial Act 2007.
896. Armed Forces Discipline Act 1971, s. 74.
897. Part II of the Act.
898. Armed Forces Discipline Act 1971, Part V.
899. Court Martial Act 2007, ss 8, 6 and 3.
900. Armed Forces Discipline Act 1971, ss 124 and 129.
901. The death penalty remained in theory until 1989 in respect of some offences.
902. Court Martial Act 2007, s. 39.

New Zealand. Identical provisions apply to the Summary Appeal Court, except that it must sit in closed court when deliberating on whether to allow an appeal.[903]

The Armed Forces Discipline Act 1971 expressly provides that outsiders, which includes the news media, can be guilty of contempt who wilfully publish any statement about the proceedings of the military tribunal or court of inquiry: that without foundation states or implies that the military tribunal or court of inquiry has not acted or is not acting impartially; or is likely to interfere with the proper administration of justice. It is also a contempt to disobey or evade any order or direction made or given by the military tribunal or court of inquiry.[904]

A person aggrieved by the decision of a court martial may appeal to a special Courts Martial Appeal Court consisting of High Court judges and barristers. This Court also sits in open court, except when it is deliberating or dealing with matters of procedure. But the court may be cleared of any persons, or classes of person, if the court considers this necessary in the interest of national safety, the due administration of justice or public morals.[905]

6. Employment Court

178. The Employment Court, established under the Employment Relations Act 2000, is a court of record.[906] It has jurisdiction over a wide range of matters arising out of employment contracts. It also hears questions of law referred to it by the Employment Relations Authority, and matters removed into the Court from the Authority.[907] There is no express provision in the Act regulating whether the Court is to sit publicly or in private.[908] However, it has been held under earlier legislation that there is a presumption that it should sit in public, and that all evidence should be in public and reportable.[909]

The Act provides that there is a power in both the Authority and the Court to prohibit publication:[910] A blanket order relating to the whole of the evidence is unlikely to survive scrutiny on appeal. Any such order should be no wider than necessary.[911] A wilful refusal without lawful excuse to comply with a non-publication order is punishable by a judge of the Employment Court, who may impose a sentence of up to three months' imprisonment or a fine of up to NZD 5,000.[912]

903. Armed Forces Discipline Act 1971, ss 138 and 139.
904. Armed Forces Discipline Act 1971, s. 150E.
905. Court Martial Appeals Act 1953, especially s. 17.
906. Employment Relations Act 2000, s. 186.
907. Employment Relations Act 2000, s. 187.
908. The Authority, which is described in the Act as 'an investigative body' (s. 157) can decide that 'an investigation meeting should not be in public, or should not be open to certain persons': (s. 160(1)(e)).
909. *Anderson v. Employment Tribunal* [1992] 1 ERNZ 500 (EC).
910. Employment Relations Act 2000, sch. 2, cl. 10; sch. 3, cl. 12.
911. *Anderson v. Employment Tribunal* [1992] 1 ERNZ 500 (EC).
912. Employment Relations Act 2000, s. 196(2).

7. Environment Court

179. The Environment Court is a court of record,[913] which has jurisdiction over matters under the Resource Management Act 1991. It has all the powers that a District Court has in the exercise of its civil jurisdiction,[914] including a power to commit to prison for disobeying its orders or for contempt in the face of the court.[915] Its hearings are held in public, although the Court may order that any evidence be heard in private, or prohibit or restrict the publication of any evidence, if it considers that there are reasons that outweigh the public interest in publicity.[916] Any prohibition or publication should be to the minimum extent required to protect the reasons.[917]

8. Māori Land Court

180. The Māori Land Court, presided over by specially appointed judges, has all the powers of a court of record.[918] It has wide power to determine claims relating to Māori land. Proceedings are to be conducted in such a way as in the opinion of the judge will best avoid unnecessary formality.[919] However, the substance of every final order must be pronounced orally in open court.[920] In addition, all the provisions of the Evidence Act 2006 apply to the Māori Land Court.[921]

9. The Tribunals

181. In New Zealand, there is a wide range of tribunals, each dealing with its own specialized area.[922] Some are concerned with the grant of licenses and permits. Some have far wider jurisdiction, for instance, the BSA and the Commerce Commission. Generally speaking, the subject-matter with which a tribunal is entrusted is of a specialist nature and requires the formulation of policy, which can be more readily handled by subject specialists than by judges.

Some of the tribunals exercise what can be described as a purely judicial function. They hear evidence in the same way as a court and reach final decisions that 'affect the rights of subjects'. Others, such as the Financial Markets Authority, can

913. Resource Management Act 1991, s. 247.
914. Resource Management Act 1991, s. 278.
915. Resource Management Act 1991, s. 282.
916. Resource Management Act 1991, s. 277.
917. *Te Ruuanga A Iwi O Ngati Tamatera v. Thames Coromandel District Court* (2001) 7 ELRNZ 27.
918. Te Ture Whenua Māori Act 1993 (Māori Land Act 1993), s. 6.
919. Te Ture Whenua Māori Act 1993 (Māori Land Act 1993), s. 66(2).
920. Te Ture Whenua Māori Act 1993 (Māori Land Act 1993), s. 41(1).
921. Te Ture Whenua Māori Act 1993 (Māori Land Act 1993), s. 69(3).
922. The Law Commission has carried out extensive work in this area: see Law Commission *Delivering Justice for All: A Vision for New Zealand Courts and Tribunals* (NZLC R85, 2004), Law Commission *Tribunal Reform* (NZLC SP20, 2008).

issue orders that have a legislative flavour.[923] Others have tasks that are more properly designated as administrative. But there is no clear division. Between the extremes are many shades of grey.

There used to be some uncertainty at common law as to whether 'tribunals' (as opposed to 'courts') need ever sit in public, even if they are exercising an undeniably 'judicial' function. The only case in which the matter has been raised drew a conflict of judicial opinion.[924] But the question is mostly academic in New Zealand, for virtually every tribunal has a constitutive statute that regulates its procedure. The procedures of the different tribunals differ widely, sometimes without any apparent reason. It would be pointless to refer to all the tribunals in detail, but the following outline will give some indication of the great variety in the matter of procedure. Persons interested in the procedure of any particular tribunal should refer to its specific statute.

The Law Commission found that procedural provisions applying to tribunals vary widely, including how the question whether hearings are in public or private is dealt with.[925] It recommended a more unitary system, in which there would be a presumption of openness such that public access to tribunals and to reporting of proceedings should be permitted, unless an overriding interest requires otherwise.[926]

10. Inquiries[927]

182. Inquiries may be set up two ways: either by the Governor-General under the letters patent (in which case they are known as royal commissions) or by the Governor-General in Council under the Inquiries Act 2013, which are called public inquiries. Additionally government inquiries can be set up by Ministers by notice in the Gazette.[928] The Law Commission found that the Commissions of Inquiry Act 1908 contains outdated and confusing provisions that have the potential to add cost and delay to the work of commissions. It also noted that there is a need for a flexible form of statutory inquiry that Ministers can use for less complex, discrete issues that require independent investigation. An Inquiries Act was passed in 2013 which now applies to all three types of inquiries.[929]

Under the new Act, an inquiry may make orders forbidding publication of the whole or any part of any evidence or submissions presented to the inquiry, any report or account of the evidence or submissions, names or particulars likely to lead to the identification of witnesses or others taking part, any rulings of the inquiry. There is also power to restrict public access to any part or aspect of the inquiry, or to hold the inquiry, or any part of it, in private. Before making any such orders, the

923. Financial Markets Authority Act 2011, s. 49.
924. *Hearts of Oak Assurance Co v. Attorney-General* [1931] 2 Ch 370; compare the judgments of Lawrence LJ and Romer LJ. The case later went to the House of Lords, but this point was not discussed.
925. Law Commission *Tribunal Reform* (NZLC SP20, 2008) at [3.18].
926. Law Commission *Tribunal Reform* (NZLC SP20, 2008) at [7.82].
927. See Law Commission *A New Inquiries Act* (NZLC R102, 2008).
928. Inquiries Act 2013, s. 6.
929. Inquiries Act 2013, s. 6.

inquiry must take into account the benefits of observing the principle of open justice, the risk of prejudice to public confidence in the proceedings of the inquiry, the need for the inquiry to ascertain the facts properly, the extent to which public proceedings may prejudice the security, defence, or economic interests of New Zealand, the privacy interests of any individual, whether not making an order would interfere with the administration of justice, including any person's right to a fair trial, and any other countervailing interests.[930]

Some statutes provide for the setting up of inquiries in specific areas. An example is special health inquiries under the New Zealand Public Health and Disability Act 2000. Typically, such statutes provide for the procedure which such inquiries must follow. Health inquiries, for example, must be held in public, although the Inquiry Board has power to go into private, and to suppress publication.[931]

V. Contempt of Court

183. Contempt of court is 'anything which plainly tends to create a disregard of the authority of courts of justice',[932] and is in the nature of a criminal offence. It is unique in New Zealand in that it is mainly common law; all other punishable wrongdoing in this country is purely statutory. Certain statutory provisions cover certain kinds of contempt,[933] but they are limited. The leading criminal statute, the Crimes Act 1961, makes it clear that the High Court retains its power to punish for anything that would have been a contempt at common law.[934]

Some courts in New Zealand, for example, the District Court, have only a limited power given to them by statute to punish for contempt, usually in relation to that type of contempt constituted by misconduct in the courtroom. However, the High Court has an overriding power to punish for contempt of all kinds, not only of itself, but also of any inferior court. It therefore exercises a kind of supervisory jurisdiction over the administration of justice as a whole.

Contempt is dealt with by summary process by a judge or judges alone. Imprisonment is a possibility, and the law did not prescribe any maximum period.[935] However, the Supreme Court recently effectively limited the period of possible imprisonment to three months,[936] but recognized that continued disobedience can be punished by repeated periods of a further three months' imprisonment after a further summary process, each penalty being for additional contempts.[937] There is also power to fine, to demand security for good behaviour and to reprimand. The persons liable to penalty are all those who were concerned with the making of the

930. Inquiries Act 2013, s. 15.
931. New Zealand Public Health and Disability Act 2000, s. 79.
932. Peter Spiller (ed.), *Butterworth's New Zealand Law Dictionary* (6th ed., LexisNexis, Wellington, 2005) and Law Commission, *Contempt in Modern New Zealand* (IP 36, 2014).
933. For example: the Criminal Procedure Act 2011, s. 365.
934. Crimes Act 1961, s. 9.
935. See *Solicitor-General v. Van der Kaap* HC Hamilton M155/97, 30 May 1997.
936. *Siemer v. Solicitor-General* [2010] NZSC 54, [2010] 3 NZLR 767.
937. *Siemer v. Solicitor-General* [2010] NZSC 54, [2010] 3 NZLR 767at [67].

offensive statement. In the case of a news medium, this will include the media company, the editor[938] and the reporter who wrote the article in question.[939] However, it is rare for proceedings to be brought against them all. Even if this does happen, they will probably not all receive the same penalty, for some will obviously be more at fault than others.[940] There is a right of appeal against both the finding and the penalty in a contempt case.[941]

A. *Types of Contempt*

184. It is a contempt of court to refuse or fail to obey a court order.[942] The most important instance of this as far as the news media are concerned is failure to comply with an injunction. Deliberate publication by one news medium of material covered by an injunction issued against another news medium can be a contempt. A number of statutory provisions now expressly cover non-publication orders. They have already been dealt with above. A *deliberate* flouting of such orders may be treated as a contempt as well as an offence under the relevant statute.

It is also contemptuous to act in breach of an undertaking given to the court. Thus, a lawyer who obtains documents on discovery in a court case undertakes that they will be used only for the purposes of the case; it is a contempt to disclose them to anyone else, for example, the media.[943] However, the courts will not attempt to uphold the administration of justice by making futile orders against the media which receives such information.[944]

Second, misbehaviour in the courtroom amounts to contempt and statutory provisions largely cover this field in New Zealand. As far as the journalist is concerned, the most important manifestation of this type of contempt is the rule that, with very few exceptions, a witness under oath in court cannot refuse to answer questions.

The next categories of contempt are so important, particularly to the journalist, that they merit extended treatment.

1. Scandalizing the Court

185. It is a contempt of court to publish disrespectful statements about a court, or the judicial system as a whole, which might undermine public confidence in the

---

938. In *Solicitor-General v. Fairfax New Zealand Ltd* HC Wellington CIV-2008-485-000705, 10 Oct. 2008, the editor of the *Dominion Post*, Tim Pankhurst, was charged as well as the publisher, although no fine was sought against him.
939. *R v. Evening Standard Co Ltd* [1954] 1 QB 578; *R v. Odhams Press Ltd* [1957] 1 QB 73. Even the printers may be proceeded against: *James v. Robinson* (1963) 109 CLR 593 (HCA).
940. For example: *R v. Thomson Newspapers Ltd* [1968] 1 WLR 1; [1968] 1 All ER 268 (QB).
941. Criminal Procedure Act 2011, s. 260.
942. See, for example, *Environment Protection Authority v. Pannowitz* [2006] NSWLEC 219 (2 May 2006).
943. *Home Office v. Harman* [1983] 1 AC 280, [1982] 1 All ER 532 (HC).
944. *Berryman v. Solicitor-General* [2005] 3 NZLR 121 (HC).

courts. However these days, action is rarely taken under this head. Court decisions, sentences imposed by judges, and the judges as individuals, are criticized in the media, sometimes in the strongest terms. A recent Australian case involved statements made about a magistrate by a radio presenter which described him as 'loony', needing a 'psychiatric bloody examination' and being a 'dirty, lousy bloody judge'.[945] In New Zealand, individual judges have used the law of defamation to redress damage to their reputations.[946]

It is wrong to assume that the law of 'scandalizing' contempt is dead. An argument that scandalizing contempt cannot survive the freedom of expression guarantee in the NZBORA 1990 failed as recently as 2004.[947] It may be used in extreme cases. The more extravagant and scurrilous the language, the greater the danger. Anything amounting to a vendetta against a judge, or a group of judges, is risky.[948] In New Zealand in 2003, a website appeared on the internet which listed fourteen judges who it said were under investigation by it, accusing them of 'corruption, incompetence and suspect character' and said evidence would be progressively published on the website to prove it. A letter from the Solicitor-General followed, and the material was removed from the website. Criticism of a court will usually be acceptable; however, criticism based on inaccurate facts may not be.[949] Accusations of bias or partiality on the part of a judge are problematic. The ideal of a fair and impartial court is at the very heart of our legal system, and attacks on this concept are therefore attacks on the basis of the system. There should be no suggestions that a judge is susceptible to pressure. Thus, when a Member of Parliament broadcast statements indicating strongly that the Family Court should return custody of a child to its parents in a pending case he was found to be in contempt.[950] The relative infrequency of recent authorities on 'scandalizing' in New Zealand suggests that sometimes the best way to deal with extravagant criticism is to ignore it.

2. Sub Judice Contempt

186. If a case is being tried in court, or even if it is due to be tried in court, no one can say or do anything that might create a real risk of prejudice to a fair trial. Such conduct not only affects the trial in question, but also can affect public confidence in the court system as a whole and may be dealt with as a contempt of court. Once a matter is sub judice, the right of outsiders, including the media, to discuss it is strictly limited. In particular, media must not publish material which could influence the minds of potential jurors, and 'poison the fountain of justice before it begins to flow'.[951]

While a case is sub judice, the media must not publish material that creates a real risk of prejudice to a fair trial. A penalty will be imposed on the defendant only if,

945. *DPP v. Francis* [2006] SASC 211.
946. See *O'Shane v. Harbour Radio Pty Ltd* [2013] NSWCA 315.
947. *Solicitor-General v. Smith* [2004] 2 NZLR 540 (HC) at 568.
948. *Secretary for Justice v. Oriental Press Group Ltd* [1998] 2 HKC 627.
949. *Solicitor-General v. Radio Avon Ltd* [1978] 1 NZLR 225 (CA).
950. *Solicitor-General v. Smith* [2004] 2 NZLR 540 (HC).
951. *R v. Parke* [1903] 2 KB 432 at 438 per Wills J.

'as a matter of practical reality, there is a real risk, as distinct from a remote possibility, of interference with a fair trial'.[952] Publishers are not punished if the risk of prejudice is slight.[953] If the real risk test is not satisfied, there is no contempt at all.[954]

It is not necessary to show that prejudice has actually occurred; it is enough that it might occur. 'It follows that, even if the accused ultimately receives a fair trial, a contempt may still be established.'[955] When answering the question of risk and assessing any prejudice created, the courts have regard to several matters: (a) the content of the publication; (b) the circumstances of publication; and (c) who is likely to be influenced by it. There may in some cases also be an additional factor of public interest. The same principles apply to criminal cases and civil cases, at least where there is a jury, although criminal cases are more prone to media publicity.

a. The Content of the Publication

i. Material Which Is Inadmissible, or Likely Not to Be Admitted, at the Trial

187. It will normally be contemptuous to publish material which will be, or which is likely to be, withheld from the jury at the trial. It is obviously a perversion of the course of justice for the jury to be informed through the media of things they are not entitled to hear in the trial itself.[956]

The publication of disallowed evidence can also be a ground of appeal against conviction.[957] Special care must be taken with retrials. If a conviction has been quashed on appeal, and a retrial ordered, on the ground that evidence was improperly admitted at the original trial, it is obviously important when reporting the second trial not to refer to that evidence.[958]

ii. Previous Record or Bad Character of Accused

188. One of the clearest examples of contempt is the publication of an accused's previous convictions or bad record. There are few things more likely to influence the mind of a juror.[959] The burden of proof is on the Solicitor-General to establish the elements of contempt beyond reasonable doubt.[960] Thus, it must be shown that

---

952. *Solicitor-General v. TV3 Network Services Ltd and Television New Zealand Ltd* HC Christchurch M520/96, 8 Apr. 1997.
953. *Solicitor-General v. W & H Specialist Publications Ltd* [2003] 3 NZLR 12 (HC) at 16.
954. *Solicitor-General v. W & H Specialist Publications Ltd* [2003] 3 NZLR 12.
955. *Solicitor-General v. Fairfax New Zealand Ltd* HC Wellington CIV-2008-485-705, 10 Oct. 2008 at [84].
956. See e.g.: *Attorney-General v. Associated Newspapers Ltd* [2012] EWHC 2029, [2012] EWHC 2981.
957. *R v. Morris* [2001] 1 NZLR 1 (CA).
958. *R v. Paniani* HC Auckland T982511, 21 Mar. 2000. Contempt proceedings were not commenced.
959. *Burns v. Howling at the Moon Magazines Ltd* [2002] 1 NZLR 381 (HC).
960. *Solicitor-General v. Fairfax New Zealand Ltd* HC Wellington CIV-2008-485-705, 10 Oct. 2008 at [77].

persons reading the article would identify the criminal record discussed in it with the person actually on trial.[961]

iii. Confessions

189. It is always dangerous to publish, before or during a trial, that the accused has confessed, whether to the police, or a fellow prison inmate, or indeed to anyone. It is common for the admissibility of an alleged confession by the accused to be challenged by the defence. If there is any suggestion that the confession was unfairly extracted, or not voluntary, it will be excluded. If the judge allows the confession to be adduced in evidence, then and only then is it safe to report it as part of the report of court proceedings.[962]

iv. Other Charges

190. One of the most difficult question arises when one or several accused persons are before the courts at about the same time on a number of charges that are being tried separately. It may not be safe to report the trial of one of the charges if there is a possibility that the report could adversely affect the subsequent trial of one of the others. Judges usually give directions to the media in this situation, to the effect that the report of the conviction or guilty plea be postponed until after the second trial. It is more difficult if no such order is made. It seems that in the absence of a judicial suppression order, it is proper and lawful to publish a report of the first trial as it takes place. Nevertheless, caution should be exercised in reporting the first trial, not to draw attention to the connection between the two trials.[963] A problem can also arise if an accused has previously been acquitted on a similar charge or charges. It may not be safe, while the current trial is sub judice, to refer to the earlier acquittals[964]

In a recent case,[965] the defendant publisher was sentenced for contempt arising from a mistake made by a journalist who was trying to comply with a suppression order. During a trial for murder, the reporter published an article which did not identify an accused but stated he was facing serious wounding charges in an upcoming trial. The reporter believed this met the requirements of a suppression order stated by the Judge, but overlooked the possibility of contempt. The report was seen by the chief reporter, the news editor, outsourced sub-editors and the editor before publication. The Judge determined that the trial could not continue and the jury was discharged, and the publisher made an early plea of guilty to a charge of contempt. The Judge noted that contempt is a serious matter, even when inadvertent as in this case, because courts jealously guard fair trial rights. However, it was noted that contempt of this kind does not arise often, and this was seen as a credit to the NZ media. After taking into account the seriousness of the contempt and its consequences, the costs

961. *Solicitor-General v. Broadcasting Corporation of New Zealand* [1987] 2 NZLR 100 (HC).
962. *R v. Clarke* (1910) 103 LT 636.
963. *Minister of Justice v. Western Australian Newspapers Ltd* [1970] WAR 202 (SC).
964. *Solicitor-General v. W & H Specialist Publications Ltd* [2003] 3 NZLR 12 (HC).
965. *Solicitor-General v. APN New Zealand Ltd* [2012] NZAR 7.

involved, and the inadequacy of the newspaper's internal procedures, the Court balanced these against the lack of intention, the prompt action to put things right, a genuine apology which had been given, and the early guilty plea. The resulting fine was NZD 26,000 and costs of NZD 14,000, not insignificant figures.

v. Contentious Detail

191. Once a matter is sub judice, a media organization should not conduct its own private investigations and publish accounts of 'evidence' it has gleaned. Once the court has jurisdiction over the matter, it alone must hear the evidence and it alone must determine the true facts. For example, media should not publish an interview with the parents of a young assault victim at a time when the jury is still considering its verdict.[966] It is also dangerous to publish any facts that could tend to connect the crime with a particular person or persons, or to publish as a fact anything that is likely to be in dispute at the trial. Such facts as are published must be completely accurate.

There has been a noticeable tendency in recent years for some of the media to go into greater detail about the facts of a crime, even after an arrest, than would previously have been regarded as acceptable. Such reports include descriptions of getaway cars, interviews with persons at the scene of the crime, and the activities of the alleged criminal as he or she tried to avoid arrest. The Crown may also attempt to limit potential contempt by firing warning shots before prominent trials.[967]

vi. Inducements to Distort Evidence

192. Attempts to threaten or dissuade witnesses, or to get them to change their evidence, are contemptuous. There appear to be no reported cases of New Zealand media being involved in cases of this kind. Media 'buying' witnesses' stories before the trial for publication afterwards is also problematic.[968]

vii. The Publication of Photographs

193. It is not automatically a contempt of court to publish photographs of an accused person. In fact, these days photographs and film of an accused leaving or entering court are common. However, the practice is not entirely risk-free. There are at least two situations where publication of photographs could be a contempt. The first is where it is apparent to a reasonable person that a question of identity may arise at the trial and a photograph is published that could confuse a witness.[969] If a witness is asked to swear that the man seen at the scene of the crime was the accused, the witness' recollection may be clouded or distorted if he or she has since seen a picture of the accused in the newspaper. If it would be prejudicial to publish

966. *Attorney-General v. Mirror Group Newspapers*, *The Guardian* (19 Apr. 2002).
967. 'Decision in Relation to the Retrial of David Bain' (media statement, 21 Jun. 2007).
968. *R v. West* [1996] TLR 207.
969. *Attorney-General v. Tonks* [1934] NZLR 141.

a photograph, it is irrelevant and no defence that the media organization had police support for what it did.[970]

The second situation where it might be risky to publish photographs is where such photographs suggest guilt or bad character. In such a case, the jury could be influenced as well as witnesses.[971] However, this is another area where, given the proliferation of images of accused persons, especially on television, the image would have to be particularly prejudicial to incur a penalty.

viii. Emotive Material

194. When a matter is sub judice, sensationalism that might arouse strong emotions in the public is best avoided. Nevertheless, each case depends on its own facts, and again it would have to be a strong case to justify the intervention of the court in its contempt jurisdiction. In a New Zealand case in 1996,[972] the Judge discharged the jury and ordered a new trial in a murder case when, during the trial, television coverage showed scenes that might have aroused prejudice against the accused. Nevertheless, despite the aborted trial, contempt proceedings against the television companies failed.[973] While the Court agreed that the impact of sensationalism can be difficult to eradicate, and that such reporting would sometimes be in contempt, it found that in this case the requisite degree of risk of prejudice had not been established. The clip in question formed a very small part of the programme, and the Court said that sympathy with the family was bound to arise from the very nature of the case; some of the evidence at the trial would be even more graphic than the television equivalent.

In 2009, New Zealand media reported extensively on the Weatherston murder trial in which, unusually, the accused pleaded guilty to killing the victim, but gave lengthy evidence in his own defence hoping to procure a verdict of manslaughter. Media broadcast the accused giving grisly evidence about how the killing occurred. The manner in which Mr Weatherston behaved while giving evidence was repugnant to some viewers and disquiet was expressed about repetition of the coverage, in particular by the use of slow motion replay.[974] However, the broadcasts did not cross the line into contempt and, arguably, Mr Weatherston contributed significantly by his own demeanour to the negative image presented.

A very clear example of prejudicial material arose in the Australian *Underbelly* case.[975] There the Court considered a proposal to broadcast a thirteen-part television series six weeks before the trial of A which dealt with the background to particular gang wars and portrayed in graphic detail as central characters the very

970. *R v. Pacini* [1956] VLR 544 (SC).

971. *Solicitor-General v. Wellington Newspapers Ltd* [1995] 1 NZLR 45 (HC); on appeal *Gisborne Herald Co Ltd v. Solicitor-General* [1995] 3 NZLR 563 (CA).

972. *R v. Lynch* HC Christchurch T59/96, 20 Aug. 1996.

973. *Solicitor-General v. TV3 Network Services Ltd New Zealand* HC Christchurch M520/96, 8 Apr. 1997.

974. See for example: David Cohen, *Clayton Weatherston is Still Guilty*, National Bus. Rev. (3 Aug. 2009).

975. *General Television Corporation Pty Ltd v. DPP* [2008] VSCA 49, (2008) 19 VR 68.

persons associated with A. The television series would run contemporaneously with the trial. Fair trial was impossible because the broadcast of the 'Underbelly' programme in the weeks leading up to and during the trial would undoubtedly create a serious risk of prejudice. The Court upheld an unusual order made by the Judge in the Court below to suppress the series on the basis of threatened contempt, although the effect of the order was confined to Victoria and the internet in Victoria.

ix. Improper Reports of Court Proceedings

195. It is fundamental that, in the absence of a suppression order, the media can fully report proceedings at a public trial. However, this protection extends only to a fair and accurate report. If the report is seriously inaccurate, and if a juror or witness reading it could be misled by it, this could be a contempt. There have not been many cases of action being taken in respect of inaccurate reports, but in an extraordinary recent case, a UK broadcaster reported online that an accused in a case had been convicted. The report included videos of pre-recorded interviews with police, and was published while the jury were still deliberating and had been sent home for the weekend. The trial did not collapse because it was found there were few hits on the material and, when surveyed, none of the jury reported seeing the highly prejudicial material. However, the matter was referred to the Attorney-General for consideration of a possible contempt action.[976]

x. Prejudgment

196. It will usually be contemptuous for the media to prejudge the very matter the court has to decide. In other words, the media cannot tell the jury, or the court, what to do. The most obvious examples would be: the publication of information, with an invitation to readers to conclude that the accused is guilty or innocent; or a prediction of the outcome of a trial; or an attempt to persuade the jury to find the accused guilty or innocent. It could also be contemptuous to assert that a crime has been committed when the facts support a more innocent interpretation.[977] Nevertheless, not every intimation of support for an accused will amount to contempt.[978]

b. The Circumstances of Publication

197. None of the types of statement discussed above will automatically be treated as a contempt. This will also depend on the circumstances in which it is published. The following aspects are relevant.

976. See: 'Judge Informs Attorney General of Channel 4 News Report That Nearly Collapsed Trial of Child Abuser', *Press Gazette*, 17 Dec. 2014: http://www.pressgazette.co.uk/judge-informs-attorney-general-channel-4-news-report-nearly-collapsed-trial-child-abuser, accessed 18 December 2014.

977. *Director of Public Prosecutions v. Wran* (1987) 7 NSWLR 616 (CA).

978. *Solicitor-General v. W & H Specialist Publications Ltd* [2003] 3 NZLR 12 (HC).

i. How Long before Trial Were the Stories Published?[979]

198. In a number of cases, there has been a finding that time has dissipated any prejudicial effect. A significant recent case in New Zealand is *Solicitor-General v. Fairfax and Pankhurst.*[980] In this case, the Solicitor-General was unsuccessful in prosecuting contempt proceedings following publication by a newspaper of an affidavit of evidence containing allegations of suspected terrorist activity in New Zealand. Although it was held the articles must have had a substantial impact on a large number of the public and had a clear potential to prejudicially affect the minds of jurors, ultimately this was cured by the fact that any trials would be up to two years away. This meant that, while some jurors might have a general recollection of publication of the extracts, it was unlikely that they would be able to recall details of them. Any risk that jurors would access the material on websites was regarded as a normal trial risk which would be addressed by appropriate jury direction. The contempt prosecution therefore failed.[981]

Nevertheless, this time factor must always be weighed against other factors.[982] If the statement is of an extreme nature, even a long lapse before the trial may not save it.[983] *Fairfax* indicates, however, that the view of what constitutes an extreme case may have relaxed somewhat.

ii. Place of Publication[984]

199. Once again, this factor of locality is not decisive: it is merely something to be weighed in the balance. Realistically, however, publication in a place remote from the trial carries the risk that it might lead to leakage of the information elsewhere, especially in the internet age.

The extent of publication and its impact are relevant also.[985] It may therefore be relevant that the offending material was published for a very short period of time in proportion to the whole.[986] However, weighed against this the medium may have a very large audience and make a significant impact in a short time. Courts now also take account of the numbers of 'hits' on a website, even though this does not necessarily determine actual readership.[987]

iii. Prior Publication

200. If the information was already well known before the defendant published it, it may be difficult to say the defendant caused the risk of prejudice. In the *Fairfax*

979. *Solicitor-General v. Broadcasting Corporation of New Zealand* [1987] 2 NZLR 100 (HC) at 115.
980. *Solicitor-General v. Fairfax and Pankhurst* HC Wellington CIV-2008-485-705, 10 Oct. 2008 (redacted version).
981. An appeal based on prejudicial media coverage was also unsuccessful, in part because of the time delay between the coverage and the trial: *Iti v. R* [2012] NZCA 492.
982. *Solicitor-General v. Fairfax and Pankhurst* HC Wellington CIV-2008-485-705, 10 Oct. 2008 (redacted version) at [119].
983. *R v. Burns* [2002] 1 NZLR 387 (CA).
984. *Gisborne Herald Co Ltd v. Solicitor-General* [1995] 3 NZLR 563 (CA).
985. *Attorney-General v. Independent Television News Ltd* [1995] 2 All ER 370 (QB).
986. *Solicitor-General v. TV3 Network Services Ltd New Zealand* HC Christchurch M520/96, 8 Apr. 1997.
987. *R v. Hinch* [2013] VSC 520.

case, any additional prejudice arising from publication by the relevant media of the offending affidavit did not add materially to potential prejudice from other sources that had also published.[988] Nevertheless, the courts do not allow the 'safety in numbers' approach to be taken to its extreme, as this could mean the more extensive and damaging the publicity the less the law can do about it. Therefore, it is not a defence that others have published the same material without facing contempt proceedings.[989] However, prior publication is assessed as part of the context to see whether a real risk exists.

iv. Identification

201. The publication in question will not be a contempt unless it is clear beyond reasonable doubt that it refers to the accused and the trial in question.[990] The prosecution must prove all aspects of the case beyond reasonable doubt. Judicial direction is also regarded as an effective method of dealing with the appearance of material on the internet – 'a normal trial risk in today's electronic environment'.[991]

c. Criminal Matters before a Judge Alone

202. Different considerations apply if the case is being heard by a judge alone. Judges have fairly consistently pronounced that they are not affected by what they see or hear in the media.[992] There is, then, much more latitude for publication when the case is before a judge, or judges, alone. Nevertheless, publications are not entirely immune in such cases, mainly because of the importance of the perception that courts be free from external influence, and the desire to avoid trial by media.

d. The Period Following Conviction

203. Once an accused has been convicted, and the tasks of the jury and witnesses have been completed, the media are much freer to comment on the case. It is not uncommon, after conviction or a guilty plea, for the media to publish 'backgrounders' on the case and the accused that contain material which they would not have ventured to publish while the trial was in progress. However, there are limits. It can be contemptuous to try to influence the judge as to the sentence to be imposed.[993] It is not beyond the bounds of possibility that a judge could be

988. *Solicitor-General v. Fairfax* HC Wellington CIV-2008-485-705, 10 Oct. 2008 (redacted versions).
989. *Solicitor-General v. W & H Specialist Publications Ltd* [2003] 3 NZLR 12 (HC) at 19. See also *Solicitor-General v. Fairfax* HC Wellington CIV-2008-485-705, 10 Oct. 2008 (redacted version) at [89] and [134].
990. *Solicitor-General v. W & H Specialist Publications Ltd* [2003] 3 NZLR 12 (HC).
991. *Solicitor-General v. Fairfax* High Court Wellington CIV-2008-485-70, 10 Oct. 2008 (redacted version) at [126].
992. However the High Court of New Zealand took a slightly softer line in *Solicitor-General v. Smith* [2004] 2 NZLR 540 (HC) at 557: 'Judges, despite their training and experience, are only human and not entirely aloof from pressure.'
993. *Attorney-General v. Tonks* [1939] NZLR 533.

'unconsciously affected' by strong comment[994] which could mean that the accused would not receive a fair hearing. Additionally, if the sentence mirrors that of the media, there will be members of the community who think that the media had influence. Therefore, taking an audience or readership poll on what an appropriate sentence would also be risky.

Any appeal will be heard by judges alone, and they are unlikely to be influenced by anything published, so for the most part it is safe to publish comment. This is not always so, because if the eventual appeal is allowed, there is the possibility of a retrial, and a jury will then again be involved. However, generally speaking, this possibility is regarded as too remote, and too distant in time, to outweigh the desirability of freedom of speech.[995] But everything depends on the degree of sensationalism involved and there could be a case where the information is of such an extreme and dramatic nature that publication of it pending appeal could constitute a significant risk, even in the remote contingency of a future retrial before a jury.[996]

Additionally, if comment is extreme (if, for example, it could be construed as an attempt to prejudge the outcome of the appeal or to put pressure on the appeal court judges) it might offend against the law of contempt by lowering public confidence in the court. Additionally, it might be taken as an attempt to dissuade the accused from exercising his rights of appeal, which is equally against principle.[997]

3. Civil Cases

204. Most civil cases nowadays are tried by a judge alone, and the judge is unlikely to be swayed by media comment. Defamation cases are among the few where juries are still used. However, the media can occasionally to be in contempt in judge alone trials. In this context, the law focuses on detriment to the administration of justice in general.

Deliberate attempts to influence the court will be held in contempt.[998] This happened in a New Zealand case where an MP criticized the Family Court and used expressions such as 'I frankly will be horrified if the Courts and the Police rip this boy out of the arms of its mother and father … ', and denigrated the possibility of custody remaining with the caregiver, saying 'that is just so blatantly wrong'. He called for a formal inquiry into how things had reached the present stage. The Court found he had demonstrated an 'intention' to put pressure on the Family Court. Even if an intention to influence is absent, conduct will still be in contempt if it carries a real risk of influencing the court.[999]

Even though the court itself may not be influenced by deliberate pressure, the public might well see it as an attempt to interfere with the independence of the judiciary and this can be a separate contempt. The media which broadcasts offending

994. *Attorney-General v. Tonks* [1939] NZLR 533 at 538 per Myers CJ.
995. *Attorney-General v. TV3 Network Services Ltd* HC Invercargill CP2/96, 8 Mar. 1996.
996. *R v. Burns* [2002] 1 NZLR 387 (CA) at 407.
997. *Attorney-General v. Crisp* [1952] NZLR 84.
998. *Solicitor-General v. Smith* [2004] 2 NZLR 540 (HC).
999. *Solicitor-General v. Smith* [2004] 2 NZLR 540 (HC) at 557.

statements with prior notice of what will be said may also be in contempt. Prejudging an issue before the court may be seen as unacceptable *trial by media* in civil cases as well as criminal'[1000] although everything depends on the facts and circumstances of the particular case.[1001]

A trial before a judge alone will normally involve witnesses. As in the case of trial by jury, anything will be a contempt which could place pressure on witnesses or confuse their recollection of what happened.

4. Public Interest and Freedom of Speech

205. Given the statutory protection of freedom of expression in section 14 of the NZBORA 1990, it has been considered whether, on some occasions, the public interest in discussing an issue should prevail over the right to a fair trial.[1002] The result of the necessary balancing exercise now appears to be as follows. Freedom of expression should not be curtailed unless there is a real risk of prejudice to a fair trial; trivial or fanciful risk is not enough to place fetters on the right to speak out. However, once it is established that there is a real risk of prejudice to a fair trial, freedom of expression must be curtailed.[1003] Even then, the interference with freedom of expression will usually not be permanent: publication is usually only suspended temporarily until the end of the trial.[1004]

The question of a public interest defence was expected to be addressed in the *Fairfax* trial. However, it did not arise because the Court found that no real risk of prejudice to fair trial rights had been established. The Court did, however, accept there was strong and justifiable public interest in the publication of material that would inform the public about suspected terrorist activity in New Zealand.[1005]

The question therefore remains whether there may not be exceptional cases where the matter under discussion is of such critical importance for the public to know that publication should be allowed, even though it creates a real risk of prejudice to a fair trial. In other words, may there be exceptional cases where freedom of expression outweighs the right to a fair trial? A 'public interest' argument might sometimes succeed, but only in very rare cases. First, there might be some cases where public safety requires publication. The best example would be the case of an accused who escapes from custody, and the police need to warn the public of the person's violent propensities. Further, a public interest argument might succeed if the publication is directed not specifically at the court case, but at a matter of general public importance to which the court case is indirectly related.[1006] The third possibility is that a publication may be more likely to escape punishment if it is merely continuing public discussion on a matter of public interest that began before the litigation was in prospect.

1000. *Solicitor-General v. Smith* [2004] 2 NZLR 540 (HC) at 560.
1001. *Greenpeace New Zealand Inc v. Minister of Fisheries* [1995] 2 NZLR 463 (HC) at 470–471.
1002. *Gisborne Herald Co Ltd v. Solicitor-General* [1995] 3 NZLR 563 (CA) at 571.
1003. *Solicitor-General v. Fairfax and Pankhurst* HC Wellington CIV-2008-485-705, 10 Oct. at [81].
1004. *R v. Burns* [2002] 1 NZLR 387 (CA) at 404–405.
1005. *Solicitor-General v. Fairfax* HC Wellington, CIV-2008-485-705, 10 Oct. 2008 at [116].
1006. *Solicitor-General v. Broadcasting Corporation of New Zealand* [1987] 2 NZLR 100 (HC) at 109.

5. Contempt and Defamation

206. An outspoken piece in a newspaper or broadcast programme may be followed by the filing of a claim for defamation by some person who alleges that the piece reflects adversely on him or her. Some such actions are brought with an incidental purpose of inhibiting further discussion in the media: they are then known as 'gagging writs'. If the news medium then continues discussion of the matter, it may lay itself open to the charges that it is attacking the character of a party to litigation, that it is stating facts on which the Court will be required to hear evidence in due course, and that it is prejudicing the trial. The courts are most reluctant to punish for contempt in such cases and where they have done so, the contempt has been of an extreme kind.[1007]

6. Strict Responsibility

207. As a general rule, a person accused of publishing harmful comment about a pending trial cannot plead that he or she did not know that the publication amounted to a contempt. This means that it is not necessary to show that the accused had any intention to pervert the course of justice. Therefore, if a report of a trial is inaccurate and misleading, it does not assist the reporter and editor at all that they honestly believed it to be accurate.[1008] However, while innocent intention will not prevent media from being found guilty of contempt, it will be relevant to the penalty.[1009]

Additionally, an article that would not otherwise be a contempt can be transformed into one by the guilty intention of the person responsible. Publication that is intended to prejudice a fair trial, or otherwise to affect the administration of justice, is contemptuous whatever the circumstances.

The strict responsibility rule has not been without its critics in recent years. New media in particular, such as bloggers who helm websites engaged in public interest discussion, have expressed concern about the effects of both contempt and suppression laws.[1010] In New Zealand, the question of whether an editor should be responsible in all situations for everything in his or her publication has yet to be answered definitively, although the courts have indicated a preference to limit online liability to those parties who have actual knowledge of some kind.

7. Police and lawyers

208. Sometimes media reports of police activities can be such as to prejudice a fair trial. Sometimes, also, statements fed to the media by the police themselves can

1007. *Wilson v. Waikato and King Country Press Ltd* HC Hamilton M248/79, 9 Feb. 1982.
1008. *R v. Evening Standard Co Ltd* [1954] 1 QB 578.
1009. See *R v. Evening Standard Co Ltd* [1954] 1 QB 578; *R v. Thompson Newspapers Ltd* [1968] 1 WLR 1 (QB).
1010. 'No more comments during trials' (12 Jul. 2009) www.kiwiblog.co.nz.

have this tendency. It is no defence to a contempt charge brought against the media for the latter to plead that the source of the information published was the police. Police-generated information has been the source of express judicial concern in several countries.[1011] In the *Gisborne Herald* case, McGechan J noted that 'the law does not grant police a facility to commit contempt, and from a media viewpoint a police source does not sanitise'.[1012]

Exceptionally, police authorization does excuse where police request media to publish a name suppressed by the courts to aid recapture of an absconder. In another situation, it might also be relevant, that is, where police request publication of the past history of a person involved in a manhunt to warn the public of the danger and to facilitate recapture.

In New Zealand, rule 13.2 of the Rules of Conduct and Client Care for lawyers provides that a lawyer must not act in a way that undermines the processes of the court or the dignity of the judiciary, which clearly encompasses any potentially contemptuous behaviour.[1013]

8. Interviewing Jurors as a Contempt

209. New Zealand case law regulates the possibility where, at the conclusion of a trial, the media interview members of the jury. Interviewing to find out how individual jurors reached their determination is contemptuous.[1014] There are three reasons for this approach. First, the jury system requires that jury verdicts be final. Moreover, juries do not give reasons, and there might be a case where different jurors in the same trial were persuaded to the same decision by different reasons. Comparing and discussing those reasons would misrepresent the very basis of the jury system. Second, it is important that jury deliberations be free and frank. Jurors should be secure in the knowledge that the views they express in the jury room will not be subsequently exposed to the world. Third, the privacy of jurors is an important consideration. Jurors serve under the impression that their privacy will be respected and their identity will remain undisclosed. If they could not be assured of that, people might be less ready to serve on jury panels.[1015]

Therefore, it appears to be unsafe either to approach a juror in an attempt to elicit comment about a decision; or to publish information about a jury's deliberations elicited from an interview with a juror. The Court seems to treat both of these things as quite separate contempts: the seeking out for interview is a contempt; the publication of the information is another contempt.

1011. *Attorney-General (NSW) v. TCN Channel Nine Pty Ltd* (1990) 20 NSWLR 368 (CA).
1012. *Solicitor-General v. Wellington Newspapers Ltd* [1995] 1 NZLR 45 (HC) at 57. See also *R v. Coghill* [1995] 3 NZLR 651, (1995) 13 CRNZ 258 (CA) at 270 per Cooke P. Compare *Rogers v. Television New Zealand* [2007] NZSC 91, [2008] 2 NZLR 277.
1013. Lawyers and Conveyancers Act (Lawyers: Conduct and Client Care) Rules 2008, Schedule. Specific prohibitions are referenced, including communicating with witnesses and jurors: rr 13.2.3 and 13. 2.4: http://www.legislation.govt.nz/regulation/public/2008/0214/latest/DLM1437811.html?search=ts_regulation_lawyers, accessed 13 Feb. 2015.
1014. *Solicitor-General v. Radio New Zealand Ltd* [1994] 1 NZLR 48 (HC).
1015. See *R v. Papadopoulos* [1979] 1 NZLR 621 (CA) at 626.

The New Zealand case law suggests that contempt may cover a case where a juror, without disclosing the secrets of the jury room, later tells the media that he or she regrets the decision or has changed his or her mind in the light of after-acquired evidence: statements of that kind can prejudice the desire for finality. However, other sorts of statements may well have no harmful tendency. An example might be the juror who gives his or her reactions to the way the case was handled by the judge (a public matter visible to all who were present in open court). In this case, it would probably make a difference whether the media sought out the juror or vice versa.

The second difficulty is whether there are any exceptions to the prohibitions laid down by the Court. It has been said that the law should not stifle 'legitimate research into how juries function'.[1016]

Media publications arising from interviews with jurors are increasingly taking place in New Zealand. Publications about a prominent murder retrial case probably disclosed more information than has ever been published before, and escaped any prosecution.[1017] Other articles reported that the behaviour of some jurors in the retrial had been questioned after they hugged the accused following his acquittal and later went to a victory party.[1018] In 2014, the *Dominion Post* newspaper published an article about twelve jurors who volunteered to share their trial experience anonymously. With identification detail and location of the trial removed, the article contained reference to whether or not verdicts were shared by all, and to the process of reaching a verdict, including jurors changing their minds. As an article about how juries function, the publication presented a rich picture of an institution about which little has been revealed in the past, while at the same time sailing somewhat close to the wind. In a small country like New Zealand, the risk of readers identifying even anonymous jurors and trials is high.[1019]

9. Where Contempt Laws Apply

a. Courts

210. Contempt laws apply to courts, however, aside from obvious cases, there is some uncertainty what amounts to a court. The Supreme Court, Court of Appeal, High Court and District Court are clearly covered, as well as the Family Court, the Youth Court and other courts declared by their statutes to be 'courts of record' such as the Māori Land Court, the Māori Appellate Court, the Environment Court, the Employment Court, the Court Martial of New Zealand and the Summary Appeal Court of New Zealand. In cases where these courts do not have jurisdiction to punish for contempt themselves, the High Court will do so: it has jurisdiction to deal with contempt of 'inferior courts'. Courts martial are protected by statute, although the court with jurisdiction to impose penalties for publication of harmful comment

1016. *Solicitor-General v. Radio New Zealand Ltd* [1994] 1 NZLR 48 (HC) at 58.
1017. David Fisher, *Bain Juror: We Were Hounded, New Zealand Herald* (7 Jun. 2009). Later articles also raised questions about the selection of jurors for the retrial: *Bain Juror Convicted of Serious Theft, New Zealand Herald* (8 Jul. 2010).
1018. Beck Eleven, 'Jurors' Behaviour Questioned', *The Press* (Christchurch, 8 Jun. 2009).
1019. 'Jury service: the verdict', Nikki Macdonald, *Dominion Post* 2 Nov. 2014, http://www.stuff.co.nz/national/crime/10688537/Jury-service-The-verdict, accessed 17 Feb. 2015.

about them is the District Court, not the High Court. The Coroners Act 2006 does not state that a Coroner's inquiry takes place in a 'court', but coroners are undoubtedly judicial officers: on appointment, they swear the judicial oath.[1020] Coroners have power to punish for contempt.[1021]

b. Tribunals

211. New Zealand has many tribunals, for instance, the Waitangi-Tribunal, the Human Rights Review Tribunal and the BSA. Many have functions that are 'court-like': they hear evidence; their determinations often affect the rights of the parties before them; they frequently decide something in the nature of a legal dispute between parties; and they often reach their decisions by the application of settled rules and principles to the facts. The relevant question for these bodies is whether they are governed by the law of contempt of court, so that disrespectful criticism of them, and publications that prejudice hearings before them, may be treated as contempt and dealt with by the High Court.

The contempt rules apply only to 'courts of law', that is, courts 'exercising the judicial power of the state', which are 'part of the judicial system of the country'.[1022] It has been held in New Zealand that the Employment Tribunal was a court;[1023] presumably, the same is true of its successor, the Employment Relations Authority.

It is open for legislation setting up tribunals specifically to provide that certain types of conduct in relation to them constitute contempt. For instance, the Residential Tenancies Act 1986 protects Tenancy Tribunals from contempt in the face of the court.[1024] Likewise, other legislation contains a prohibition on attempting to influence the tribunal in question.[1025]

c. Commissions of Inquiry

212. An inquiry (commissions of inquiry, government inquiries and public inquiries) is not a court. Inquiries have power to regulate their own processes[1026] and to summon witnesses and hear evidence.[1027] Witnesses have all the privileges and immunities of witnesses in a court of law,[1028] and they are subject to prosecution for perjury if their evidence is false.[1029] However, in New Zealand, inquiries are unable to punish for contempt in the same way courts can, in part because although current or former judges have the judicial experience and temperament to

1020. See *Burns v. Legal Services Board* [1995] 1 NZLR 594 (HC) at 600.
1021. Coroners Act 2006, s. 117(3)(e).
1022. *Attorney-General v. British Broadcasting Corporation* [1981] AC 303 (HL), followed in New Zealand in *Attorney-General v. Reid* [2000] 2 NZLR 377 (HC).
1023. *Attorney-General v. Reid* [2000] 2 NZLR 377 (HC).
1024. Residential Tenancies Act 1986, s. 112.
1025. For example, State Sector Act 1988, s. 85.
1026. Inquiries Act 2013, s. 14.
1027. Inquiries Act 2013, s. 23.
1028. Inquiries Act 2013, s. 27.
1029. Crimes Act 1961, s. 108(4).

exercise the power, an inquiry is simply not a court, and inquiries can also be headed by non-judicially qualified individuals. New Zealand inquires rely primarily on specified offences for conduct in the face of and on the periphery of inquiries, and the Solicitor-General can commence proceedings in the High Court if necessary.[1030]

10. Reform

213. It is regularly asked whether the law of contempt would benefit from legislative reform and clarification. The New Zealand Law Commission is examining the topic, and has proposed a statutory codification approach.[1031] A final report is currently being prepared.

1030. Inquiries Act 2013, ss 29 and 31.
1031. *Contempt in Modern New Zealand*, LCIP 36, May 2014.

Chapter 6. Press Council

214. In 1972, a Press Council was formed in New Zealand along the lines of the English model. The Council has no legislative backing, but is a purely voluntary organization with no legally enforceable punitive powers. It is financially supported by four metropolitan newspapers, twenty-two provincial newspapers, three Sunday newspapers, four community newspaper interests, two business weeklies, three magazine publishers and their associations, and three digital members.[1032] The Council extended its membership to non-newspaper digital media in 2014.[1033]

The Council consists of eleven permanent members: an independent Chair (so far always a retired judge), five persons representing the public, and five industry representatives (two from the Newspaper Publishers' Association, one representing magazine publishers, and two from the NZ Engineering, Printing and Manufacturing Union (Media Division)). It is now actively seeking members who can deal with complaints arising from digital media publications. The Council has so far had six chairmen: Sir Alfred North, Sir Thaddeus McCarthy, Sir Joseph Ongley, Sir John Jeffries, Barry Paterson CNZM, OBE, QC, and currently, Sir John Hansen, KNZN. Its main objective is to provide the public with an independent forum for resolving complaints involving the press. The Council is also concerned with promoting press freedom and maintaining the press in accordance with the highest professional standards.[1034]

Most of the Council's time is taken up in considering complaints and, following a recent extensive independent review,[1035] it now has a detailed complaints procedure.[1036] All complaints against a print or digital publication must first be made to the publication concerned in order to give the editor the opportunity of dealing with the matter first.[1037] If the editor does not respond within ten working days, or the complainant is unsatisfied with the editor's decision, the complaint can be referred to the Council.[1038] Complaints may be about publication and non-publication. Complaints about a particular article must be made within one calendar month of the date of publication of the article; those arising from a series of articles, within one calendar month of the earlier of the date from which the substance of the complaint would have been reasonably apparent to the complainant, or the publication of the last article in the series. Complaints concerning non-publication of any material

1032. See www.presscouncil.org.nz/principles_3.php, accessed 10 Apr. 2015. All have agreed to abide by the Council's guiding principles.

1033. See press release *NZ Press Council to extend coverage, gain new powers*, 23 Mar. 2014: http://www.presscouncil.org.nz/articles/Press_Council_-_Press%20statement_230314.pdf, accessed 10 Apr. 2015. Membership fees depend on the size of the digital entity and its commercial or non-commercial status and are stated on the Press Council website: Press Council Membership: http://www.presscouncil.org.nz/application.php. Digital entities not part of the existing permanent bodies can apply for associate membership: http://www.presscouncil.org.nz/application.php, accessed 10 Apr. 2015.

1034. See www.presscouncil.org.nz/principles.php, accessed 10 Apr. 2015.

1035. *Review of the New Zealand Press Council*, Ian Barker & Lewis Evans, NPA, EPMU, MPA, November 2007, see www.presscouncil.org.nz/articles.php, accessed 28 May 2010.

1036. See www.presscouncil.org.nz/complain.php, accessed 10 Apr. 2015.

1037. See www.presscouncil.org.nz/complain.php Complaints Procedure at 1.

1038. See www.presscouncil.org.nz/complain.php Complaints Procedure at 3.

must be made within two calendar months of the date on which the request to publish was received by the publication, and complaints arising from matters other than publication, within one month of the incident giving rise to the complaint. A complaint about an online article or blog must be made within one calendar month of the date of first publication, but the complaint option is kept open for two years if the offending article remains uncorrected electronically, or longer at the Chairperson's discretion.[1039]

Most complaints are dealt with on the papers only, but there is provision for both sides to be heard, and the Council conducts the hearing not unlike judicial proceedings.[1040] However, the complainant has no entitlement to be represented by a lawyer, and the hearings are not open to the public. Newspapers named in any complaint are expected to publish the Council's decision, giving it fair prominence. Decisions must be published unedited and unaccompanied by editorial comment, though publications can comment on the decision elsewhere. If a complaint is not upheld, the publication may determine whether to publish the decision and where it should be published.

The Council will provide a shortened version for publication if the decision is a long one.[1041] If the complained-about article has been published on the publication's website, or distributed to other media, the Council now requires that all electronic copy that is enduring and deemed to be conveying inaccuracy must be noted as having been found incorrect and why. In cases where a potential harm outweighs the need to keep public record intact, the Council may go so far as to require the removal of story elements or the taking down of a story in its entirety. Additionally, on the website, the article must be flagged as being subject to a ruling by the Press Council and a link to the decision at www.presscouncil.org.nz provided. The Council will also provide a short statement to be published in each hard-copy publication known to have published the original item.[1042] Publications, websites and blogs must not give undue publicity to a complaint until it has been resolved or adjudicated. However, the fact a complaint has been made can be reported.

The great majority of matters dealt with by the Council involve questions of journalistic practice and ethics rather than questions of law. However, where the circumstances suggest that the complainant may have a legally actionable issue, the complainant is required to provide a written undertaking that he or she will not take or continue proceedings against the publication or journalist concerned.[1043] This is to avoid any possibility of a Council inquiry being used as a 'trial run' for litigation.

As it is a self-regulatory body reliant on the voluntary adherence of members of the print media to its rulings, the Council has never had comprehensive coverage. The Council had jurisdiction over nearly all metropolitan and provincial newspapers and the great majority of community newspapers. The Council's website now states that it considers complaints against newspapers, magazines and periodicals in public circulation in New Zealand (including their websites) as well as other digital

1039. See www.presscouncil.org.nz/complain.php Complaints Procedure at 2.
1040. See www.presscouncil.org.nz/complain.php Time Limits at 4.
1041. See www.presscouncil.org.nz/complain.php Publication of adjudications at 1.
1042. See www.presscouncil.org.nz/complain.php Publication of adjudications at 5–7.
1043. See www.presscouncil.org.nz/complain.php Other requirements at 1.

sites with news content, including blogs characterized by news commentary. Published material includes audio and video streams. The Council retains the discretion to decline a complaint if the publication has limited readership or the circumstances make the complaint inappropriate for resolution by the Council.[1044] The extension of jurisdiction to include digital media has in part been a response to the Law Commission report on new media and to the government response to that report rejecting the recommendations but stating an expectation that existing forms of media self-regulation would continue to adapt to digital media.[1045]

The Council may now also consider third-party complaints, but if the circumstances appear to require the consent of an individual involved or referred to in the article, it reserves the right to require his or her consent in writing to the Council's adjudication on the issue.[1046]

§1. Complaints

215. The range of complaints dealt with by the Council is vast and includes complaints about: inaccuracy, distortion and failure to verify facts; lack of balance; unprofessional and unethical conduct; subterfuge; bias; misrepresentation; censorship and suppression of facts; breach of confidence and failure to observe embargoes; some aspects of letters to the editor; refusal to allow a right of reply; offensive or sensational language, particularly in headlines; unnecessary publication of the names of persons or schools involved in sensitive matters; invasions of privacy; intrusions into private grief; wrongful or unnecessarily upsetting use of photographs; racist reporting; the insensitive reporting of suicide and tragedy; and lack of good taste generally. Complaints have been received, not just about published articles, but about pictures, cartoons, advertisements and billboards; also about breaches of good journalistic practice in obtaining information. Not all complaints have been *against* the media; journalists and newspapers have themselves complained (although infrequently) about treatment of them by other persons, in particular politicians, and sometimes other media.[1047]

The Council refers to its previous adjudications when investigating complaints, and is thus building up a body of precedent. Its adjudications, all of which have been summarized in its *Annual Reports* since 1999,[1048] constitute a guide to the requirements of ethical journalism in New Zealand.

The complaints system is based on a *Statement of Principles*, which has been recently reviewed and reissued.[1049]

1044. See www.presscouncil.org.nz/complain.php Complain.
1045. See *The News Media Meets 'New Media'* LC R128, (2013) and press statement of Press Council, 23 Mar. 2014: http://www.presscouncil.org.nz/articles/Press_Council_-_Press%20statement_230314.pdf, accessed 10 Apr. 2015.
1046. See www.presscouncil.org.nz/complain.php, Other requirements at 2.
1047. *Sky Network Television Against Manawatu Standard* (Press Council, Case Number 2286, September 2012).
1048. Decisions can also be searched on the Council's website: www.presscouncil.org.nz.
1049. These are reproduced in each annual report and also on www.presscouncil.org.nz.

I. Statement of Principles

216. The Principles currently are:

(1) Accuracy, Fairness and Balance
Publications should be bound at all times by accuracy, fairness and balance, and should not deliberately mislead or misinform readers by commission or omission. In articles of controversy or disagreement, a fair voice must be given to the opposition view.
Exceptions may apply for long-running issues where every side of an issue or argument cannot reasonably be repeated on every occasion and in reportage of proceedings where balance is to be judged on a number of stories, rather than a single report.

(2) Privacy
Everyone is normally entitled to privacy of person, space and personal information, and these rights should be respected by publications. Nevertheless, the right of privacy should not interfere with publication of significant matters of public record or public interest.
Publications should exercise particular care and discretion before identifying relatives of persons convicted or accused of crime where the reference to them is not relevant to the matter reported.
Those suffering from trauma or grief call for special consideration.

(3) Children and Young People
In cases involving children and young people, editors must demonstrate an exceptional degree of public interest to override the interests of the child or young person.

(4) Comment and Fact
A clear distinction should be drawn between factual information and comment or opinion. An article that is essentially comment or opinion should be clearly presented as such. Material facts on which an opinion is based should be accurate.

(5) Columns, Blogs, Opinion and Letters
Opinion, whether newspaper column or internet blog, must be clearly identified as such unless a column, blog or other expression of opinion is widely understood to consist largely of the writer's own opinions. Though requirements for a foundation of fact pertain, with comment and opinion balance is not essential. Cartoons are understood to be opinion.
Letters for publication are the prerogative of editors who are to be guided by fairness, balance and public interest. Abridgement is acceptable but should not distort meaning.

(6) Headlines and Captions
Headlines, sub-headings and captions should accurately and fairly convey the substance or a key element of the report they are designed to cover.

(7) Discrimination and Diversity
Issues of gender, religion, minority groups, sexual orientation, age, race, colour or physical or mental disability are legitimate subjects for discussion where they are relevant and in the public interest, and publications may report

and express opinions in these areas. Publications should not, however, place gratuitous emphasis on any such category in their reporting.

(8) Confidentiality
Publications have a strong obligation to protect against disclosure of the identity of confidential sources. They also have a duty to take reasonable steps to satisfy themselves that such sources are well informed and that the information they provide is reliable. Care should be taken to ensure both source and publication agrees over what has been meant by 'off-the-record'.

(9) Subterfuge
Information or news obtained by subterfuge, misrepresentation or dishonest means is not permitted unless there is an overriding public interest and the news or information cannot be obtained by any other means.

(10) Conflicts of Interest
To fulfil their proper watchdog role, publications must be independent and free of obligations to their news sources. They should avoid any situations that might compromise such independence. Where a story is enabled by sponsorship, gift or financial inducement, that sponsorship, gift or financial inducement should be declared.
Where an author's link to a subject is deemed to be justified, the relationship of author to subject should be declared.

(11) Photographs and Graphics
Editors should take care in photographic and image selection and treatment. Any technical manipulation that could mislead readers should be noted and explained.
Photographs showing distressing or shocking situations should be handled with special consideration for those affected.

(12) Corrections
A publication's willingness to correct errors enhances its credibility and, often, defuses complaint. Significant errors should be promptly corrected with fair prominence. In some circumstances, it will be appropriate to offer an apology and a right of reply to an affected person or persons.

The principles may be used by complainants when they wish to advise the Council of their complaint. However, a complainant may nominate other ethical grounds for consideration.[1050]

In the preamble, the Council also notes that in dealing with complaints, it will give primary consideration to freedom of expression and the public interest. The latter is defined as involving a matter capable of affecting the people at large so that they might be legitimately interested in, or concerned about, what is going on, or what may happen to them or to others.[1051]

1050. See www.presscouncil.org.nz/principles.php, accessed 11 Apr. 2015.
1051. See www.presscouncil.org.nz/principles_3.php n 3, accessed 11 Apr. 2015.

The Council now also specifically endorses the principles and spirit of the Treaty of Waitangi and the Bill of Rights Act.[1052] The Council has a fast-track procedure for dealing with complaints arising out general elections.[1053]

II. Decisions

A. *Letters to the Editor*

217. The Council has stated:[1054]

> A newspaper serves its readers when published letters illustrate a wide range of opinion, when it does not allow its letters page to become a mouth-piece for one side of an argument and when it does not allow one group to intimidate, even by constant complaint, the views of others.

The Council filters these complaints rigorously and rarely accepts complaints regarding letters to the editor column unless there are substantive issues beyond non-publication, abridgement and editing. The Council has ruled that it is the editor's right to determine which letters to publish, which letters to edit (provided the correspondent's views are correctly represented) and when to draw correspondence on a particular topic to a close.[1055]

B. *Fairness and Balance*

218. In articles of controversy or disagreement, a fair voice must be given to the opposition view. Exceptions may apply for long-running issues where every side cannot reasonably be repeated on every occasion and in reportage of proceedings where balance is to be judged on a number of stories, rather than a single report.[1056]

The Press Council has made it clear that in ordinary circumstances it is unacceptable, where serious accusations are made, not to provide an opportunity for the opposing side to give its viewpoint.[1057] Deadlines or nominal attempts at making contact are not adequate reasons for failing to provide balance.[1058] However, balance can be provided in a variety of ways such as by articles in other publications and the giving opposing views fair treatment in opinion columns.[1059] The Council recognizes that it would place an impossible burden on newspapers and readers to require that every article, report or quotation in each issue cover all sides on every topic.

1052. See Principles, Preamble: http://www.presscouncil.org.nz/principles.php, accessed 4 May 2015.
1053. See, e.g.: Case 2053, *Helen Kelly v. New Zealand Herald* (2008).
1054. Case 2107, *Kiwis for Balanced Reporting on the Middle East v. the Press* (2010).
1055. See e.g.: Case 2346, *John Nelson v. the Dominion Post* (2013.
1056. Principle 1: http://www.presscouncil.org.nz/principles_2.php, accessed 4 May 2015.
1057. *29th Annual Report* (2001), Balance in News Reporting at 16.
1058. *29th Annual Report* (2001), Balance in News Reporting at 16.
1059. Case 2110, *Professor Charlotte Paul v. the New Zealand Listener* (2010).

Publication which facilitates a vendetta will breach the fairness requirement,[1060] even if it is humorous. The Council will also consider overall unfairness of a publication.[1061] In one case, the Council found the combined use of a headline, a dominant position on the front page, repeated phrasing, and details of previous charges faced by the complainant sensationalized the story so that it became overcooked and therefore unfair.

C. Accuracy

219. Publications should be bound at all times by accuracy, and should not deliberately mislead or misinform readers by commission or omission.[1062] The Council will uphold complaints about inaccuracy and connected complaints that attempts to publish corrections have not been given appropriate prominence.[1063]

Journalists should not contrive debates from separate interviews where the interviewees do not know the premises on which an opposing argument is based, particularly where the argument is about scientific evidence.[1064] Headlines that present two opposing views, with neither party able to question the assertions of the other, are misleading. Attributions should not be the reporter's words, opinions or thoughts.[1065]

The onus to get it right for front-page material is high.[1066] Media need to take particular care in making statements of fact about medical research. It is possible to take a robust critical attitude to products or practices that promote health outcomes, but caution is required in choosing how to treat a particular topic. Ill-judged inflammatory news stories and even cartoons may be unfair. Although cartoons have some leeway in terms of being opinion with more licence to offend, in one case the cartoon illustrated a serious (and inaccurate) news item and was therefore treated according to the same standards as the news article.[1067]

D. Headlines and Captions

220. Headlines, sub-headings and captions should accurately and fairly convey the substance or a key element of the report they are designed to cover.[1068] However, it appears women's magazines are exempt from this principle. A headline

1060. Case 2095, *M Laurence Withy v. Vibrant Hutt* (2009).
1061. Case Number 2198, *Devlin v. New Zealand Herald* (2011).
1062. Principle 1: http://www.presscouncil.org.nz/principles_2.php, accessed 4 May 2015.
1063. Case 779, *Sam Knowles v. the National Business Review* (2000).
1064. Case 957, *Steven Courtney v. Wairarapa Times-Age* (2003).
1065. Case 957, *Steven Courtney v. Wairarapa Times-Age* (2003).
1066. Case 2320, *Clive Stuart Against North & South* (2013). See also Case 2198, *Devlin v. New Zealand Herald*, (2011).
1067. Cases 354-2357 *Smyth et al against the Press* (2013).
1068. Principle 6: http://www.presscouncil.org.nz/principles_2.php, accessed 12 Dec. 2014. See e.g.: Case 1087 *Denise Dalziel v. New Zealand Listener*, (2007).

which said 'R-Patz & Katy's Wedding Shock' on the cover of *Woman's Day* magazine of June 2013 was complained about as misleading. The article dealt with relationship issues of celebrity couple Katy Perry and Robert Pattinson and contained nothing to substantiate the teaser in the headline. The majority of the Council took the position that the article was clearly gossip, which by its very nature, can be ambiguous or mislead. Furthermore, the majority thought that if the magazine was misleading its readers, the readers were accepting of the possibility, since the nature of such magazines is well known. In other words, no one takes such magazines too seriously, so the ordinary stringencies do not apply.

Cover montages or composite photos should be clearly acknowledged and should not be misleading.[1069] Even when a cover montage is acknowledged as such inside the cover, it will breach the principle if readers do not realize they are not looking at a genuine photograph at first glance.

However, publications are entitled to use the most newsworthy aspect of a story for the headline and are not expected to cram every detail in. Context is all. The Council did not uphold a complaint from Air New Zealand about a headline which stated 'Air NZ plans $20 bag charge' when the article itself made it clear the plan was to charge between NZD 10 and NZD 20 a bag.[1070]

E. Comment and Fact

221. A clear distinction should be drawn between factual information and comment or opinion, and any article that is essentially comment or opinion should be clearly presented as such.[1071] Cartoons are understood to be opinion.

F. Discrimination and Diversity

222. From once simply covering racism, the principles now require avoidance of gratuitous emphasis on gender, religion, minority groups, sexual orientation, age, race, colour, or physical or mental disability.[1072] It is rare that such complaints are upheld.

Complaints about articles with racist overtones, or which appear to incite racial hatred, fall into this category.[1073] Material which discriminates is also likely to be inaccurate. In 2007, a discrimination complaint was upheld in relation to an in-depth article in the magazine *North & South* by Deborah Coddington reporting on Asian immigration and crime.[1074] In the article, Ms Coddington stated that in 2001 Asians made up 6.6% of the population but were responsible for just 1.7% of all criminal

1069. Case 2023, *Air New Zealand v. Investigate Magazine* (2008).
1070. Case 2032, *Air New Zealand v. New Zealand Herald* (2008).
1071. Principle 4: http://www.presscouncil.org.nz/principles_2.php, accessed 4 May 2015. Case 2379, *EQC v. NBR NZ Property Investor* (2014).
1072. Principle 7: http://www.presscouncil.org.nz/principles_2.php, accessed 4 May 2015.
1073. See, for example: *23rd Annual Report* (1995), at 10, 21.
1074. Case 1090 *Tze Ming Mok and Ors v. North and South* (2007).

convictions. The writer then went on to say that total offences by Asiatics aged 17–50 rose 53% in the years 1996–2005. The article spoke of 'the gathering crime tide' and 'the Asian menace ... steadily creeping up on us'. The cover line was: 'Is it time to send some back?' The presentation of the statistics was inaccurate, and taking account of the increased Asian population over the period revealed that the overall crime rate had actually fallen. There was also a gratuitous emphasis on dehumanizing racial stereotypes and fear-mongering. Although the magazine had published many letters critical of the original article, any ameliorating effect had been cancelled out by negative comments and failure to acknowledge the statistical inaccuracies.

Opinion pieces will be subject to the principle if they are extreme enough.[1075] The Council has upheld complaints made about a newspaper column containing a number of generalizations about the Maori race while contending that a national holiday celebrating the bi-cultural nature of New Zealand was a 'bullshit day' and 'a day of lies'.[1076]

G. Journalistic Ethics

223. The news-gathering methods employed by reporters are generally covered by the principles dealing with confidentiality, subterfuge and conflicts of interest. Editors have a strong obligation to protect against disclosure of the identity of confidential sources. They also have a duty to take reasonable steps to satisfy themselves that such sources are well informed and that the information they provide is reliable. Care should be taken to ensure both source and publication agrees over what has been meant by 'off-the-record'.[1077] The use of deceit and subterfuge is only condoned in cases when the information sought is in the public interest and cannot be obtained by any other means. Publications must be independent and free of obligations to their news sources and should avoid any situations that might compromise such independence.[1078] Where a story is enabled by sponsorship, gift or financial inducement, these inducements should be declared. Where an author's link to a subject is deemed to be justified, the relationship of author to subject should be declared.[1079]

It has been held to be a breach of journalistic ethics for a newspaper to publish discussions that were clearly meant to be 'off-the-record', even though that was not stated in so many words.[1080] The Council has also endorsed the provision in the code of ethics of the New Zealand Journalists' Union to the effect that journalists ought normally to reveal their identity.[1081] However, it accepted that a newspaper

1075. Case 2253, *Michael Harcourt Against Sunday Star-Times* (2012).
1076. Case 2260, *Diane White Against The Weekend Herald* (2012).
1077. Principle 8: http://www.presscouncil.org.nz/principles_2.php, accessed 4 May 2015.
1078. Principle 9: http://www.presscouncil.org.nz/principles_2.php, accessed 4 May 2015.
1079. Principle 10: http://www.presscouncil.org.nz/principles_2.php, accessed 4 May 2015.
1080. *6th Annual Report* (1978), 9.
1081. Case 2455, *Woodhall & Os v. NZ Herald* (2015).

might be justified in resorting to subterfuge in exceptional cases involving the public interest or the exposure of crime, although any such exception should be a matter for careful senior editorial judgment.[1082] It has also held that a newspaper which comes legitimately into possession of a document issued confidentially to members of an organization is not bound by the confidence enjoined on the person to whom it is addressed, provided the editor is satisfied that publication of the document is directed to serving the public interest, and provided the newspaper presents the information in an accurate and balanced way.[1083]

The Council has affirmed that newspapers are not obliged to disclose sources of 'leaks' in such circumstances.[1084] To do so could jeopardize legitimate newsgathering. The Council has also stressed that when conditions for interviews are laid down, such as not reporting on a particular subject, particular care should be taken that they are understood clearly and unambiguously by both parties.[1085]

There have also been adjudications relating to the familiar practice of Ministers and others imposing an embargo on the release of a statement until a specified time. The Council has emphasized the importance of such embargoes being observed by the media, although it has said that they are not binding if a newspaper, before it has received the embargoed document, has obtained all the information from another, non-embargoed source.[1086] However, another copy of a document which is generally embargoed but has been received from a non-official source is still regarded as being embargoed.

However, the Council will uphold the terms of an embargo, provided that it is reasonably imposed. The Council's concern is that such a form of restraint on freedom of the press could be misused by agencies or officials seeking to advance special agendas. There is therefore no requirement to accept embargoes without question. Editors are entitled to inquire into the reasons for an embargo and, where appropriate, negotiate a change of terms. On rare occasions, the proper approach may be to publish and take the consequences.[1087]

When dealing with journalistic ethics complaints, the Council can also consider whether the writing is irresponsible and malicious. In one prominent case, the Council found a consistently irresponsible and malicious purpose in an opinion article about suicide published by a student magazine.[1088] The article described the grim details and pain of suicide methods in a hard-hitting way which was, nonetheless, acceptable. However, the introductory page had a provocative heading 'SUICIDE And how to do it'. This appeared to introduce a guide with instructions, the Council found, but the descriptions of painful deaths in the article were anything but a guide. The headline was therefore unacceptable because it grabbed the attention but led the reader astray.

1082. *3rd Annual Report* (1975) at 10.
1083. *2nd Annual Report* (1974) at 1011.
1084. *9th Annual Report* (1981) at 1012.
1085. *24th Annual Report* (1996) at 30.
1086. *13th Annual Report* (1985) at 510.
1087. Case 2002, *West Coast District Health Board v. Westport News* (2007).
1088. Case 784, *Ministry of Health v. Craccum* (2000).

H. Privacy

224. The principles recognize that everyone is normally entitled to privacy of person, space and personal information, and these rights should be respected by publications. Nevertheless, the right of privacy will not interfere with publication of significant matters of public record or public interest. Publications must exercise particular care and discretion before identifying relatives of persons convicted or accused of crime where the reference to them is not relevant to the matter reported. Those suffering from trauma or grief call for special consideration.[1089] A further principle, requiring editors to demonstrate an exceptional public interest to override the interests of children or young persons,[1090] may also be relevant, as will that requiring care in photographic and image selection and treatment.[1091]

Children or young people are being treated with some concern reasonably consistently by the Council,[1092] and it will often draw attention to the adverse effects of undue publicity on children, even where it finds the principles have not been breached.[1093] The Council strongly criticized a newspaper which ran a photograph on its front page of two young girls involved in an alleged abduction, at the time when the newspaper knew one of the children had made up the story. The newspaper had blurred the faces of the girls, but the Council expressed its great concern that the photograph was used at all. This was an example of unnecessary media attention; there was an overriding public interest in protecting young people and children from it.[1094]

Significant public interest in a story can outweigh privacy. The Council has stated that most political coverage is unquestionably in the public interest – this includes coverage of Parliament, select committees, council meetings, elections, political parties, pay and allowances.[1095] However, stories about the children of Members of Parliament are not in this category.[1096] The Council upheld a complaint where a newspaper had identified an MP's 14-year-old son by name and published 'selected comments' from his Bebo site in the context of a story about another piece from a gay website which had suggested that the comments were provocative. The Council confirmed that the need to protect young people from being harmed by the glare of publicity requires greater circumspection and sensitivity than might apply to adults, to the extent that material otherwise publishable about adults would not appear in the case of children. The Council also accepted that a public figure has the same right as every other citizen to expect his or her young children to be protected, unless there is a demonstrable justification for drawing the young person into the limelight.

Care is required in relation to the use of photographs, especially where children or other vulnerable people are involved. The Council upheld two complaints against

1089. Principle 2: http://www.presscouncil.org.nz/principles_2.php, accessed 4 May 2015.
1090. Principle 3: http://www.presscouncil.org.nz/principles_2.php, accessed 4 May 2015.
1091. Principle 11: http://www.presscouncil.org.nz/principles_2.php accessed 4 May 2015.
1092. See Principle 3.
1093. *25th Annual Report* (1997), at 13.
1094. *25th Annual Report* (1997), at 14.
1095. *28th Annual Report* (2000), at 13.
1096. Case 2019, *Hon Bill English v. the Southland Times* (2008).

the *New Zealand Herald* over a photograph of a young girl which filled about 60% of a front-page boxed story about an 11-year-old who drove a stolen car and was stopped by police.[1097] The child's eyes were blocked out by a black rectangle. The Council accepted this was a dramatic and highly newsworthy incident. However, it considered that the steps taken to conceal the identity of the child were insufficient, and that it was an error of judgment to treat the child's eyes as her sole identifying feature. There were no compelling reasons for allowing the child's privacy to be intruded on, and it was not essential to show the child's face to bring home to readers the central point of the story. Inconsistent pixilation of children's faces in another article, combined with the fact that identifying children with their father in a story about him was a clear breach of the principles.[1098]

The Council has also upheld a complaint about the use of a photograph of a homeless man to illustrate an article on poverty and wealth in New Zealand, where the subject of the photograph had not been consulted.[1099] The man should have been accorded dignity beyond his usefulness in terms of providing an appropriate image. The vulnerability of accident victims in public has also been recognized. One upheld complaint concerned a photograph on the front page of the weekend *Manawatu Standard* that accompanied a report about a car accident in which two people had been killed and three injured.[1100] The photograph showed a woman who was the driver of one of the two cars receiving help from fire fighters and paramedics. She was clearly visible and the headline was 'Two Die and Three Taken to Hospital After Horror Crash', but the names of those who died had not been released at the time of publication. Public interest in a report of a road accident, even such a tragic accident, did not outweigh the vulnerability of the family involved, especially when the names of those who had died had not been released.

The Council has also recognized that a person's home is essentially private and should be free of intrusion although its approach has not been consistent in this area.[1101]

I. Bad Taste and Offensiveness

225. A significant group of complaints are based on bad taste and offensiveness.[1102] Complaints about sexist, sexual or degrading references could be said to fall into this general category and are also covered by the discrimination and diversity principle referred to above.

1097. Case 811, *Youthlaw and the Department of Child, Youth and Family v. the New Zealand Herald* (2000); see also Case 812, *Youthlaw and the Department of Child, Youth and Family v. the New Zealand Herald* (2000).
1098. Case 2440 *Cronin v. Herald on Sunday* (2015).
1099. Case 773, *Page v. Sunday Star Times* (2000).
1100. Case 2273, *Campbell Family Against Manawatu Standard* (2012).
1101. Case 929, *Simon Hayes v. Mountain Scene* (2003). But cf Case 2048, *Hart v. Herald on Sunday* (2008).
1102. There is no specific principle covering this general heading, but the public persist with such complaints. See, e.g.: Case 2144, *Otago Mental Health Support Trust v. Critic-Te-Aroha* (2010). However, no substantive complaint appears to have been made since 2010.

It is clear that the issue of offensiveness is challenging and has divided the Council. In one case,[1103] a majority decision of 6:4 did not uphold a complaint about a series of 'jokes' inserted by a newspaper among classified advertisements in an edition of the newspaper. The jokes were a series of definitions of political correctness and all related to women. The Council did not believe the material was humorous and most members thought it was puerile and offensive. However, the majority did not believe the newspaper transgressed the standard.

In general, spoofs and parodies that are well signposted escape censure. An article with associated advertisements on the front page of a newspaper on April Fool's day reporting a visit of a mythical Sheik Osama bin Hidin to Wanganui was not intended to be taken seriously and was therefore not in poor taste.[1104] Cartoons are generally given some artistic licence in this category of complaints.[1105] Cartoons are accepted as vehicles for social and political comment.[1106]

In a case arising from two articles about suicide in a student magazine,[1107] the Council upheld a complaint against the introductory page and its headline because it was 'ill considered', 'ill advised', 'irresponsible' and 'offensive'. However, the Council concluded that the article itself was an unvarnished and ugly story about a subject distasteful to many, but informative on more than one level and, because of its grim revelations, might well be a deterrent. The Council found the second article an opinion piece whose tone was nasty, repellent and obnoxious, and went far beyond measured arguments about the right to die.

An article reporting on a case of indecencies involving horses attracted a complaint that it represented moral dangers to children in much the same way as exposure to pornography.[1108] The complaint was rejected because the newspaper was entitled to report what was revealed in open court and had not sensationalized or used the material to titillate.

Editors of websites who invite comments should be particularly vigilant they do not create a forum for personal attacks, and close monitoring is required. The growth of online news editions, where comments from readers are also solicited and published, has resulted in publication of robust material which might offend at times. In *Francken v. Stuff*,[1109] the Council dealt with a complaint which arose after the website published the news that a woman Member of Parliament was to resign as a member of Parliament, and published readers' comments on her. After noting that such commentary is analogous to letters to editors in a newspaper, the Council held that similar principles apply. These are that politicians may be subject to more robust criticism than others, comments can include disparaging remarks that are newsworthy, a correspondent can express strong and even prejudiced views, a comment must not incite violence, but nevertheless a politician is entitled to fair treatment and online commentary is not a forum for personal attacks. In this case, the

1103. Case 768, *Hall v. the Northland Age* (1999).
1104. Case 930, *Little v. Wanganui Chronicle* (2003). See also Case 959, *Hobden v. New Zealand Listener* (2003).
1105. Case 918, *Brailsford v. Dominion Post* (2003).
1106. See also Case 1055, *Sloan v. Dominion Post* (2006).
1107. Cases 783–786, *Various v. Craccum* (2000).
1108. Case 846, *Conway v. Upper Hutt Leader* (2001).
1109. Case 2087, *Francken v. Stuff* (2009).

Council found both positive and negative views had been posted online, and this was a Member of Parliament who was high profile and was in many respects a crusader. On balance, it did not uphold the complaint.

An increased tendency to publish challenging sexual material in mainstream publications has also attracted complaints; however, extreme circumstances involving gratuitous offence to a particular group is required. Clear warnings may assist. In one case,[1110] the Council refused to uphold a complaint about a three-page feature and photographs published in a newspaper on a Saturday. This was a lengthy account of an investigation into the activities of members of Uncommon Bonds – a bondage and discipline community. The first page included a warning: 'Warning: Story features adult sexual themes' on the bottom right hand corner. No one was identified. The Council noted how difficult it is for it to adjudicate on such matters, and that decency and taste are constantly evolving to reflect changing attitudes and values. While the material in the article would be distasteful to some readers, the text was straightforward and unsensational, and also enlightening rather than lurid in its detail. The photographs were borderline, but the warning was completely inadequate and should have been more prominent and published on the first page of the edition as well as with the article. Overall, however, the piece did not cross the line.

III. Review of Press Council

226. An independent review was carried out of the Press Council in 2007.[1111] The main recommendations of the review were as follows. The Council should become an independent legal entity, with a new constitution and better resources, and ongoing independent reviews every five years. Processes should be enhanced in various ways. A Chief Executive Officer (CEO) should act as a 'gatekeeper' to filter either vexatious or misdirected complaints, and deal with simple complaints, using mediation and conciliation where possible. There should be an established 'fast-track' Complaints Committee with delegated powers to deal with complaints continuously where such a process is appropriate. This Committee would also deal with appeals from refusal by the CEO to accept a complaint, and there should be a right of appeal from decisions of this Committee to the Press Council itself. Time limits should be reduced and processes simplified. A waiver from bringing suit against the publication should not be required of complainants. Decisions should be streamlined, in particular to remove any impression of a compromised decision. The Council should maintain more control over how its decisions are published and full decisions should be published on the Council website. The *Statement of Principles* should be reviewed and updated regularly. Penalties should be graduated and there should be a majority of public members participating in any decision on a complaint. The jurisdiction of the Press Council should encompass e-publications in the same manner as for hard-copy print publications. Management processes should

1110. Case 2083, *Ken Orr v. the Press* (2009).

1111. *Review of the New Zealand Press Council*, Ian Barker & Lewis Evans, NPA, EPMU, MPA, November 2007, see www.presscouncil.org.nz/articles.php, accessed 28 May 2010.

become more formalized and streamlined. The Council should be made more accessible through greater publication of its details and functions, and improvements to its website and use of other technology.

By 2013, almost all of these recommendations of the Review Committee had been carried out.[1112] The Council has also been developing forms of mediation, however, in 2012 it mediated or resolved only 6% of complaints, and in 2013, even less, at 4%. This may be because there is a concern not to displace the development of a clear body of precedent in the form of actual decisions. There has been an attempt to make decisions shorter where possible and more accessible, although this may be countered to some degree by the fact that complaints appear to be becoming more complex.

The Council's decisions still lack the penalties which a court of law or the BSA can impose, in that, apart from the Council website database, decisions against a print publication only receive publicity in the relevant publication itself. However, the Council has attempted to strengthen its sanctions process by taking to itself powers to direct where an adjudication should appear in a publication, based on a requirement for fair prominence. For example, where an article has been published on one or more of the first three pages of a newspaper, the council is now able to direct an adjudication to be published on page three. Similar placement requirements cover magazines and websites. All electronic copy that persists and is deemed to be conveying inaccuracy must be noted as having been found incorrect and why. Where the potential harm outweighs the need to keep the public record intact, the Council may go so far as to require the removal of story elements or the taking down of a story in its entirety.[1113]

1112. *Annual Report of the New Zealand Press Council* (2013) Chairman's Foreword, at 4, and *Annual Report of the New Zealand Press Council* (2009) Chairman's Foreword at 7.

1113. Press Statement 23 Mar. 2014 – NZ Press Council to extend coverage, gain new powers, http://www.presscouncil.org.nz/articles/Press_Council_-_Press%20statement_230314.pdf, accessed 4 May 2015.

Part III. Regulation of Audio-Visual Media (Broadcasting)

Chapter 1. Public Service Broadcasting

§1. THE CONCEPT AND MISSION OF PUBLIC SERVICE BROADCASTING

227. Most broadcasting services in New Zealand were originally provided by Government. A statutory corporation, the Broadcasting Corporation of New Zealand (BCNZ), monopolized television services until 1987, when the New Zealand economy was radically de-regulated and opened up to completion generally. In 1988 BCNZ was replaced with what are now two Crown Entity companies,[1114] Radio New Zealand (RNZ)[1115] and Television New Zealand Limited (TVNZ).[1116] A Crown Ownership Monitoring Unit, which is part of the Treasury, provides commercial and ownership monitoring for these enterprises.[1117] Regulation of the radio spectrum was opened up to an auction process under the Radiocommunications Act 1989,[1118] now administered by the Ministry of Business, Innovation and Employment (MBIE).

Since deregulation, there has been continuous tinkering with public service broadcasting, in New Zealand, much of it based on a drive to increase cost-efficiencies by various governments. In 1989, a funding body called NZ On Air was established[1119] with responsibilities focused on cultural identity rather than public service outcomes, and this approach has continued to dominate government priorities for public television.

In 2001, the Government approved a Charter for TVNZ that applied to all parts of TVNZ's operations and was to be fulfilled through free-to-air broadcasting.[1120] The Charter provided that in its programming TVNZ had to meet a number of diverse social and cultural objectives, including providing shared experiences that

---

1114. Under the Crown Entities Act 2004, sch. 2.
1115. http://www.radionz.co.nz/, accessed 25 Jul. 2015.
1116. http://tvnz.co.nz/tvnz-corporate-comms/tvnz-4880728, accessed 25 Jul. 2015.
1117. http://www.dpmc.govt.nz/cabinet/portfolios/broadcasting, accessed 25 Jul. 2015.
1118. http://www.rsm.govt.nz/about-rsm/who-is-radio-spectrum-management/new-zealand-radiocommunications-history, accessed 25 Jul. 2015.
1119. NZ on Air is the funding agency that delivers government funding under Part 4 of the Broadcasting Act 1989.
1120. http://tvnz.co.nz/about-tvnz-profile/charter-3401112, accessed 28 Jul. 2015.

contributed to a sense of citizenship and national identity, ensuring in its programmes and programme planning the participation of Maori and the presence of a significant Maori voice, catering to all age groups, interests and information needs of New Zealanders, maintaining balance between mainstream and minority programming and supporting and promoting the talents and creative resources of New Zealanders and of the New Zealand film and television industry. The Charter was to be reviewed every five years, but ultimately was abandoned in 2011.[1121]

TVNZ now operates on a commercial footing under legislation with commercial objectives based on efficiency.[1122] Its functions are to be a successful national television and digital media company providing a range of content and services on a choice of delivery platforms and maintaining its commercial performance. In doing so, it must do no more than provide high quality content that is relevant to, and enjoyed and valued by, New Zealand audiences, and encompasses both New Zealand and international content and reflects Māori perspectives. TVNZ's services must include the provision of channels that are free of charge and available to audiences throughout New Zealand.[1123]

Radio New Zealand is now the only form of fully funded public broadcasting, although its funding has been frozen for seven years.[1124] The Radio New Zealand Act 1995 sets out functions of and a charter for, Radio New Zealand, and these provisions impact on the content of material broadcast by it. The functions of Radio New Zealand are to provide innovative, comprehensive and independent broadcasting services of a high standard and, to provide:

(a) programmes which contribute towards intellectual, scientific, and cultural, spiritual, and ethical development, promote informed debate, and stimulate critical thought; and
(b) a range of New Zealand programmes, including information, special interest, and entertainment programmes, and programmes which reflect New Zealand's cultural diversity, including Maori language and culture; and
(c) programmes which provide for varied interests and a full range of age groups within the community, including information, educational, special interest and entertainment programmes; and
(d) programmes which encourage and promote the musical, dramatic and other performing arts, including programmes featuring New Zealand and international composers, performers and artists; and
(e) a nationwide service providing programming of the highest quality to as many New Zealanders as possible, thereby engendering a sense of citizenship and national identity; and
(f) comprehensive, independent, impartial, and balanced national-news services and current affairs, including items with a regional perspective; and

1121. TVNZ charter extinguished, *Stuff National*, 12 Jul. 2011, http://www.stuff.co.nz/national/5275457/TVNZ-charter-extinguished, accessed 28 Jul. 2015.
1122. Television New Zealand Act 2003.
1123. Television New Zealand Act 2003, s. 12.
1124. 'Job cuts show threat to Radio NZ – funding frozen since 2008' http://wellington.scoop.co.nz/?p=79986, accessed 25 Jul. 2015.

(g) comprehensive, independent, impartial and balanced international news services and current affairs; and

(ga) an international radio service to the South Pacific (Radio New Zealand International), which may include a range of programmes in English and Pacific languages; and

(h) archiving of programmes which are likely to be of historical interest in New Zealand.[1125]

In providing broadcasting services, National Radio must take account of recognized standards of excellence, its responsibility as the provider of an independent national broadcasting service to provide balance between programmes of wide appeal and programmes of interest to minority audiences, the broadcasting services provided by other broadcasters, annual surveys of persons who are members of its current audiences to establish whether those members consider that the quality and quantity of its services are being maintained and occasional surveys outside its usual audience.[1126] It must demonstrate responsiveness to audience surveying.[1127]

Radio New Zealand's Charter is reviewed by the House of Representatives at five-yearly intervals.[1128] In fulfilling its Charter, National Radio must exhibit a sense of social responsibility by having regard to the interests of the community in which it operates and by endeavouring to accommodate or encourage those interests when able to do so.[1129] It must also operate in a financially responsible manner.[1130] The Charter is currently being amended to allow it to pursue 'new opportunities that do not detract' from its commercial free character.[1131]

In 2004, Māori television was established under the Māori Television Service Act 2003.[1132] The service has a statutory function to be a high quality, cost effective television provider which informs, educates, and entertains and enriches New Zealand's society, culture and heritage. It must broadcast mainly in the Māori language, and is required to consider the needs of children participating in immersion education and anyone else learning Māori. It must provide broadcast services that are technically available throughout New Zealand and practicably accessible to as many people as is reasonably possible.[1133] The service broadcasts at least 90% locally made programming, in bi-lingual Māori and English language and offers a range of genre including arts, culture, film, sports, music, New Zealand's environment and history, and issues of relevance to New Zealanders. It also operates a Te Reo channel that

---

1125. Radio New Zealand Act 1995, s. 7(1).
1126. Radio New Zealand Act 1995, s. 7(2).
1127. Radio New Zealand Act 1995, s. 7(2A).
1128. Radio New Zealand Act 1995, s. 7(4).
1129. Radio New Zealand Act 1995, s. 8(1).
1130. Radio New Zealand Act 1995, s. 8(2).
1131. Press Release of the Minister of Broadcasting, Amy Adams, 'Bill to Update Radio NZ charter passes second reading', 20 May 2015, http://www.beehive.govt.nz/release/bill-update-radio-nz-charter-passes-second-reading, accessed 30 Jul. 2015.
1132. Briefing to incoming Ministers of Māori Development and Finance, October 2014: http://www.maoritelevision.com/sites/default/files/attachments/Briefing%20to%20Incoming%20Ministers%202014.pdf, accessed 28 Jul. 2015.
1133. Māori Television Service (Te Aratuku Whakaata Irirangi Māori) Act 2003, s. 8.

aims to broadcast in 100% te reo Māori and focuses on the core Māori audiences and advanced language learners, as well as an online service.[1134]

The service reports to the Crown and to Te Pūtahi Paohoa (Māori Television Electoral College). It is run by a Board appointed by the Minister of Māori Affairs and the Minister of Finance and the College. The Board is made up of up to seven non-executive directors. Te Pūtahi Paoho appoint four directors and the remaining three directors are appointed by the Crown. The Ministers and the College determine the remuneration and other benefits for the Board of Māori Television.[1135]

Currently, there appears to be no clear political concept of public service broadcasting and the mission for TVNZ, Māori Television and RNZ remains one of meeting the policy requirements of the government of the day while maintaining limited editorial independence. The Māori Television service is perceived by many as New Zealand's true public service television broadcaster.

§2. The Organization of Public Service Broadcasting

228. Crown entity companies, TVNZ, Māori Television and RNZ, form the core of public broadcasting in New Zealand. In addition to the provisions impacting on content in the specific Acts detailed above that apply to the three entities, the Broadcasting Act 1989 controls broadcasting content. Importantly, however, it applies to both public and private broadcasters. The Act provides for the maintenance of programme standards in broadcasting and a complaints process by establishing a BSA.[1136] The government implements various social policies through the Broadcasting Commission,[1137] and attempts to promote and protect New Zealand's indigenous language through the agency Te Reo Whakapuaki Irirangi.[1138] The Act also regulates broadcast of election programmes for Parliamentary elections free of charge,[1139] and places very limited restrictions on advertising hours.[1140]

I. The BSA

229. The Broadcasting Act 1989 set up the BSA,[1141] and gives legal force to codes of practice developed by broadcasters themselves. This could be described as

1134. Briefing to incoming Ministers of Māori Development and Finance, October 2014: http://www.maoritelevision.com/sites/default/files/attachments/Briefing%20to%20Incoming%20Ministers%202014.pdf, accessed 28 Jul. 2015, at 8.
1135. Māori Television Service (Te Aratuku Whakaata Irirangi Māori) Act 2003, Part 1, Subpart 3. See also Briefing to incoming Ministers of Māori Development and Finance, October 2014, http://www.maoritelevision.com/sites/default/files/attachments/Briefing%20to%20Incoming%20Ministers%202014.pdf, accessed 28 Jul. 2015, at 5.
1136. Broadcasting Act 1989, Part 3.
1137. Broadcasting Act 1989, Part 4.
1138. Broadcasting Act 1989, Part 4A. This is the Māori Broadcasting Funding Agency.
1139. Broadcasting Act 1989, Part 6.
1140. Broadcasting Act 1989, s. 81.
1141. See www.bsa.govt.nz; and also Steven Price, *Media Minefield: A Journalists' Guide to Media Regulation in New Zealand* (New Zealand Journalists Training Organization, 2007).

a form of induced self-regulation. The BSA is a Crown entity which consists of four members appointed by the Governor-General on the recommendation of the Minister of Broadcasting. One member is appointed after consultation by the Minister with representatives of the broadcasting industry, and one member is appointed after consultation with such representatives of public interest groups in relation to broadcasting as the Minister thinks fit.[1142] It may also co-opt persons with special expertise. The Authority's main sources of funds are money appropriated by Parliament,[1143] and levies on broadcasters.[1144]

II. The Broadcasting Commission (NZ on Air)

230. The Broadcasting Commission[1145] was established under the Broadcasting Act 1989 and is an autonomous Crown entity under the Crown Entities Act 2004.[1146] It has a number of connected social functions. It must reflect and develop New Zealand identity and culture by promoting programmes about New Zealand and New Zealand interests, and by promoting Maori language and Maori culture.[1147] In exercising its functions, the Commission must consult from time to time with persons who have an interest in New Zealand broadcasting and the production of programmes in New Zealand, representatives of consumer interests in relation to broadcasting, and representatives of Maori interests.

The Commission must maintain and, where it considers that it is appropriate, extend the coverage of television and sound radio broadcasting to New Zealand communities that would otherwise not receive a commercially viable signal.[1148] It must ensure that a range of broadcasts is available to provide for the interests of women, youth, children, persons with disabilities, and minorities in the community including ethnic minorities.[1149] It must encourage a range of broadcasts that reflects the diverse religious and ethical beliefs of New Zealanders.[1150] Finally, the Commission must encourage the establishment and operation of archives of programmes that are likely to be of historical interest in New Zealand.[1151]

The Commission carries out these functions by making funds available, on such terms and conditions as it thinks fit, for broadcasting, the production of programmes to be broadcast, and the archiving of programmes.[1152] The Commission

---

1142. Broadcasting Act 1989, s. 26.
1143. Broadcasting Act 1989, s. 31.
1144. Broadcasting Act 1989, ss 30A–30G.
1145. The funding body is known as New Zealand on Air: http://www.nzonair.govt.nz/about-nz-on-air/#anchor-vision-and-mission, accessed 25 Jul. 2015.
1146. Crown Entities Act 2004, sch. 1, Part 2.
1147. Broadcasting Act 1989, s. 36. *Haliburton v. Broadcasting Commission* (Court of Appeal, CA 14/99, 15 Jul. 1999, Richardson P, et al.), *New Zealand Maori Council v. Attorney-General* [1994] 1 NZLR 513 (PC).
1148. Broadcasting Act 1989, s. 36(b).
1149. Broadcasting Act 1989, s. 36(c).
1150. Broadcasting Act 1989, s. 36(ca).
1151. Broadcasting Act 1989, s. (d).
1152. Broadcasting Act 1989, s. 36(e)-(g).

must promote, in its funding of the production of programmes, a sustained commitment by television and radio broadcasters to programming reflecting New Zealand identity and culture, ensure that, in its funding of the production of television programmes, reasonable provision is made to assist in the production of drama and documentary programmes, and ensure that, in its funding of sound radio broadcasting, reasonable provision is made to assist in the production and broadcasting of drama programmes and in the broadcasting of New Zealand music.[1153]

In assessing any proposal to make funds available for broadcasting or for the production of a programme or programmes to be broadcast, the Commission must have regard to the following matters:[1154]

(a) the extent to which the persons seeking the funding for the project to which the proposal relates have sought and secured funding or other resources for the project from sources other than the Commission;
(b) the potential size of the audience likely to benefit from the project to which the proposal relates;
(c) in the case of a project to maintain or extend the coverage of television broadcasting or sound radio broadcasting, the extent of the likely benefit to the consumers of broadcasting services affected by the project in relation to the cost of the project;
(d) in the case of a proposal for the production of a programme or programmes, the extent to which the proposed programme or content would contribute to the Commission meeting its objectives under more than one of the categories specified in the Act, and the availability of a balanced range of programmes providing for varied interests in the community; and
(e) in the case of a proposal for the production of a programme or programmes, the likelihood that the proposed programme or programmes, if produced, would be broadcast or transmitted on demand.

The Commission must require undertakings that the programme or programmes will be consistent programming standards from recipients of its funding.[1155] The Commission cannot give editorial direction to any person to whom it has made funds available, in respect of a particular programme.[1156] It must, to the extent that it is practicable to do so, invite competitive proposals for the use of the funds made available by the Commission, and ensure under contract that specified standards of performance and accountability of the funds are maintained.[1157] In carrying out its functions under the Act, the Commission must also have regard to the funding policies adopted by Te Reo Whakapuaki Irirangi.[1158]

No Minister or person acting by or on behalf of or at the direction of a Minister, may give a direction in respect of any programme or content, or the gathering or

1153. Broadcasting Act 1989, s. 37(b)-(d).
1154. Broadcasting Act 1989, s. 39.
1155. Broadcasting Act 1989, s. 40.
1156. Broadcasting Act 1989, s. 42.
1157. Broadcasting Act 1989, s. 43.
1158. Broadcasting Act 1989, s. 39A. This is a reciprocal requirement for both entities.

presentation of news or the preparation or presentation of any current affairs programme or content. The Minister must notify the Commission of its policies and provide the Commission with an appropriate direction in respect of the funding of Radio New Zealand Limited, although the statute does not direct the Commission to take account of these, except in the heading to the relevant provision.[1159] The Minister may not give a direction to the Commission in relation to cultural matters.[1160]

The Commission is governed by a six-member Board, and members are appointed by the Governor-General on the recommendation of the Minister and carry out their duties under the Crown Entities Act 2004.[1161] A member must be a person who, in the responsible Minister's opinion, has the appropriate knowledge, skills and experience to assist the statutory entity to achieve its objectives and perform its functions, and the Minister must take account of the desirability of promoting diversity in the membership.[1162] Appointment is for up to five years and the member may be reappointed,[1163] or indeed, removed for just cause.[1164] Members have duties of honesty and integrity, good faith and reasonable care.[1165]

The Commission is publicly funded.[1166] The income of the Commission is exempt from income tax.[1167]

§3. The Financing of Public Service Broadcasting

231. The New Zealand equivalent of a licensing fee for broadcasting was permitted to gradually decline, leaving TVNZ around 85% reliant on advertising revenue by 1988.[1168] TVNZ now operates on a commercial footing under legislation with commercial objectives based on efficiency.[1169] Only approximately 5% of TVNZ revenue now comes from government, with the balance earned from commercial activity – mainly advertising.[1170] TVNZ carries advertising every day of the week,[1171] the only form of regulation being the self-regulatory codes provided by the Advertising Standards Authority (ASA).

Radio New Zealand is fully publicly funded in New Zealand, although its funding has been frozen for seven years.[1172] RNZ is bulk-funded for its two main

1159. There is, however, a clear direction that applies under the Crown Entities Act 2004, s. 103.
1160. Broadcasting Act 1989, s. 44.
1161. Crown Entities Act 2004, ss 25 and 28 and see Part 2, subpart 1.
1162. Crown Entities Act 2004, s. 29.
1163. Crown Entities Act 2004, s. 32.
1164. Crown Entities Act 2004, ss 39–40.
1165. Crown Entities Act 2004, ss 57.
1166. Annual Report of New Zealand on Air, 2013–14, http://www.nzonair.govt.nz/about-nz-on-air/#anchor-vision-and-mission, accessed 25 Jul. 2015.
1167. Broadcasting Act 1989, s. 51.
1168. http://www.teara.govt.nz/en/television/page-1, accessed 25 Jul. 2015.
1169. Television New Zealand Act 2003.
1170. http://tvnz.co.nz/tvnz-corporate-comms/tvnz-4880728, accessed 25 Jul. 2015.
1171. Except for six hours on Sundays and four public holidays: Broadcasting Act 1989, s. 81.
1172. 'Job cuts show threat to Radio NZ – funding frozen since 2008' http://wellington.scoop.co.nz/?p=79986, accessed 25 Jul. 2015.

domestic networks through a contract with NZ On Air, in accordance with a ministerial directive.[1173] Its major responsibilities are National Radio, Concert FM and Radio New Zealand International.[1174]

Māori Television has a mixed funding model, with significant funding provided by the Ministry of Māori Affairs and Te Manghai Paho – the Māori Broadcasting Funding Agency. Māori Television also relies on additional programming produced by the independent production sector using contestable funding available from Te Māngai Pāho (see below). There is no guarantee that Te Māngai Pāho will agree to fund the type of programmes Māori Television wants for its schedules.[1175]

The government funds community radio and regional television services through New Zealand on Air.[1176] However, it appears the government made it very difficult for regional and independent television broadcasters to transition from analogue to digital, and these broadcasters were badly affected by the charging of market rates for digital spectrum and transmission services. One professionally run independent channel, Stratos[1177] was apparently forced to close because of lack of government support.

1173. Minstry of Culture and Heritage 'Cultural Industries' (2015), http://www.mch.govt.nz/what-we-do/cultural-sector-overviews/cultural-policy-new-zealand/5-cultural-industries, accessed 31 Jul. 2015.

1174. http://www.radionz.co.nz/about, accessed 25 Jul. 2015.

1175. Briefing to incoming Ministers of Māori Development and Finance, October 2014, http://www.maoritelevision.com/sites/default/files/attachments/Briefing%20to%20Incoming%20Ministers%202014.pdf, accessed 28 Jul. 2015, at 9.

1176. See para. 230 above.

1177. *Plug Pulled on Stratos Television*, National Bus. Rev., 23 Dec. 2011, http://www.nbr.co.nz/article/plug-pulled-stratos-television-ne-107044, accessed 27 Aug. 2015.

Chapter 2. Private Broadcasting

§1. Different Categories of Private Broadcasters

232. All and any forms of broadcasting can operate in New Zealand by use of the New Zealand radio spectrum which supplies the frequency bands required for broadcasting. Legislation does not regulate which spectrum should be brought into the rights-based regime, and the means by which it should subsequently be allocated. However, the Radiocommunications Act 1989 allows for management of the spectrum using an administrative-based licensing regime and a regime of tradable rights. Provision is made in the Act for the establishment of management rights of up to twenty years[1178] and for transfers and subdivision of such rights. Broadcasters operating under warrants issued by the Broadcasting Tribunal on 1 July 1989, (including TV1, TV2 (state-owned) and TV3 (privately owned by MediaWorks), and Radio New Zealand Limited), were entitled to a licence under the Radiocommunications Act. It is the Government's general policy that where the demand for such rights or licenses exists, supply of those rights will be tendered. The Government administers an auction process as the means by which it makes spectrum available and controls trading and operation of spectrum rights.[1179]

Although regulation of broadcasting is now minimal, the Government maintains social objectives in broadcasting. It does this by preserving special access to radio and television for particular groups in the community. The Radiocommunications Act 1989 included special provisions for non-commercial broadcasters. Long-standing non-commercial broadcasters were guaranteed limited rights to continue broadcasting free of charge, other than an administration fee, and special arrangements were made for Radio New Zealand's non-advertising funded National Radio, Concert Programme and AM Network services providing national programmes, and for access (or community) radio and the broadcast of the proceedings of Parliament. In addition, many non-commercial broadcasters purchased frequencies at tenders. Many Māori tribal (iwi) radio stations broadcast on frequencies reserved for the promotion of Maori language and culture.[1180] A set of UHF television frequencies was reserved for non-commercial purposes.[1181]

Few non-commercial broadcasting frequencies are rarely available now but if they are, allocation is governed by the Regional and Community Broadcasting Policy Framework maintained by the Ministry of Culture and Heritage. Frequencies will only be issued to operators of radio stations that show a strong geographic or community of interest connection with the target audience. Programming must be focussed on the needs of that audience, and the station must be situated within the

1178. Radiocommunications Act 1989, s. 34(g).

1179. Radio Spectrum Management, Radiocommunications History in New Zealand, Ministry of Business, Innovation and Employment, http://www.rsm.govt.nz/about-rsm/pdf-and-documents-library/who-is-rsm/radiocommunications-history-in-new-zealand.pdf, accessed 30 Jul. 2015.

1180. http://www.irirangi.net/iwi-stations/punga-net-2.aspx, accessed 31 Jul. 2015.

1181. Minstry of Culture and Heritage 'Cultural Industries' (2015), http://www.mch.govt.nz/what-we-do/cultural-sector-overviews/cultural-policy-new-zealand/5-cultural-industries, accessed 31 Jul. 2015.

coverage area. Such broadcasters must be a company or incorporated society or charitable trust or other entity operated as a charity or on a not-for-profit basis. Stations may derive funding from advertising of no more than six minutes per clock hour, and no more than 50% if revenue can come from advertising.[1182]

§2. Licensing Requirements

233. Economic restrictions were relaxed in 1989 to provide open entry to the industry for new television and radio services. All special restrictions on overseas ownership of broadcasters were removed in 1991, allowing investment by overseas investors. Entry into the market is now provided for by the general law of competition as set out in the Commerce Act 1986. There are no longer limitations on which technologies may be used to supply broadcasting services. Broadcasters may use cable, microwave-distributed services, and satellites as well as traditional broadcasting techniques to broadcast radio and television services. Pay television services are also permitted.

Until 1989, entry into the commercial radio market was controlled by a Broadcasting Tribunal that considered a wide range of economic, social and commercial issues when granting broadcasting rights. However, now anyone can broadcast using radio spectrum purchased at auction, so long as they are a legal entity and have also obtained a suitable licence under the Radiocommunications Act 1989.[1183] Broadcast licences are for individuals or other legal entities that own and operate a radio broadcast station in the AM or FM broadcast bands; or a television broadcast station in the UHF television broadcast band.[1184] Licences are registered on the Register of Radio Frequencies,[1185] and annual licence fees must be paid for renewal of the licence.[1186]

All non-commercial radio licences are subject to a licence agreement governing the broadcaster, the Ministry of Culture and Heritage, and the MBIE. Conditions include that the service must feature local news, information, stories and history, discussion of community issues, programming that informs, entertains and involves a specified or under-served local community. Complaints about matters such as equitable allocation of air time for all interested users and other conditions of the licence that are not covered by the BSA must be responded to by the broadcaster

1182. Ministry of Culture and Heritage Regional and Community Broadcasting Policy Framework (July 2006), http://www.mch.govt.nz/what-we-do/non-commercial-broadcasting-licences, accessed 31 Jul. 2015.

1183. Legal entities for the purposes of the Radiocommunications Act 1989 (PIB 47), December 2014, http://www.rsm.govt.nz/online-services-resources/pdf-and-documents-library/publications-and-guides/pibs/pib47, accessed 30 Jul. 2015.

1184. Radio Spectrum Management, Ministry of Business, Innovation and Employment, http://www.rsm.govt.nz/licensing/how-do-i/get-a-licence, accessed 30 Jul. 2015.

1185. Radio Spectrum Management, Ministry of Business, Innovation and Employment, http://www.rsm.govt.nz/online-services-resources/the-register-of-radio-frequencies, accessed 30 Jul. 2015.

1186. Radio Spectrum Management, Ministry of Business, Innovation and Employment, Radio Spectrum Management, Ministry of Business, Innovation and Employment, http://www.rsm.govt.nz/licensing/how-do-i/renew-a-licence, accessed 30 Jul. 2015.

within twenty-one days. Renewal of licences depends on the broadcaster continuing to meet the special requirements of the licence, and continued failure to do so will result in revocation of the licence.[1187]

1187. Ministry of Culture and Heritage Regional and Community Broadcasting Policy Framework (July 2006), http://www.mch.govt.nz/what-we-do/non-commercial-broadcasting-licences, accessed 31 Jul. 2015.

Chapter 3. Programme Standards

234. Under the Broadcasting Act 1989, every broadcaster is responsible for maintaining, in programmes and their presentation, standards which are consistent with:[1188]

(a) the observance of good taste and decency;
(b) the maintenance of law and order;
(c) the privacy of the individual;
(d) the principle that when controversial issues of public importance are discussed, reasonable efforts are made, or reasonable opportunities are given, to present significant points of view either in the same programme or in other programmes within the period of current interest; and
(e) any approved code of broadcasting practice applying to the programmes.

The BSA[1189] has as one of its functions the encouragement of broadcasters to develop codes of broadcasting practice in relation to the protection of children, the portrayal of violence, fair and accurate programmes and procedures for correcting factual errors, safeguards against the portrayal of persons in a manner that encourages denigration of or discrimination against sections of the community, restrictions on the promotion of alcohol, the presentation of appropriate warnings in respect of programmes, and the privacy of the individual.[1190]

The BSA is also to encourage consultation by broadcasters with interested persons when developing codes.[1191] Once a code has been developed by a broadcaster, the BSA may approve it;[1192] it may also issue codes of practice of its own where it considers that appropriate.[1193] Codes, once approved or issued, are to be published by the Authority, and are to be available for purchase.[1194] The BSA must publish in the *Gazette* notices stating that such codes have been issued or approved.[1195]

There are currently four codes, standardized as much as possible, which cover radio,[1196] free-to-air television[1197] and Pay TV,[1198] and election programmes.[1199] The codes contain ethical requirements set out in a number of standards, each accompanied by associated interpretative guidelines. A programme which does not comply exactly with a particular guideline may not be in breach, as this depends on whether there is overall compliance with the relevant standard.[1200]

1188. Broadcasting Act 1989, s. 4(l). See *Ransfield v. Radio Network Ltd* [2005] 1 NZLR 233 (HC).
1189. www.bsa.govt.nz.
1190. Broadcasting Act 1989, s. 21(l)(e).
1191. Broadcasting Act 1989, s. 21(2). Codes are reviewed at least every five years.
1192. Broadcasting Act 1989, s. 21(l)(g).
1193. Broadcasting Act 1989, s. 21(l)(f).
1194. Broadcasting Act 1989, s. 22.
1195. Broadcasting Act 1989, s. 22.
1196. Revised from 1 Jul. 2008.
1197. Revised from May 2011.
1198. Revised from January 2008.
1199. Revised from May 2011.
1200. See http://bsa.govt.nz/standards/overview, accessed 7 Apr. 2015.

In addition, the BSA may issue advisory opinions to broadcasters about broadcasting standards and ethical conduct,[1201] and conduct research and publish findings on matters relating to standards.[1202] It may also promulgate rules about the retention of tapes of programmes.[1203] Following dissatisfaction with some radio broadcasters' tape retention practices, the current Radio Code contains express provision to ensure the Authority can have access to relevant material.[1204]

The Act specifically states that failure to comply with standards is not a matter to be dealt with by civil action in the courts.[1205] The main mode of enforcement is through the complaints procedure which is laid down by the Act. This procedure is based on the principle that complaints should be made in the first instance to the broadcaster concerned. 'An independent complaints procedure is not a substitute for proper consideration of complaints by the broadcaster.'[1206] However, an independent body must be available to ensure that broadcasters discharge their responsibilities.[1207]

The Act provides that every broadcaster is under a duty to receive and consider complaints about programmes which are alleged to have failed to comply with the standards,[1208] and consistency with an approved code of broadcasting practice is one of them. Every broadcaster must publicize the procedures for making complaints, and establish procedures for investigating them. Complaints need not be considered unless they are made in writing within twenty working days of the broadcast concerned.[1209] The broadcaster, having investigated the complaint, must notify the complainant of its decision. If the complaint is found to be justified, the broadcaster must take appropriate action and notify the complainant of that action.[1210]

If the complainant is not satisfied with the decision or action taken, or has not been notified of some action, within twenty working days of the complaint being received by the broadcaster, the complainant may refer the complaint to the BSA.[1211] If the complaint relates to alleged infringement of privacy, the complainant may elect to complain direct to the BSA in the first instance.[1212] The BSA will not accept complaints that are referred to it after certain time limits laid down by the Act. (In the normal case, that limit is twenty days after receipt of the decision of

---

1201. Broadcasting Act 1989, s. 21(l)(d).
1202. Broadcasting Act 1989, s. 21(l)(h). A list of BSA publications is available on its website: see www.bsa.govt.nz.
1203. Broadcasting Act 1989, s. 30.
1204. *Hydrabadi v. Radio Tarana (NZ) Ltd* 2003-128, 20 Nov. 2003.
1205. Broadcasting Act 1989, s. 4(3). *Ransfield v. Radio Network Ltd* [2005] 1 NZLR 233 (HC).
1206. Broadcasting Act 1989, s. 5(d).
1207. Broadcasting Act 1989, s. 5(b).
1208. Broadcasting Act 1989, s. 6. The complaint should be about a specific programme, not a series: *Frewen v. TVNZ* 2004-053-054, 6 May 2004. It is not necessary for a complainant to actually hear or view the programme complained about: *James v. Radio New Zealand Ltd* 2002-190, 28 Nov. 2002.
1209. Broadcasting Act 1989, s. 6(2). The BSA may also decline to determine a complaint which is trivial under s. 11(a) of the Broadcasting Act 1989: *Mowat v. Television New Zealand Ltd* 2004-163.
1210. Broadcasting Act 1989, s. 7(1).
1211. Broadcasting Act 1989, s. 8. *TV3 Network Services Ltd v. The Prime Minister (Rt Hon Helen Clark)* HC Wellington CIV-2003-485-1655 and CIV-2003-485-1816, 10 Feb. 2004.
1212. Broadcasting Act 1989, s. 8(1A).

the broadcaster.)[1213] The BSA may determine a complaint without a formal hearing, but in such a case, it must give the complainant and the broadcaster a reasonable opportunity to make written submissions.[1214] In all cases, the BSA should consider the complaint with as little formality and technicality as the law permits.[1215]

If the BSA decides that a complaint is justified, it has considerable powers of enforcement. It may do any of the following:[1216]

(a) It may direct the broadcaster to publish a statement approved by the Authority.
(b) It may direct the broadcaster to refrain from broadcasting at all, or from broadcasting advertising programmes, for a period of up to twenty-four hours.
(c) It may refer the complaint back to the broadcaster.
(d) If it finds the broadcaster has failed to maintain standards that are consistent with the privacy of an individual, it may order the broadcaster to pay the individual compensation of up to NZD 5,000.

The BSA must notify both complainant and broadcaster of its decision.[1217] It must also give public notice of the decision, and copies of the decision are to be available to purchase.[1218] The broadcaster must comply with any order made, and notify the BSA in writing of the manner in which it has been complied with.[1219] Failure to comply with an order is an offence which renders the broadcaster liable to a fine of NZD 100,000.[1220]

Decisions of the BSA may be appealed to the High Court, which will treat the decisions as if they were made in the exercise of a discretion. This means that the appellant must establish that the Authority acted on a wrong principle, failed to take into account a relevant matter or had regard to an irrelevant matter, or was plainly wrong.[1221] The Court may confirm, modify or reverse the decision or order made, or any part of it.[1222] It may also send the decision back to the Authority for reconsideration.[1223]

The standards cover accuracy, good taste and decency, fairness, balance on controversial issues, children's interests, privacy, law and order, violence, discrimination and denigration, liquor, and responsible programming.[1224] The *Annual Report of the BSA 2014* shows that most complaints still concern news, current affairs and

1213. Broadcasting Act 1989, s. 9(4).
1214. Broadcasting Act 1989, s. 10(l).
1215. Broadcasting Act 1989, s. 10(2).
1216. Broadcasting Act 1989, s. 13.
1217. Broadcasting Act 1989, s. 13(2).
1218. Broadcasting Act 1989, s. 15. Decisions from 1994 are available on the internet: see www.bsa.govt.nz.
1219. Broadcasting Act 1989, s. 13(3).
1220. Broadcasting Act 1989, s. 14.
1221. *TV3 Network Services Ltd v. The Prime Minister (Rt Hon Helen Clark)* HC Wellington CIV-2003-485-1655 and CIV-2003-485-1816, 10 Feb. 2004 at [8].
1222. Broadcasting Act 1989, s. 18.
1223. This power was said to be implied in s. 18 by the High Court in *TV3 Network Services Ltd v. The Prime Minister (Rt Hon Helen Clark)* HC Wellington CIV-2003-485-1655 and CIV-2003-485-1816, 10 Feb. 2004 at [27]–[30].
1224. See http://bsa.govt.nz/standards/overview, accessed 7 Apr. 2015.

talk radio,[1225] and the standards most often complained under were accuracy, and good taste and decency.[1226]

§1. IMPARTIALITY

235. Broadcasters should make reasonable efforts to ensure that news, current affairs and factual programming are accurate in relation to all material points of fact and do not mislead.[1227] The accuracy requirements do not cover expressions of opinion, comment or analysis.[1228] Minor and unintentional mistakes no longer constitute a breach of the standards.[1229] However, extravagant, sensationalized and exaggerated claims that cannot be substantiated should not be made.[1230] Broadcasters should take care not to report implications as explicitly stated facts.[1231] However, reporting speculative theories without supporting any one in particular is acceptable, because allegations of inaccuracy will be difficult to establish.[1232] Matters of excuse such as extent of intention to mislead, and degree of carelessness or inaccuracy will be relevant to any order made.[1233] When using experts, broadcasters need to be confident of the quality of the expert evidence offered, and also need to explain clearly at the outset if the views of experts are controversial.[1234]

If factual errors are material, they should be corrected as soon as possible,[1235] but broadcasters do not have the onus of proof to establish accuracy.[1236] Assertions of fact have to be objectively correct, but the broadcaster does not bear the onus of proving such accuracy, because the Broadcasting Act 1989 does not impose an onus of proof on either broadcasters or complainants. This suggests that the Authority should make findings of fact if at all possible,[1237] and it has been held that a finding of inaccuracy is a threshold requirement for the accuracy standard to engage.[1238] This does impose an extra burden on the Authority. Talkback radio is not usually

1225. *Annual Report of the Broadcasting Standards Authority* 2014 at 57.
1226. *Annual Report of the Broadcasting Standards Authority* 2014 at 58.
1227. See Standards 5 of the TV and Radio Code. The Pay TV Code requires only that significant errors of fact should be corrected at the earliest opportunity: Standard P8.
1228. Guidelines 5a in both codes.
1229. See *McDonald v. Television New Zealand Limited* (unreported, High Court, Wellington, CIV-2011-485-1836, Simon France J) and *McDonald v. Television New Zealand Limited* 2011-136; *RNZ v. Bolton* HC, Wellington, CIV-2010-485-225, 19 Jul. 2010.
1230. See *Ministry of Social Development v. TVNZ* 2004-067, 17 Jun. 2004.
1231. *Associate Minister of Health (the Hon Jim Anderton) v. Radio NZ* 2004-081, 15 Jul. 2004.
1232. *Boyce v. Television New Zealand Ltd* 2002-207, 17 Dec. 2002.
1233. *Dickson, Dunlop and McMillan v. TV3 Network Services Ltd* 1998-025-027, 12 Mar. 1998.
1234. *NZ Chiropractors' Association and TVNZ* 2009-058, 17 Sep. 2009.
1235. Guideline 5b in the TV Code; Guideline 5c in the Radio Code. *Cheer v. TVWorks Ltd* 2008-034, 2 Oct. 2008.
1236. *Television New Zealand Ltd (TVNZ) v. KW* HC Auckland CIV-2007-485-1609 and CIV-2007-485-1610, 18 Dec. 2008.
1237. *Television New Zealand Ltd (TVNZ) v. KW* HC Auckland CIV-2007-485-1609 and CIV-2007-485-1610, 18 Dec. 2008.
1238. *RNZ v. Bolton* HC, Wellington, CIV-2010-485-225, 19 Jul. 2010, [49]–[56].

subject to the accuracy standard, except where the presenter makes an unqualified statement of fact.[1239]

§2. Cultural Diversity

I. Māori Television

236. Māori television was established in 2004 under the Māori Television Service Act 2003.[1240] The service has a statutory function to be a high quality, cost effective television provider which informs, educates and entertains; it must broadcast mainly in the Māori language, and is required to consider the needs of children participating in immersion education and anyone else learning Māori. It informs, educates and entertains viewers, and enriches New Zealand's society, culture and heritage.[1241]

II. Te Reo Whakapuaki Irirangi (Te Manghai Paho)

237. The Broadcasting Act 1989 established an agency called Te Reo Whakapuaki Irirangi (Te Manghai Paho).[1242] Te Manghai Paho is an autonomous Crown Entity under the Crown Entities Act 2004.[1243] The function of Te Manghai Paho is to promote Maori language and Maori culture by making funds available for broadcasting, the production of programmes and archiving.[1244] In exercising its function under the Act, Te Manghai Paho must consult from time to time with representatives of Maori interests, broadcasters, persons who transmit on demand and others who can assist in the development of its funding policies.[1245]

In assessing any proposal for the agency to make funds available for broadcasting or for the production of a programme or programmes to be broadcast, Te Manghai Paho must have regard to the following:[1246]

(a) the extent to which the persons seeking the funding for the project to which the proposal relates have sought and secured funding or other resources for the project from sources other than Te Reo Whakapuaki Irirangi;

1239. Guideline 5b of the Radio Code. *Kinsella v. Canwest Radioworks* 2007-059, 25 Sep. 2007; *Lochead v. RadioWorks Ltd – Mazer v. RadioWorks Ltd* 2010-021, 27 Apr. 2010.

1240. Briefing to incoming Ministers of Māori Development and Finance, October 2014: http://www.maoritelevision.com/sites/default/files/attachments/Briefing%20to%20Incoming%20Ministers%202014.pdf, accessed 28 Jul. 2015.

1241. Māori Television Service (Te Aratuku Whakaata Irirangi Māori) Act 2003, s. 8(1).

1242. Broadcasting Act 1989, s. 53A(1). The agency is known as Te Manghai Paho – the Māori Broadcasting Funding Agency: http://www.tmp.govt.nz/, accessed 25 Jul. 2015. See *New Zealand Maori Council v. Attorney-General*[1992] 2 NZLR 576 (CA), *New Zealand Maori Council v. Attorney-General* [1994] 1 NZLR 513 (PC).

1243. Crown Entities Act 2004, sch. 1, Part 2.

1244. Broadcasting Act 1989, s. 53B.

1245. Broadcasting Act 1989, s. 53C.

1246. Broadcasting Act 1989, s. 53E.

(b) the potential size of the audience likely to benefit from the project to which the proposal relates;
(c) the extent to which the intended audience involved has access to services that have as their primary aim the promotion of Maori language and Maori culture;
(d) in the case of a proposal for the production of a programme or programmes, the extent to which the proposed programme or programmes would contribute to Te Reo Whakapuaki Irirangi meeting its objective of promoting Maori language and Maori culture;
(e) in the case of a proposal for the production of a programme or programmes, the likelihood that the proposed programme or programmes, if produced, would be broadcast or transmitted on demand; and
(f) the needs and preferences of children participating in te reo Māori immersion education, and all persons learning te reo Māori.

Te Manghai Paho must require from recipients of its funding in relation to the production of a programme or programmes, undertakings that the programme or programmes will be consistent with the programme standards specified in the Broadcasting Act 1989, in such form as it determines.[1247] In carrying out its functions under the Act, the Agency must also have regard to the funding policies adopted by New Zealand on Air.[1248]

In making funds available under the Act, Te Manghai Paho must, to the extent that, in its opinion it is practicable to do so, invite competitive proposals for the use of its available funds, ensure by the terms of contracts that the recipients of the funds are obliged both to attain specified standards of performance and to account for the use of the funds, and adopt measures to ensure that recipients of funds comply with the terms of such contracts.[1249]

No Minister or person acting by or on behalf of or at the direction of a Minister, may give a direction in respect of any programme or content, or the gathering or presentation of news or the preparation or presentation of any current affairs programme or content.[1250] The agency must also take account of government policy under the Crown Entities Act 2004.[1251]

Te Manghai Paho consists of not more than seven members.[1252] Members are appointed by the Governor-General on the recommendation of the Minister and carry out their duties under the Crown Entities Act 2004.[1253] A member must be a person who, in the responsible Minister's opinion, has the appropriate knowledge, skills and experience to assist the statutory entity to achieve its objectives and perform its functions, and the Minister must take account of the desirability of promoting diversity in the membership.[1254] Appointment is for up to five years, and the

1247. Broadcasting Act 1989, s. 53F.
1248. Broadcasting Act 1989, s. 53G. This is a reciprocal requirement for both entities.
1249. Broadcasting Act 1989, s. 53H.
1250. Broadcasting Act 1989, s. 53S.
1251. Crown Entities Act 2004, s. 103.
1252. Broadcasting Act 1989, s. 53I.
1253. Crown Entities Act 2004, ss 25 and 28 and see Part 2, subpart 1.
1254. Crown Entities Act 2004, s. 29.

member may be reappointed,[1255] or indeed, removed for just cause.[1256] Members have duties of honesty and integrity, good faith and reasonable care.[1257]

Te Manghai Pahou is publicly funded, and the income of the agency is exempt from income tax.[1258]

III. Radio New Zealand

238. The Radio New Zealand Act 1995 specifies as its second function the broadcast of 'a range of New Zealand programmes, including information, special interest, and entertainment programmes, and programmes which reflect New Zealand's cultural diversity, including Maori language and culture'.[1259]

§3. Protection of Minors (Indecency and Violence)

I. Children's Interests

239. The Free-to-Air television Code (TV code) established under the Broadcasting Act 1989 has a specific standard dealing with children's interests, whereby broadcasters are required to consider the interests of child viewers during children's normally accepted viewing times.[1260] The guidelines cover: promos; the scheduling of adult material; being mindful of children's viewing habits in the holidays and on Friday nights and in the weekend and the need for warnings; the need to deal sensitively with depictions of disturbing social and domestic friction or sequences in which people, especially children, or animals may be humiliated or badly treated; and the need to avoid gratuitous violence in children's cartoons. The Radio Code has no specific standard. However, the Fairness and Privacy standards in particular will be relevant, as well as those relating to Responsible Programming.[1261]

The Pay TV Code requires broadcasters to ensure that child viewers are protected from unsuitable content, and has guidelines which highlight the need to classify and promote correctly, to deal sensitively with sexual, violent and other disturbing material, and to promote filtering technology for the protection of children.[1262] Obviously enough, the BSA has held that the purpose of the children's interests standards is to protect children from broadcasts which might adversely affect them.[1263]

1255. Crown Entities Act 2004, s. 32.
1256. Crown Entities Act 2004, ss 39–40.
1257. Crown Entities Act 2004, ss 57.
1258. Broadcasting Act 1989, s. 53O.
1259. Radio New Zealand Act 1995, s. 7(1)(b).
1260. TV Code, Standard 9. Appendix 1 of the TV Code sets out programme classifications. A child is a boy or girl under the age of 14 years: Appendix 1.
1261. Radio Code, Standards 3, 6 and 8. The Privacy Principles are dealt with at paras 99–108 above.
1262. Pay TV Code, Standard P3.
1263. *Harrison v. TVNZ* 2008-066, 18 Sep. 2008.

Programmes which breach good taste and decency, and which might be watched by children, will infringe the standard. Footage on a current affairs programme of a man jumping on a blow-up doll, together with firearm use and alcohol consumption, did so.[1264] Promos and programmes for mature audiences should also be shown at appropriate times,[1265] although there is more latitude where they are shown during unclassified programming, such as the news.[1266] In fact, the news generally has considerable leeway.[1267] It is accepted that generally children will not watch the news unsupervised.[1268] However, some news items shown during children's normally accepted viewing times may require warnings, as in the case of 'One News' which broadcast two items covering a grisly trial.[1269]

Warnings must be effective. The Authority held that a warning from a TV3 newsreader that a story contained 'disturbing images' was inadequate to prepare viewers for witnessing a horrific execution during a report about a massacre in a Kenyan shopping mall. Although there was very high public interest in the story and in the footage, viewers were not given a reasonable opportunity to exercise discretion or make a different viewing choice.[1270]

Cruel or callous treatment of animals during the times children might watch is risky.[1271] Sex scenes should be discreet if shown during a PGR time slot.[1272] Non-sexualized nudity may be acceptable if accompanied by a warning.[1273] Stylized, theatrical, farcical and light-hearted treatments are unlikely to be seen as potentially disturbing.[1274]

Programmes which breach the classification standard are highly likely to breach the children's interests standard too.[1275] The popular TV programme, 'Outrageous Fortune', was well known for use by the characters of frequent coarse and obscene language. Frequent coarse language before 8.40 pm in one episode was found to be unacceptable in context, despite the AO classification and the expectations of regular viewers.[1276]

In fact, the fairness standards in both the TV and the Radio Codes require that broadcasters recognize the rights of children and young people not to be exploited, humiliated or unnecessarily identified.[1277] This will often overlap with privacy complaints.[1278]

1264. *Cotsilinis v. Television New Zealand* 2009-069, 20 Oct. 2009.
1265. *Harrison v. TVNZ* 2008-066, 18 Sep. 2008.
1266. *Oosterbroek v. TVNZ* 2008-102, 17 Feb. 2009.
1267. *VoTE v. TVNZ* 2006-033, 28 Jun. 2006; *Kiro v. Television New Zealand* 2007-111, 26 Mar. 2008.
1268. *Lewes v. TVNZ* 2008-085, 10 Nov. 2008.
1269. *Coates v. TVNZ* 2009-116, 25 Nov. 2009.
1270. *Warwick and TVWorks Ltd* 2013-089, 1 Apr. 2014.
1271. *Irwin v. TVNZ* 2009-162, 31 May 2010.
1272. *Painter v. Television New Zealand* 2009-155.
1273. *Cheyne v. Television New Zealand* 2007-116, 19 Feb. 2008.
1274. *Boulton v. TVNZ* 2009-031, 10 Jun. 2009.
1275. *Wong and World TV Ltd* 2012-031.
1276. *Binks and 20 Others and TVWorks Ltd* – 2010-141.
1277. TV Code and Radio Code, Standard 6, Guideline 6e. Standard 7 and 7e in the Pay TV code.
1278. *Hastings v. TVWorks* 2009-088, 2 Mar. 2010.

II. Violence[1279]

240. The current TV Code has a special standard requiring that broadcasters should exercise care and discretion when dealing with the issue of violence, together with five detailed guidelines: one requiring that any violence be justified in the context of screening and not be gratuitous; one cautioning against the cumulative effect of violence; one requiring care to be taken with programmes in which rape or sexual violence is a theme; one requiring news, current affairs and factual programmes which contain disturbing or alarming material to be justified in the public interest; and one warning against gratuitous repetition of violence in sports programmes.[1280] The Authority sees the objective of the standard as being to ensure that broadcasters use care and discretion to exclude unsuitable violent material and to promote the use of warnings where necessary to protect viewers, particularly child viewers.[1281]

Because it applies to a non-visual media, the Radio Code has fewer requirements, and few of them are specifically directed at violence. In radio, broadcasters are required to maintain standards that are consistent with the maintenance of law and order,[1282] programmes cannot be presented in such a way as to cause panic, or unwarranted alarm or undue distress,[1283] broadcasters must be mindful of the effect that any programme may have on children during their normally accepted listening times,[1284] the time of transmission and the station profile is an important consideration in the scheduling of programmes that contain violent themes,[1285] and if a programme is likely to disturb, an appropriate warning should be broadcast.[1286]

The requirements of the Pay TV Code are less strict and require that violent content should be appropriate to the context of the programme and classified carefully.[1287] The associated guidelines suggest that violent content should be appropriately classified, with warnings if necessary, that content should not include any combination of violence and sex designed to titillate, that rape as a theme should be treated with utmost care and explicit detail, and prolonged focus on sexually violent contact should be avoided, that devices and methods of inflicting pain or injury, particularly when capable of easy imitation, should not screen without the most careful consideration, and that violent incidents during or surrounding play in sporting coverage should not be gratuitously repeated.

Breaches of the relevant standards are regarded in a serious light. The inclusion of violence in a broadcast has to be justified in the context[1288] and in the time slot

1279. See Broadcasting Act 1989, s. 4(1)(b); TV Code, Standard 10 and Guidelines; Radio Code, Standard 8, Guidelines 8a–8c; Pay TV Code, Standard 4. The *BSA Annual Report 2014* records that one upheld complaint (1% of the decisions issued in 2013/14) was based on the violence standard: at 56.

1280. TV Code, Standard 10, Guidelines 10a–e.

1281. *Knight v. TVWorks Ltd* 2008-137, 3 Mar. 2009.

1282. Radio Code, Standard 2.

1283. Radio Code, Standard 2, Responsible Programming, Guideline 8e.

1284. Radio Code, Standard 2, Guideline 8a.

1285. Radio Code, Standard 2, Guideline 8b.

1286. Radio Code, Standard 2, Guideline 8c.

1287. Pay TV Code, Standard P4.

1288. *Howard v. TVWorks* 2009-105, 20 Oct. 2009.

given. Brief, non-explicit violence is less likely to offend.[1289] Slapstick humour is unlikely to be a breach.[1290] Where the time slot is appropriate, warnings are given, the violence is in context, the programme is targeted at an adult audience and the classification is correct, no breach will occur.[1291]

The slasher film, 'Wolf Creek' was, in the Authority's view, an extremely cruel, unusual and sickening variety of film that carried sexual connotations.[1292] It had received a classification of 'R18 Contains Sadistic Violence, Sexual Themes and Offensive Language' from the Office of Film and Literature Classification in New Zealand. TVNZ classified it AO and screened it at 8.30 pm with a pre-broadcast warning for 'graphic violence'. The Authority found that the film should not have been broadcast at 8.30 pm even though no violence occurred until after 9.30 pm. Programmes are considered as a whole and the start time of 8.30 pm signalled to viewers that the movie would contain a lesser degree of violence than was actually shown. Further, the warning for 'graphic violence' was inadequate, and the title 'Wolf Creek' did not signal that it was in fact a horror film.

Three complaints were upheld against the New Zealand soap opera, 'Shortland Street', for violence that was unsuitable for children even when supervised by an adult (the show goes to air at 7 pm weekdays).[1293] The episodes involved murder, gang violence and being taken away to be killed. Although necessary to the storyline, the violence was realistic and the implication from the decisions is that implied violence could have been shown in the time slot.

More complaints appear to now arise in relation to news programmes. With the rise of terrorism, it is perhaps more common to see depictions of torture or the results of torture on the news. These will not be seen as likely to disturb or alarm children if brief and restrained, and if they contain no specific images of violence or injury.[1294]

Although news, current affairs and factual programmes have some natural immunity to the violence standards because, by their nature, reporting on violence and brutality may be a necessity, warnings may still be required without unjustifiably breaching freedom of expression.[1295] Verbal warnings will do if appropriate in the context.[1296] The BSA has emphasized that if a warning is used, it must be effective.[1297]

Complaints about violence are uncommon. The Authority has carried out research exploring comfort levels of the public with violent depictions and attitudes towards it.[1298] It found that gender and age had the most significant effects on perception.

1289. *Garlick v. TVNZ* 2009-086, 17 Sep. 2009; *Findlay v. TVNZ* 2008-100, 25 Nov. 2008; *Child v. TVNZ* 2007-064, 25 Sep. 2007; *Orsulich v. Television New Zealand* 2006-036, 28 Jun. 2006.
1290. *Stranaghan v. TVNZ* 2007-127, 26 Mar. 2008.
1291. *Dobson v. TVWorks* 2008-067, 18 Sep. 2008, *Howard v. TVWorks* 2009-105, 20 Oct. 2009.
1292. *McIntosh v. TVNZ* 2008-039, 4 Jul. 2008.
1293. *Turner and TVNZ* 2008-112, 19 Dec. 2008; *Buxton and TVNZ* 2009-016-017, 6 May 2009.
1294. *Pratt v. Television New Zealand Ltd* 2004-120, 30 Sep. 2004.
1295. *Kiro v. Television New Zealand* 2007-111, 26 Mar. 2008.
1296. *Monkton v. TVNZ* 2007-023.
1297. *Warwick and TVWorks Ltd* 2013-089, 1 Apr. 2014.
1298. *Viewing Violence: Audience Perceptions of Violent Content in Audio-Visual Entertainment*, November 2008: www.bsa.govt.nz/publications-booksandreports.php#reports, accessed 26 May 2010.

Women participants were more likely to anticipate harmful effects than men. Teenagers displayed less ability to interpret context than older teenagers and adults. Participants were particularly concerned about effects on children.[1299]

III. Censorship

241. On 1 October 1994, the previous tripartite system of classification of films, videos, and books and magazines was replaced by a streamlined, comprehensive classification system enforced and administered from one Office of Film and Literature Classification ('the Office') under the empowering legislative umbrella of the Films, Videos and Publications Classification Act 1993 ('the Act'). The censorship regime centres on a finding that material is 'objectionable'.[1300] Publications that promote or support, or tend to promote or support, certain types of behaviour listed in section 3(2) of the Act are automatically deemed likely to be injurious to the public good. Other publications must be considered giving particular weight to other factors set out in section 3(3), which are the manner, extent and degree to which the publication describes, depicts or deals with matters such as torture, physical cruelty, acts of sexual violence, sexual acts with children, acts of a degrading or dehumanizing nature, or of a sado-masochistic character, or which represent a particular class of persons as inherently inferior. Under section 3(4), matters such as the character of the work, including any merit, value or importance that the publication has in relation to literary, artistic, social, cultural, educational, scientific or other matters are also to be considered, as are the overall effect of the publication as a whole, the impact of the form in which the publication is presented, the likely or intended audience, and the purpose for which the publication is intended to be used.

The Act establishes an office of Film and Literature Classification,[1301] consisting of a Chief Censor, a Deputy Chief Censor and such classification officers as are required. The main function of the Office is to classify any publications submitted to it under the Act as objectionable or otherwise.[1302] The punishment of offences is left to the ordinary courts, although the Office's jurisdiction is very wide. Section 2 defines 'publication' as:

(a) any film, book, sound recording, picture, newspaper, photograph, photographic negative, photographic plate, or photographic slide:
(b) any print or writing:

1299. *BSA Annual Report* 2009 at 6–7.
1300. Films, Videos and Publications Classification Act 1993, s. 3.
1301. Films, Videos and Publications Classification Act 1993, s. 76. See http://www.classificationoffice.govt.nz/.
1302. Films, Videos and Publications Classification Act 1993, s. 77 of the Act sets out this function, and that of determining any question relating to the character of a publication referred by a court, determining any restrictions that might apply as part of classification, examining film posters and determining any exemptions from the Act's provisions. The Office must act independently.

(c) a paper or other thing that has printed or impressed upon it, or otherwise shown upon it, 1 or more (or a combination of 1 or more) images, representations, signs, statements, or words:

(d) a thing (including, but not limited to, a disc, or an electronic or computer file) on which is recorded or stored information that, by the use of a computer or other electronic device, is capable of being reproduced or shown as 1 or more (or a combination of 1 or more) images, representations, signs, statements, or words.

The Office is responsible for the classification of a wide range of material, including films, videos, newspapers, magazines, computer discs, video games, CD-ROMS, printed clothing, posters and playing cards.[1303] Hard drives of computers and stored images are also covered.[1304] The Office does not deal with three-dimensional publications, such as statuary, or live performances. The courts would deal with such items under other criminal provisions.

The Act does not apply to broadcasting in general. The definition of exhibiting a film to the public in the Act does not include broadcasting the film.[1305] However, a broadcaster may broadcast a film that has been classified as objectionable or contains a part required to be excised only with the consent of the Chief Censor.[1306] Any other classification, including restricted (where the film is classified as objectionable except in the hands of specified individuals or groups), does not require such permission.[1307] Such broadcasts would be subject to the post-broadcast complaints jurisdiction of the BSA and would be judged according to the relevant code provisions dealing with good taste and decency, and violence.[1308] This separation of jurisdiction is somewhat anomalous in that the print media are subject to the Act, which contains draconian offence provisions, while broadcasters are subject in the main to the less onerous complaints jurisdiction of the BSA.

It appears that live broadcasts on television or radio are not covered by the Act since no recording exists until after the broadcast.[1309] In any event, classification in such a situation is impossible and pointless. Ordinary criminal provisions might again cover such broadcasts, where for example indecent or obscene language was used, although these provisions would apply to the speaker, not the broadcaster. The latter risks a complaint to the BSA.

The BSA has additional powers to make orders in respect of series that contain objectionable material. Under section 13A of the Broadcasting Act, the Authority may consider broadcast series dealing with sex, violence, degrading, dehumanizing or demeaning sexual or physical conduct, sexual conduct with or by children, exploitation of the nudity of children, or promoting or encouraging criminal acts or

1303. *Annual Report* (2003) 24.

1304. *R v. Spark* [2009] 3 NZLR 625 (CA), upheld on appeal: [2010] 1 NZLR 599 (SC).

1305. Section 2 of the Act.

1306. Broadcasting Act 1989, s. 4(2).

1307. *Re Baise-Moi* [2005] NZAR 214 (CA).

1308. See *In re Baise-Moi v. Society for the Promotion of Community Standards* [2005] NZAR 214 (CA) at [29].

1309. 'Exhibit' in relation to a sound recording means to play that sound recording: Films, Videos and Publications Classification Act 1993, s. 2.

acts of terrorism,[1310] and determine whether the manner in which these themes are dealt with are injurious to the public good. The Authority must have regard to contextual matters in making its decision.[1311] It may look at recordings and transcripts relating to further programmes in the series and direct withdrawal of any programme or impose conditions,[1312] or order withdrawal of the entire series or part of it.[1313] Failure to comply with an order or contravention of an order attracts a fine of up to NZD 100,000.

§4. Human Dignity

242. Broadcasters are required not to encourage discrimination against, or denigration of, any section of the community on account of sex, sexual orientation, race, age, disability, occupational status, or as a consequence of legitimate expression of religion, culture or political belief.[1314]

A high level of denigration is required in the sense of the blackening of the reputation of a group.[1315] The requirements of the NZBORA 1990 are seen to require this.[1316] Comments that reinforce negative stereotypes do not therefore reach the threshold.[1317]

Decisions have given prominence to the issue of 'hate speech', and these illustrate when the level of denigration is sufficient. Celebrity broadcaster Paul Holmes made comments about the United Nations and its Secretary-General Kofi Annan on his radio breakfast show, referring to him as a 'cheeky darkie' five times. The Radio Network received numerous complaints and responded internally by various means. The host also broadcast a radio apology and a voluntary apology on his evening current affairs television programme.[1318] The Authority received ten complaints and agreed that the comments were a serious breach of programme standards.[1319] The Authority considered that whether or not the comments were intentionally racist did not matter; they supported a racist view of the world, which the host had later stated in his apology he abhorred. Thus, intention is irrelevant to this standard. However, it declined to uphold the complaints because sufficient action had been taken by the broadcaster.

1310. Broadcasting Act 1989, s. 13A.

1311. Broadcasting Act 1989, s. 13A(2): The dominant effect of: the programme as a whole; the impact of the programme given the medium in which the programme is presented; the character of the programme, including any merit, value or importance the programme has in relation to artistic, social, cultural, educational, scientific or other matters; the persons, class of persons, or age of persons by whom the programme was intended, or is likely, to be viewed; the purpose of the programme; and any other relevant matter relating to the broadcasting of the programme.

1312. Broadcasting Act 1989, s. 13A(3).

1313. Broadcasting Act 1989, s. 13A(4).

1314. Standard 7 in the TV Code and the Radio Code. In the Pay TV Code, fairness guidelines under Standard P7 cover this area.

1315. *Browne v. CanWest* 2005-112; *Petros v. The Radio Network* 2009-040, 10 Jun. 2009; *Lee v. UPFM* 2010-011, 27 Apr. 2010.

1316. *Gibson v. RadioWorks* 2010-020, 27 Apr. 2010.

1317. *Broughton v. Television New Zealand* 2009-097.

1318. *TVNZ v. Hooker* 2004-011, 4 Mar. 2004.

1319. *Smith v. The Radio Network Ltd* 2003-174-183, 19 Dec. 2003.

In the same programme, the host had interviewed a journalist about the dominance of women in journalism. At one point, Holmes put the question: 'Is it, do you think, making our journalism ignorant and bitchy do you think?' He later asked: 'At certain times of the month do the newspapers get particularly judgmental?' These comments were also the subject of a complaint alleging denigration of or discrimination on account of gender. This complaint was rejected by the Authority, which considered that a high level of denigration was required to constitute a breach.[1320] The Authority found the comments had been made during an exchange between the host and an interviewee and were clearly intended to be provocative.

Shortly thereafter, a programme broadcast by Triangle Television between 3 pm and 4 pm on a Monday included a lecture titled: 'Challenges Facing Muslims in the New Millennium'. The lecture was delivered by a Brother Abdullah Hakim Quick, who stated that AIDS is caused by the 'filthy practices' of homosexuals, that homosexuals are dropping dead from AIDs and 'want to take us all down with them', that the Islamic position on homosexuality is 'death', that homosexuals are 'sick' and 'not natural', and that 'Muslims are going to have to take a stand [against homosexuals] and it's not enough to call names'. This broadcast was found by the BSA to unlawfully encourage discrimination and denigration.[1321] The Authority considered the statements to be 'hate speech', in particular those advocating death and taking a stand were seen as an incitement to violence.

'Discrimination' has been defined as encouraging the different treatment of the members of a particular group to their detriment.[1322] The standards cover sections or classes of the community rather than individuals.[1323] The Radio Code has been held to cover comments about: doctors as an occupational group;[1324] the denigration of Africans arising from a statement read on talkback radio which observed that an individual well-known African living in New Zealand should be 'swinging in trees in the Congo';[1325] and a statement made on a breakfast show on Newstalk ZB describing women who attended parties with rugby league players as 'moles' and implying that they were inviting sexual abuse.[1326] However in other decisions, a group of campaigners for responsible consumerism was not a group within the same code because it was not bound together by religious, cultural or political beliefs, as required by the standard;[1327] a programme focusing on the disruption caused by an employee with a mental health disability did not discriminate against the mentally disabled generally;[1328] and the Authority questioned, but did not decide, whether tobacco company executives are a group which can be discriminated against, before it ultimately rejected a complaint that a documentary about cigarette smoking in

1320. *Smith v. The Radio Network Ltd* 2003-174-183, 19 Dec. 2003. Clearly, by implication, the 'cheeky darkie' comments had met this high standard.
1321. *Clayton v. Triangle Television Ltd* 2004-001, 26 Feb. 2004. Standard 6 and Guideline 6g of the TV Code.
1322. *Teoh v. TVNZ* 2008-091, 25 Nov. 2008; *Duff v. TVWorks* 2010-003, 23 Mar. 2010.
1323. *Towl v. RadioWorks* 2009-136, 21 Dec. 2009.
1324. *Sawyers v. Radio Pacific Ltd* 1996-076, 18 Jul. 1996: doctors who carried out abortions were described as 'baby murderers'.
1325. *Keir v. Radio Pacific Ltd* 1996-133, 10 Oct. 1996.
1326. *Whitla v. Newstalk ZB* 2004-104, 2 Sep. 2004.
1327. *Caddie v. Channel Z* 1998-037, 23 Apr. 1998.
1328. *Boyce v. TVNZ* 2004-119, 30 Sep. 2004.

New Zealand portrayed tobacco executives in a manner which would encourage discrimination against them.[1329]

The requirement does not prevent the broadcast of material that is factual, or the expression of genuinely held opinion in news, current affairs or other factual programmes, or legitimate humour, drama or satire.[1330] In the *Triangle Television* decision discussed above,[1331] the programme could not fall within the exception for genuinely held opinion in factual programmes as it was a sermon and not a factual programme. In all, the comments were an unacceptable tirade against homosexuals and homosexuality. However, the potentially discriminatory inferences and statements made about tobacco executives and Māori women in a documentary programme about cigarette smoking in New Zealand were exempt as genuinely held opinions.[1332]

The content of a satirical or humorous work has to move towards the realm of vitriol or hate speech before it can breach the denigration and discrimination standard. A complaint was made about 'Nightline' which incorporated an item on Māori TV's bid for the free-to-air broadcasting rights to the Rugby World Cup, included a satirical sketch about what Māori TV's coverage would look like.[1333] The Authority noted that Māori TV is not, in fact, a 'section of the community' to which the standard applies, but addressed it because of the strong connection now made between Māori TV and Māori in general. The BSA found the item did not mock Māori in general, but rather satirized Māori TV's proposed coverage and its view that Māori language and culture could be promoted through its coverage of the Rugby World Cup. Overall, nothing in the item could be said to have 'blackened the reputation' of Māori, or to encourage the different treatment of Māori to their detriment.

Once again, talkback and controversial hosts appear to have some leeway in this area. Extreme comments may be acceptable if they encourage discussion of a legitimate issue in the robust environment of talkback.[1334]

There have been few recent complaints upheld in this area in the last five years.[1335]

Under the Broadcasting Act 1989, the BSA has jurisdiction to deal with complaints that a broadcaster has breached some aspect of privacy of the individual. These are discussed above.[1336]

1329. *The Tobacco Institute of New Zealand Ltd v. TVNZ* 2000-036, 9 Mar. 2000.
1330. Guideline 7a in both the TV and Radio Code. There are minor variations in the wording used, for example Standard 7 and Guideline 7a of the Radio Code exempt a genuine expression of serious comment, analysis or opinion.
1331. *Clayton v. Triangle Television Ltd* 2004-001, 26 Feb. 2004.
1332. *The Tobacco Institute of New Zealand Ltd v. TVNZ* 2000-036, 9 Mar. 2000.
1333. *Adair v. TVWorks* 2009-138, 21 Dec. 2009.
1334. *Cage v. TVNZ* 2009-125, 15 Feb. 2010.
1335. *Ashurst and Others v. Television New Zealand Ltd* 2010-001.
1336. See paras 99–108 above.

§5. Right of Reply

I. Fairness

243. Broadcasters should deal fairly with any person or organization taking part or referred to in a broadcast.[1337] A broadcast will invariably be unfair if it fails to give a party adversely affected by it or presented in a bad light an opportunity to give their side of the story.[1338] The purpose of filming and use of footage has to be made known clearly, and broadcasters cannot delegate the role to police or others in authority either. There is a higher threshold for breach of fairness where public figures are involved. However, the line may still be crossed where comments are sustained personal abuse masquerading as satire.[1339]

Serious allegations require forceful (although not necessarily aggressive) challenges in interviews, especially if they are uncorroborated, hearsay or made by unidentified parties. If parties who are the subject of the allegations are given an opportunity to be interviewed, the offer of an interview must be a reasonable one so that there is no element of surprise. The individual should be advised of the purpose of the interview unless reasons of public interest prevent this. It is acceptable not to supply interviewees in advance with specific questions, but in some cases, giving only a general indication of the subject-matter of the interview will be inadequate, especially if the allegations to be raised will have serious implications for the interviewee.[1340] The fact that a party refuses to be interviewed does not excuse the broadcaster from meeting its code obligations. Any programme in which unidentified accusers allege that an identified person has committed serious but unspecified criminal offences is likely to be inherently unfair to the accused.[1341]

The use of subterfuge or deceptive practices will often be relevant to whether or not an issue has been dealt with fairly. Footage taken by a hidden camera or filmed without consent, even if in a public place, can be risky.[1342] This approach has a significant exception carved out where there is high public interest in the subject of the broadcast and a reasonable belief by the broadcaster that there is no other method of obtaining the information.[1343] The BSA has consistently held that while 'door-stepping' (confronting individuals without notice with a camera or tape-recorder and reporter, and asking questions) will not always be a breach of a code, it is normally not a method to be used if there are alternative legitimate modes of obtaining information or the person being investigated can be given an opportunity to respond with plenty of notice. In other words, it is an approach of last resort.[1344] The practice is generally assumed to be potentially most unfair and intimidating, and the media

1337. See Standards 6 of the TV Code and the Radio Code. Standard 7 of the Pay TV Code states that: 'People and organisations taking part or referred to in programmes should be dealt with fairly'.

1338. *Diocese of Dunedin v. TV3 Network Services Ltd* 1999-125-137, 9 Sep. 1999.

1339. *Craig v. Television New Zealand Ltd* 2013-034.

1340. *Ministry of Health and Canwest TVWorks Ltd* (2007-012).

1341. *Ellis v. Radio NZ* 2004-115, 3 Sep. 2004.

1342. *Dr Z v. Television New Zealand Ltd* 2012-074 (2 May 2014).

1343. *Hart, Cameron and Cotter v. TV3 Network Services Ltd* 2000-108-113, 10 Aug. 2000.

1344. *The Prime Minister (Rt Hon Helen Clark) v. TV3 Network Services Ltd* 2003-055-061, 3 Jul. 2003.

should accordingly exercise discretion in using it. Contrived incidents will fall foul of the fairness requirement.[1345]

The requirement to deal fairly will be breached where a presenter adopts an extreme or inappropriately partisan response. Similarly, if a presenter reacts strongly and inaccurately to a stance taken by an interviewee, the fairness standard may be breached. Aggressively talking over the top of an invited interviewee may also be going too far.[1346] Juxtaposition of news items may also raise fairness concerns if a misleading impression is created[1347] and material should not be edited to unfair effect.[1348]

The character of the broadcast is relevant to a finding of fairness.[1349] News and current affairs programmes are given less leeway than programmes which provide advocacy for particular interest groups, for example, programmes which represent consumers.[1350] However, with regard to news and current affairs programmes, the BSA has noted that if a matter is controversial, complex and one of public interest, it is inevitable that some strands of argument will be highlighted and others not.[1351] The implication is that this would be acceptable.

Inevitably, the degree of unfairness will be relevant to any order made and it is quite common for the BSA not to impose an order where the breach is minor or where the broadcaster has apologized.[1352]

II. Controversial Issues: Viewpoints

244. When discussing controversial issues of public importance in news, current affairs or factual programmes, broadcasters should make reasonable efforts, or give reasonable opportunities, to present significant points of view either in the same programme or in other programmes within the period of current interest.[1353] This is essentially an obligation to provide balance and requires objectivity in the sense that competing arguments must be advanced with sufficient purpose to enable a viewer to arrive at an informed and reasoned opinion.[1354] The Authority will take into account the programme introduction, whether the programme approaches a topic from a particular perspective (e.g., authorial documentaries, public access and

1345. *Road Transport of New Zealand v. TV3 Network Services Ltd* 1997-114.
1346. *Beckett, Cox and Warren v. TVWorks Ltd* 2011-047.
1347. *The Warehouse v. Television New Zealand Ltd* 2004-019, 11 Mar. 2004.
1348. Guideline 6b of the TV Code now provides: 'Broadcasters should exercise care in editing programme material to ensure that the extracts used are not a distortion of the original event or the overall views expressed.'
1349. See Guideline 6a in the TV Code and the Radio Code.
1350. See *Lancaster Sales and Service Ltd v. Television New Zealand Ltd* 1997-113.
1351. *New Zealand Police v. TV3 Network Services Ltd* 1997-160, 4 Dec. 1997.
1352. See, e.g.: *Beckett, Cox and Warren v. TVWorks Ltd* 2011-047.
1353. See Broadcasting Act 1989, s. 4(1)(d); Standard 4 of the TV Code and the Radio Code. Standard P6 of the Pay TV Code provides: 'News and current affairs content dealing with controversial issues of public importance should be balanced, with significant sides to these issues presented in as fair a way as possible.'
1354. *The Prime Minister (Rt Hon Helen Clark) v. TV3 Network Services Ltd* 2003-055-061, 3 Jul. 2003 at [357].

advocacy programmes), and whether viewers or listeners could reasonably be expected to be aware of views expressed in other coverage.[1355]

For radio, the programme type is also relevant.[1356] For example, talkback programmes may be subject to a lesser requirement to present a range of views.[1357] This is because in considering the viewpoints standard, the Authority must consider not only whether a controversial issue of public importance was actually raised, but also the full context of the broadcast, including the treatment of the issue and how a reasonable listener or viewer would have understood it. The standard also ensures audiences are presented with a wide range of significant viewpoints so that they can reach a reasoned and informed opinion.

There is no set formula to determine the issue of balance and each case is considered in its context.[1358] The higher the impact and the more serious the allegations, the greater the onus to provide balance.[1359] Programmes said to provide balance in the period of current interest are first assessed individually and then cumulatively to determine overall effect. Sheer numbers of broadcasts dealing with the topic will not automatically determine the matter since their content is all-important.

An offer of participation in a broadcast does not negate the need to provide balance. A party may reasonably decline to take part in an interview and not lose the right to have their side of the story made known.[1360] As a general rule, when a person declines to participate in a broadcast, the broadcaster must make sure that viewers and/or listeners are aware that the matter being discussed is controversial and that there exist other significant perspectives. A straightforward method of achieving this would be the interviewer explaining the other points of view and possibly adopting a devil's advocate approach. However, balance will be very difficult to achieve by any method where unsubstantiated, vague allegations are raised without more, unless they are strongly challenged and probed, and a reasonable opportunity to respond is given contemporaneously or within a short time after the allegations are broadcast.

The issue of what constitutes a period of current interest is assessed by the Authority methodically considering the totality of coverage.[1361] Reasonable efforts and reasonable opportunities to present significant points of view on the issue across programmes within the period of current interest will be sufficient.

The requirement is not that every current affairs programme has to be mathematically balanced and every perspective covered. The Authority has stated its views as

1355. TV Code, Guideline 4b; Radio Code, Guideline 4a. The Pay TV Code provides that factual content which clearly approaches such issues from a particular perspective may not be required to be balanced, but should be fair, and no set formula is advanced for the allocation of time to interested parties on controversial issues.
1356. Radio Code, Guideline 4a.
1357. *Cindy Kiro, Children's Commissioner v. RadioWorks* Ltd 2008-108, 19 Dec. 2008.
1358. TV Code, Guideline 4a. *The Prime Minister (Rt Hon Helen Clark) v. TV3 Network Services Ltd* 2003-055-061, 3 Jul. 2003.
1359. *Brooking and TVWorks Ltd* 2012–121, 27 Feb. 2013.
1360. *Radio New Zealand Ltd v. McCully* [1998] NZAR 293 (HC).
1361. *NZORD v. TVNZ* 2009-131, 15 Feb. 2010.

to balance in relation to what it calls 'authorial documentaries'.[1362] While there is an overriding obligation to ensure balance, absolute neutrality on every issue is not possible, as this would not be consistent with fundamental democratic principles, nor can it be achieved in any simple mathematical sense. Broadcasters may therefore broadcast authorial documentaries in the public interest.[1363]

The requirements as to balance and impartiality have no application to fictional programmes,[1364] or to satirical or glib editorial observations.[1365]

1362. *Anderson v. Television New Zealand Ltd* 2003-028-030, 15 Apr. 2003.
1363. *Anderson v. TVNZ* 2004-127A, 15 Oct. 2004.
1364. *Mental Health Foundation of New Zealand v. TVNZ* 2002-074-075, 13 Jun. 2002.
1365. *Duggan v. the Radio Network Ltd* 2004-086, 29 Jul. 2004.

Chapter 4. Political Broadcasting

§1. Rules on Political Independence of Broadcasters

245. Under the Television New Zealand Act 2003, no Minister or person acting at the direction of a Minister may give a direction to TVNZ or to any of its subsidiaries, or to any director or officer or employee of TVNZ or of any of its subsidiaries, in respect of any programme or other content, any allegation or complaint relating to a programme or other content, the gathering or presentation of news or the preparation or presentation of any current affairs programme or content, or the broadcasting standards under the Broadcasting Act 1989. Further, no director of TVNZ or of any of its subsidiaries may be removed for any reason relating to any of those same things. The protection applies regardless of the type of delivery platform TVNZ uses to deliver any programmes or other content.[1366] Additionally, TVNZ must also pay a dividend to the Crown each financial year, and the Minister must give written notice of the amount and consult with the company when it does so.[1367]

No Minister of the Crown may give a direction to Radio New Zealand, or any subsidiary of it in respect of a particular programme or a particular allegation or a particular complaint, the gathering or presentation of news or the preparation or presentation of current affairs programmes, or the responsibility of the company for programme standards. No director of Radio New Zealand or of any subsidiary of it may be removed for any reason relating to a particular programme or a particular allegation or a particular complaint, the gathering or presentation of news or the preparation or presentation of current affairs programmes, or the responsibility of the company for programme standards.[1368]

The Māori Television Service cannot be politically directed as to particular programmes in relation to allegations or complaints relating to particular programmes, the gathering or presentation of news or the preparation or presentation of current affairs programmes, or programme standards.[1369]

§2. Fair Representation in Election Periods

I. Broadcasting Act 1989

246. Part 6 of the Broadcasting Act[1370] lays down important provisions about parliamentary election programmes. Part 6 regulates the broadcasting of election programmes in an 'election period', which is defined to cover the period beginning with writ day and ending with the close of the day before polling day. An election

1366. Television New Zealand Act 2003, s. 28.
1367. Television New Zealand Act 2003, ss 27 and 29. See also s. 115 of the Crown Entities Act 2004.
1368. Radio New Zealand Act 1995, s. 13.
1369. Māori Television Service (Te Aratuku Whakaata Irirangi Māori) Act 2003, s. 10.
1370. As amended in 1996 and 2004. See *Alliance Party v. Electoral Commission* [2010] NZAR 222 (CA).

programme is a programme used to persuade voters to vote for or against a political party or the election of any person at an election, or which opposes a candidate or a political party, or notifies meetings held or to be held in connection with an election.[1371] The Electoral Commission determines allocation of time and money for election broadcasting.

There is a prohibition on paid election programmes, whether within or outside an election period.[1372] However, this does not apply to: any election programme broadcast for a political party or group of related political parties during broadcasting time allocated under the Act; any election programme broadcast for a political party or group of related political parties and paid for with money allocated to that political party or group of related political parties under the Act; any programme promoting one named candidate for a particular election and broadcast by the candidate or with the candidate's authority within the election period; or to an advertisement placed by the Electoral Commission, a Registrar of Electors, a Returning Officer or other official for the purposes of the Electoral Act 1993; or to a non-partisan advertisement broadcast as a community service. Nor does the prohibition restrict the broadcasting of news, comment or current affairs programmes about the election. However, these exceptions aside, a party may not use its own money to purchase more time nor, if it receives no allocation, may it purchase any time at all. This does not prevent lobby groups from using their own resources to purchase broadcasting time or space.

Television New Zealand (TVNZ) and Radio New Zealand (Radio NZ) must each provide time, free of charge, for the broadcasting in an election period of the opening addresses and closing addresses of political parties.[1373] TVNZ must broadcast opening addresses and closing addresses on one free-to-air channel with national coverage. Radio NZ must broadcast opening addresses and closing addresses on the service known as National Radio. Opening addresses and closing addresses must be broadcast in accordance with the Act.[1374]

The Electoral Commission seeks a statement from the state broadcasters about time available, and they must reply within a reasonable time and may give their own views of how time should be allocated.[1375] The Commission allocates the time offered in such proportions as it sees fit.[1376] It also allocates to the parties moneys appropriated by Parliament for the purpose of meeting all or part of the costs of broadcasting election programmes.[1377] Conditions may be imposed on the monetary allocation, including a requirement that the party advise the Commission of the value of its election programme bookings.[1378] Money allocated may only be

1371. Broadcasting Act 1989, s. 69.
1372. Broadcasting Act 1989, s. 70.
1373. Broadcasting Act 1989, s. 71(1). See *Alliance Party v. Electoral Commission* [2010] NZAR 222 (CA).
1374. Broadcasting Act 1989, s. 77A.
1375. Broadcasting Act 1989, s. 71A.
1376. Broadcasting Act 1989, s. 73. It may modify the broadcasters' allocation suggestions.
1377. 'Broadcasting allocation 2014 General Election' (2014) Electoral Commission New Zealand, http://www.elections.org.nz/events/2014-general-election/2014-parties-candidates-and-third-parties/broadcasting-allocation-2014, accessed 9 Mar. 2015.
1378. Broadcasting Act 1989, s. 74A.

used to meet the production costs or the cost of broadcasting time of any election programme broadcast during the election period.[1379] By using its own funds for production costs (which have been accepted as election expenses),[1380] a political party may use its allocated time or money exclusively for actual broadcasting. It may also approach a broadcaster directly to buy time at usual rates using its allocated funds if it is dissatisfied with its allocation of free or discounted time.

The Commission may allocate time and money only to a party that was registered on the Register of Political Parties at the time of the dissolution of Parliament for the election or, as the case requires, at the time that Parliament expired, and that party has given to the Electoral Commission, in relation to that election, a notice that it is eligible.[1381] The Commission must have regard to: the number of votes the party and its candidates received at the last election; the number of votes its candidate received at any by-election held since the last election; the number of Members of Parliament it had before the dissolution of Parliament for a general election; any relationship between the party and any other political party; any other indications of public support for the party, such as polls and membership; and the need to provide a fair opportunity for each political party to convey its policies to the public by broadcasting an election programme on television.[1382]

TVNZ and Radio NZ have the opportunity to comment on the proposed allocation of free time, as do the political parties.[1383] Failure by the broadcasters or parties to take advantage of these opportunities does not prevent valid allocation being made. The state broadcasters must broadcast as allocated, and on the terms offered. Any disputes are resolved by the Commission.[1384]

The principle contained in section 4(1)(d) of the Broadcasting Act, that when controversial issues of public importance are discussed, reasonable efforts are made or reasonable opportunities are given to present significant points of view either in the same programme or in other programmes within the period of current interest, does not apply in relation to election programmes broadcast under the Act.[1385] Election programmes may not be broadcast on television during the hours between 6 am and noon on Sunday or Anzac Day, or on television or radio all day on Christmas Day, Good Friday or Easter Sunday.[1386]

Broadcasters cannot offer or give to any political party or candidate terms more favourable for broadcasting time than those offered or given to any other political party or candidate that buys or expresses an interest in buying comparable time from the broadcaster.[1387] This provision means if a broadcaster agrees to sell or give time, it must sell or give it to all comers on equal terms. A broadcaster can also simply refuse to sell or give broadcasting time altogether, but if it does so, apparently it

1379. Broadcasting Act 1989, s. 74B.
1380. See s. 205(1) of the Electoral Act 1993.
1381. Broadcasting Act 1989, s. 75(1).
1382. Broadcasting Act 1989, s. 75(2).
1383. Broadcasting Act 1989, ss 75A and 76.
1384. Broadcasting Act 1989, s. 77.
1385. Broadcasting Act 1989, s. 79.
1386. Broadcasting Act 1989, s. 79A.
1387. Broadcasting Act 1989, s. 79B.

must refuse all other approaches as well. Although this is intended to prevent partisan refusal to give broadcast time to particular parties, arguably it still allows a broadcaster to hamper a particular party if it is prepared also to refuse others.

Anyone who infringes the provisions of the Act about election programmes commits an offence and is liable on conviction to a fine of up to NZD 100,000.[1388]

Additionally, decisions about airtime for party leaders in debates and the like can still be challenged under judicial review.[1389]

§3. News and Current Affairs

I. The Electoral Act 1993, the Local Electoral Act 2001 and the Citizens Initiated Referenda Act 1993

247. With respect to general elections and referenda, it is an offence at any time on polling day before the close of the poll to publish, distribute or broadcast any statement advising or intended or likely to influence any person as to the candidate or party for whom he or she should or should not vote, or to abstain from voting.[1390] So no political views can be expressed in the media on that day. This rule does not apply to anything in a newspaper published before 6 pm on the day before polling day;[1391] this covers the case of a paper published the previous afternoon, but still on the stands on the morning of polling day. There is also provision that in the periods mentioned it is not permissible to publish any party name or logo. However, this does not apply to mention of a party name in a news item about the election in the media, or the name of a proponent of any answer to a question to which the indicative referendum relates.

It is a defence in relation to the exhibition in or in view of a public place of a statement, name, emblem, slogan or logo if the defendant proves that the exhibition was inadvertent and the defendant caused the exhibition to cease as soon as the defendant was notified by a returning officer or a manager of the polling place that the exhibition was taking place.[1392] In respect of general elections, there is also a defence that relates to the publication on an internet website of a relevant statement or other material if the defendant proves that the statement or material was placed on the website before polling day, and the defendant did not operate or permit access to the website statement on polling day to persons other than persons who voluntarily access the website, and did not, on polling day, distribute, broadcast or exhibit in or in view of a public place, or publish, or cause to be published, in an issue of

1388. Broadcasting Act 1989, s. 80.
1389. In 2014, leader of the Conservative Party, Colin Craig, obtained an interim injunction against TV3 to restrain it from broadcasting an election debate with the leaders of six minor parties which excluded Mr Craig: *Craig v. MediaWorks Ltd* [2014] NZHC 1875. Cf: *Dunne v. Canwest TVworks Ltd* HC Wellington CIV-2005-495-1596, 11 Aug. 2005.
1390. Electoral Act 1993, s. 197(1)(g); Citizens Initiated Referenda Act 1993, s. 52(1)(g).
1391. Electoral Act 1993, s. 197(1)(g).
1392. Electoral Act 1993, s. 197(2); s. 52(2).

a newspaper or magazine issued on polling day, any material promoting or advertising the website.[1393]

With respect to general elections and referenda, it is an offence at any time on polling day before the close of the poll to make any statement having reference to the poll or the indicative referendum 'by means of any … … … cinematograph or television apparatus'. However, this does not restrict a publication by a broadcaster of advertisements placed by the Chief Electoral Officer, or any non-partisan advertisement broadcast as a community service, or any news in relation to the election or indicative referendum.[1394]

With respect to general elections and referenda, it is an offence at any time on polling day before the close of the poll, or at any time on any of the three days preceding it, to print or distribute any imitation ballot paper with candidates' names on it together with any indications as to the candidate for whom one should vote, or containing any matter likely to influence any vote.[1395] This might extend to mock ballot forms in the media. Similar provisions apply with respect to local elections, except that there is no time limit; such imitation ballot papers are totally forbidden.[1396]

With respect to general elections and referenda, it is an offence on polling day before the close of the poll to print, distribute or deliver to any person any card or paper having thereon the names of any candidates or the question to which the indicative referendum relates.[1397] Although this provision is no doubt capable of very wide application, it would probably be held to be confined to persons thrusting advertising leaflets at voters on election day.

With respect to local elections, it is an offence to print, publish or distribute any instruction on the method of marking the voting paper that differs from the official instructions required to be included in the voting paper, so as to be likely to cause confusion or mislead voters.[1398]

With respect to general elections and referenda, it is an offence on polling day, before the close of the poll, to conduct a public opinion poll in relation to the election or referendum;[1399] it is also an offence to poll people who vote before polling day or any time before the close of the poll.[1400]

With respect to both general and local elections, officials at a polling booth must not communicate to anyone any information acquired by them in that capacity except in accordance with their official duty.[1401] Nor must anyone attempt to obtain at a polling booth any information about how a person has voted, or communicate any such information to anyone.[1402] There are further specific provisions with respect to local elections that it is an offence to make known or pretend to make

1393. Electoral Act 1993, s. 197(2A).
1394. Electoral Act 1993, s. 197(1)(c); s. 52(1)(c).
1395. Electoral Act 1993, s. 197(1)(f); s. 52(1)(f).
1396. Local Electoral Act 2001, s. 122(1)(b).
1397. Electoral Act 1993, s. 197(1)(h); Citizens Initiated Referenda Act 1993, s. 52(1)(i).
1398. Local Electoral Act 2001, s. 122(1)(c).
1399. Electoral Act 1993, s. 197(1)(e); Citizens Initiated Referenda Act 1993, s. 52(1)(e).
1400. Electoral Act 1993, s. 197(1)(d); Citizens Initiated Referenda Act 1993, s. 52(1)(d).
1401. Electoral Act 1993, s. 203(1); Local Electoral Act 2001, s. 129(1).
1402. Electoral Act 1993, s. 203(2), (3); Local Electoral Act 2001, s. 129(2).

known before the close of voting any information by which the state of the election may be known.[1403]

It is an offence to knowingly and wilfully supply, receive or use information supplied in electronic form, or derived from information supplied in electronic form for a purpose other than those authorized under the Electoral Act 1993.[1404] Offenders are liable on summary conviction to a fine not exceeding NZD 50,000 where the information is supplied, received or used for a commercial purpose, and, in any other case, to a fine not exceeding NZD 10,000.

§4. Political Advertising

248. With respect to general elections, a person may only publish an election advertisement if the advertisement includes a promoter statement. This must state the name and address of the promoter of the election advertisement. If the election advertisement is published in a visual form, the promoter statement must be clearly displayed in the advertisement, but if the advertisement is published only in an audible form, the promoter statement must be no less audible than the other content of the advertisement.[1405]

For local elections, no person may publish or broadcast any advertisement to procure the election of any constituency candidate or party unless the candidate or secretary of the party has authorized the advertisement in writing and the advertisement contains the name and address of the person for whom or at whose direction it is published. Nothing in this provision is to restrict the publication in the media of any news or comments relating to an election.[1406]

Further, no one may publish any advertisement that is not an election advertisement but relates to a general election, unless the advertisement contains a statement setting out the true name of the person for whom or at whose direction it is published and the address of that person's place of residence or business. Similarly, this does not restrict the publication of any news or comments relating to an election.[1407]

1403. Local Electoral Act 2001, s. 130(1).

1404. Electoral Act 1993, s. 116. An authorized purpose is one such as that under s. 112, being for scientific purposes or for the purposes of a health study.

1405. Electoral Act 1993, s. 204F. 'Advertisement' is defined in s. 3A as an advertisement in any medium that may reasonably be regarded as encouraging or persuading voters to vote or not vote for a candidate or party. See *Watson v. Electoral Commission* [2014] NZHC 666 (video and song not an advertisement), and *Greenpeace of New Zealand Inc v. Electoral Commission* [2014] NZHC 2135 (website content).

1406. Local Electoral Act, s. 113. Publication is also permitted if the publication of the advertisement is endorsed by an organization or body representing residents or ratepayers in the community or district in which the advertisement is published, and the advertisement contains a statement setting out the true name of the person or persons for whom or at whose direction it is published and the address of his or her residence or place of business, and the true name of the organization or body that has endorsed the publication of the advertisement and the address of the place of business of that organization or body: *ibid.*, s. 113(4).

1407. Electoral Act 1993, s. 221A. *Watson v. Electoral Commission* [2014] NZHC 666.

Part 6AA of the Electoral Act 1993, inserted into the Act in 2010, was intended to provide greater certainty and transparency in the conduct of the electoral process. The Part affects promoters of election advertisements, electoral advertising, the regulated campaign period, campaign expenditure limits and donations. It also amends the advance voting rules.

With respect to local restoration polls, no one may publish an advertisement promoting one of the options in the poll unless it shows the name and address of the person at whose direction it is published. This is just to restrict the publication of views or comment about the poll in a newspaper or in a broadcast.[1408]

1408. Local Restoration Polls Act 1990, s. 21.

Chapter 5. Advertising Rules

§1. Various Forms of Commercial Communications

249. Advertising in New Zealand is self-regulated, that is, voluntarily regulated by the advertising industry as opposed to the government.[1409] The relevant bodies are the ASA and the Advertising Standards Complaints Board (ASCB) and Appeal Board (ASCAB).

The ASA, previously known as the Committee of Advertising Practice, was formed in 1973 and incorporated under the Incorporated Societies Act 1908 in 1990. Rule 5 of the ASA's constitution provides that media proprietors, advertising agencies and advertisers, either individually or through organizations representing them, are eligible for membership. There are two classes of members: associations and individuals. The ASA is unusual in including other trade organizations as members.[1410] In 2014, the membership was made up of representatives from:

- Association of New Zealand Advertisers (Inc);
- Communication Agencies Association of New Zealand;
- Community Newspapers Association Inc;
- Interactive Advertising Bureau New Zealand;
- Letterbox Media Association;
- Magazine Publishers Association (Inc);
- New Zealand Cinema Advertising Council;
- New Zealand Marketing Association (Inc);
- Newspaper Publishers Association of New Zealand (Inc);
- New Zealand Post Ltd;
- Think TV;
- Outdoor Media Advertising Association;
- Pay TV Group; and
- Radio Broadcasters Association (Inc).

The ASA has as one of its objects the promulgation of codes which the members undertake to uphold.[1411] The ASA has developed codes of practice inspired by those of the International Chamber of Commerce.[1412] These codes are intended to guide the professional behaviour of members and provide the basis for the complaints process. If an advertisement is found to have breached one or more of the codes, the advertiser, advertising agency or media in question are requested to withdraw the advertisement. The ASA reports a 100% compliance rate with this request.[1413]

1409. See the ASA website: http://www.asa.co.nz/ and, in particular, Advertising Codes of Practice 2014 Handbook, http://www.asa.co.nz/pdfs/ASA%20CoP%202014%20(Web).pdf, accessed 7 May 2015.

1410. Fabrice Desmarais, *New Zealand Law for Marketers* 520 (2d ed., LexisNexis NZ Ltd 2014). 520.

1411. Advertising Standards Authority *Advertising Codes of Practice* January 2013, 3(d).

1412. Fabrice Desmarais, *New Zealand Law for Marketers* 522 (2d ed., LexisNexis NZ Ltd 2014).

1413. Fabrice Desmarais, *New Zealand Law for Marketers* 522 (2d ed., LexisNexis NZ Ltd 2014).

Misleading advertising is the issue most often complained about, followed by issues relating to offensiveness and/or social responsibility.[1414]

The codes in force as at January 2015 were:

- Code for Advertising and Promotion of Alcohol;
- Code for Advertising to Children;
- Children's Code for Advertising Food;
- Code for Comparative Advertising;
- Code for Environmental Claims;
- Advertising Code of Ethics;
- Code for Financial Advertising;
- Code for Advertising of Food;
- Code for Advertising Gaming and Gambling;
- Code for People in Advertising;
- Therapeutic Products Advertising Code;
- Therapeutic Services Advertising Code;
- Code for Advertising Vehicles; and
- Code for Advertising of Weight Management.

Advertisers may submit advertisements to an independent approvals process specific to the particular industry. It is possible for advertisements to be subject to codes implemented by bodies outside the advertising industry (made up of advertisers, advertising agencies and media).[1415] The codes of practice of other trade associations may overlap the ASA codes. For example, the New Zealand Television Broadcasters' Council has policies and rules that supplement the ASA's codes. The liquor industry instigated the Liquor Advertising, Promotion and Pre-vetting Service (LAPPS), which is administered by the Association of New Zealand Advertisers (Inc) (ANZA). ANZA initiated the Therapeutic Advertising Pre-vetting System (TAPS) for the advertisement of therapeutic products and services. Under these systems, each advertisement is submitted to an adjudicator who advises the advertiser whether the proposed advertisement complies with the relevant codes of practice.

Advertisements may be submitted to a media approvals body. In 1989, the Television Commercial Approvals Bureau (now Commercial Approvals Bureau or CAB) was established to maintain standards for television commercials. Television commercials must be accepted and classified by the CAB before they are supplied for broadcast. If an advertisement has passed through the approvals processes, it can be broadcast or published. It may subsequently become the subject of a complaint by a member of the public before the ASCB. An advertisement that has the approval before it is broadcast or displayed to the public is more likely to withstand complaints made by members of the public. Indeed, commercials that have been approved by CAB are less likely to have judgments of the ASCB held against them than other commercials.[1416] Nevertheless, approval by a pre-vetting service does not guarantee that an advertisement will be judged to comply with the codes.

1414. Advertising Standards Authority, *Annual Report 2012*, at 23.
1415. Fabrice Desmarais, *New Zealand Law for Marketers* 517 (2d ed., LexisNexis NZ Ltd 2014).
1416. http://www.commercialapprovals.co.nz/cab_story.php.

Any member of the public who considers that an advertisement has breached the advertising codes of practice may make a complaint, free of charge. Advertising complaints go directly to a Complaints Board, and there is no requirement to complain to the broadcaster in the first instance. In March 1988, the ASA established a separate self-regulatory body called the ASCB,[1417] formerly known as the Advertising Standards Council. Its main role is to adjudicate on complaints received about advertisements that may breach the codes of practice. Its other roles are to advise the ASA on the interpretation of the codes and possible improvements to the codes and to report to the ASA on any aspect of advertising that is causing concern. The ASCB considers complaints about advertisements in all media.

Decisions of the ASCB and the Panel are notified to the parties as soon as practicable (generally within forty-eight hours for ASCB decisions).[1418] Decisions are also made available to other parties and form a body of precedent which the ASCB may refer to in the same way as the courts cite judgments. If a complaint is upheld, the breaching advertiser is required to withdraw the advertisement with immediate effect and media members of the ASA are required not to publish or broadcast the breaching advertisement. These requirements are not legally binding obligations, but all members of the ASA invariably comply with them.[1419] If a complaint is not upheld, the advertisement can continue to be broadcast, published or displayed. If it has been held that an advertisement does not breach a particular provision, this will not prevent a later decision that it breached another.[1420]

Any party to a complaint may appeal a decision of the ASCB within fourteen days of receipt of the ASCB's written decision.[1421] The chairperson of the ASCB decides whether or not to accept the appeal application. If the appeal is accepted, the chairperson will order that the appeal either be referred to the ASCAB or to the ASCB for rehearing. The grounds for appeal are:

(i) the proper procedures have not been followed;
(ii) there is new evidence of sufficient substance to affect the decision;
(iii) evidence provided to the ASCB has been misinterpreted to the extent that it has affected the decision;
(iv) the decision is against the weight of evidence; and
(v) it is in the interests of natural justice that the matter be reheard.

If a party is dissatisfied with the outcome of the appeal process, it may be subject to judicial review.

The Advertising Code of Practice states that the codes apply to the entire content of an advertisement, including all words and numbers (spoken and written), visual

---

1417. See http://www.asa.co.nz/ascb.php.
1418. Advertising Standards Authority Constitution, Second Schedule – Rules of the Advertising Standards Complaints Board Complaints Procedures, 5.
1419. Advertising Standards Complaints Board *Decision 95/334*, 6.
1420. *Unilever Australasia* 07/155 (ASCB Acting Chair, 16 Apr. 2007) and *Unilever Australasia Ltd – Lynx* 07/147 (ASCB, 12 Jun. 2007).
1421. Advertising Standards Authority Constitution, Second Schedule – Rules of the Advertising Standards Complaints Board Complaints Procedures, 5.

presentations, music and sound effects.[1422] Where there is any doubt about whether a breach has in fact occurred, the interpretation that best serves the purpose and intent of the code in question and the Code of Ethics is adopted.

An 'advertisement' is defined by the Codes of Practice as:[1423]

> The word 'advertisement' is to be taken in its broadest sense to embrace any form of advertising and includes advertising which promotes the interest of any person, product or service, imparts information, educates, or advocates an idea, belief, political viewpoint or opportunity. The definition includes advertising in all traditional media and digital media such as online advertising, including websites. Emails and SMS messaging that are selling or promoting a product, service, idea or opportunity are also covered by the codes, as are neck labels or promotions attached to a product. Other examples include posters, pamphlets and billboards (whether stationary or mobile) and addressed or unaddressed mail.

The definition of advertisement has been widely interpreted by the ASCB and the ASCAB.[1424] It can cover church signs and billboards, for example.[1425] However, instructional information is unlikely to be held to be an advertisement. In 2014, the ASCB held it had no jurisdiction over an Air New Zealand safety video because overall it was a compulsory instructional video and not an advertisement.[1426]

A 'product' is defined to include goods, services and facilities whether paid or given free. A 'consumer' refers to any person to whom an advertisement is addressed or is likely to be reached by it whether as a final consumer or as a trade customer or user.[1427]

As noted in the Codes of Practice Handbook, all of the codes are to be applied taking into account the 'spirit and intention', as well as the specific requirements[1428] of the codes. The Boards first undertake a literal analysis in order to decide if an advertisement complies with the specific written principles and rules of the code in question. They then take a purposive approach by considering whether the spirit and intention of the code have been complied with. This often involves taking a common sense approach.

The codes complement rather than replace the law of New Zealand. There are about fifty pieces of legislation that impact on, or in some way restrict, advertising in New Zealand,[1429] for example, the Fair Trading Act 1986, Consumer Guarantees Act 1993 and the Bill of Rights Act 1990. The Code for Financial Advertising states

1422. Advertising Standards Authority *Advertising Codes of Practice* January 2013.
1423. See Advertising Codes of Practice 2014 Booklet, 11, http://www.asa.co.nz/pdfs/ASA%20CoP%202014%20(Web).pdf, accessed 7 May 2015.
1424. Advertising Standards Authority Complaints Board *Decision 13/514.*
1425. Advertising Standards Complaints Appeal Board *Decision 14/005.*
1426. Advertising Standards Complaints Board *Decision 14/155.*
1427. See Advertising Codes of Practice 2014 Booklet, 11, http://www.asa.co.nz/pdfs/ASA%20CoP%202014%20(Web).pdf, accessed 7 May 2015.
1428. Advertising Codes of Practice 2014 Booklet, 11, http://www.asa.co.nz/pdfs/ASA%20CoP%202014%20(Web).pdf, accessed 7 May 2015.
1429. Advertising Standards Authority, *The Case for Advertising Self-Regulation.*

that the code should be read in conjunction with legislation, in particular the Securities Act 1978, the Securities Regulations 1983, the Credit Contracts and Consumer Finance Act 2003 and the Fair Trading Act 1986.

Advertisements are judged primarily in terms of their impact upon the type of person who is likely to be exposed to the message. The ASCB and ASCAB take into account the context of an advertisement and so consider factors such as the placement and form of the advertisement and the demographics likely to be exposed to it. Also examined are the time that an advertisement screens during the day, the nature of the programme in which an advertisement is placed, the location of a billboard and the nature of any limitations placed on access to advertisements.[1430] The ASA effectively considers whether an advertisement fits within its intended media context.[1431]

For advertisements that originate and intended for audiences outside New Zealand that also reach New Zealand audiences, the Boards take into account the compliance with the advertising rules in the country of origin, the size and composition of the New Zealand audience, whether the advertising is targeted at New Zealand consumers, the accessibility of the product to New Zealand consumers and whether the best endeavours have been made to exclude advertisements which would clearly breach the Codes of Practice (which could be particularly relevant in the case of live presentations of overseas events to a substantial number of New Zealanders).[1432] New Zealand broadcasters may transmit live presentations originating in other countries, such as live sporting events, which may contain advertisements over which the New Zealand broadcaster has no control. For example, an advertisement for Miller beer was screened in the period between 6 am and 9 pm during the screening of the US Golf Open on Sky TV, which breached the Code for Advertising Liquor.[1433] In refusing to uphold a complaint against Sky TV, the ASCB held that, although it technically breached the code, the spirit of the code had not been breached. It was stated that it would be unreasonable to expect advertisements which are contained in a programme originating in the United States of America to comply with the rules of every country of reception.

The advertising codes require that the advertisements comply with the laws of New Zealand.[1434] However, these provisions are seldom invoked. Basic Principle 1 of the Code for People in Advertising requires advertisements to comply with the laws of New Zealand, including the Human Rights Act 1993 and the NZBORA 1990.

1430. Advertising Standards Complaints Board *Decision 13/095*.
1431. Fabrice Desmarais, *New Zealand Law for Marketers* 536 (2d ed., LexisNexis NZ Ltd 2014).
1432. Advertising Codes of Practice 2014 Booklet, 12, http://www.asa.co.nz/pdfs/ASA%20CoP%202014%20(Web).pdf, accessed 7 May 2015.
1433. Discussed in Fabrice Desmarais, *New Zealand Law for Marketers* 537 (2d ed., LexisNexis NZ Ltd 2014).
1434. Basic Principle 1 of the Code of Ethics, Basic Principle 1 of the Code for People in Advertising, Principle 1 of the Code for Advertising Gaming and Gambling, Principle 1 of the Therapeutic Products Advertising Code, Principle 1 of the Therapeutic Services Advertising Code, Principle 1 of the Code for Advertising Vehicles, Principle 1 of the Code for Advertising of Weight Management.

The right to freedom of expression contained in section 14 of the NZBORA makes no distinction between commercial and non-commercial speech, although it is subject to section 5 which permits reasonable limits on freedom of expression that can be demonstrably justified in a free and democratic society. It is unclear whether the NZBORA applies to advertising regulation.[1435] Section 3(b) of the NZBORA states that the Act applies to acts done by 'any person or any body in the performance of any public function, power, or duty conferred or imposed on that person or body by or pursuant to law'. It is arguable that the regulation of advertising is a public function even though it is carried out by the industry itself.[1436] This is because a public function is not the same as a government function.[1437]

§2. Restrictions on Content

I. Social Responsibility

250. Basic Principle 4 of the Code of Ethics provides that all advertisements 'should be prepared with a due sense of social responsibility to consumers and to society'. Social responsibility is also contained in other advertising codes.[1438] However, social responsibility is a rather imprecise concept, and there may be no agreement or consensus in society as to what social responsibility involves.[1439] Basic Principle 4 is cited in many complaints and is often cited together with other provisions such as Rule 2 of the Code of Ethics which refers to truthful presentation and Ethics Rule 5 pertaining to offensiveness.

Advertisers must take care to ensure that their advertisements comply with the codes in order to be deemed socially responsible. A failure to match the advertisement to the target market may lead to a breach, particularly the case where children are exposed to advertisements which are considered to contain inappropriate material.[1440] Email advertisements must also be directed at the target audience.[1441] If the advertiser uses a medium that targets the intended audience, the advertisement is likely to be considered to meet the requirement of social responsibility.[1442]

1435. Selene Mize, *From Goldstein to the Burger King Babes: People Issues in Advertising*, *The Real Deal! Essays in Law and Advertising* 11 (Ursula Cheer ed., The Centre for Commercial and Corporate Law Inc 2008).
1436. Selene Mize, *From Goldstein to the Burger King Babes: People Issues in Advertising*, *The Real Deal! Essays in Law and Advertising*, 111 (Ursula Cheer ed., The Centre for Commercial and Corporate Law Inc 2008) footnote 12.
1437. A. Butler & P. Butler, *The New Zealand Bill of Rights Act: A Commentary* (2005) para. 5.7.12.
1438. Principle 1 of the Code for Advertising to Children, Principle 1 of the Children's Code for Advertising Food 2010, Principle 1 of the Code for Advertising of Food, Principle 2 of the Code for Advertising Gaming and Gambling, Principle 3 of the Therapeutic Products Advertising Code, Principle 2 of the Therapeutic Services Advertising Code, Principle 2 of the Code for Advertising of Weight Management, Basic Principle 2 of the Code for Financial Advertising.
1439. Selene Mize, *From Goldstein to the Burger King Babes: People Issues in Advertising*, *The Real Deal! Essays in Law and Advertising* 141 (Ursula Cheer ed., The Centre for Commercial and Corporate Law Inc 2008).
1440. Advertising Standards Complaints Board *Decision 12/628*.
1441. Advertising Standards Complaints Board *Decision 13/581*.
1442. Advertising Standards Complaints Board *Decision 13/217*.

The content of the advertisement must also appeal to the target market.[1443] Advertisers of television commercials can demonstrate social responsibility by complying with the limitations settled on by CAB, or by voluntarily submitting to greater limitations.[1444] Complaints about depictions in advertisements are not usually successful unless there is widespread public dissemination of the advertisement or the content is sufficiently problematic that the advertisement is found to breach other advertising codes.[1445]

Advertisements that encourage copycat behaviour may exhibit a lack of social responsibility, but particularly problematic behaviour is required.[1446]

Where an advertisement makes claims that cannot be substantiated, it will lack the required social responsibility. This is particularly the case with regard to claims about therapeutic products and services, and weight loss. Where such claims are made, the onus is on the advertiser to produce sufficient evidence to justify the claim.[1447] Indicating the existence of scientific tests online or elsewhere is generally not sufficient to substantiate claims made. However, claims about the performance or capability of a product or service which require substantiation may be distinguished from puffery, in which clearly exaggerated claims are used in order to praise the product or service.[1448]

The use of the TAPS process by advertisers to help ensure code compliance may assist them in demonstrating social responsibility.[1449] However, this does not guarantee compliance.[1450]

The use of hyperbole in an advertisement can mean it lacks social responsibility. However, there must be a clear exaggeration and complaints may nonetheless succeed if the advertisement is particularly problematic.[1451] Humour and hyperbole used in an advertisement may not mitigate the depiction of illegal and dangerous practices.[1452]

II. Misleading or Deceptive Advertisements

251. Basic Principle 3 of the Code of Ethics states, 'No advertisement should be misleading or deceptive or likely to mislead or deceive the consumer' and Ethics Rule 2 states:

> Advertisements should not contain any statement or visual presentation or create an overall impression which directly or by implication, omission, ambiguity or exaggerated claim is misleading or deceptive, is likely to deceive or

1443. Advertising Standards Complaints Board *Decision 182.*
1444. Advertising Standards Complaints Board *Decision 14/142.*
1445. Advertising Standards Complaints Board *Decision 05/396.*
1446. Advertising Standards Complaints Board *Decision 12/653.*
1447. Advertising Standards Complaints Board *Decision 13/010.*
1448. Advertising Standards Complaints Board *Decision 13/011.*
1449. Advertising Standards Complaints Board *Decision 13/537.*
1450. Advertising Standards Complaints Board *Decision 13/430.*
1451. Advertising Standards Complaints Board *Decision 14/076.*
1452. Advertising Standards Complaints Board *Decision 13/592.*

> mislead the consumer, makes false and misleading representation, abuses the trust of the consumer or exploits his or her lack of experience or knowledge. (Obvious hyperbole, identifiable as such, is not considered to be misleading.)

Misleading or deceptive advertisements are also prohibited under the other advertising codes.[1453]

In deciding whether an advertisement is misleading or deceptive, or likely to mislead or deceive, the ASCB considers what the target audience would understand the advertisement to mean. This is known as the consumer take out, in that the Board determines what the likely consumer would 'take out' of the advertisement.[1454] The consumer take out is determined on a general understanding of the advertisement, by taking an overall impression of all of the elements.[1455] The entire context of the advertisement must be taken into account, rather than considering the claims made in the advertisement in isolation.[1456] The likely consumer take out may differ from the literal interpretation of the words contained in an advertisement.[1457]

Advertisements must clearly specify key terms and conditions. If they fail to do so, they may be adjudged to mislead or deceive consumers. This is particularly the case where an advertisement conceals the true cost of a product or service.[1458] Omitting key information will also lead to a finding that the advertisement is misleading or deceptive.[1459] However, terms and conditions need not be recited in the advertisement itself, provided sufficiently clear reference is made to their existence and where to find them. If terms and conditions conflict with the overall impression ascertained from the advertisement, it may mislead or deceive consumers.[1460]

Where an advertisement creates ambiguity, it may likely mislead or deceive its audience. Absolute terms and phrases may mislead consumers, even if conditions are provided in the advertisement in an attempt to qualify their meaning.[1461] The use of clichés may also create ambiguity.[1462] Nonetheless, simplification of the content contained in an advertisement may be permitted.[1463] Advertisers must be careful not to generalize advertisements in such a way that claims in them cannot be supported by the facts.[1464] However, qualifying an absolute claim may save an advertisement from being found in breach.[1465]

1453. Principle 2 of the Code for Advertising to Children, Principle 2 of the Children's Code for Advertising Food 2010, Principle 2 of the Code for Environmental Claims, Principle 3 of the Code for Advertising Gaming and Gambling, Principle 2 of the Therapeutic Products Advertising Code, Principle 3 of the Therapeutic Services Advertising Code, Principle 3 of the Code for Advertising of Weight Management.
1454. Advertising Standards Complaints Board *Decision 13/283*.
1455. Advertising Standards Complaints Board *Decision 13/120*.
1456. Advertising Standards Complaints Board *Decision 12/100*.
1457. Advertising Standards Complaints Board *Decision 13/307*.
1458. Advertising Standards Complaints Board *Decision 13/200*.
1459. Advertising Standards Complaints Board *Decision 13/433*.
1460. Advertising Standards Complaints Board *Decision 13/426*.
1461. Advertising Standards Complaints Board *Decision 13/497*.
1462. Advertising Standards Complaints Board *Decision 13/311*.
1463. Advertising Standards Complaints Board *Decision 13/151*.
1464. Advertising Standards Complaints Board *Decision 13/406*.
1465. Advertising Standards Complaints Board *Decision 13/320*.

Advertisements must use images that are representative of the product or service itself.[1466] This means the use of stock images can be risky, but will be acceptable if it is generally accepted that, in a particular industry, images are not always representative of the product.[1467] In relation to the Code for Advertising of Weight Management, the use of a product must show realistic outcomes and not mislead consumers as to the effectiveness of a weight loss product.[1468] Weight loss shown should be representative of the average consumer if that is the target audience.

Advertisements that would otherwise be misleading or deceptive may be saved by hyperbole and/or humour.[1469] Positioning statements used to promote the unique aspects of a product or service, rather than absolute claims about the effectiveness or performance of the product or service, may not be interpreted as misleading or deceptive, for example, the expression '100% Pure New Zealand'.[1470] The Warehouse positioning statement 'Everyone gets a bargain' was seen as a catch phrase or slogan used as a general statement across a range of products and not a statement to be interpreted literally in terms of each individual product.[1471]

III. Decency and Offensiveness

252. Rules 4 and 5 of the Code of Ethics concern decency and offensiveness respectively in light of generally prevailing community standards. Rule 4 provides 'Advertisements should not contain anything which clearly offends against generally prevailing community standards taking into account the context, medium, audience and product (including services).' Rule 5 states: Advertisements should not contain anything which in the light of generally prevailing community standards is likely to cause serious or widespread offence taking into account the context, medium, audience and product (including services). Basic Principle 3 of the Code for People in Advertising states:

Advertisements should not portray people in a manner which, taking into account generally prevailing community standards, is reasonably likely to cause serious or widespread offence on the grounds of their gender; race; colour, ethnic or national origin; age; cultural, religious, political or ethical belief; sexual orientation; marital status; family status; education; disability; occupational or employment status.

These provisions all contain offence standards. The Concise Oxford Dictionary defines 'offence' as including a wounded feeling, annoyance or umbrage.[1472] Rule 4 requires that an advertisement should not contain anything that 'clearly offends' against generally prevailing community standards, whereas Rule 5 requires that an advertisement should not contain anything that 'is likely to cause serious or widespread offence' in the light of generally prevailing community standards. Therefore,

1466. Advertising Standards Complaints Board *Decision 13/529.*
1467. Advertising Standards Complaints Board *Decision 13/282.*
1468. Advertising Standards Complaints Board *Decision 13/279.*
1469. Advertising Standards Complaints Board *Decision 14/076.*
1470. Advertising Standards Complaints Board *Decision 13/100.*
1471. Advertising Standards Complaints Board *Decision 12/006.*
1472. 7th edition 1982.

it is not necessary to show actual serious or widespread offence to uphold a complaint for offending community standards under the latter provision.[1473]

In determining a complaint about offensiveness, the Board will first consider the application of Rules 4 and 5 of the Code of Ethics, followed by Ethics Rule 5 and then Basic Principle 3 of the Code for People in Advertising. Relatively few complaints under Rule 4 have succeeded. Complaints have been made about sexual content in advertisements. Such advertisements must be sufficiently beyond the parameters of decency in the particular context.[1474] However, a television advertisement for Burger King that depicted three women dressed in bikinis together in a number of scenes in the advertisement, including 'showering' in a fountain, with close-ups and a script that had arguably sexual connotations was held to have clearly offended against generally prevailing community standards and therefore breached Rule 4.[1475]

The placement and medium of an advertisement is particularly important in relation to whether or not an advertisement has breached Rule 4.[1476] A rental van which featured a cartoon of a man behind a woman, accompanied by text which said: 'Up the bum. No babies!' was found to offend against generally prevailing community standards.[1477] The ASCB noted the medium of a rental van and its high visibility and mobility which meant that a wide range of people could potentially view it, including those under 18 years of age. The context of an advertisement is also relevant in determining whether an advertisement has breached Rule 4.[1478] Deliberate ambiguity may prevent an advertisement from breaching Rule 4.[1479] However, if the advertisement has the potential to be seen by a large section of the public, such as on billboards, intended ambiguity may not save it.

Pursuant to Ethics Rule 5, an advertisement must not contain anything that is likely to cause serious or widespread offence in the light of generally prevailing community standards. Basic Principle 5 of the Code for People in Advertising concerns sexual appeal in advertisements, but only in relation to unrelated products. It thus contains no limitations on the use of sexual appeal to draw attention to related products, as long as it is not carried out in a manner that is exploitative or degrading. In this case, Ethics Rule 5 is the relevant provision.[1480] Ethics Rule 5 is also relevant where a person is implied but not actually portrayed in an advertisement.[1481]

In order for a complaint to be upheld under Ethics Rule 5, the advertisement must be likely to cause serious or widespread offence. This is the same offence standard that is contained in Basic Principle 3 of the Code for People in Advertising, except that any offence under the latter code must be 'reasonably likely' to occur, and that the offence caused must be on one of the prohibited grounds. In determining the

1473. Advertising Standards Complaints Board *Decision 00/02.*
1474. Advertising Standards Complaints Board *Decision 13/510.*
1475. Advertising Standards Complaints Board *Decision 07/209.*
1476. Advertising Standards Complaints Board *Decision 14/008.*
1477. Advertising Standards Complaints Board *Decision 14/097.*
1478. Advertising Standards Complaints Board *Decision 13/284.*
1479. Advertising Standards Complaints Board *Decision 13/533.*
1480. Advertising Standards Complaints Board *Decision 06/389.*
1481. Advertising Standards Complaints Board *Decision 05/413.*

likelihood of the advertisement to cause serious or widespread offence under both codes, the ASCB will consider the context in which it is placed.[1482]

The offence likely to be caused by an advertisement in order to breach Ethics Rule 5 or People Basic Principle 3 must be serious or widespread, but need not be both. Whether the offence is serious depends on the intensity of the effect.[1483] On the other hand, whether the offence is widespread depends on the portion of the audience that suffers offence.[1484] Minority views may not be included in generally prevailing community standards.

The ASCB may sometimes take into consideration the number of complaints made about a particular advertisement.[1485] However, it has also stated that the number of complaints is irrelevant to its decisions.[1486] Therefore, the ASCB has taken conflicting approaches regarding the number of complaints in relation to widespread offence. This may be reconciled by suggesting that while the broad number of complaints should not affect how compelling each individual complaint is seen to be, numbers may be relevant to the specific issue of whether offence is widespread or not. The ASCB may also consider quantitative surveys in determining whether an advertisement is likely to cause serious or widespread offence.[1487]

Sexual content in an advertisement may breach Ethics Rule 5. The depiction of women dressed in bikinis together in a number of scenes in an advertisement, including 'showering' in a fountain and sharing the same bed, was likely to cause serious or widespread offence when taking into account the context, medium, audience and product.[1488] An advertisement by the Ministry of Health stated, 'If you don't got the rubber, there'll be no hubba hubba'.[1489] The context of the advertisement was a public health education message to reduce the incidence of HIV and did not breach Rule 5.

Bad language contained in an advertisement may also be likely to cause serious or widespread offence pursuant to Ethics Rule 5.[1490] In this decision, the ASCB noted that the word 'fuck' and its variations appeared as the third, fourth, sixth, seventh and eighth most offensive expletives out of 31 in the BSA's 2013 survey entitled 'What Not to Swear. The Acceptability of Words in Broadcasting 2013', which the Board used as a guide to generally prevailing community standards. Complaints about the use of this word are commonly upheld.[1491]

Advertisements that demean religion may be considered offensive, thereby breaching Ethics Rule 5. An advertisement for the Dancing Butchers that depicted Hare Krishnas, who believe in vegetarianism, was held to breach Rule 5.[1492] However, not all such treatments cross the line. During a television advertisement for

1482. Advertising Standards Complaints Board *Decision 05/133.*
1483. Mize, at 116.
1484. Advertising Standards Complaints Board *Decision 99/23.*
1485. Advertising Standards Complaints Board *Decision 00/195.*
1486. Advertising Standards Complaints Board *Decision 13/510.*
1487. Advertising Standards Complaints Board *Decision 00/314.*
1488. Advertising Standards Complaints Board *Decision 07/209.*
1489. Advertising Standards Complaints Board *Decision 05/022.*
1490. Advertising Standards Complaints Board *Decision 14/052.*
1491. Advertising Standards Complaints Board *Decision 07/255* (band poster: 'Fuckin' shit up tour 07'); *11/432* (café poster: 'Kill Fuck Die').
1492. Advertising Standards Complaints Board *Decision 03/20.*

Hell Pizza which promoted their thin base pizza, an upside down cross could be seen. Taking into account the more secular nature of New Zealand society and the fleeting glimpse of the image, the chairperson ruled that there were no grounds to proceed.[1493] Objectionable conduct has also been held to breach Rule 5. However, context may be determinative.[1494]

As indicated above, in order for a complaint to be upheld under Basic Principle 3 of the Code for People in Advertising, two requirements must be met. First, the advertisement must be reasonably likely to cause serious or widespread offence. Second, the offence must be on a prohibited ground. The prohibited grounds are similar to those in the Human Rights Act 1993, with some minor wording changes (such as political belief instead of political opinion) and including cultural belief, occupational status and education.[1495] It is unclear what 'on the ground of', as stated in Basic Principle 3, means. It must be distinguished from stereotyping, which is specifically provided for by Basic Principle 4 of the Code for People in Advertising. Nevertheless, it is clear that there must be some relationship between the serious or widespread offence to a group and at least one of the prohibited grounds. For example, a clothing advertisement that showed only Caucasian models gave no grounds for a complaint to proceed.[1496] Complaints must be based on the treatment or portrayal of a group that is shown in the advertisement and not on the absence of a group.

It has also been suggested that because the Human Rights Act's primary focus is on differential treatment by reason of a prohibited ground, this may be the intended ambit of Basic Principle 3.[1497] Then the test would be whether or not a people was portrayed differently in an advertisement because of their race, or religion, etc, and whether or not this portrayal was reasonably likely to cause serious or widespread offence, taking into account community standards.[1498]

IV. Advocacy Advertising

253. Rule 11 of the Code of Ethics states that 'expression of opinion in advocacy advertising is an essential and desirable part of the functioning of a democratic society. Therefore such opinions may be robust. However, an opinion should be clearly distinguishable from factual information. The identity of an advertiser in matters of public interest or political issue should be clear'. The basic premise of

---

1493. Advertising Standards Chairman *Decision 12/379.*
1494. Advertising Standards Authority Chairman *Decision 12/585.*
1495. Selene Mize, *From Goldstein to the Burger King Babes: People Issues in Advertisin, The Real Deal! Essays in Law and Advertising*, 120 (Ursula Cheer ed., The Centre for Commercial and Corporate Law Inc 2008).
1496. Advertising Standards Authority Chairman *Decision 07/276.*
1497. Selene Mize, *From Goldstein to the Burger King Babes: People Issues in Advertising, The Real Deal! Essays in Law and Advertising* 121 (Ursula Cheer ed., The Centre for Commercial and Corporate Law Inc 2008).
1498. Advertising Standards Authority Complaints Board *Decision 13/163.*

this provision is that it protects the right to freedom of expression contained in section 14 of the NZBORA. The ASCB has developed advocacy principles for the application of Rule 11 in its decisions. These are that:[1499]

- Section 14 of the NZBORA, in granting the right of freedom of expression, allows advertisers to impart information and opinions but, in exercising that right, what is factual information and what is opinion should be clearly distinguishable.
- The right of freedom of expression as stated in section 14 is not absolute as there could be an infringement of other people's rights; care should be taken to ensure that this does not occur.
- The codes fetter the right granted by section 14 to ensure there is fair play between all parties on controversial issues. Therefore in advocacy advertising and particularly on political matters the spirit of the code is more important than technical breaches. People have the right to express their views and this right should not be unduly or unreasonably restricted by the Rules.
- Robust debate in a democratic society is to be encouraged by the media and advertisers and the codes should be interpreted liberally to ensure fair play by the contestants.
- It is essential in all advocacy advertisements that the identity of the advertiser is clear.

In order for Rule 11 to apply, it must be an expression of opinion. A newspaper advertisement for the Wellington City Council proposed a rezoning change for a piece of residential land in order to allow business activities.[1500] The ASCB held that Rule 11 did not apply because the advertisement was more of a public notice than an expression of opinion. The ASCAB has acknowledged that while Rule 11 provides for a certain amount of latitude, the right is not unfettered and strong opinion requires robust substantiation.[1501] For example, a series of quizzes that promoted the removal of fluoridation from water supplies in New Zealand failed to distinguish opinion from fact.[1502] The ASCAB held that the quiz format was widely recognized as providing absolute answers.

Advertisements seeking to rely on the advocacy provision must also clearly identify the advertiser.[1503] Where the advertiser has a statutory duty to provide information to the public, it is seen as an expert body and the ASCB will 'tread carefully' to ensure that it does not substitute its own opinion for that of the expert body.[1504]

Where Rule 11 is considered by the ASCB, it is often in relation to the rules regarding decency and offensiveness.[1505]

1499. Advertising Standards Complaints Board *Decision 14/044*.
1500. Advertising Standards Complaints Board *Decision 13/044*.
1501. Advertising Standards Complaints Board *Decision 13/410, Appeal 13/036*.
1502. Advertising Standards Authority Complaints Board *Decision 14/044, Appeal 14/004*.
1503. Advertising Standards Authority Complaints Board *Decision 13/480*.
1504. Advertising Standards Authority Complaints Board *Decision 13/501*.
1505. Advertising Standards Authority Complaints Board *Decision 13/450*.

V. Violence

254. Rule 7 of the Code of Ethics provides that 'advertisements should not contain anything which lends support to unacceptable violent behaviour'. Complaints against advertisements that portray unacceptable violent behaviour will offend, particularly where the advertisement reaches a wide ranging audience.[1506] Highly visible and graphic material will breach the requirement,[1507] as may the use of weapons in advertisements.[1508]

The context is also taken into account when Ethics Rule 7 is considered.[1509] However, even if an advertisement's content is placed in context, it may nonetheless go too far. Once again, billboards are risky because, in a public place, the message in the advertisement may become a more general endorsement of aggressive, violent behaviour, as can placement of the advertisement in an 'untargeted web environment'. If behaviour in an advertisement is exaggerated and lacks seriousness, it may not breach Rule 7.[1510]

VI. Hostility, Contempt, Abuse or Ridicule

255. Basic Principle 2 of the Code for People in Advertising states that advertisements should not portray people in a manner which is reasonably likely to cause serious or widespread hostility, contempt, abuse or ridicule. Complaints made under this provision are seldom successful. Between 2007 and 2014, only two out of sixty-eight complaints (excluding complaints that have been settled and withdrawn), or 2.9% of all complaints made under Basic Principle 2, have been upheld. It has been suggested that an advertisement could breach this principle either by showing a person in a negative light, thereby provoking a hostile reaction to the person depicted or to people of a similar type, or by expressing hostility against an individual or group and encouraging others to do the same.[1511]

VII. Stereotyping

256. Basic Principle 4 of the Code for People in Advertising deals with the issue of stereotyping:

1506. Advertising Standards Authority Complaints Board *Decision 09/750.*
1507. Advertising Standards Authority Complaints Board *Decision 09/756.*
1508. Advertising Standards Authority Complaints Board *Decision 10/180.*
1509. Advertising Standards Authority Complaints Board *Decision 08/139.*
1510. Advertising Standards Authority Complaints Board *Decision 07/159.*
1511. Selene Mize, *From Goldstein to the Burger King Babes: People Issues in Advertising, The Real Deal! Essays in Law and Advertising* 112 (Ursula Cheer ed., The Centre for Commercial and Corporate Law Inc 2008). See e.g.: Advertising Standards Authority Complaints Board *Decision 12/616.*

> Stereotypes may be used to simplify the process of communication in relation to both the product offered and the intended consumer. However, advertisements should not use stereotypes in the portrayal of the role, character and behaviour of groups of people in society which, taking into account generally prevailing community standards, is reasonably likely to cause serious or widespread offence, hostility, contempt, abuse or ridicule.

It has been suggested that this principle could be redundant.[1512] This is because the use of stereotypes in a way that is reasonably likely to cause serious or widespread hostility, contempt, abuse or ridicule would also breach Basic Principle 2 of the same code, which states that advertisements should not portray people in a manner which is reasonably likely to cause serious or widespread hostility, contempt, abuse or ridicule. It could also be a breach of Rule 5 of the Code of Ethics which provides that advertisements should not contain anything which is likely to cause serious or widespread offence.

In order for a complaint to be upheld by the ASCB under Basic Principle 4, the advertisement must contain a stereotype in the portrayal of the role, character and behaviour of groups of people in society. Stereotypes imply uniformity within a group of people, whereby a role, character or behaviour is regarded as applicable to an entire group of people based on their association with the group. For example, an advertisement which stated that men could not multi-task was considered to be a stereotype.[1513] The stereotype must also be inaccurate in some way. It must at least involve an over-generalization or over-simplification.[1514]

According to the first part of Basic Principle 4, stereotypes may be used to simplify the process of communication in relation to both the product offered and the intended consumer. For instance, an advertisement for a new pizza flavour depicted a female taking on the characteristics of a male as she chewed the pizza.[1515] However, it appears that the use of racial stereotypes in order to simplify the process of communication in relation to the product offered and the intended consumer is not acceptable.[1516]

It is also clear that the threshold of being reasonably likely to cause serious or widespread offence, hostility, contempt, abuse or ridicule is a high threshold. Between 2007 and 2014, only 7 out of 151 complaints (excluding complaints that have been withdrawn or settled), or 4.6% of complaints, have been upheld under Basic Principle 4.[1517]

1512. Selene Mize, *From Goldstein to the Burger King Babes: People Issues in Advertising*, *The Real Deal! Essays in Law and Advertising* 123 (Ursula Cheer ed., The Centre for Commercial and Corporate Law Inc 2008).
1513. Advertising Standards Authority Complaints Board *Decision 07/102*.
1514. Selene Mize, *From Goldstein to the Burger King Babes: People Issues in Advertising*, *The Real Deal! Essays in Law and Advertising*, 125 (Ursula Cheer ed., The Centre for Commercial and Corporate Law Inc 2008).
1515. Advertising Standards Authority Chairman *Decision 06/385*.
1516. Advertising Standards Authority Complaints Board *Decision 08/139*.
1517. Advertising Standards Authority Complaints Board *Decision 09/536*.

VIII. Sexual Appeal

257. Basic Principle 5 states:

> Advertisements should not employ sexual appeal in a manner which is exploitative and degrading of any individual or group of people in society to promote the sale of products or services. In particular people should not be portrayed in a manner which uses sexual appeal simply to draw attention to an unrelated product. Children must not be portrayed in a manner which treats them as objects of sexual appeal.

The ASCB appears to use two independent tests when applying Basic Principle 5.[1518] 'Sexual appeal' requires something more than portraying attractive, fully clothed people in advertisements.[1519] It has been used in depictions of risqué complete or partial nudity;[1520] sexual behaviour;[1521] provocative or suggestive behaviour;[1522] and provocative dress.[1523] Partial or complete nudity does not always mean that sexual appeal is employed.[1524] It is also used when there are subtle or explicit links between a product and one's sexual attractiveness or performance.[1525] As with other code provisions, the ASCB takes the context of the advertisement into account.[1526]

The use of sexual appeal must also be exploitative and degrading.[1527] Advertisements that use sexual appeal in order to advertise related and unrelated products may also breach Basic Principle 5. The following products have been found to be related to sexual appeal in certain contexts:[1528] hotel rooms,[1529] deodorant,[1530] fashionable clothing,[1531] jeans,[1532] men's shirts,[1533]

1518. Advertising Standards Authority Complaints Board *Decisions 07/284; 05/098; 02/376.*
1519. Selene Mize, *From Goldstein to the Burger King Babes: People Issues in Advertising, The Real Deal! Essays in Law and Advertising*, 133 (Ursula Cheer ed., The Centre for Commercial and Corporate Law Inc 2008).
1520. Advertising Standards Authority Complaints Board *Decision 03/371.*
1521. Advertising Standards Authority Complaints Board *Decision 03/64.*
1522. Advertising Standards Authority Complaints Board *Decision 07/209.*
1523. Advertising Standards Authority Complaints Board *Decision 04/325.*
1524. Advertising Standards Authority Complaints Board *Decision 14/119.*
1525. Selene Mize, *From Goldstein to the Burger King Babes: People Issues in Advertising, The Real Deal! Essays in Law and Advertising* 133 (Ursula Cheer ed., The Centre for Commercial and Corporate Law Inc 2008).
1526. Advertising Standards Authority Complaints Board *Decision 14/064.*
1527. Advertising Standards Authority Complaints Board *Decision 12/628.*
1528. Noted by Selene Mize, *From Goldstein to the Burger King Babes: People Issues in Advertising, The Real Deal! Essays in Law and Advertising* 135 (Ursula Cheer ed., The Centre for Commercial and Corporate Law Inc 2008).
1529. Advertising Standards Authority Complaints Board *Decision 06/446.*
1530. Advertising Standards Authority Complaints Board *Decision 05/107.*
1531. Advertising Standards Authority Complaints Board *Decision 05/098.*
1532. Advertising Standards Authority Complaints Board *Decision 05/235.*
1533. Advertising Standards Authority Complaints Board *Decision 02/163.*

vehicles,[1534] body wash,[1535] underwear,[1536] 'women's magazines'[1537] and perfume.[1538] Products which were held to be unrelated, lacking a sufficient nexus with the sexual context, include:[1539] cell phones,[1540] ice cream,[1541] a shoe store,[1542] stationery dividers,[1543] surfboards,[1544] homes in the city,[1545] the FA Cup,[1546] burgers,[1547] machinery[1548] and forklifts.[1549]

IX. Humour

258. Basic Principle 6 of the Code for People in Advertising states:

> Humour and satire are natural and accepted features of the relationship between individuals and groups within the community. Humorous and satirical treatment of people and groups of people is acceptable, provided that, taking into account generally prevailing community standards, the portrayal in not likely to cause serious or widespread offence, hostility, abuse or ridicule.

It has been argued that Basic Principle 6 should not apply to other parts of the Code for People in Advertising. One complainant argued that the codes do not contain anything that suggests that one principle can override another, and that being 'clever' or 'satirical' should not render acceptable advertisements that would otherwise breach the codes.[1550] But the chairperson rejected this argument, holding that if an advertisement was considered to have breach the codes, Basic Principle 6 could save it if the offending portrayal was humorous and unlikely to cause serious or widespread offence. Basic Principle 6 has been referred to as discretionary,[1551] but it is regularly used to save advertisements.[1552]

1534. Advertising Standards Authority Complaints Board *Decision 06/191.*
1535. Advertising Standards Authority Complaints Board *Decision 00/177.*
1536. Advertising Standards Authority Complaints Board *Decision 01/220.*
1537. Advertising Standards Authority Complaints Board *Decision 02/56; 05/293; 12/335.*
1538. Advertising Standards Authority Complaints Board *Decision 02/376; 02/377.*
1539. Noted by Selene Mize, *From Goldstein to the Burger King Babes: People Issues in Advertising, The Real Deal! Essays in Law and Advertising* 136 (Ursula Cheer ed., The Centre for Commercial and Corporate Law Inc 2008).
1540. Advertising Standards Authority Complaints Board *Decision 06/438.*
1541. Advertising Standards Authority Complaints Board *Decision 03/64; 01/314* & *01/314a.*
1542. Advertising Standards Authority Complaints Board *Decision 04/362.*
1543. Advertising Standards Authority Complaints Board *Decision 00/41.*
1544. Advertising Standards Authority Complaints Board *Decision 00/84.*
1545. Advertising Standards Authority Complaints Board *Decision 00/19.*
1546. Advertising Standards Authority Complaints Board *Decision 01/116.*
1547. Advertising Standards Authority Complaints Board *Decisions 07/209; 07/016; 13/045.*
1548. Advertising Standards Authority Complaints Board *Decision 12/691.*
1549. Advertising Standards Authority Complaints Board *Decision 12/628.*
1550. Advertising Standards Authority Complaints Board *Decision 03/142, Appeal 03/23.*
1551. Advertising Standards Authority Complaints Board *Decision 01/116.*
1552. Selene Mize, *From Goldstein to the Burger King Babes: People Issues in Advertising, The Real Deal! Essays in Law and Advertising* 137 (Ursula Cheer ed., The Centre for Commercial and Corporate Law Inc 2008).

It is unclear what definition of humour the ASCB uses. Therefore, it is also unclear what types of humour may qualify for recognition by the ASCB.[1553] It appears that humour need not be particularly sophisticated in order to save an advertisement under Basic Principle 6, and that slapstick humour can be sufficient.[1554] It may also be employed through the use of stock characters.[1555]

Humour may not save advertisements in certain circumstances. The correct targeting of the advertisement to the market may be required for humour to save the advertisement.[1556] Additionally, if an advertisement contains particularly problematic content, it is unlikely to be saved by any intended humour on the part of the advertiser.[1557]

X. Safety

259. Rule 12 of the Code of Ethics provides that advertisements should not, unless justifiable on educational or social grounds, contain any visual presentation or any description of dangerous or illegal practices or situations which encourage a disregard for safety. Additionally, Principle 2 of the Code for Advertising Vehicles states that advertisements 'should not encourage unsafe practices'. It provides four guidelines to be considered in determining whether this provision has been breached, including that advertisements:

- Should not glorify excessive speed and/or unsafe driving practices.
- Should not portray unsafe practices (such as cyclists, motorcyclists and ATV drivers not wearing approved safety helmets, or persons not wearing seatbelts where they are normally worn) in off-road activities.
- Should not associate driving with alcohol consumption unless the consumption is clearly after the completion of driving or the advertising has the aim of discouraging unlawful practices.
- Should not depict unsafe road practices which may not breach the law but are undesirable from a safety point of view, for example skateboarders or roller skaters on the roadway.

A distinction is to be drawn between fiction and reality. If an advertisement clearly depicts fiction through the use of hyperbole and exaggeration, it is less likely to breach the codes concerning the encouragement of a disregard of safety.[1558]

1553. Selene Mize, *From Goldstein to the Burger King Babes: People Issues in Advertising*, *The Real Deal! Essays in Law and Advertising*, 138 (Ursula Cheer ed., The Centre for Commercial and Corporate Law Inc 2008).
1554. Advertising Standards Authority Complaints Board *Decision 13/272*.
1555. Advertising Standards Authority Complaints Board *Decision 13/045*.
1556. Selene Mize, *From Goldstein to the Burger King Babes: People Issues in Advertising*, *The Real Deal! Essays in Law and Advertising* 140 (Ursula Cheer ed., The Centre for Commercial and Corporate Law Inc 2008).
1557. Advertising Standards Authority Complaints Board *Decision 13/163*.
1558. Advertising Standards Authority Complaints Board *Decision 13/327*.

However, advertisements are likely to reach the threshold if they contain particularly dangerous or illegal behaviour.[1559] Advertisements that do not contain humour or hyperbole may nonetheless fail to reach the threshold.[1560]

XI. Comparative Advertising

260. Comparative advertising occurs when an advertiser compares their product or service with a competing product or service in order to demonstrate why their product or service should be preferred over that of the competitor. This type of advertising is specifically provided for by the Code for Comparative Advertising. Principle 1 states that comparisons in advertisements should not mislead or deceive or be likely to mislead or deceive consumers. Obvious hyperbole is not considered to be misleading. Principle 2 provides that advertisements that make comparative claims should fairly and properly identify the competitors and not denigrate them or identifiable products.

Certain information that should be included in advertisements using price comparisons has been identified in decisions of the ASCB in relation to advertisements for supermarkets:

- the name and location of the advertiser's supermarket;
- the name and location of the supermarket being used in the price comparison;
- the date the shopping was done; and
- reference to the basket selection of goods.

Advertisers must ensure that advertisements are placed in context and do not make generalizations, otherwise, the advertisement may be held to be in breach of the code.[1561] It must be possible to infer a comparison between two or more competing products or services from an advertisement in order for the Code for Comparative Advertising to apply.[1562]

XII. Alcohol

A. Advertising Standards Authority

261. The advertising and promotion of alcohol were formerly dealt with by two separate codes: the Code for Advertising Liquor and the Code for the Naming, Packaging and Promotion of Liquor. However, both codes were replaced by the Code for Advertising and Promotion of Alcohol on 1 January 2013. A key difference is that the new code covers the packaging of alcohol products and branded

1559. Advertising Standards Complaints Board *Decision 13/592*.
1560. Advertising Standards Complaints Board *Decision 13/546*.
1561. Advertising Standards Authority Complaints Board *Decision 13/203*.
1562. Advertising Standards Authority Complaints Board *Decision 13/064*.

merchandise, in addition to media advertising, sponsorship and any branding associated with alcohol products. Guideline 1(d) has been introduced, which provides that alcohol advertising and promotions shall not depict alcohol as a necessity, nor required for relaxation, nor suggest it offers any therapeutic benefit.

The new code is designed to ensure that alcohol advertising and promotion is consistent with the need for responsibility and moderation in merchandising and consumption, and does not encourage consumption by minors. A key factor in determining compliance with this code is the likely audience of the alcohol advertisement. For example, point of sale materials and other promotions for alcohol must not be made available in unrestricted areas or events where more than 25% of the expected audience is made up of minors.[1563] The new code also takes into account social media as a new form for advertising alcohol. The code requires that all alcohol branded websites must have an age verification entry page, where visitors are required to enter their birth date. On social media, advertisers will be responsible for any material they own or manage. It is expected that advertisers will moderate user generated content regularly to ensure that it complies with the code.

Alcohol advertising and promotion is defined as an advertisement, packaging, point of sale or other promotions, activities and materials (including dispenser units) generated by an alcohol producer, distributor or retailer that promotes alcohol by product, brand or outlet. This includes media releases, branded merchandise, competitions, word of mouth marketing, advergaming, product displays and sampling, but does not include a sponsorship advertisement or an advertisement in which reference to, or the depiction of, alcohol or alcohol packaging or an alcohol outlet is incidental to its purpose. An advertisement including a reference to licensed premises is not automatically an alcohol advertisement – the intent of the advertisement must be to promote the consumption of alcohol.[1564]

Under Principle 1 of the Alcohol Code, alcohol advertising and promotions must observe a high standard of social responsibility. An example of this is Guideline 1(b) which states that while alcohol advertising and promotions may depict the consumption of alcohol as incidental to a friendly and happy social environment, it shall not promote drinking alcohol as a better or more attractive lifestyle choice or imply that the success of a social occasion depends on the presence or consumption of alcohol. Guideline 1(c) states that such advertising and promotions shall not suggest that alcohol can lead to sexual, social, sporting or business success or popularity or is necessary to achieve social status with peers.[1565] Implying that liquor would create a desirable change in mood may also breach the code.[1566]

Alcohol advertisements must also be consistent with the need for responsibility and moderation in alcohol consumption.[1567] Suggesting that excessive consumption of alcohol is amusing and comical may be in breach.[1568] Alcohol advertisements

1563. Guideline 3(g) of the Code for Advertising and Promotion of Alcohol.
1564. Code for Advertising and Promotion of Alcohol, Definitions, http://www.asa.co.nz/code_promo_advert_liquor.php, accessed 8 May 2015.
1565. Advertising Standards Authority Complaints Board *Decision 13/541*.
1566. Advertising Standards Authority Complaints Board *Decision 13/026*, *Appeal 13/012*.
1567. Principle 2 of the Code for Advertising and Promotion of Alcohol.
1568. Advertising Standards Authority Complaints Board *Decision 13/331*.

must also be directed at adult audiences and should not be directed at minors or have strong or evident appeal to minors.[1569] This applies to the content and the placement of an advertisement. When considering an advertisement for alcohol which was displayed in a supermarket, a majority of the ASCB noted that while minors would be present in a non-restricted environment such as supermarkets, it accepted the figures provided by the advertiser that suggested that the percentage of adults in supermarkets was sufficiently high to surpass the 75% threshold referred to by Guideline 3(g) of the Code.[1570]

Alcohol advertising and promotion in non-restricted areas must not use or refer to identifiable heroes or heroines of the young.[1571] Heroes and/or heroines of the young are defined as persons or characters (including groups or teams) whose example is likely to be followed by minors or who have strong appeal to minors.[1572] This differs from the definition contained in the Code for Advertising Liquor which defined heroes and/or heroines of the young as individuals or groups of people who have achieved particular celebrity status with minors and includes cartoon and other imaginative characters. Therefore, the new definition appears to require more than just recognition and requires that the person in question must be a person young people would want to be or would want to connect with.[1573] The All Blacks have been considered to be heroes of the young under the Code for Advertising Liquor.[1574]

B. Incidental Alcohol Promotion

262. While jurisdiction for most aspects of alcohol advertising lies with the ASA, the BSA still has jurisdiction for incidental promotion of alcohol.[1575] On 1 December 2004, the Promotion of Liquor Code was abolished.[1576] Standards are now contained in the TV Code, the Radio Code and the Pay TV Code. The requirements in the TV and Radio Codes are almost identical.

In general, broadcasters should observe restrictions on the promotion of liquor appropriate to the programme genre being broadcast. Liquor promotion should be socially responsible and must not encourage consumption by people who are under the legal age to purchase liquor.[1577] 'Liquor promotion' is defined as promotion of a liquor product, brand or outlet, liquor sponsorship of a programme, and advocacy of liquor consumption.[1578] Saturation of liquor promotions, separately or together,

1569. Principle 3 of the Code for Advertising and Promotion of Alcohol.
1570. Advertising Standards Authority Complaints Board *Decision 13/245.*
1571. Guideline 3(a) of the Code for Advertising and Promotion of Alcohol.
1572. Code for Advertising and Promotion of Alcohol, Definitions, http://www.asa.co.nz/code_promo_advert_liquor.php, accessed 8 May 2015.
1573. Advertising Standards Authority Complaints Board *Decision 12/657.*
1574. Advertising Standards Authority Complaints Board Panel *Decision 13/245.*
1575. See *Patel v. Access Radio* 2004-006, 26 Feb. 2004.
1576. See http://bsa.govt.nz/standards/practice-notes/liquor-promotion, accessed 9 Apr. 2015.
1577. Free-to-Air TV Code Standard 11; Radio Code Standard 9; Pay TV Code Standard P10.
1578. Free-to-Air TV Code Standard 11; Radio Code Standard 9; Pay TV Code Standard P10.

must be avoided. Where it has occurred repeatedly, the BSA has not accepted that an apology blaming human error is sufficient and has imposed a costs order instead.[1579] In the same case, an argument that the breach was acceptable because it occurred in a limited region where audience surveys suggested that only 12,500 viewers were watching was rejected, although it could be relevant to a costs order. Furthermore, the excuse that the breach was only technical has also been rejected.[1580]

A two-stage test is used to determine whether there has been a breach. The Authority decides whether the broadcast constituted 'liquor promotion' and, if so, it then considers whether the liquor promotion was socially responsible.[1581] The portrayal of the consumption of excessive amounts of liquor as enjoyable and acceptable, combined with minimization of the negative effects of drinking to excess, is likely to breach the requirements.[1582] In a rare complaint about a radio broadcast where a 'ZM Breakfast' presenter drank a yard glass on his twenty-first birthday, the BSA found the tone of the item accepted the practice as normal and was therefore socially irresponsible promotion of liquor.[1583]

Liquor complaints do not arise very often. There were none in the 2013/14 year, and the last time a complaint was upheld was in 2011, when the BSA found that a C4 broadcast of a music video for a song called 'Shots by LMFAO' promoted liquor in breach of the code requirements.[1584]

C. *Criminal Offence for Promoting Alcohol*

263. The Sale and Supply of Alcohol Act 2012 penalizes irresponsible promotion of alcohol and applies to any platform used for promotion, not just broadcasting. Under the Act, a person commits an offence if, in the course of carrying on a business, that person does anything that encourages people to consume alcohol to an excessive extent, promotes discounts on alcohol leading people to believe the price is 25% or more below ordinary price, promotes alcohol is free of charge, offers any goods or services on the condition that alcohol is bought, or promotes alcohol in a manner aimed to have appeal to minors.[1585] A licensee is liable to either or both of a fine not more than NZD 10,000 or suspension of licence. Any other person is liable to a fine of not more than NZD 10,000.

1579. *GALA v. Television New Zealand Ltd* 1997-011, 13 Feb. 1997. Costs of NZD 500.
1580. *GALA v. TVNZ* 1999-153, 23 Sep. 1999.
1581. *Memelink v. TVWorks* 2009-045, 8 Jul. 2009.
1582. *Harrop v. CanWest TVWorks* 2007-063, 4 Dec. 2007. Compare *Howard v. TVWorks* 2009-105, 20 Oct. 2009, where the programme 'Skins' which depicted teenagers drinking excessive amounts of alcohol and taking drugs did not breach the Code requirements because it did not promote liquor consumption and, in fact, showed the perils of excessive alcohol consumption.
1583. *Regional Public Health v. the Radio Network* 2007-030, 14 Aug. 2007.
1584. *BSA Annual Report* 2014 at 58; *O'Neill and TVWorks Ltd* 2011-127.
1585. Sale and Supply of Alcohol Act 2012 s. 237.

XIII. Criminal Offences for Advertising: All Media

A. Prohibition on Tobacco Advertising

264. The Smoke-free Environments Act 1990 restricts the advertising of tobacco products. Section 22(1) provides that no person can publish, or arrange for any other person to publish, any tobacco product advertisement in New Zealand.[1586] This does not apply to any advertisement included in any book, magazine or newspaper printed outside New Zealand, or in any radio or television transmission originating outside New Zealand, or in any film or video recording made outside New Zealand, unless the principal purpose of the book, magazine, newspaper, transmission, film or video recording is the promotion of the use of tobacco products, or the book, magazine, newspaper, film or video recording is intended for sale, distribution or exhibition primarily in New Zealand, or, in the case of an advertisement in any radio or television transmission, the advertisement is targeted primarily at a New Zealand audience. Nor does it apply to the dissemination, broadcasting or exhibition of any film, video recording or sound recording where that film, video recording or sound recording was made before 16 December 1990 and the tobacco product advertisement included in that film, video recording or sound recording is in the form of a reference to, or a depiction of, a tobacco product trademark that is only an incidental part of that film, video recording or sound recording. Advertisements made outside New Zealand, price lists, advertisements to employees of the manufacturer, artefact exhibitions and incidental references are also exempt.[1587]

Every person who publishes any advertisement for a tobacco product in contravention of the Act without reasonable excuse is liable, where not a manufacturer, an importer or a distributor, to a fine not exceeding NZD 10,000.[1588] Further, no person can publish an advertisement for a tobacco product that directly or indirectly states or suggests that the product is suitable for chewing or for any other oral use (other than smoking).[1589] This offence attracts liability for persons other than a manufacturer, an importer or a distributor to a fine not exceeding NZD 5,000.

'Tobacco product advertisement' means any words, whether written, printed or spoken, including on film, video recording, or other medium, broadcast or telecast, and any pictorial representation, design, or device, used to encourage the use or notify the availability or promote the sale of any tobacco product or to promote smoking behaviour; and includes any trade circular, any label, and any advertisement in any trade journal, any depiction, in a film, video recording, telecast, or other visual medium, of a tobacco product or a tobacco product trademark, where in return for that depiction any money is paid, or any valuable thing is given, whether to the maker or producer of that film, video recording, telecast, or visual medium or to any other person, and the use in any advertisement or promotion to the public of

1586. Smoke-free Environments Act 1990, s. 22A(b).
1587. Smoke-free Environments Act 1990, s. 36.
1588. Smoke-free Environments Act 1990, s. 29(1).
1589. Smoke-free Environments Act 1990, s. 36.

a tobacco product manufacturer's company name where that name or any part of that name is used as, or is included in, a tobacco product trademark.[1590]

No person may knowingly distribute an advertisement relating to the purchase or sale in New Zealand of human tissue.[1591] 'Distribute' means to publish or otherwise disseminate, by newspaper, magazine, periodical, book, billboard, radio, television, cinematograph film or any other means such as the internet, or to exhibit to public view in any premises or place, or to deposit in any area, yard, garden or enclosure comprising part of or appurtenant to any premises. Every person who commits the offence is liable to imprisonment for a term not exceeding three months or a fine not exceeding NZD 20,000.[1592]

B. Medical Products

265. It is an offence under the Medicines Act 1981 to publish anything promoting any medical product or method of treatment claimed to be infallible or to be able to alleviate, prevent or cure one of the long list of ailments specified in the schedules to the Act: the illnesses include cancer, heart disease, sexual impotence and even baldness. Articles by or interviews with those engaging in fringe medicines must therefore be carefully watched.[1593] Where parties operated a web-based mail order pharmaceuticals business and, following a number of convictions, they changed their method of operation so that the website was hosted in the United States, it was held that the offences were committed within New Zealand because the fact that websites are able to be viewed in this country establishes advertising in New Zealand.[1594]

C. Food

266. Under the Food Act 1981,[1595] no person can, for the purpose of effecting or promoting the sale of a food, publish or cause to be published any advertisement relating or likely to cause any person to believe that it relates to the food, or to any ingredient or nutrient or other constituent of the food, that breaches the requirements of the Act or is false, or is likely to deceive a purchaser with regard to the nature, quality, strength, purity, composition, origin, age or effects of the food or of any ingredient or nutrient or other constituent of the food. If the advertisement appears on television or in an otherwise transitory manner on screen, the words must be exposed in clearly legible lettering for a length of time sufficient to enable them to be read by the ordinary viewer. The offence attracts a fine of up to NZD 5,000 for an individual where the court is satisfied that the individual intended to commit the

---

1590. Smoke-free Environments Act 1990, s. 2.
1591. Human Tissue Act 2008, s. 61.
1592. Human Tissue Act 2008, s. 92F(3).
1593. Medicines Act 1981, s. 58. See also ss 57 and 59.
1594. *Ink Media Ltd v. Ministry of Health* HC Hamilton CRI-2006-419-67, 22 Aug. 2007.
1595. Food Act 1981, s. 11. A new Food Act 2014 will be fully in force 1 Mar. 2016 and this provision will be replaced by s. 238 in that Act.

offence and where the court is satisfied that a body corporate intended to commit the offence, to a fine not exceeding NZD 20,000. Any other case attracts a fine not exceeding NZD 3,000 for an individual and NZD 5,000 for a body corporate.

D. *Sexual Services*

267. The Prostitution Reform Act 2003 contains restrictions on advertising commercial sexual services.[1596] Advertisements for these services may not be broadcast on radio or television, or published in a newspaper or periodical, except in the classified advertisements section, or screened at a public cinema. 'Advertisement' means any words, or any pictorial or other representation, used to notify the availability of, or promote the sale of, commercial sexual services, either generally or specifically. A person who thus advertises or who authorizes such advertising is liable on summary conviction to a fine not exceeding NZD 50,000 if a body corporate and, in any other case, a fine not exceeding NZD 10,000.

E. *Resource Management Act*

268. Under the Resource Management Act 1991, a local authority may make an order prohibiting or restricting the publication or communication of any information supplied to it or obtained by it in the course of any proceeding, to avoid serious offence to tikanga Māori or to avoid the disclosure of the location of waahi tapu, or to avoid the disclosure of a trade secret or unreasonable prejudice to the commercial position of the person who supplied, or is the subject of, the information. In the circumstances of the particular case, the importance of avoiding such offence, disclosure or prejudice must outweigh the public interest in making that information available.[1597] It is an offence to contravene or permit a contravention of such an order.[1598]

F. *Gambling Advertisements*

269. Under the Gambling Act 2003,[1599] a person must not publish or arrange to publish in New Zealand an overseas gambling advertisement. This does not apply to publishing or arranging to publish a health message concerning gambling, an advertisement for services to prevent, minimize or treat harm, a message about preventing, minimizing or treating harm, an advertisement for gambling equipment

1596. Prostitution Reform Act 2003, s. 11.
1597. Resource Management Act 1991, s. 42.
1598. Resource Management Act 1991, s. 338.
1599. Gambling Act 2003, s. 16(1). See *TVWorks Ltd v. Department of Internal Affairs* [2012] NZCA 160, [2012] NZAR 534. Gambling is not just games of pure chance. In this case, advertisements for a poker tournament involving an entry fee which also provided a prize pool and acted as a stake in the game offended against the Act.

intended for distribution only to buyers of gambling equipment, or an overseas gambling advertisement in which the publicizing or promotion of gambling or a gambling operator is incidental to the purpose of the advertisement.[1600]

G. Approved Psychoactive Substances

270. The Psychoactive Substances Act 2013 provides that a person must not advertise an approved product on TV or radio, in any newspaper or other publication or medium in any way that conveys the product is safe, is appealing to minors, or encourages persons to buy an approved product. Any advertising may only be done in accordance with the Act.[1601]

H. Cheating Services

271. The Education Act 1989 creates an offence where a person advertises or publishes an advertisement for cheating services,[1602] attracting liability for a fine not exceeding NZD 10,000.

§3. TIME AND FREQUENCY RESTRICTIONS

272. There is no specific regulation in New Zealand limiting the frequency of advertising within broadcast programming. Broadcasters run advertising as often as audiences will tolerate. Online advertising within on-demand services is spliced into programmes at any point without using natural breaks and cannot be avoided. A voluntary policy agreed by the main broadcasters, TVNZ and MediaWorks, operates in relation to advertising to children. No advertising or sponsorship is run in programming produced for pre-school children. Additionally, advertising in school-age children's programming is reduced to a maximum of ten minutes per hour. Advertisements during school-age children's programming are not to be repeated excessively, and no advertisement may be played more than twice within an hour per channel per day. No advertisement may be played more than three times within each specified school-age children's programming time period per channel per day.[1603]

A miscellaneous offence under the Broadcasting Act 1989 attracts a fine of NZD 100,000 relating to broadcasting advertising generally. No broadcaster may broadcast advertising programmes on television during the hours between 6 am and noon on Sunday or Anzac Day, or on television or sound radio all day on Christmas Day,

1600. Gambling Act 2003, s. 11(2).
1601. Psychoactive Substances Act 2013, s. 56.
1602. Education Act 1989, s. 292E.
1603. ThinkTV, Standards and Regulations, Advertising on Television – Getting it Right For Children, http://www.thinktv.co.nz/wp-content/uploads/TTV0005_Childrens_BookletV5-final.pdf, accessed 31 Jul. 2015.

Good Friday or Easter Sunday. This does not include credits for sponsorship or underwriting, or apply to programme signals that originate overseas, are produced and transmitted simultaneously to both New Zealand and outside audiences, and are targeted primarily at the latter.299

In April 2009, this provision was tested for the first time when TV3 was convicted for broadcasting commercials on three consecutive Sunday mornings during the Rugby World Cup in 2007.300 The Ministry of Culture and Heritage brought the action and explained that it has a legal obligation to do so. TV3 relied on a subsection of the provision which exempts any programme where the programme signal originates outside New Zealand and is produced and transmitted simultaneously to both New Zealand audiences and audiences outside the country.301 TV3's argument was that it had an arrangement with Fiji TV to broadcast the signal for the cup to more than 9 million people in the Pacific Islands. The broadcaster was convicted and discharged on each of the three charges it faced, the Judge holding that this would both deter and denounce the conduct.302 Prosecution costs of NZD 5,000 were also awarded.

Under the provision, advertising is also banned on television for the same time period on Anzac Day, Christmas Day, Good Friday and Easter Sunday. However, it is banned on radio only for the latter three, which appears inconsistent. The periods involved do seem a drop in the bucket, nonetheless, and there are no controls whatever on online advertising.

§4. Sponsorship

273. Under the ASA Code for Advertising and Promotion of Alcohol, sponsored liquor advertisements must clearly and primarily promote the sponsored activity, team or individual, and the sponsor, the sponsorship and items incidental to them may only be featured in a subordinate manner.[1604] 'Sponsorship' means any agreement or part of an agreement involving payment or other consideration in lieu of payment by a liquor producer, distributor or retailer to support a sporting or cultural property, event or activity, in return for which the sponsored party agrees to be associated with or promote the sponsor's drink(s) or outlet. The Code applies to the overall sponsorship agreement, including any material bearing the sponsor's logo or trademark. It does not apply to any use to which that material might subsequently be put, or to the behaviour or activities of sponsored parties, if that is not required or specifically permitted by the sponsorship agreement. Alcohol companies can sponsor teams and events as well as individuals and activities. 'Sponsorship advertisement' means an advertisement which clearly indicates that the advertiser is sponsoring a person, competition, activity or event. Approximately 15% of the advertising space or time available can be used to mention the sponsor's name, brand name or logo, however, consideration is given to the overall look and feel of the material and whether the advertisement is promoting the event or product. Teams and individuals who may otherwise be considered heroes of the young and

1604. Principle 4 of the ASA Code for Advertising and Promotion of Alcohol.

prevented from being included in alcohol advertisements, may be included in sponsorship advertisements as long as the requirements set out in the Guidelines are met.

A voluntary policy agreed by the main broadcasters, TVNZ and MediaWorks, operates in relation to sponsorship advertising to children. Sponsorship during children's programming is to be limited and socially responsible. Alcohol sponsorship is not allowed. Sponsors can promote their association with the programme through other avenues such as press or sales promotion. Any commercial acknowledgement associated with the actual programme on air must not be dominant. No advertising footage will be allowed in the opening and closing credits.[1605]

§5. Product Placement

274. There is no direct regulation of advertising product placement in New Zealand such as that which exists in the United Kingdom.[1606] The ASA codes may have indirect impact through requirements that advertisements should be clearly distinguishable as such, whatever their form and whatever the medium used. However, it seems these have never been used to challenge or legitimize forms of product placement.

1605. ThinkTV, Standards and Regulations, Advertising on Television – Getting it Right For Children, http://www.thinktv.co.nz/wp-content/uploads/TTV0005_Childrens_BookletV5-final.pdf, accessed 31 Jul. 2015.

1606. OFCOM Broadcasting Code 2015, http://stakeholders.ofcom.org.uk/binaries/broadcast/code-july-15/Ofcom_Broadcast_Code_July_2015.pdf, accessed 31 Jul. 2015.

Chapter 6. Right to Information

§1. Access to Major Events

275. The Major Events Management Act 2007 establishes a procedure for appropriate events (like the Rugby World Cup) to be declared by the government to be major events and, among other things, it prohibits representations that suggest persons, brands, goods or services have an association with a major event when they do not.[1607] Provisions in the Act intended to prevent ambush advertising could impact on media. For example, once a clean zone is declared around an event, no person may advertise there during a specified period without the written authorization of the major event organizer.[1608] A person advertises if that person pays for, commissions or authorizes the advertisement, or receives consideration for the placement or the location of the advertisement.[1609] The offence does not apply if, in accordance with honest practices in industrial or commercial matters, the advertising is done by an existing organization continuing to carry out its ordinary activities, or to advertising in a newspaper or magazine, or on a television, radio, or electronic device, being used for personal use, unless it is being used with the intention that the advertising intrude on a major event activity or the attention of the associated audience.[1610] Knowing breach of the provision attracts liability on conviction to a fine not exceeding NZD 150,000.[1611]

The Major Events Management Act 2007 also contains a provision dealing with the unauthorized use of emblems and words relating to Olympic Games and Commonwealth Games which attracts similar liability.[1612] There is a defence where the defendant's business includes publishing or arranging for the publication of advertisements and the defendant received the advertisement, or the emblem or word contained in the advertisement, in the ordinary course of that business and did not know, and had no reason to believe, that the publication of the advertisement or the publication of the advertisement containing the emblem or word would constitute a breach.[1613] Charges of ticket scalping and unauthorized use of emblems may be laid up to three years after they occur.[1614]

1607. Major Events Management Act 2007, s. 10.
1608. Major Events Management Act 2007, s. 18. 'Advertise' means any form of communication (including selling or giving away any goods or services, but excluding communications of personal opinion made by a natural person for no commercial gain) made to the public or a section of the public in relation to any goods or services, or brand of goods or services, or person who provides goods or services: s. 4.
1609. Major Events Management Act 2007, s. 21.
1610. Major Events Management Act 2007, s. 22.
1611. Major Events Management Act 2007, s. 23.
1612. Major Events Management Act 2007, ss 28 and 31.
1613. Major Events Management Act 2007, s. 32.
1614. Major Events Management Act 2007, s. 64. Otherwise, s. 25 of the Criminal Procedure Act 2011 applies providing for varied time limits depending on the offence.

§2. SHORT NEWS REPORTING

276. New Zealand does not regulate broadcasters to prevent exclusive broadcasting of major events. However, informal agreements by way of convention, and copyright law, can have impact in this area.

The most prominent example is that of sports coverage, particularly in relation to the broadcast of international rugby matches featuring the male New Zealand All Black team. In 1992, New Zealand's main pay television provider, Sky Network Television, secured the rights to an All Black tour of South Africa. This was the first time a major sporting event could no longer be seen live on free-to-air channels. In 1996, Sky secured a ten-year global deal involving the rights to most major rugby games. Sky went on to partner with the state broadcaster, TVNZ and later with its rival, TV3, to sell delayed coverage rights. Legislation to prevent this sort of siphoning off of key sporting events from the free-to-air platform to pay TV has never been considered in New Zealand.[1615]

Broadcasters have used informal conventions to deal with the issue as to how footage of major events to which one broadcaster had exclusive rights might be used by other broadcasters. In July 2007 however, TV3, Sky and Television New Zealand (TVNZ) entered into a New Zealand Television Broadcasters News Access Agreement which permitted use in bona fide news programmes and set out other permissible degrees of use. Such agreements have no impact in law and may be overridden by copyright law.

The Copyright Act 1994 provides that fair dealing with a work is not a breach, provided it is for the purposes of criticism or review, whether of that work or another work, or a performance of a work, and is accompanied by a sufficient acknowledgment.[1616] A work includes a communications work, which is a transmission of sounds, visual images or other information, or a combination of these, for reception by members of the public, and includes a broadcast or cable programme.[1617] There is also a fair dealing defence for reporting news and current events.[1618] Both these defences are usually interpreted broadly. A leading case is *MediaWorks v. Sky Television*,[1619] where Justice Winkelmann found in favour of MediaWorks NZ Ltd and TV3, in a claim against Sky Television Network Ltd for using exclusive footage of the 2007 Rugby World Cup matches to which TV3 had rights and which Sky had access to under the 2007 agreement described above. Sky had used TV3's footage intensively in a number of different programme formats including news, current events and sports and magazine-style programmes, and across a number of its channels. The Judge held that fair dealing is a question of impression and degree, including a key question as to whether the challenged use

1615. Paul Norris, *News Media Ownership in New Zealand*, in *What's News? Reclaiming journalism in New Zealand* 51 (Judy McGregor & Margie Comrie eds, Dunmore Press 2002).

1616. Copyright Act 1994, s. 42(1).

1617. Copyright Act 1994, s. 2. A cable programme may include an internet website service: *Shetland Times Ltd v. Wills* [1997] EMLR 277.

1618. Sections 40–43. This prevents 'place shifting' transmission of broadcasts from Korea to New Zealand: see *Munhwa Broadcasting Corporation v. Young International 2009 Ltd* HC Auckland CIV-2010-404-203, 17 Dec. 2010.

1619. *MediaWorks v. Sky Television* (2007) 74 IPR 205 (HC).

competes with the exploitation of copyright by the copyright owner.[1620] In this case, Sky's use was intensive – at times viewers were able to access TV3 footage on Sky in excess of forty-eight times a day. The rate of repetition alone was found to be excessive, but use in the magazine-style programmes was also unfair. Sky's use was therefore in breach of TV3's copyright.

1620. *MediaWorks v. Sky Television* (2007) 74 IPR 205 (HC) at [61].

Chapter 7. Access to Networks

§1. Must Carry Rules

277. There are no 'must carry' rules. Under the Radiocommunications Act 1990, the government allocates spectrum through the price mechanism to those who are prepared to pay the highest price. Tenders and auctions are used to allocate spectrum. Following initial allocation of spectrum rights can be freely traded, and spectrum managers can make decisions about whether and how to get involved in the market.

§2. Other Access Obligations for Networks

278. Access obligations are not imposed. The Crown allocates and reserves spectrum licences to give effect to government policy for commercial uses, such as the digital television switchover, or public policy uses such as to meet its obligations under the Treaty of Waitangi to Maori, or to develop access radio. Where there is no competition for spectrum, allocation is through an administrative process where radio licences are issued by Radio Spectrum Management (RSM).[1621] Allocations are reviewed from time to time, and changes can occur where public policy objectives change.[1622]

In 2008, as part of the move to digital, the government rolled out a free-to-air digital platform called Free view with NZD 25 million in funding. Free view is a consortium of public and private broadcasters made up of Television New Zealand, MediaWorks, Māori Television, and Radio New Zealand. It broadcasts using both satellite and terrestrial transmission systems, and delivers a range of channels including TVNZ's four channels, MediaWorks' four channels, two Māori Television channels, Radio New Zealand's two networks, Prime, Choice TV, Parliament TV, Chinese Television and a number of regional broadcasters.[1623]

Sky Television, the main pay television provider, now carries free-to-air channels as part of its entertainment packages. However, it only pays licensing fees for this if a channel is exclusive to its platform.

Otherwise, ordinary competition law governs business acquisition and behaviour in the area of broadcasting and communications generally.

1621. See Policy Rules for Crown Spectrum Management Rights, PIB 59, RSM, Ministry of Business, Innovation and Development, August 2014, http://www.rsm.govt.nz/online-services-resources/pdf-and-documents-library/publications-and-guides/pibs/pib59, accessed 31 Jul. 2015.

1622. Ministry of Business, Innovation & Employment, Radio Spectrum Management, Allocation of Spectrum, http://www.rsm.govt.nz/about-rsm/spectrum-policy/allocation-of-spectrum, accessed 31 Jul. 2015.

1623. Minstry of Culture and Heritage 'Cultural Industries' (2015), http://www.mch.govt.nz/what-we-do/cultural-sector-overviews/cultural-policy-new-zealand/5-cultural-industries, accessed 31 Jul. 2015.

Chapter 8. Standards and Interoperability

279. In New Zealand, radio spectrum is managed under the Radiocommunications Act 1989 by the Radio Spectrum Management (RSM) which is a business unit of the MBIE.[1624] This role includes allocating rights for the use of the spectrum, and enforcing compliance with the requirements to ensure legitimate users are able to enjoy their rights.

RSM also prescribe standards to ensure safe and satisfactory products fit for their intended use. The Electromagnetic Compatibility (EMC) and Radio Standards also protect the radio spectrum, minimize interference and allow effective use of radiocommunications services. Joint Australia and New Zealand standards (AS/NZS) and international standards (IEC-CISPR, ETS, EN, & FCC), are used in New Zealand where possible, to maximize trade opportunities, equipment availability and minimize compliance costs. There are joint agreements which provide for direct acceptance of compliant, correctly labelled electrical and electronic products sold in reciprocal markets in Australia and China. New Zealand also gives mutual recognition to testing bodies in the EU, Singapore, Taiwan and the APEC countries.[1625]

New Zealand is a signatory to several international agreements that impact on usage of the radio spectrum or relevant standards and equipment specifications. The primary covenant concerning radio spectrum usage, licensing and interference management is the International Telecommunication Union International Radio Regulations (IRRs), which form a part of the Constitution and Convention of the International Telecommunication Union (Geneva, 1992). The IRRs create obligations to other countries regarding coordination, licensing and interference management.

The primary purpose of the IRRs is to prevent harmful interference between countries. However, because in many frequency bands New Zealand's geographic isolation makes harmful interference to and from other countries unlikely, this is not a significant issue. The IRRs do impact on equipment standardization and interoperability for some applications, however. Currently the Radiocommunications Act 1989 requires compliance with the IRRs for radio and spectrum licences.[1626] The Act is being reviewed.[1627]

There is no requirement for interoperability of analogue and digital television sets because New Zealand switched to digital television by 2013.

1624. See http://www.rsm.govt.nz/.

1625. See Compliance Standards for EMC and Radio, http://www.rsm.govt.nz/compliance/supplier-requirements/compliance-standards-for-emc-radio, accessed 27 Aug. 2015.

1626. Radiocommunications Act 1989, ss 101, 111 and sch. 1.

1627. See Review of the Radiocommunications Act 1994 Discussion Document July 2014, http://www.rsm.govt.nz/projects-auctions/current-projects/review-of-the-radiocommunications-act-1989, accessed 27 Aug. 2015.

Part IV. Cross Ownership Regulation

280. There is no special regulatory scheme directed at preventing cross ownership of media in New Zealand. However, the Commerce Commission monitors and prohibits mergers and acquisitions that substantially lessen competition under the Commerce Act 1986. The Act also prohibits anti-competitive agreements between businesses such as agreements to fix prices or to carve up markets and makes it illegal for companies to abuse a dominant market position.

The business acquisition clearance regime is a permissive one of general application that includes the acquisition of broadcasting enterprises.[1628] A person who proposes to acquire assets of a business or shares may give the Commerce Commission a notice seeking clearance for the acquisition. The Commission will give a written clearance for the acquisition if it is satisfied that it will not have or be likely to have, the effect of substantially lessening competition in a market.[1629]

In broadcasting, lessening competition is not automatically found where one party proposes the acquisition of all or most of a particular kind of broadcast spectrum rights. The nature of broadcast technology, where services are delivered in multitudinous media, means the sector is seen as less susceptible to competition problems associated with acquisition of traditional business assets.[1630] Content concerns such as the increasing homogenization of news services through business

1628. Commerce Act 1986, Parts III and V. See http://www.comcom.govt.nz/business-competition, accessed 31 Jul. 2015.

1629. Commerce Act 1986, ss 47 and 66. In *Broadcast Communications Ltd and the Crown* [1990] NZAR 433, Broadcast Communications Ltd was given clearance to acquire Crown licences to utilize one UHF network and up to nineteen supplementary UHF channels for medium or low power transmission even though it was a wholly owned subsidiary of TVNZ. The members of the Commission could not reach agreement on the issue of the strengthening of dominance in the various markets, and the decision was made by the casting vote of the Chairman.

1630. In *Telecable Holdings Ltd and the Crown* (Commerce Commission Decision No 257, 12 Dec. 1990), clearance was given to a proposed merger or takeover from the Crown of management rights for twelve channels in the 2.3 – 2.396 Ghz range.The Commission held that the relevant markets were the buying and selling of management rights for transmission vehicles and provision of television broadcasting services. It considered that competition existed from users in the neighbouring spectrum and other spectrums with similar characteristics, and cable and satellite. There was also potential for operators in other bands to operate the same applications. See also *Fairfax New Zealand Ltd and Times Media Group Ltd, Re* (Commerce Commission Decision No 561, 14 Oct. 2005), *Canwest Radioworks Ltd and Radio FM Licenses in Northland, Re* (Commerce Commission Decision 557, 31 Aug. 2005), *Wilson & Horton Ltd and Power Plant Productions Ltd, Re* (Commerce Commission Decision 445, 7 Dec. 2001) *Independent News Auckland Ltd and Review Publishing Co Ltd, Re* (Commerce Commission Decision 395, 16 Jun. 2000).

acquisition have no influence on the Commission's determination of what makes a competitive market.

Lessening of competition in the market is the only relevant factor in achieving a clearance. However, the Commission may grant an authorization instead of a clearance if it considers the acquisition will result, or will be likely to result, in such a benefit to the public that it should be permitted.[1631]

Where no clearance has been obtained, it is illegal to acquire a broadcasting business or shares in it if market dominance results.[1632] Penalties for breach of the requirement can be very severe.[1633]

Part II of the Commerce Act 1986 which deals with practices regarded as substantially lessening competition, has effect in the broadcasting sector, as does Part IV, providing for control of prices.[1634] These provisions have been rarely triggered; however, the convergence of conventional broadcasters with new platform providers has the potential to concern the monitoring body. Under the Commerce Act, it is illegal to 'enter into a contract or arrangement, or arrive at an understanding, containing a provision that has the purpose, or has or is likely to have the effect, of substantially lessening competition in a market'.[1635] The provision also prohibits giving effect to such a contract, arrangement or understanding. In other words, both entering into and giving effect to such an agreement is illegal. In 2013, the Commission investigated whether provisions in contracts of New Zealand's main pay television provider Sky Network Television with telecommunications retail service providers were likely to have previously breached these provisions of the Act. The Commission issued Sky with a warning after finding the provisions did appear to have had such an effect in the past but were unlikely to have the effect of substantially lessening competition in the future due to the appearance of competitors in the market which were providing alternative pay TV packages. However, the Commission put Sky on notice that it would continue to monitor the company's contracts and conduct.[1636]

1631. Commerce Act 1986, s. 67(3)(b) and see Part V.
1632. Commerce Act 1986, s. 47(1).
1633. Section 83 provides for pecuniary penalties payable to the Crown not exceeding NZD 500,000 in the case of a person not a body corporate, or NZD 5,000,000 in the case of a body corporate. Section 84 provides for the granting of injunctions, s. 84A allows actions for damages, and under s. 85 the court may order divestiture of assets or shares.
1634. However, there is apparently no substantive case law arising from such practices, possibly because the diverse technology available to deliver services renders such practices unnecessary. No price control has been imposed.
1635. Commerce Act 1986, s. 27.
1636. Media Release, Commerce Commission, 'Commerce Commission issues warning to Sky', 8 Oct. 2013, http://www.comcom.govt.nz/the-commission/media-centre/media-releases/detail/2013/commerce-commission-issues-warning-to-sky, accessed 31 Jul. 2015.

Part V. Supervision: Media Regulator

Chapter 1. Law Commission Recommendations

281. New Zealand does not have a grand media regulator. However, like the United Kingdom and Australia, New Zealand recently examined how its media is specifically regulated. Rather than investigating the legality of media conduct, the particular task for the New Zealand Law Commission was to investigate whether the growth of new media had led to gaps in the regulatory regime which required addressing.

In a report released in March 2013 after two years investigating the current state of regulation and consulting closely with mainstream media, new media and other stakeholders, the Commission recommended that the then current complex system of media regulation involving a statutory authority for broadcasters, the BSA and a self-regulatory Press Council for the print media, be replaced with one over-arching regulator known as the News Media Standards Authority (NMSA).[1637]

The Law Commission recommended that NMSA should enforce one set of standards across all publishers of news irrespective of format or method of distribution. It would accept and resolve complaints relating to news, current affairs, news commentary, and content like documentaries and factual programming. As recommended by the Commission, membership of NMSA would be voluntary, but mainstream media would be incentivized by being promised in return the privileges in laws such as those which give media presumptive access to courts, exemptions from the operation of the likes of the Privacy and Fair Trading Act, and access to certain defences in the Defamation Act so long as reports are fair and accurate. NMSA would be independent of both media and government. An independent panel would be appointed to work on its membership.

Members of NMSA would fund the body, although the government would provide some funding for its recommended research function. The Authority would be a 'one-stop shop' covering three previously separate media platforms – print media, broadcasters, and online and anything between. It would also develop a mediation service, and appeal would be into an independent body. NMSA would have power to make take down orders, correction orders, apologies, rights of reply and censure. The members of NMSA would not be compelled to comply with orders made, but would agree to be bound by its rulings by signing a contract beforehand.

1637. See 'The news media meets new media', NZLC R 128, (2013), http://r128.publications.lawcom.govt.nz/, accessed 31 Jul. 2015.

The Commission also recommended that all statutes which give privileges or exemptions specifically to the news media should be amended to include a new and consistent definition of 'news media', which would include new media. Under this definition, news media would have to meet specified statutory criteria:

- a significant element of their publishing activities involves the generation and/or aggregation of news, information and opinion of current value;
- they disseminate this information to a public audience;
- publication is regular and not occasional; and
- the publisher must be accountable to a code of ethics and to the NMSA.

Bloggers could therefore meet this definition and take advantage of journalistic privileges and exemptions if they are prepared to develop a code of ethics.

Voluntary membership of the Authority was recommended to make the body as attractive to media as possible. The Commission observed that non-members would still be covered by other laws such as those relating to defamation and privacy, and statutes like the Privacy Act. They would also be subject to new laws recommended by the Commission in a Briefing Paper on cyberbullying – a criminal offence, and access to special jurisdiction in the District Court which would deal with speech that causes serious harm online.[1638]

The recommendations about NMSA and cyberbullying were somewhat co-dependent for the full symmetry of the review reforms to be realized. However, the Government cherry-picked the cyberbullying recommendations and agreed to implement those but not the more major recommendations about on media regulation generally. Justice Minister Judith Collins noted that the regulatory review was not driven by a crisis of confidence in the mainstream media, and thought the media in New Zealand have already made good progress in dealing with these challenges. She concluded there is no pressing need for statutory or institutional change of the regulatory bodies.[1639]

1638. The Harmful Digital Communications Act which implements the Law Commission Briefing Paper on Cyberbullying is discussed at para. 280 below. See Law Commission, *Harmful Digital Communications: The Adequacy of the Current Sanctions and Remedies* (Ministerial Briefing, 15 Aug. 2012) http://www.lawcom.govt.nz/project/review-regulatory-gaps-and-new-media/publication/ministerial-briefing/2012/ministerial-briefing-harmful-digital-communications-adequacy-current-sanctions-and-remedies, accessed October 2013.

1639. New Zealand Ministry of Justice, *Government Response to Law Commission Report 'News Media Meets New Media'* (October 2013) http://www.justice.govt.nz/publications/global-publications/n/news-media-meets-new-media-government-response-to-law-commission-report, accessed October 2013.

Chapter 2. Harmful Digital Publications

282. In November 2013, the Government introduced the Harmful Digital Communications Bill,[1640] which passed into law two years later.[1641] The Act provides a civil regime based on a set of communication principles and an approved Agency with the power to receive and assess complaints about harm caused by digital communications. The Agency will focus on mediating the complaint and seeking voluntary take-down if appropriate, but has no powers to make orders. If the complaint cannot be resolved at this level, the complainant may take the matter to the District Court.

The Act also contains a criminal offence of posting a harmful digital communication with intent to cause serious emotional distress punishable by up to two years imprisonment, or a fine.[1642] Online content hosts have protection from criminal or civil liability if they follow a complaint and take-down procedure in the Act.[1643] Only these provisions are currently in effect. The civil regime will not commence until the government appoints an appropriate Agency by 2017.

The regime is based on a set of Digital Communication Principles, which are:

Principal 1
A digital communication should not disclose sensitive personal facts about an individual.
Principal 2
A digital communication should not be threatening, intimidating or menacing.
Principal 3
A digital communication should not be grossly offensive to a reasonable person in the position of the affected individual.
Principal 4
A digital communication should not be indecent or obscene.
Principal 5
A digital communication should not be used to harass an individual.
Principal 6
A digital communication should not make a false allegation.
Principal 7
A digital communication should not contain a matter that is published in breach of confidence.
Principal 8
A digital communication should not incite or encourage anyone to send a message to an individual for the purpose of causing harm to the individual.

1640. Harmful Digital Communications Bill 2013, 168-1: http://www.legislation.govt.nz/bill/government/2013/0168/latest/DLM5711810.html, accessed August 2015.
1641. Harmful Digital Communications Act 2015.
1642. Harmful Digital Communications Act 2015, s. 22.
1643. Harmful Digital Communications Act 2015, ss 23–25.

Principal 9
A digital communication should not incite or encourage an individual to commit suicide.
Principal 10
A digital communication should not denigrate an individual by reason of his or her colour, race, ethnic or national origins, religion, gender, sexual orientation or disability.

Both the approved Agency and courts must take account of the communication principles and act consistently with the rights and freedoms contained in the NZBORA 1990 when operating under the Act.[1644]

The principles cover most of the forms of harmful speech recognized in New Zealand law. It is possible, then, that they would regulate more speech and have more serious effects than regulation of offline speech. The Act contains a number of safeguards against this. First, only an individual who has suffered harm can make a complaint. Harm is defined as serious emotional distress.[1645] Thus, the threshold is high. Second, a Court can only consider a complaint if the Agency has already attempted to deal with it, and then only if there has been a serious, repeated or threatened breach of one or more of the Principles, and this has caused or is likely to have caused harm.[1646]

The remedial powers in the Act are practical and extensive. The Court may make interim orders pending determination of an application for a final order.[1647] Both interim or final orders can take the following forms:

- an order to take-down or disable material;
- an order that the defendant cease the conduct concerned;
- an order that the defendant not encourage any other persons to engage in similar communications towards the affected individual;
- an order that a correction be published;
- an order that a right of reply be given to the affected individual;
- an order that an apology be published.[1648]

The following orders can be made against content hosts:

- an order to take-down or disable public access to material;
- an order that the identity of the author of an anonymous or pseudonymous communication be released to the court;
- an order that a correction be published;
- an order that a right of reply be given to the affected individual.[1649]

1644. Harmful Digital Communications Act 2015, s. 6(2).
1645. Harmful Digital Communications Act 2015, s. 4.
1646. Harmful Digital Communications Act 2015, s. 11.
1647. Harmful Digital Communications Act 2015, s. 18.
1648. Harmful Digital Communications Act 2015, s. 19(1).
1649. Harmful Digital Communications Act 2015, s. 19(2).

There is also power to direct orders to apply to third parties, to order a declaration that a Principle has been breached, and to order suppression of names.[1650] Such declarations would not bind host of offshore websites, but are intended to have symbolic effect.

A court is required to consider a number of factors before making an order, including the purpose of the communicator, and whether the communication was intended to harm. This does not mean lack of fault will result in no order being made. In some cases, even if there is no fault at all, it may still be a good idea to order removal of material from the internet, or publication of a correction in a relevant form. However, the inclusion of this factor means that the issue of fault must be addressed and weighed in some way before any order is made. The Act also requires the question whether the communication is in the public interest to be addressed, as well as the truth or falsity of the statement. Additionally, a court must consider the occasion, context and subject-matter of the communication, the content of the communication and the level of harm caused, the extent to which the communication has spread beyond the original parties, the age and vulnerability of the affected individual, the conduct of the defendant, including any attempt to minimize the harm, the conduct of the affected individual or complainant, the technical and operational practicalities and the costs of an order, and the appropriate individual or other person who should be subject to the order.[1651]

The Harmful Digital Communications Act 2015 establishes an unknown, new and quite complex legal regime that will impact on online speech differently to the same speech in another medium. Its effects will be closely monitored.

1650. Harmful Digital Communications Act 2015, s. 19(4).
1651. Harmful Digital Communications Act 2015, s. 19(5).

Chapter 3. Online Media Standards Authority

283. While the Government was considering the recent Law Commission recommendations for regulatory reform of media in New Zealand,[1652] the main broadcasters TVNZ, SKY/Prime, MediaWorks TV, and Maori Television, Radio New Zealand, The Radio Network and MediaWorks Radio developed an industry-led body to regulate the identified unregulated area of online news and current affairs content. The New Zealand Online Media Standards Authority (OMSA) came into being on 1 July 2013. It is an industry-funded, self-regulatory body which oversees online news and current affairs content standards.[1653]

Any media proprietor who publishes news and current affairs content online can apply to be a member of OMSA. The media proprietor must be an individual or organization which carries on activities aimed at a public audience online.[1654] The founding broadcasters referred to above were the original members, but two bloggers have since become members also.[1655] A member must seek at all times to maintain proper and generally acceptable standards when publishing content online, submit to the jurisdiction of the OMSA's complaints process and comply with all orders made in the course of the OMSA's complaints process.[1656]

OMSA aims to provide a cost effective and consumer-friendly solution to complaints,[1657] and is similar in structure to the ASA and the New Zealand Press Council.[1658] OMSA's free complaints process is overseen by a Complaints Committee with a separate Appeals Committee. One specific object of the OMSA, as stated in the Constitution, is to encourage the media to voluntarily co-operate in the process of self-regulation.[1659]

The OMSA is the body responsible for establishing and upholding a Code of Standards (the Code) for all news and current affairs content published online by their members.[1660] The objective of the Code is to set out agreed standards for the publication of news and current affairs content published on the websites of OMSA

1652. See 'The news media meets new media', NZLC R 128, (2013), http://r128.publications.lawcom.govt.nz/, accessed 11 Jun. 2014. The recommendations were ultimately rejected: New Zealand Ministry of Justice, *Government Response to Law Commission Report 'News Media Meets New Media'* (October 2013) http://www.justice.govt.nz/publications/global-publications/n/news-media-meets-new-media-government-response-to-law-commission-report, accessed October 2013. See para. 281 above.
1653. Online Media Standards Authority 'Broadcasting Industry to Launch Online News and Current Affairs Self-Regulatory Body' (media release, 14 Feb. 2013); Online Media Standards Authority 'New Online Media Standards Authority to Launch on 1 July 2013' (media release, 7 May 2013).
1654. OMSA membership application form, http://www.omsa.co.nz/constitution/current-membership/, accessed 31 Jul. 2015.
1655. OMSA Membership, http://www.omsa.co.nz/constitution/current-membership/, accessed 31 Jul. 2015.
1656. www.omsa.co.nz/constitution/current-membership.
1657. Online Media Standards Authority, 'Online Media Standards Authority Open for Business' (media release, 27 Jun. 2013).
1658. See www.omsa.co.nz/how-we-work/what-we-do/, accessed 31 Jul. 2015.
1659. Online Media Standards Authority Constitution cl. 3(c), http://www.omsa.co.nz/constitution/, accessed 31 Jul. 2015.
1660. See www.omsa.co.nz, accessed 31 Jul. 2015.

members.[1661] Freedom of speech and social responsibility are said to underpin the Code, which is to be applied consistently on the principles of natural justice.[1662]

Part A of the Code contains two standards that relate to the information published. Standard 1 governs accuracy and provides that publishers should make reasonable efforts to ensure that news and current affairs content is accurate and/or does not mislead in relation to all material points of fact. Standard 2 governs balancing of controversial issues: taking account of the context in which the content is published, publishers should make reasonable efforts to ensure that, where the content deals with controversial issues of public importance, it makes due reference to a reasonable range of significant viewpoints on the issue.

Part B of the Code contains two standards that relate to those participating or referred to in the content. Complaints under this part may only be brought by the person or organization taking part or referred to in the publication. Standard 3 governs fairness: publishers should deal fairly with any person or organization taking part or referred to in online news and current affairs publications. Standard 4 governs privacy and provides that publishers of news and current affairs content should respect an individual's right to privacy and refrain from publishing content that is a breach of that right. It is a defence to a privacy complaint if publication is in the public interest or consent has been given to publication.[1663] But where publication involves the privacy interests of a child or a vulnerable person (even if consent is given on behalf of the child or vulnerable person) publishers must exercise particular care and discretion.[1664]

Part C of the Code deals with social responsibilities. Standard 5 governs responsible content: publishers should ensure news and current affairs content: is responsible, is not presented in such a way as to cause panic, or unwarranted alarm or undue distress, and does not deceive. Standard 6 governs discrimination and denigration: publishers of news and current affairs content should not encourage discrimination against, or denigration of, any section of the New Zealand community on account of gender, sexual orientation, race, age, disability, occupational status, or as a consequence of legitimate expression of religion, culture or political belief.

Part D of the Code deals with remedy principles. Where a complaint has been upheld, publishers will publish OMSA's decision, or a fair summary of it, on their website with similar prominence to the original publication. All OMSA decisions will be published on its website. Complaints should identify any other remedy sought in the event that the complaint is upheld. The OMSA remedy principles are:

- Errors should be acknowledged and promptly corrected by amending or removing the relevant content.
- Corrections should be clearly labelled, dated and given appropriate prominence having regard to the original publication.

1661. See www.omsa.co.nz/how-we-work/code/, accessed 31 Jul. 2015.
1662. See www.omsa.co.nz/how-we-work/code/, accessed 31 Jul. 2015.
1663. OMSA Code of Standards 4a. and 4b, http://www.omsa.co.nz/how-we-work/code/, accessed 31 Jul. 2015.
1664. OMSA Code of Standards 4c, http://www.omsa.co.nz/how-we-work/code/, 31 Jul. 2015.

- Rights of reply (which may include relevant links to other material) should be offered and published with due prominence where appropriate.
- Apologies should be offered and published where justified in the circumstances.

Under the remedy principles, the Committee has no authority to order a financial penalty (the complainant had asked for a remedy of the publisher to donate to a charity).[1665]

Any person or organization within New Zealand can complain about any news and current affairs material published online by the members that they consider breaches the Code of Standards.[1666] The complaints process is free and is overseen by the independent Complaints Committee which upholds and reviews the Code.[1667] The Committee is currently chaired by a retired Court of Appeal Judge and is made up of seven members – four from the public (including the Chair) and three nominated by the media industry.[1668]

The Committee uses the Code when considering the merits of any complaint.[1669] The Complaints Committee may deliberate on any standards under the Code it considers appropriate, whether or not specified by the complainant, provided they fall within the tenor of the original complaint and the publisher has been notified and given an opportunity to comment.[1670] Complaints are to be determined in accordance with the rules of natural justice, in writing and with as little technicality and formality as possible.[1671]

The Complaints Committee's jurisdiction extends solely to complaints about news and current affairs content published online by any of the Authority's members that do not fall within the jurisdiction of any other media content regulator.[1672] Jurisdiction does not extend to factual content outside news and current affairs, complaints made by a person or an organization outside New Zealand (subject to the discretion of the Chairman), or complaints under the privacy and fairness standards brought by someone other than the person or organization referred to.[1673]

A complaint may only be brought against a member of OMSA. Complaints must be lodged within fourteen days of the content first being posted. The Chair can summarily dismiss complaints that fall outside OMSA's jurisdiction, are trivial or vexatious, or do not disclose an arguable breach of the Code of Standards. This is

---

1665. *Hopping v. MediaWorks* [2014] NZOMSA 14/011 (8 Sep. 2014).
1666. See www.omsa.co.nz/how-we-work/complaints-form/, accessed 31 Jul. 2015.
1667. Online Media Standards Authority, 'New Online Media Standards Authority to Launch on 1 July 2013' (media release, 7 May 2013); www.omsa.co.nz/how-we-work/, accessed 31 Jul. 2015.
1668. See www.omsa.co.nz/how-we-work/what-we-do/; Online Media Standards Authority Constitution First Schedule Rule 2, accessed 12 Dec. 2014.
1669. See www.omsa.co.nz/how-we-work/what-we-do/, accessed 31 Jul. 2015.
1670. See Online Media Standards Authority Constitution Second Schedule cl. 4(f), http://www.omsa.co.nz/constitution/complaints-procedures/, accessed 31 Jul. 2015.
1671. See Online Media Standards Authority Constitution Second Schedule cl. 4(h), http://www.omsa.co.nz/constitution/complaints-procedures/, accessed 31 Jul. 2015.
1672. See www.omsa.co.nz/how-we-work/our-jurisdiction/; Online Media Standards Authority Constitution Second Schedule cl. 1(a), http://www.omsa.co.nz/constitution/complaints-procedures/, accessed 31 Jul. 2015.
1673. See www.omsa.co.nz/how-we-work/our-jurisdiction/; Online Media Standards Authority Constitution Second Schedule cl. 1(b), http://www.omsa.co.nz/constitution/complaints-procedures/, accessed 31 Jul. 2015.

modelled on the ASA model and is useful in weeding out claims with no foundation but leaves considerable power in the Chair. If complaints get through this step, OMSA will investigate and mediate if possible. The Chairman must decide and notify parties within fourteen days of receipt of the complaint if it is within OMSA's jurisdiction and demonstrates an arguable breach. Complaints may be withdrawn and/or settled between the parties at any time.[1674]

If a matter is referred to the Complaints Committee, the Committee is to make its formal written decision within ten days of receipt of the publisher's comments or supplementary material. This decision must be notified to the parties within seven days of the decision and posted on the OMSA's website. The Complaints Committee will issue a formal written decision for all complaints, setting out the reasons for its decision.[1675]

If a complaint is upheld in whole or in part, the publisher must post a summary and link to the Complaints Committee's decision and take any other action stipulated by the Complaints Committee. Where the decision leads to the removal or modification of content, the publisher shall take all reasonable steps to remove or modify third-party sites where the material has been published. If a complaint is not upheld, the publisher is at liberty to take any action regarding the content.[1676]

The Complaints Committee may also direct the publisher to remove the material under investigation pending final determination of the complaint if it appears that the Code has been breached and the material gives rise to a real risk of significant harm to an individual or group.[1677]

The Complaints Appeals Committee reviews any appeals deemed appropriate by the Chair of the Appeals Committee.[1678] The Complaints Appeals Committee consists of a three-person board made up of two members of the public, including the Chair and one broadcasting industry representative.[1679] There is a limited right to appeal to the Appeal Committee – only the following grounds provide a right to appeal:[1680]

- significant new evidence is available;
- the rules of natural justice were not followed;
- the Code of Standards was not correctly applied.

1674. Online Media Standards Authority Constitution Second Schedule, http://www.omsa.co.nz/constitution/complaints-procedures/, accessed 31 Jul. 2015.

1675. Online Media Standards Authority Constitution Second Schedule cl. 5(a), http://www.omsa.co.nz/constitution/complaints-procedures/, accessed 31 Jul. 2015.

1676. Online Media Standards Authority Constitution Second Schedule, http://www.omsa.co.nz/constitution/complaints-procedures/, accessed 31 Jul. 2015.

1677. Online Media Standards Authority Constitution Second Schedule, http://www.omsa.co.nz/constitution/complaints-procedures/, accessed 31 Jul. 2015.

1678. See www.omsa.co.nz/how-we-work/complaints-committee/, accessed 31 Jul. 2015.

1679. See www.omsa.co.nz/how-we-work/complaints-committee/; Online Media Standards Authority Constitution Third Schedule, http://www.omsa.co.nz/constitution/rules-of-the-complaints-appeals-committee/, accessed 5 May 2015.

1680. Online Media Standards Authority Constitution Fourth Schedule 4, http://www.omsa.co.nz/constitution/appeals-board-procedures/, accessed 31 Jul. 2015.

An appeal must be made online and submitted within ten days of receipt of the decision. Where the Chairman of the Appeal Committee decides to hear the appeal, the Committee is to notify all parties to the complaint and seek their response. The Appeal Committee is to consider the Complaints Committee's decision, the full details, the publication, and any comments and opinions.[1681]

The Appeal Committee must notify all interested parties of the decision either orally or in writing as soon as practical and within forty-eight hours. Reasons for the determination are not given except by direction of the Chairman of the Appeal Committee. The Appeal Committee members must not give any information to the media unless directed by the Chairman. The Chairman can make any information public, provided it has first been conveyed to all interested parties to the appeal.[1682]

By the end of 2014, few complaints had reached the OMSA committee. A number of complaints have been rejected because they were filed out of time.[1683] The complaints procedures require a complaint to be lodged within fourteen days of the content first being posted on the publisher's website. The fourteen-day requirement does not really meet the stated objective of reflecting a balance between the immediacy and ongoing nature of online publications, the need to provide a reasonable opportunity to complain and the time needed for proper consideration of complaints. Requiring a complaint to be made within fourteen days from first posting gives priority to immediacy rather than to the fact that information can remain online indefinitely, and, when compared to the BSA, which requires a complaint to be made within twenty working days of the broadcast concerned, appears miserly. If more apparently weighty complaints are rejected in future because of this requirement, or the Chair is regularly asked to grant exceptions to the time limits, the fourteen-day period may be unfair and require revisiting.

It appears content on Facebook pages is unlikely to be seen as news and current affairs, and that comments posted in response to such content are seen as providing balance in any event.[1684] However, a time lapse between events in one country and reporting them in another does not necessarily exclude an item from being news.[1685] An online book review can be current affairs.[1686]

One of the few decisions so far to reach the Complaints Committee[1687] concerned the accuracy standard. The complainant argued that the opening sentence of an article put words into the mouth of the interviewee that were never said and were denied on the spot. Radio New Zealand argued it was reasonable paraphrasing, and

---

1681. Online Media Standards Authority Constitution Fourth Schedule, http://www.omsa.co.nz/constitution/appeals-board-procedures/, accessed 31 Jul. 2015.

1682. Online Media Standards Authority Constitution Fourth Schedule 4, http://www.omsa.co.nz/constitution/appeals-board-procedures/, accessed 31 Jul. 2015.

1683. *Maurice v. TVNZ* [2013] NZOMSA 14/005 (14 Jan. 2014), *Didier v. Radio New Zealand* [2014] NZOMSA 14/005 (16 Jun. 2014). In *Hopping v. MediaWorks* [2014] NZOMSA 10/011 (8 Sep. 2014), the complaint was raised out of time, but the Chairman thought it reasonable to allow an extension of time because there were similarities in the content broadcast and the online article which confused the complaint when determining where to file the complaint.

1684. [2014] NZOMSA 14/001 (14 Jan. 2014) and *Ngaro v. The Radio Network* [2014] NZOMSA 14/003 (12 Mar. 2014).

1685. *Bicknell v. Television New Zealand* [2014] NZOMSA 14/001 (23 Jul. 2014).

1686. *Kowalczewski v. The Radio Network* [2014] NZOMSA 14/004 (28 May 2014).

1687. *Munro v. Radio New Zealand* [2014] NZOMSA 14/006 (2 Jul. 2014).

that the sentence did not compromise audience understanding. A majority of the Committee ruled the sentence did accurately reflect and paraphrase what was said, and the sentence was unlikely to be misinterpreted by an online reader. In another decision,[1688] the Chairman noted that TVNZ had acknowledged there was a possible breach of Standard 1 Accuracy where an inaccurate photo accompanied a story but there was no inaccuracy identified in the story itself. TVNZ had removed the photo and included a note on the story advising the photo had been removed and why. These self-regulatory actions meant there was no further benefit in placing the matter before the Complaints Committee. The Chairman determined the complaint was settled.

OMSA has also noted that it is important story headlines as well as content comply with the code requirements, especially in the online environment where audiences are most likely to browse using headlines.[1689]

In a complaint objecting to an article headline about a person coming out as a transgender woman, the Chairman found the use of names and feminine and masculine pronouns in the story reflected the timing of the public transition and did not meet the threshold of encouraging discrimination or denigration.[1690]

There is no special reference to freedom of expression in the OMSA code, but Schedule 2 to the Constitution provides that, in deliberating complaints, the Complaints Committee must give primary consideration to freedom of expression guaranteed under the NZBORA 1990. There have been very few decisions which have raised the issue of freedom of expression, and where it has been raised, it has not been addressed by the Chairman or Complaints Committee.[1691]

An examination of the first OMSA decisions reveals the system is operating in a practical fashion with an emphasis on robust decisions by the Chair at the initial consideration stage. Currently, OMSA appears to provide a serious and efficient complaints process, though the small number of complaints received has not placed it under any real pressure as yet, and uphold rates are yet to be established.

The appearance of OMSA and the passing of the Harmful Digital Publications Act 2015 unfortunately adds to the proliferation of regulatory schemes dealing with speech in New Zealand to the point of incoherence. An individual wishing to complain about published speech is faced with a series of confusing choices. For example, if a person currently wishes to complain to OMSA that something seriously untrue was broadcast on a broadcaster's website, she or he must first establish the story is not exactly the same as any, which was actually broadcast outside the website. If it is the same, then the complaint should go to the broadcaster concerned, and perhaps ultimately to the BSA. If it is a unique online story, then a complaint can be made to OMSA, provided the broadcaster is a signed-up member. Alternatively, in future, a complaint could be made to the approved Harmful Digital Communications Agency so long as the individual can show he or she suffered serious emotional harm and is interested in the complaint being mediated between the

1688. *Mitchell v. Television New Zealand* [2014] NZOMSA 14/002 (7 Feb. 2014).
1689. *Cumming v. Radio New Zealand* [2013] NZOMSA 13/003 (4 Dec. 2013).
1690. *Wood v. Radio New Zealand* [2013] NZOMSA 13/002 (5 Sep. 2013).
1691. *Hopping v. MediaWorks Ltd* [2014] NZOMSA 14/011 (8 Sep. 2014), *Cumming v. Radio New Zealand* [2013] NZOMSA 13/003 (4 Dec. 2013).

parties by the Agency. If the complaint cannot be resolved, the matter will go to the District Court so long as there is serious, repeated or threatened emotional harm, but not if there is only pecuniary loss. The individual may prefer to bring a civil action using the tort of defamation to pursue pecuniary loss and would need to be advised about this.

Each complaint path is based on different codes, standards, guidelines, principles or elements of liability. Some are industry-based, some are not. Some provide light remedies, some provide a full range of remedies. While regulatory bodies maintain excellent websites such as that of the BSA, (which outlines how to complain), and make the process as easy as possible, (as the Press Council and OMSA websites attempt to do), it is inevitable that potential complainants will need some sort of legal advice to negotiate a path through the remedial minefield. It appears the simplicity of the schemes themselves is outweighed by the complexity of the overall remedial landscape. In this context, it could be seen as a mistake for the Government to reject the idea of a grand regulator in the form of a New Media Standards Authority put forward by the Law Commission in 2013.[1692]

1692. See the discussion at para. 279 above of the Law Commission report, 'The News Media Meets New Media', *Report 128* (March 2013) http://r128.publications.lawcom.govt.nz/, accessed 31 Jul. 2015.

Chapter 4. Convergence and the Future

284. The government has started work on the issue of convergence again and has recently issued a number of papers, one of which is a discussion document examining whether all audio-visual publications may be regulated in some way.[1693] One suggestion is one new Media Content Standards Act to replace the existing Classification Office regime and the broadcasting regime. Other possibilities include the status quo in which on-demand material is not covered but the numerous existing regimes could attempt to cover it; voluntary codes with no state intervention; the Broadcasting Act regime could be extended to cover on-demand content; the Classification Act could be extended to cover it; or the broadcasting regime could be made more self-regulatory. Submissions to the papers in this expansive review are to be made within a very short time frame of about two months, in October 2015.

1693. Content Regulation in a Converged World, Discussion Document, Ministry for Culture and Heritage, 25 Aug. 2015: http://www.mch.govt.nz/contentregulation. Other discussion papers have been issued as part of the government Convergence programme: see the New Zealand Government Convergence Programme: http://convergencediscussion.nz/. The government is also carrying out a review of telecommunications law and policy: Review of the Telecommunications Act, 2001, http://www.mbie.govt.nz/info-services/sectors-industries/technology-communications/communications/regulating-the-telecommunications-sector/review-of-the-telecommunications-act-2001.

Selected Bibliography

Butler & Butler. *The New Zealand Bill of Rights Act: A Commentary*. Wellington: LexisNexis, 2005.

Cheer. *Burrows and Cheer on Media Law in New Zealand.* 7th ed. Wellington: LexisNexis, 2015.

Cheer, Caldwell & Tully. 'The Family Court, Families and the Public Gaze'. *Families Commission Blue Skies Report* 16/07 (2007).

Desmarais. *New Zealand Law for Marketers.* 2nd ed. Wellington: LexisNexis, 2014.

Geiringer. 'The Principle of Legality and the Bill of Rights Act: A Critical Examination of *R v Hansen*'. *NZ Journal of Public and International Law* 6 (2008): 59.

Joseph. 'Sampling the "Wine Box"'. *NZLJ* (1994): 292.

Joseph. *Constitutional and Administrative Law in New Zealand.* 4th ed. Wellington: Brookers Ltd, 2014.

Koltay. *Freedom of Speech.* Hungary: Complex Publisher Ltd, 2013.

Mize. 'From Goldstein to the Burger King Babes: People Issues in Advertising'. In *The Real Deal! Essays in Law and Advertising*, edited by Ursula Cheer. The Centre for Commercial and Corporate Law Inc, 2008.

Mullis & Scott. 'Tilting at Windmills: The Defamation Act 2013'. *Modern Law Review* 77 (2014): 87.

New Zealand Law Commission Issues Paper No. 13. *Suppressing Names and Evidence.* Wellington, 2008.

New Zealand Law Commission Issues Paper No. 27. *The News Media Meets New Media.* Wellington, 2011.

New Zealand Law Commission Issues Paper No 36. *Contempt in Modern New Zealand.* Wellington, 2014.

New Zealand Law Commission Report No. 58. *Electronic Commerce Part Two.* Wellington, 1999.

New Zealand Law Commission Report No. 68. *Electronic Commerce Part Three.* Wellington, 2000.

New Zealand Law Commission Report No. 85. *Delivering Justice for All: A Vision for New Zealand Courts and Tribunals.* Wellington, 2004.

New Zealand Law Commission Report No. 109. *Suppressing Names and Evidence.* Wellington, 2009.

New Zealand Law Commission Report No. 128. *The News Media Meets New Media.* Wellington, 2013.

New Zealand Law Commission Supplementary Paper No. 20. *Tribunal Reform.* Wellington, 2008.

Norris. 'News Media Ownership in New Zealand'. In *What's News? Reclaiming Journalism in New Zealand*, edited by Judy McGregor & Margie Comrie. Dunmore Press, 2002.

Norton. '*Hosking v Runting* and the Role of Freedom of Expression'. *AULR* 10 (2004): 245.

Penk & Tobin (eds). *Privacy Law in New Zealand.* Wellington: Brookers, 2010.

Price. *Media Minefield: A Journalists' Guide to Media Regulation in New Zealand.* Wellington: New Zealand Journalists Training Organisation, 2007.

Rishworth. 'Human Rights'. *NZLRev* 1 (2005): 87.

Rolph. 'Irreconcilable Differences? Interlocutory Injunctions for Defamation and Privacy'. *Media and Arts Law Review* 17 (2012): 170.

Spiller (ed). *Butterworths New Zealand Law Dictionary.* 6th ed. Wellington: LexisNexis, 2005.

Zwaga, Stace & Brunton. *Real Media, Real People: Privacy and Informed Consent in Broadcasting*. Wellington: BSA, 2004.

Index

The numbers here refer to paragraph numbers.

Index

Index

www.ingramcontent.com/pod-product-compliance
Lightning Source LLC
Chambersburg PA
CBHW071430230926
51846CB00001B/176
9789041167583